Patriot Hearts

W.T. Coffey Jr.

Always Out Front!

PATRIOT HEARTS

An Anthology of American Patriotism

True stories and insights from American warriors, veterans, and patriots about the values and sacrifices that created the freedoms now enjoyed by all Americans.

Compiled and Edited by
Major William T. Coffey, Jr.

Credits:

Book Cover Photography: Earl W. Barcome, Barcome Photography,
Colorado Springs, Colorado

Text and Cover Design: Daniel Maio, Graphics West

Production and Composition: Graphics West, Inc.,
Colorado Springs, Colorado

Editor: Sharon Green, Graphics West

Cover Design and Composition: Jesse Epting, Graphics West

Printing: Publishers Press, Salt Lake City, Utah

Published by Purple Mountain Publishing

**Purple Mountain
Publishing**

ISBN: 0-9704124-2-8
          0-9704124-0-1 (pbk.)

FOREWORD

Patriot Hearts is must reading for every person who loves our country and is devoted to make the 21st Century the finest in our country's history. *Patriot Hearts* makes it very clear that FREEDOM IS NOT FREE.

While tens of millions of Americans have already served and sacrificed for this country, well over a million have given their very lives to protect our great country and freedoms. All of us need to understand and appreciate their courage, commitment, and the sacrifices they made to give us the greatest country in the world.

We will have to make these same sacrifices and commitments to protect and keep our country safe in the future.

I particularly encourage young people in high school, college, and those beginning their military service to read this book, so they can understand and appreciate the sacrifices of prior generations.

Ross Perot

DEDICATION

☆

To those who took up arms,
to all who gave some,
to those who gave all,
to all who serve to protect our freedoms.

To those who are also affectionately known as:

Warriors, Joes, Sarges, Yanks, Troops, Airmen, and Cannon Cockers. Eltees, NCOs, Os, COs, AOs, ALOs, SIGOs, BSOs, XOs, FOs, and GOs. Rebels, Docs, Medics, and Corpsmen. Zoomies, Green Suiters, Lifers, Night Fighters, and Light Fighters. Johnny Rebs, JAGs, Jarheads, and Jet Jockies. Blue Suiters, Blue Bellies, and Green Tabbers. Frogs, Squids, SEALs, Turtles, Full Bulls, Wolfhounds, and Doggies. Short Timers, Skippers, Smages, Swabbies, Scouts, Sailors, and Spoons. Red Legs, Grey Liners, and Blue Liners. CINCs, WACs, Tops, TACs, Tailhookers, and Tread Heads. Seabees, Soldiers, Seamen, SCUD Busters, Spooks, and Snake Eaters. Buffalo Soldiers, Bonus Babies, Butter Bars, and 11-Bang Bangs. Green Berets, Black Berets, Maroon Berets, and Black Hats. Rough Riders, Leathernecks, Lurps, and Loggies. Ground Pounders, Gunnies, GIs, Grunts, Fly Boys, Gun Bunnies, and Wire Dogs. Frontliners and REMFs. Rotor Heads, Rangers, Reservists, Freedom Fighters, Liberators, and Peacekeepers. Weekend Warriors, Warfighters, and Wrenches. Guardsmen, Coast Guardsmen, D-Boys, Duckhunters, Dogfaces, and Doughboys. 1s, 2s, 3s, and 4s. KPs, MPs, SPs, and FNGs. Recruits, Minutemen, Merchant Mariners, and Marines.

All together,
nothing short of the finest,
most selfless, courageous and honorable
men and women of this country.

In short … American heroes all.

Contents

☆

AUTHOR'S INTRODUCTION

☆

These words of inspiration and wisdom come from the hearts of soldiers, sailors, airmen, marines, veterans, and civilians alike. The vast majority are from Americans about America and in a couple of cases, from foreigners about America. These words focus on the values, ideals, and sacrifices that created and maintain America. They are the values embodied in the American warrior spirit and our nation at large. They are the standards from our history and the basis for our Nation's future.

Most of the words in this book are from the citizens who took up arms in the defense of America. Their service to our country within the profession of arms is the pinnacle of patriotism. Their words will inspire and motivate you. They remind us of the price already paid for our freedoms and the price needed for continued strength and vigilance. They allow us to better appreciate our history, their sacrifices and heartbeats, and stimulate a sense of pride in our country and in our fellow citizens.

Throughout this book you may discover or reaffirm for yourself the uniqueness of America and its history, its military, and the values that created and sustain America. In the end, I hope each reader can better appreciate the experiences and sacrifices made by the legions of American warriors and patriots, past and present, who served, loved, defended, and supported this nation to keep us free ... lest we forget.

William T. Coffey Jr.
Citizen and Soldier
Colorado Springs, Colorado
October 9, 2000

Heart is what makes
the American soldier.

SFC Barbara J. Ray
"Letters to the Editor"
Noncommissioned Officer (NCO) Journal
Summer 1993

War is conflict; fighting is an elemental
exposition of the age-old effort to survive.
It is the cold glitter of the attacker's
eye, not the point of the questing
bayonet, that breaks the line.
It is the fierce determination of the
driver to close with the enemy,
not the mechanical perfection of the
tank, that conquers the trench.
It is the cataclysmic ecstasy of conflict
in the flier, not the perfection of his
machine gun, which drops the
enemy in flaming ruin.
Yet volumes are devoted to armament;
pages to inspiration.

General George Smith Patton, Jr.
"Old Blood and Guts"
1885–1945

The mind, the soul, the heart, the spirit
(or whatever you wish to call it),
of the soldier is everything.
In comparison, numbers and
resources are nothing.

Powell

Outstanding leaders appeal to the hearts
Of their followers, not their minds.

Author Unknown

In order to take a full part in the life which is before you,
I think that you must in effect relive the past so that
you may turn to the present with deep convictions and
an understanding of what manner of country this is for
which men for generations have laid down their lives.

General George Catlett Marshall
Speech at Princeton University
February 22, 1947

I always enjoy reading military history. I tell people that
history strengthens me—it helps me and, I would hope,
others realize that mortal man can overcome the
obstacles in his path, transforming his situation
through sound decisions and steadfast application
of his will … . My point is: read to relax,
to learn, and to expand your horizons.
You will be better for it as you will grow
personally and professionally.

General Gordon Sullivan
Army Chief of Staff
(1991–1995)

CHAPTER ONE

Duty

Duty is the single most important word to describe what this book is about, what America is about, and what patriotism requires of us. "Duty First" is a common term that sets our priority. Duty to our country, duty to our government and military, duty to our communities, duty to our assigned missions, duty to our comrades, and duty to ourselves in our chosen profession is the focus of this chapter, appropriately the first chapter in this book. This chapter also includes stories, articles, and quotations concerning national will, commitment, loyalty, vigilance, and military service.

We were going to stand or die.
That's all there was to it.
This was not an order from HQ;
it was the determined
opinion of the men.

Albert M. Ettinger
A Doughboy with the
Fighting Sixty-Ninth
World War I
(1914–1918)

WHEN DUTY WHISPERS

It may be laid down as a primary position, and the basis of our system, that every citizen who enjoys the protection of a free Government, owes not only a proportion of his property, but even of his personal services to the defense of it.

George Washington
1st President of the United States
(1789–1797)

General George Washington
Continental Army
1732–1799

Thus the great and hazardous enterprise we have been engaged in is, God be praised, happily completed. A few years of peace will improve, will restore and increase our strength; but our future will depend on our union and our virtue. Let us, therefore, beware of being lulled into a dangerous security; and of being both enervated and impoverished by luxury; of being weakened by internal contentions and divisions.

Benjamin Franklin
in a letter to Charles Thomson,
from Paris, 1784,
just after signing the Peace Treaty
1706–1790
Statesman, Diplomat, Scientist, Inventor

*W*hen duty whispers low, thou must,—
you must reply, I can.

Ralph Waldo Emerson
1803–1882
American Poet, Author, Philosopher

I am a soldier
I fight where I'm told to
And I win where I fight.

General George S. Patton, Jr.

DO THIS ...

*T*he genius of this nation is not in the least to be compared
with that of the Prussians, Austrians, or French. You say to
your soldiers, "Do this," and he doeth it;
but I am obliged to say "This is the reason why
you ought to do that," and then he does it.

MG Frederick von Steuben
(in a letter about American soldiers during the American revolution)

MG Frederick von Steuben
1730–1794
*Former Aide-de-Camp to Frederick the Great
German General in service to
the Continental Army*

Daniel Webster
1782–1852
Statesman, State Representative,
Senator, Secretary of State

*L*et our object be, OUR COUNTRY, OUR WHOLE
COUNTRY, AND NOTHING BUT OUR COUNTRY.
And, by the blessing of God, may that country itself become
a vast and splendid monument, not of oppression and
terror, but of Wisdom, of Peace, and of Liberty, upon which
the world may gaze with admiration for ever!!

Daniel Webster
closing remarks of his address at the Bunker Hill Monument, 1825

I now take up a resolution to do for the future all that
lies in my way for the service of my countrymen.

Benjamin Franklin

*T*o prepare for its vital role, the military must insist
upon a respect for duty and a discipline without
counterpart in civilian life.

The U.S. Supreme Court

It is not the dangerous days of battle which most strongly test the soldier's resolution, but the years of peace, when many voices, offering many counsels, bewilder and confound him.

General Matthew Ridgway
U.S. Army
World War II and Korean War

Unless I Won

I have never taken any command into battle with the slightest desire to come out of it alive unless I won.

General Sheridan

**General
Phillip Henry Sheridan**
1831–1888
Union General, Civil War

THE FIERY TRAIL

Fellow citizens, we cannot escape history. We of this Congress and this administration, will be remembered in spite of ourselves. No personal significance, or insignificance, can spare one or another of us. The fiery trail through which we pass will light us down, in honor or dishonor, to the last generation. We say we are for the Union. The world will not forget that we say this. We know how to save the Union. The world knows we do know how to save it. We—even we here—hold the power, and bear the responsibility. In giving freedom to the slave, we assure freedom to the free—honorable alike in what we give, and what we preserve. We shall nobly save, or meanly lose, the last best hope of earth. Other means may succeed; this could not fail. The way is plain, peaceful, generous, just—a way which, if followed, the world will forever applaud, and God must forever bless.

President Abraham "Honest Abe" Lincoln
In his second annual message to Congress
December 1, 1862

Abraham Lincoln
1809–1865
16th President of the United States
(1861–1865)

HEADQUARTERS
THIRD UNITED STATES ARMY

Office of The Commanding General

APO 403

13 March, 1945

My dear General Marshall:

When the operations against Germany are brought to a successful conclusion, I should like to be considered for any type of combat command from a division up against the Japanese. I am sure that my method of fighting would be successful.

I also am of such an age that this is my last war, and I would therefore like to see it through to the end.

Please pardon my bothering you with personal matters.

With warm regards to Mrs. Marshall, I am,

Very Respectfully,

G. S. Patton, Jr.,
Lieutenant General, U.S. Army
Commanding

General of the Army George C. Marshall
Chief of Staff
War Department
Washington, D.C.
U.S.A.

*D*o *your duty in all things,*
you cannot do more,
you should never wish to do less.

General Robert Edward Lee
1807–1870
Confederate General, Civil War

No symbol of resolve is more persuasive than a U.S. soldier, well trained, well equipped, well supplied, well led, and determined to hold his ground … . The soldier is the ultimate symbol of resolve of this great nation.

General Carl E. Vuono
Army Chief of Staff
(1987–1991)

STILL THE NOBLEST CALLING

I visited with three old friends recently at a park near my town. It seemed like only yesterday that we were all together, but actually it had been 28 years. There was a crowd at the park that day, and it took us a while to connect, but with aid of a computer we made it. I found Lance at Panel 54W, line 037, Lynn over at panel 51W, line 032, and Vince down at panel 27W, line 103. In 1968 we were gung-ho young fighter pilots in Vietnam, the cream of the crop of the US Air Force pilot training system, and now their names are on that 250-foot-long, half-size model of Washington's Vietnam War Memorial that moves around the country.

I had intentionally avoided visiting the wall when it came to town in years past because I did not trust myself to keep my composure. But after nearly three decades it was time to try for some closure on this issue. I told my wife that I preferred to go alone, if that was all right. Truth be known, I nearly backed out at that. Dancing the Wild Blue. Standing in front of that somber wall, I tried to keep it light, reminiscing about how things were back then. We used to joke about our passionate love affair with an inanimate flying object. We flew F-100s and we marveled at the thought that we actually got paid to do it. We were not draftees but college graduates in Vietnam by choice, opting for the cramped confines of a jet fighter cockpit over the comfort of corporate America. In all my life I've not been so passionate about any other work. If that sounds like an exaggeration, then you've never danced the wild blue with a supersonic angel.

I vividly remember the Sunday afternoon, in the summer of '68, when we flew out of Travis Air Force Base, California, on a troop transport headed for Vietnam. Lynn, Lance and I crowded around the same porthole and watched the Golden Gate Bridge disappear below broken clouds. We had gone through fighter pilot school together and had done some serious bonding. In an exceedingly rare moment of youthful fighter pilot humility, I wondered if I would live to see that bridge again. For reasons I still don't understand, I was the only one of the three of us who did.

Once in Vietnam, we passed the long, lonely off-duty hours at Dusty's Pub, a lounge that we lieutenants built on the beach of the South China Sea at Tuy Hoa Airbase. The roof at Dusty's doubled as a sun deck and the walls were nonexistent. The complaint heard most often around the bar, in the standard gallows humor of a combat squadron, was, "It's a lousy war, but it's the only one we have." (I've cleaned up the language a bit.) We sang mostly raunchy songs that never seemed to end. Someone was always writing new verses and, as an antidote to loneliness, fear in the night and the sadness over dead friends, we often drank too much.

Vince joined us at Dusty's Pub halfway through my tour of duty, and since he was a like-minded country kid from Montana, we hit it off. He had a wide grin, slightly stooped shoulders and his own way of walking. He just threw his feet out and stepped on them. But what he lacked in military bearing he made up for with the heart of a tiger. He often flew as my wingman, and we volunteered for the night missions on the Ho Chi Minh Trail.

One starless night, the longest, saddest night of my life, we got into a nasty gun duel with some antiaircraft artillery batteries. I watched Vince die in a mushroom-shaped fireball that for a moment turned night into day. Lance, a New York boy who took unmerciful grief from us because he talked like a New Yawker, crashed into the side of a mountain in the central Vietnamese highlands while attacking a target. Lynn, a happy-go-lucky jock from Pennsylvania's Slippery Rock College with a hound named John the Basset, returned to his base on a stormy night in July after weather aborted his mission. Two miles of wet runway weren't enough to stop an F-100 landing at 160 knots with all its bombs still on board. He ran off the end, flipped over, and slid through the minefield at the perimeter fence, setting off a gruesome sound and light show.

At the wall, I told the guys only about the good parts of the last 28 years. Lacy, one of our associates from Dusty's Pub, became an astronaut, and a few summers ago I watched from my backyard, near Tampa, as he blasted off. His voice over the radio from space was at least an octave lower than it was the day I heard him radio for help while swinging from his parachute hung in a tree in Laos. Another Dusty's patron, Rick, is now a two-star general, and I reminded them what we used to say about the military promotion system. It's like a septic tank, only the really big chunks float to the top. I didn't tell them about how ostracized Vietnam vets still are, that during that same week, one of the nation's leading newspapers had run an article that implied we Vietnam vets were, to quote one syndicated columnist, either suckers or psychos, victims or monsters. I didn't tell them that Hanoi Jane, who shot at us and helped torture our POWs, had married one of the richest guys in the United States. I didn't tell them that the secretary of defense (MacNamara) they fought for back then, has now declared that he was not a believer in the cause for which he assigned them all to their destiny. I didn't tell them that a dope-doing, muck-sucking, lecherous, draft-age kid from Arkansas who hid out in England and the Soviet Union to dodge his duty while they were fighting and dying, is now the commander-in-chief. And I didn't tell them we lost that lousy war. I gave them the same story I've used since the Nixon administration: We were winning when I left.

I relived that final day as I stared at the black onyx wall. The dawn came up like thunder after 268 combat missions in 360 days in the valley of the shadow. The ground trembled as 33 F-100s roared off the runway, across the beach and out over the South China Sea, climbing into the rising sun. On the eastern horizon, a line of towering deep-purple clouds stood shoulder-to-shoulder before a brilliant orange sky that slowly turned powder blue from the top down. From somewhere on that stage, above the whine of spinning turbine blades, I could hear a choir singing Handel's Hallelujah Chorus in fortissimo: "The Lord God omnipotent reigneth," and He was bringing me home, while Lance and Lynn and Vince will remain as part of the dust of Southeast Asia until the end of time. I was not the only one talking to the wall through tears. A leather-vested, bare-chested biker two panels to my left was in even worse shape. I backed about 25 yards away from the wall and sat down on the grass under a clear blue sky and midday sun that perfectly matched the tropical weather of the war zone.

The wall, with all 58,200 names, consumed my field of vision. I tried to wrap my mind around the megatonnage of violence, carnage and ruined lives that it represented. Then I thought of how Vietnam was only one small war in the history of the human race. I was overwhelmed with a sense of mankind's wickedness.

My heart felt like wax in the blazing sun and I was on the verge of becoming a spectacle in the park. I arose and walked back up to the wall to say goodbye and ran my fingers over the engraved names Lance and Lynn and Vince as if I could communicate with them in some kind of spiritual Braille. I wanted them to know that God, duty, honor and country will always remain the noblest calling.

Revisionist history from elite draft dodgers trying to justify and rationalize their own actions will never change that. I have been a productive member of society since the day I left Vietnam. I am proud of what I did there, and I am especially proud of my friends—heroes who voluntarily, enthusiastically gave their all. They demonstrated no greater love to a nation whose highbrow opinion makers are still trying to disavow them. May their names, indelibly engraved on that memorial wall, likewise be found in the Book of Life, a novel based on service in Vietnam.

by J. D. Wetterling, May 24, 1996
<http://www.jdwetterling.com>

*B*eing a soldier is different—not an occupation,
but a profession, a calling.

General Edward C. Meyer
Army Chief of Staff
(1979–1983)

No More Than My Troops Received

On July 15, 1948, John J. Pershing died after attaining the highest rank ever reached by an army officer, General of the Armies. He was the first to achieve this rank. Before his death, Pershing was asked if he wanted a memorial at his gravesite. Pershing said that even in death he wanted to be with the troops, and asked to have the same government-issue gravestone that all troops receive. Today as you walk through Arlington National Cemetery, you will find General Pershing's gravestone, a government-issue gravestone, on top of a hill, watching over thousands of troops, just as he had done throughout his life.

THE BOYS OF POINTE DU HOC

by President Ronald Reagan
at the 40th Anniversary of the D-Day Ceremony
Pointe du Hoc, Normandy, France, June 6, 1984

We're here to mark that day in history when the Allied peoples joined in battle to reclaim this continent to liberty. For four long years, much of Europe had been under a terrible shadow. Free nations had fallen, Jews cried out in the camps, millions cried out for liberation. Europe was enslaved, and the world prayed for its rescue. Here in Normandy the rescue began. Here the Allies stood and fought against tyranny in a giant undertaking unparalleled in human history.

We stand on a lonely, windswept point on the northern shore of France. The air is soft, but forty years ago at this moment, the air was dense with smoke and the cries of men, and the air was filled with the crack of rifle fire and the roar of cannon. At dawn, on the morning of the 6th of June 1944, 225 Rangers jumped off the British landing craft and ran to the bottom of these cliffs.

Their mission was one of the most difficult and daring of the invasion: to climb these sheer and desolate cliffs and take out the enemy guns. The Allies had been told that some of the mightiest of these guns were here and they would be trained on the beaches to stop the Allied advance.

The Rangers looked up and saw the enemy soldiers—at the edge of the cliffs shooting down at them with machine-guns and throwing grenades. And the American Rangers began to climb. They shot rope ladders over the face of these cliffs and began to pull themselves up. When one Ranger fell, another would take his place. When one rope was cut, a Ranger would grab another and begin his climb again. They climbed, shot back, and held their footing. Soon, one by one, the Rangers pulled themselves over the top, and in seizing the firm land at the top of these cliffs, they began to seize back the continent of Europe. Two hundred and twenty-five came here. After two days of fighting only ninety could still bear arms.

Behind me is a memorial that symbolizes the Ranger daggers that were thrust into the top of these cliffs. And before me are the men who put them there.

These are the boys of Pointe du Hoc. These are the men who took the cliffs. These are the champions who helped free a continent. These are the heroes who helped end a war.

Gentlemen, I look at you and I think of the words of Stephen Spender's poem. You are men who in your "lives fought for life ... and left the vivid air signed with your honor"... .

President Ronald Reagan
1911–
40th President of the United States
(1981–1989)

Forty summers have passed since the battle that you fought here. You were young the day you took these cliffs; some of you were hardly more than boys, with the deepest joys of life before you. Yet you risked everything here. Why? Why did you do it? What impelled you to put aside the instinct for self-preservation and risk your lives to take these cliffs? What inspired all the men of the armies that met here? We look at you, and somehow we know the answer. It was faith, and belief; it was loyalty and love.

The men of Normandy had faith that what they were doing was right, faith that they fought for all humanity, faith that a just God would grant them mercy on this beachhead or on the next. It was the deep knowledge—and pray God we have not lost it—that there is a profound moral difference between the use of force for liberation and the use of force for conquest. You were here to liberate, not to conquer, and so you and those others did not doubt your cause. And you were right not to doubt.

You all knew that some things are worth dying for. One's country is worth dying for, and democracy is worth dying for, because it's the most deeply honorable form of government ever devised by man. All of you loved liberty.

All of you were willing to fight tyranny, and you knew the people of your countries were behind you.

You and I have a rendezvous with destiny. We will preserve for our children this, the last best hope of man on earth, or we will sentence them to take the first step into a thousand years of darkness. If we fail, at least let our children and our children's children say of us we justified our brief moment here. We did all that could be done.

The One Lesson

During a televised interview in March of 1991 (shortly after the ground war), between David Frost and General H. Norman Schwarzkopf, Mr. Frost asked "What, if anything, was the one lesson from Operation Desert Storm?"
The General responded:

Although we had many advanced weapons and incredible firepower, when it came right down to it, the bottom line, the number one lesson, was the individual soldier … . The will to win, the character to go into battle, the belief that what you are doing is right, the support of the country … without this, all else is meaningless.

General H. Norman
"Stormin' Norman"
Schwarzkopf
1934–
Army General, Desert Storm

A basic question a soldier must answer in making the decision to serve his nation under arms is "What makes this nation, this way of life, worth defending?" At the most fundamental level, the answer is most often found in the freedoms, peace and human rights we each enjoy.

General John A. Wickham, Jr.
Army Chief of Staff
(1983–1987)

It Is A Privilege

The United States does not consider it a sacrifice to do all one can, to give one's best to our nation, when the nation is fighting for its existence and its future life. It is not a sacrifice for any man, old or young, to be in the Army or the Navy of the United States. Rather it is a privilege. It is not a sacrifice for the industrialist or the wage earner, the farmer or the shopkeeper, the trainman or the doctor, to pay more taxes, to buy more bonds, to forego extra profits, to work longer or harder at the task for which he is best fitted. Rather it is a privilege. It is not a sacrifice to do without many things to which we are accustomed if the national defense calls for doing without it.

President Franklin D. Roosevelt
from his "Fireside Chat," December 9, 1941
1882–1945
32nd President of the United States
(1933–1945)

The American has been harassed by rifle and automatic weapons, pounded by hand grenades, by artillery and rocket shells, attacked by tanks and

airplane bombs! He has faced the hazards of countless mines and booby traps and every form of static obstacle. He has conquered them all!

Dwight D. Eisenhower
in his address before a joint session on Congress
1890–1969

As our boat touched sand and the ramp went down, I became a visitor to Hell.

Pvt. Charles Neighbor
29th Division
Omaha Beach, World War II

TO ALL THE MEN OF HONOR AND COURAGE

President Ronald Reagan
Address at the U.S.-French Ceremony at Omaha Beach
on the 40th Anniversary of D-Day, June 6, 1984
Normandy, France

We stand today at a place of battle, one that 40 years ago saw and felt the worst of war. Men bled and died here for a few feet of—or inches of sand, as bullets and shellfire cut through their ranks. About them, General Omar Bradley later said, "Every man who set foot on Omaha Beach that day was a hero."

Some who survived the battle of June 6, 1944, are here today. Others who hoped to return never did.

"Someday, Lis, I'll go back," said Private First Class Peter Robert Zannata, of the 37th Engineer Combat Battalion, and first assault wave to hit Omaha Beach. "I'll go back, and I'll see it all again. I'll see the beach, the barricades, and the graves."

Those words of Private Zanatta come to us from his daughter, Lisa Zanatta Henn, in a heartrending story about the event her father spoke of so often. "In his words, the Normandy invasion would change his life forever," she said. She tells some of his stories of World War II but says of her father, "the story to end all stories was D-Day."

Crossed rifles in the sand   A comrade's tribute to this American soldier who sprang ashore from a landing barge and died at the barricades of Western Europe, 1944. ©National Archives.

"He made me feel the fear of being on the boat waiting to land. I can smell the ocean and feel the seasickness. I can see the looks on his fellow soldiers' faces—the fear, the anguish, the uncertainty of what lay ahead. And when they landed, I can feel the strength and courage of the men who took those first steps through the tide to what must have surely looked like instant death."

Private Zannata's daughter wrote to me, "I don't know how or why I can feel this emptiness, this fear, or this determination, but I do. Maybe it's the bond I had with my father. All I know is that it brings tears to my eyes to think about my father as a 20-year old boy having to face that beach."

The anniversary of D-Day was always special to her family. And like all the families of those who went to war, she describes how she came to realize her own father's survival was a miracle: "So many men died. I know that my father watched many of his friends killed. I know that he must have died inside a little each time. But his explanation to me was, 'You did what you had to do, and you kept on going'."

When men like Private Zannata and all our Allied forces stormed the beaches of Normandy 40 years ago they came not as conquerors, but as liberators. When these troops swept across the French countryside and into the forests of Belgium and Luxembourg they came not to take, but to return what had been wrongfully seized. When our forces marched into Germany they came not to prey on a brave and defeated people, but to nurture the seeds of democracy among those who yearned to be free again.

We salute them today. But, Mr. President [François Mitterand of France], we also salute those who, like yourself, were already engaging the enemy inside your beloved country—the French Resistance. Your valiant struggle for France did so much to cripple the enemy and spur the advance of the armies of liberation. The French Forces of the Interior will forever personify courage and national spirit. They will be a timeless inspiration to all who are free and to all who would be free.

Today, in their memory, and for all who fought here, we celebrate the triumph of democracy. We reaffirm the unity of democratic people who fought a war and then joined with the vanquished in a firm resolve to keep the peace.

From a terrible war we learned that unity made us invincible; now, in peace, that same unity makes us secure. We sought to bring all freedom-loving nations together in a community dedicated to the defense and preservation of our sacred values. Our alliance, forged in the crucible of war, tempered and shaped by the realities of the post-war world, has succeeded. In Europe, the threat has been contained, the peace has been kept.

Today, the living here assembled—officials, veterans, citizens—are a tribute to what was achieved here 40 years ago. This land is secure. We are free. These things are worth fighting and dying for.

Lisa Zannata Henn began her story by quoting her father, who promised that he would return to Normandy. She ended with a promise to her father, who died 8 years ago of cancer: "I'm going there, Dad, and I'll see the beaches and the barricades and the monuments. I'll see the graves, and I'll put flowers there just like you wanted to do. I'll never forget what you went through, Dad, nor will I let anyone else forget. And, Dad, I'll always be proud."

Through the words of his loving daughter, who is here with us today, a D-Day veteran has shown us the meaning of this day far better than any President can. It is enough to say about Private Zannata and all the men of honor and courage who fought beside him four decades ago: We will always remember. We will always be proud. We will always be prepared, so we may always be free.

Thank you.

*A*n *Army lieutenant returning from the Gulf [War]
was asked what it was that allowed him to survive
six months in the desert and gave him courage in
combat. He thought for a minute and answered
with a wisdom far beyond his years, "It was a
commitment to a cause greater than myself."*

General Carl E. Vuono

FAITH IN TODAY'S SOLDIERS

General Dennis Reimer
United States Army, Chief of Staff
December 1998

I had my faith in America, but, specifically in the youth of our country and the Army, restored several weeks ago.

A soldier of the '90s decides to sign a contract to join the Army. He attends OSUT (One Station Unit Training) here at Fort Benning and graduates in the summer of 1998. Following graduation from OSUT, he continues his training as part of his contract, and in-processes with the 1st Battalion (Airborne) 507th Infantry—Airborne School.

During jump week, on jump number two, his reserve parachute activates in the aircraft while the doors are open. As the reserve canopy inflates and moves to the door, the soldier reacts to the training that has been drilled into him over the last three weeks—Beat the canopy out the door! As the soldier races down the length of the aircraft, he pushes the canopy away from him to reach the door and get out first. Unfortunately the canopy won the race, it reached the door before the soldier did. During the course of the race to the door, a few static lines wrapped around his fingers. The result was an instant detachment of his middle two fingers (below the second knuckle) from his left hand.

Now at this point could you blame the soldier for not completing Airborne School and proceeding on to his unit? He has sacrificed parts of two fingers to the Army. I could not blame him. The soldier remained at the Airborne School as a medical hold, in order for his hand to heal.

At the beginning of December, the soldier received a medical clearance to move on to his unit. But, he decided to complete what he started and return to the airborne course. He still needed three jumps to earn his airborne wings. I met the soldier on 8 December and had the opportunity to talk with him— Private Newell—Joe American—normal, clean cut kid with a high and tight.

He had the appearance of your little kid brother dressed up in BDUs. On Thursday, 10 December 1998, five months after donating parts of his body to Fryar Drop Zone—Private Newell completed his fifth jump, received his airborne wings and graduated Airborne School. But the story does not end here.

The soldier could have quit—and many would have thought he would—but, he didn't. He probably could have gotten a medical drop from the Army and taken the money and run—but, he didn't.

On Monday, 14 December Private Newell reported to the 75th Ranger Regiment. He went to the Ranger Regiment to complete his portion of the Airborne/Ranger contract that he signed when he enlisted in the Army. He went because he wanted to complete the Ranger Indoctrination Program (RIP) and become a Ranger.

When I talked with Private Newell, his concern was that he would have a hard time in RIP. He was concerned with his ability to grasp a rope, because he was still getting used to only having two complete fingers and a thumb on his left hand. He said he wanted to complete RIP and become a Ranger.

I told Private Newell that he had already accomplished something of great importance early in his career. He did not quit. He had demonstrated the will to drive-on and persevere—he possessed discipline and the Infantry Spirit. I told Private Newell that all he needed to do is continue to drive-on. Make them tap him on the shoulder and pull him from the course, but not quit, maintain that fighting spirit. I told Private Newell that quitting was like a disease—like AIDS—once you have it, once you get it, it only gets worse.

In a time where: Officers coming into the resident courses here at Benning want to resign, or quit. In a time where: A soldier tells a 1st Sgt., "I have been training for four months in OSUT, I have been training too hard and I need a break," and quits Airborne School before his third jump (after completing ground and tower weeks). In a time where: You really wonder what's happening to the Army—There is a Private Newell.

I would take a company of Private Newell's as a company commander. I think that any battalion commander would take 700 Private Newell's. He is the kind of soldier I want in My Army. He is the kind of soldier we need in Our Army.

My faith in the generations of today has been restored. Just when I really wondered about what was going on in the Army, and happening to the Army, I meet a soldier that eliminates those thoughts.

If there is one Private Newell out there—there has to be others. We probably see those soldiers every day and never know it. It does not take losing a body part to discover them. We need to cultivate, train, mentor and nurture those soldiers.

Private Newell is the soldier that we need to meet the 21st century with and win with in the future. Keep an eye out for your Private Newell.

Just some thoughts from my fighting position.

Oath of Office
for United States Military Personnel

... I do solemnly swear that I will support and defend the constitution of the United States against all enemies, foreign and domestic, that I will bear true faith and allegiance to the same; that I take this obligation freely, without any mental reservation or purpose of evasion; and that I will well and faithfully discharge the duties of the office upon which I am about to enter; so help me God.

Those of us in the Total Army who take an oath of service have sworn to "support and defend the Constitution of the United States." By doing so, we stand shoulder to shoulder with the framers of the Constitution who mutually pledged their lives, their fortunes, and their sacred honor. We do this freely because it is the Constitution which guarantees all citizens the rights and obligations which are the essence of being an American. And it is the Constitution that our comrades have, in other times and in other places, sacrificed to preserve.

General John A. Wickham, Jr.

SLEEP TIGHT MRS. HARVEY

The following is an editorial response to a complaining resident, as printed in the *San Diego Union Tribune*, February 8, 1999:

Re: "Is harassment of residents the role of the military?" (Letters, February 4):

Responding to Maura Harvey's letter wondering if the Marine helicopter training flights that passed above her Del Mar home were simply to harass residents, I can say that, yes, our mission is to harass residents, specifically Mrs. Harvey. We do not train 24 hours a day, seven days a week to provide freedom and security to all residents of the United States. We exist only to annoy the very people we are sworn to protect, against all enemies, foreign and domestic. We spend months and years overseas, away from our families and loved ones, in some cases making less than minimum wage, choosing to live a life in which many qualify for food stamps, just to have the chance, one day, to annoy people like Mrs. Harvey.

There is no more sought-after position in the military than the Maura Harvey Annoyance Task Force. As a matter of fact, the Marines who spent Christmas dug into fighting positions in northern Kuwait and their brothers in the sky, braving anti-aircraft missiles and artillery, were just training to come back to the States and fly missions over Mrs. Harvey's house. It has nothing to do with the security of the nation. It has no impact on our ability to carry out missions in Africa, the Middle East and Eastern Europe, and it has no bearing on Mrs. Harvey's ability to enjoy "nature and peaceful, quiet living." The "strange, almost science fiction war scene" she described was put on solely to make noise and to destroy her "scenic view corridors" in Del Mar Terrace. It certainly was not valuable and necessary training to help sustain the lives of those who ensure this nation's freedom, sent into harm's way to do just that.

Next time, Mrs. Harvey may want to look upon those loud machines and think about the men and women, who fly, ride in, and maintain them. Ponder the sacrifices they make in providing this nation with the warm blanket of freedom we all enjoy. Maybe she might even imagine how much more disturbing it would be if she were not sure what country the helicopters were from, or whether they were going to attack her beautiful neighborhood. But she shouldn't worry too much about that, because we will not let it happen.

Capt. John R. Peterson,
USMC Pacific Beach

IT SURE WASN'T FUN

These words (excerpts from his speech) were spoken "extemporaneously" and recorded at an informal retirement farewell for Marine Colonel Wayne Shaw who retired after more than 28 years of service.

In recent years I've heard many Marines on the occasion of retirements, farewells, promotions and changes of command refer to the "fun" they've had in the Marine Corps. "I loved every day of it and had a lot of fun" has been voiced far too often. Their definition of "fun" must be radically different than mine. Since first signing my name on the dotted line 28½ years ago I have had very little fun. Devoting my entire physical and mental energies training to kill the young men of some other country was not fun. Worrying about how many of my own men might die or return home maimed was not fun. Knowing that we did not have the money or time to train as best we should have, was not fun either. It was no fun to be separated from my wife for months on end, nor was it fun to freeze at night in snow and rain and mud. It was not much fun to miss my father's funeral because my Battalion Commander was convinced our peacetime training deployment just couldn't succeed without me. Missing countless school and athletic events my sons very much wanted me to attend was not much fun either. Not being at my son's high school graduation wasn't fun.

Somehow it didn't seem like fun when the movers showed up with day laborers from the street corner and [then have to deal with] the destroyed personal effects that were predictable from folks who couldn't hold a job. The lost and damaged items, often-irreplaceable family heirlooms, weren't much fun to try to "replace" for pennies on the dollar. There wasn't much fun for a Colonel with a family of four to live in a 1700-square-foot apartment with one bathroom that no welfare family would have moved into. It was not much fun to watch the downsizing of the services after Desert Storm as we handed out pink slips to men who risked their lives just weeks before. It has not been much fun to watch mid-grade officers and senior Staff NCOs, after living frugal lives and investing money where they could, realize that they cannot afford to send their sons and daughters to college. Nor do I consider it much fun to reflect on the fact that our medical system is simply broken. It is not much fun to watch my Marines board helicopters that are just too old and train with gear that just isn't what is should be anymore. It is not much fun to receive the advanced copies of promotion results and call those who have been passed over for promotion. It just wasn't much fun to watch the infrastructure at our bases and stations sink deeper into the abyss because funding wasn't provided for the latest "crisis." It just wasn't much fun to discharge good Marines for being a few pounds overweight and have to reenlist Marines who were HIV positive and not worldwide deployable. It sure wasn't much fun to look at the dead Marines in the wake of the Beirut bombing and ask yourself what in the hell we were doing there. I could go on and on. There hasn't been much fun in a career that spans a quarter century of frustration, sacrifice and work.

So, why did you serve you might ask? Let me answer that: I joined the service out of a profound sense of patriotism. As the son of a career Air Force Senior NCO I grew up on military bases often within minutes flying time from Soviet airfields in East Germany. I remember the Cuban Missile Crisis, the construction of the Berlin Wall, the nuclear attack drills in school and was not many miles away when Soviet tanks crushed the aspirations of citizens in Czechoslovakia. To me there was never any doubt that our great Republic and the last best hope of free people, needed to prevail in this ultimate contest.

I knew I had to serve. When our nation was in turmoil over our involvement in Vietnam I knew that we were right in the macro-strategic sense and in the moral sense, even if in the execution we may have been flawed. I still believe to this day that we did the right thing. Many of our elites in the nation today continue to justify their opposition in spite of all evidence that shows they were wrong and their motives either naive or worse. This nation needed to survive and I was going to join others like me to ensure it did. We joined long before anyone had ever referred to service in the infantry units of the Marine Corps as an "opportunity." We knew the pay was lousy, the work hard and the rewards would be few. We had a cause, we knew we were right and we were willing when others were not. Even without a direct threat to our Nation many still join and serve for patriotic reasons.

I joined the Marines out of a sense of adventure. I expected to go to foreign countries and do challenging things. I expected that, should I stick around, my responsibilities would grow, as would my rewards. It was exciting to be given missions and great Marines to be responsible for. Finally, I joined for the camaraderie. I expected to lead good men and be led by good men. Marines, who would speak frankly and freely, follow orders once the decision was made and who would place the good of the organization above all else—Marines who would be willing to sacrifice for this great nation. These were men I could trust with anything and they could trust me. It was the camaraderie that sustained me when the adventure had faded and the patriotism was tested.

I was a Marine for all of these years because it was necessary, because it was rewarding, because our nation needed individuals like us and because I liked and admired the Marines I served with ... but it sure wasn't fun.

I can't promise you "fun," but I can promise you the reward and satisfaction of being able to look in the mirror for the rest of your life and say: "I gave more to America than I ever took from America ... and I'm proud of that."

Semper Fi and God Bless you all!

I WILL FIGHT FOR YOU

Vernon Baker, author of *Lasting Valor*, fought in Italy in World War II and earned a Purple Heart, a Bronze Star, a Distinguished Service Cross (DSC), and ultimately, the Medal of Honor. Lieutenant Baker was one of five African-Americans who won the DSC in WWII, which was upgraded in 1998 to the Medal of Honor. At the 1998 annual dinner and meeting of The Retired Officers Association (TROA), in October, Captain Al Hersh introduced Lt. Baker by describing not only his bravery as stated in the Medal of Honor citation but also his commitment to tomorrow's leaders. At the meeting, Baker shared these thoughts with his fellow TROA members.

You know, I thought the war was over. But looking out here on these faces, it seems like we're still fighting the war, not with bullets, but with ballots and courage. We are trying to keep the armed forces, the civilian soldier, in the spotlight, and it's people like you out here who have been in the armed services, active duty, winning your stars, your gold and silver leaves, silver bars, that have kept this country in the forefront of the world.

I have a little saying that I say to everybody whenever I go someplace and speak. And I say again, and I will continue to say it until I no longer can ... that as I look out on a crowd, I don't see color, I don't see black, I don't see white, I don't see green, but I see America. America, I love you. And if I have to do it again, I will fight for you until I die.

A Marine's Creed

I was that which others did not want to be. I went where others feared to go, and did what others failed to do. I asked nothing from those who gave nothing and reluctantly accepted the thought of eternal loneliness should I fail. I have seen the face of terror, felt the stinging cold of fear, and enjoyed the sweet taste of a moment's love. But most of all I have lived times others would say were best forgotten. At least some day I will be able to say, I was proud of what I was and always will be ... A United States Marine.

Battle-weary Marine   Back to a Coast Guard assault transport comes this Marine after two days and nights of Hell on the beach on Eniwetok in the Marshall Islands. His face is grimy with coral dust and the terror of battle in his eyes.
©National Archives.

A decade after the restructuring that began with the fall of the Berlin Wall, we have the best Army on earth. That's no accident. We succeeded because we have soldiers and leaders who were not afraid of change, willing to roll up their sleeves and do the right thing for the Nation. That's why we will continue to succeed ... we are an Army poised for the future.

General Dennis Reimer, CSA
January 4, 1999
Army Chief of Staff
(1995–1999)

The highest reward for a person's toil is not what they get for it, but what they become by it.

Representative Helen Chenoweth
May 20, 1999

Great thoughts speak only to the thoughtful mind, but great actions speak to all mankind.

Emily P. Bissel

My fellow citizens, our Nation is poised for greatness. We must do what we know is right and do it with all our might. Let history say of us, "These were golden years—when the American Revolution was reborn, when freedom gained new life, when America reached for her best."

President Ronald Reagan
from his Second Inaugural Address
January 21, 1985

In the final measure, nothing speaks like deeds.

General John A. Wickham, Jr.

Absolute Obedience

Gentlemen,—you have now reached the last point. If anyone of you doesn't mean business let him say so now. An hour from now will be too late to back out. Once in, you've got to see it through. You've got to perform without flinching, whatever duty is assigned you, regardless of the difficulty or the danger attending it. If it is garrison duty, you must attend to it, if it is meeting fever, you must be willing, if it is the closest kind of fighting, [you must be] anxious for it. Absolute obedience to every command is your first lesson. No matter what comes you mustn't squeal. Think it over—all of you. If any man wishes to withdraw he will be gladly excused, for others are ready to take his place.

Theodore Roosevelt
Remarks to Recruits, 1898

Theodore Roosevelt
1858–1919
26th President of the United States
(1901–1909)

We live by General Order 100: Men who take up
arms against one another in public war do not cease on this
account to be moral beings responsible to one another.
As leaders, we do not simply take action to achieve an end.
We must act responsibly. We must accomplish our tasks in
a manner consistent with our values. The importance of
those values to the nation and to us as leaders cannot be
overstated. For the nation, an Army rooted in values is
the surest defense against tyranny from within and defeat
from without. The antithesis of a value-based army is a
mercenary force, whose disadvantages were clearly laid out
by Machiavelli: "Troops of this sort are disunited,
ambitious, undisciplined, and faithless, swaggering when
among friends and cowardly in the face of the enemy; they
have neither the fear of God nor loyalty to men." Our
institutional values are not a luxury; they are part of the
nation's soul, and they are essential to victory in battle.

General Gordon Sullivan
Army Chief of Staff
(1991–1995)

People sleep peaceably in their beds at night only because
rough men stand ready to do violence on their behalf.

George Orwell
1903–1940

Seeing That It Is Carried Out

General John J. Pershing, while inspecting one of his units during World War I, found a project that was not going too well, even though the officer in charge seemed to have a good plan. The general asked the lieutenant how much pay he received, and when the lieutenant replied: "$141.67 per month sir," General Pershing said: "Just remember that you get $1.67 for making your plan and issuing the order, and $140.00 for seeing that it is carried out."

From the book, *Bradley*, 1966

FROM MY GRID SQUARE

"Sir, could you please tell me where the real Army is?"

This is my story I have always referred to as "The Bill Coffey *Real Army* Story." It is a story I have told to most of my soldiers and other soldiers' soldiers many times. I believe it is a timeless story and worth telling again.

I was born in 1961 to an Infantry Captain and his wife. We grew up in Smalltown USA with my Mom staying at home raising my two sisters and myself while my dad served with the Connecticut National Guard as a full time Guardsman. As a child I remembered how decent and proud he looked in his uniform. He was always proud of his uniform, his soldiers, and his military career. He never really stated that he loved the Army and its soldiers; his actions and his bearing spoke louder than any words ever could. The Army he was in was the only Army I knew—to a small boy it was the "real" Army. I remember sometimes after Dad got home from his day's work, we would head down to the Armory where we kids would play in the Armory's gym while my Dad worked on paperwork in his office. We played with Army equipment, uniforms, etc. It was always fun. Being a soldier seemed like a really neat thing to do, and I figured that one day I wanted to be like my Dad. I remember his monthly weekend deployments, his summer training, and his many TDYs; but most of all I remember when he received his orders in early 1969 to go to Vietnam. I was 8 years old at that time. I was old enough to know that war was bad and that Vietnam was a dangerous place for my Dad to be, but I was not old enough to understand why he had to go. It took nearly two more decades before I understood. In June 1969 we all loaded into our stationwagon and took my Dad to the airport where he departed for Vietnam. Funny thing is I absolutely cannot remember our "good-byes" at the terminal gate. Thirty years later the only thing I can remember about that day is the long ride home after leaving the airport—three kids under 10 years old in the backseat and my mom driving. We cried all the way home, actually I think we howled. It was a very sad day for all of us—literally not knowing if we were ever going to see our Dad again.

Years later my Mom told me I cried every day throughout Dad's first six months in Vietnam. During Christmas of 1969 we met up with Dad in Hawaii for about 10 days during his R&R. That family reunion made his second six months bearable for all of us. It was a blessing that we really didn't know the danger he was really in. While in Vietnam my Dad served as the Battalion S-3 of the 1/12th Infantry and XO of the 1/22th Infantry Battalion, 2nd Brigade, 4th Infantry Division. Living on a fire base, he was in the thick of that war. On one occasion his OH-6 "Loach" helicopter was hit by a rocket fired from an RPG-7. The rocket was a dud and only left a large dent in the helicopter's tailboom. On another occasion in May 1970 his battalion air assaulted into Cambodia to attack a Vietcong training base where he caught some Vietcong mortar shrapnel in the shoulder. All this happened while life and my childhood pretty much went on undisturbed in Smalltown USA.

In June 1970 my Dad returned home safely to us. Soon after his return he began a series of active duty tours taking us to Carlisle PA, Northern VA, and finally Leavenworth KS before I went off to college. After 18 years as an "Army brat," I saw what I thought was the real Army and I knew I wanted to be part of it.

While in Army ROTC at the University of Kansas I continued with a perception of what I thought the Army was: an opportunity to travel, to be challenged, to lead and be led, assume responsibilities, be part of a profession that was respected by our nation serving a worthy cause, be part of organizations led by competent and caring leaders, and have an opportunity to pay something back to this Nation. The mentor I appreciated and respected most during this period was our ROTC Sergeant Major. His name was Sergeant Major Strong—Franklin Delano Roosevelt Strong (to be complete). He was an Infantryman and a Vietnam veteran with several "tours" in Nam. I considered him one of those NCOs from the "old mold," a mold that must have been broken after they made him. He was all American, all Army, a true patriot, a mentor, a leader, and a role model. His blood was more than red; it was also white and blue. SGM Strong taught me what was required of officers, what an officer's job was and wasn't. He was the first person ever to tell me what it was like to hold a wounded comrade on the battlefield and watch him die—that kind of stuck with me. He never really stated that he loved the Army and its soldiers; his actions and his bearing spoke louder than any words ever could. To a young ROTC cadet, SGM Strong was a one-of-a-kind, although years later I realized that this country had always had soldiers like SGM Strong who fought America's wars, led and trained American soldiers, and woke each morning really giving a damn about something more than their own personal safety, comfort, and career progression. SGM Strong represented the *real Army* to me. A nickname like "SGM Sam Damon" would have fit him well. He inspired and encouraged me, and with this inspiration I was ready to sign up for and excel at the best the *real Army* had to offer me. The notions of "distance lends enchantment" and "glory's on the horizon" began to set in. My personal race toward this ideal and the *real Army* had begun.

While in college I completed Air Assault School and Airborne School—this was real "Hooah" stuff, it wet my whistle and I loved the taste. In May 1983 my Dad, an Army Colonel on Active Duty, had me raise my right hand while he administered the oath of office. I was duly sworn into the Army as a newly commissioned 2LT. Life was good, my parents were proud of me, and me of them. Later that same afternoon, General "Shy" Meyer, the Chief of Staff of the Army (at that time), ceremonially administered the oath of office to about 20 of us newly commissioned officers in the KU Student Union Auditorium. After the ceremony I spoke with General Meyer. In my hand I held a

10-year-old photo of then BG Meyer and 12-year-old Bill Coffey. In the photo BG Meyer, then Deputy Commandant of the U.S. Army War College at Carlisle Barracks, was handing me a Junior National Rifle Association medal I had won at one of the Carlisle Barracks NRA club competitions. I remember showing him that photo of him and me taken 10 years earlier and commenting to him "Sir, our paths had crossed before, and I have to tell you, we've come a long way in 10 years." Here I was, talking with the CSA, my parents by my side, Ronald Reagan was our Commander in Chief, we had "an enemy" called the Warsaw Pact, ... we had good reason to serve and serve proudly. The *real Army* was just around the corner.

In January 1984, I entered Active Duty and reported to Fort Huachuca for the Military Intelligence Officer's Basic Course (MIOBC). This was when reality started setting in for me. Shortly after our course began it was obvious to all of us 2LTs that the OBC course was in disarray. The Intelligence Center and School had just begun the new "TASIO" (Tactical All Source Intelligence Officer's) course. It was a mess and really disillusioned many of us formidable 2LTs. Soon the permanent party cadre started telling us "Don't form your opinions about the Army from this place, this is not the *real Army*. Wait till you get to the *real Army* to form your opinions, this is just a TRADOC school, **not** the *real Army*." OK, so I had to wait, no biggie, I'm heading to Germany via Ranger School and I guess I'll just have to wait a little longer to get to the *real Army*.

I began Ranger School in August 1984; I had trained like hell the previous six months and was 158 pounds of lean mean green—I was hooah all the way. I learned a lot in Ranger School, primarily things about myself, my physical and mental capacities, my limits, my abilities, how to ... and how not to ... lead and motivate soldiers and make decisions under very strenuous conditions. I learned that I could go days without sleep, that thirst was worse than hunger, and being cold and wet was worse than thirst—that all three together really sucked. I realized that MREs were a precious gift—when we got them. Those little packets of powdered ketchup could really take the edge off your hunger (if you were disciplined enough to save one for those really long all night patrols).

At one point in Ranger School our class was aboard a C-141 aircraft that was flying us to a dry lake bed that would serve as our Drop Zone (DZ) somewhere north of El Paso in the New Mexico desert. This airborne insertion began our "desert phase" of Ranger training. After a long and tiring night aboard the C-141 from Fort Benning Georgia to New Mexico we all got rigged up in our parachutes, stood up, hooked up, and shuffled to the door. The back doors of the C-141 opened several miles out from the DZ. Being the 3rd man in "the stick" I was no more than three feet from the door, giving me a clear view of the ground below and the 1st man in the stick, a much older man, a soldier with a large unlit cigar in his mouth, **not** a soldier from our Ranger class. "Who the hell is that?" I thought. "Doesn't he know you can't have smokes on the plane?" In the fog and haze of absolute fatigue I was unable to process any logic from this scene ... until, that is, I caught a glimpse of his name tag and rank. Four stars and "FOSS" on his helmet band, General Foss, at that time, was Commander of the Training and Doctrine Command (TRADOC). General Foss was more to me than just the TRADOC commander. I had known his name and had seen pictures of him from my childhood days. He was my Dad's Brigade XO in Vietnam. In some way, he was responsible for keeping my Dad alive in Vietnam. Whatever he did, or didn't do, in Vietnam allowed my family to remain in tact; it allowed me to have a father for the second part of my childhood. On that jet, over an unnamed part of the desert, a part of me wanted to tap General Foss on the shoulder and yell to him, over the deafening noise of the jet engines, "General Foss, my name is Bill Coffey, son of Major Coffey—he was one of your Battalion XOs in Vietnam. Thank you for getting him home alive." Between the jet engine noise, my fatigue, and the nervousness of the approaching drop zone, I just intermittently looked at him and the floating ground below and said nothing. The green light flashed and in a moment we were all out of the jet and floating to the ground. On that aircraft was the first and last time I ever saw General Foss. After thirty-one years since my Dad left for Vietnam, wherever you are General Foss, let me take this opportunity to thank you and all the soldiers of the 4th Infantry Division for fighting the fight and getting my Dad back home.

After 42 days in Ranger School, my "patrols passed percentage" fell below 50% and I was dropped from the course for what they called "Training Deficiencies." My bubble was popped. At that time the Infantry Center had an unofficial policy that noncombat arms officers would not be recycled. I left Fort Benning in mid October with an attitude and a chip on my shoulder. Ranger School was certainly not the *real Army* as I had earlier envisioned it might be. I had a Platoon Leader job awaiting me in Germany and I just couldn't wait to get there.

During my 30 days of post-Ranger School "Leave" I managed to bring my Ranger School exit weight of 144 pounds to 172 in a mere three weeks. I had lots of food—ate tons, life was on the upswing and my attitude was in repair. In November 1984, I reported into B Company, 165th MI Battalion (Tactical Exploitation), 205th MI Bde, V Corps, Germany. I became the Platoon Leader for the battalion's three MSQ-103 ("Teampack") track-mounted radar intercept and direction finding systems. I had a great Platoon Sergeant and Company Commander. At the time of my arrival the battalion had just finished reorganizing from the 331st Army Security Agency (ASA) to the 165th MI Bn (CEWI). We were going through a TO&E change under the J Series "Army of Excellence" TO&E; we were also going through fleet vehicle change from M151 (jeeps) to CUCVs. REFORGER '85 was just two months away and we were working long hours to prepare for that too. I worked like hell with great soldiers, loved it, but was told by many that the 165th was not the *real Army*. My Company Commander, whose opinion I respected, grabbed me one day and told me "the 165th is the most messed up unit I've ever seen in the Army, please don't form your opinions about the Army based on this place.

After the 165th you will hopefully get to a *real* unit". "Really?" I thought. After hearing this story in different forms from different soldiers, I actually began to believe it.

After a year as a Platoon Leader I PCSed within Germany to the 56th Field Artillery Command (Pershing II Missiles), I became the Battalion S-2 of a newly forming battalion. I was the 35th person to sign into the unit and within four months we capped off at a strength of 915 soldiers. "Fit to Fight" was our motto. We were big and bad and worked like hell. The 56th had 108 missiles in country with 16 "on pad" with nuclear-tipped warheads 24 hours a day, 365 days a year—ready to fire at a moment's notice. The Pershing II missiles epitomized the Cold War. We trained continuously, had a rigorous PT program, and actually studied the enemy. The Soviets had us on the top of their PIR (Priority Intelligence Requirements) list, we had many demonstrators, and it seemed everyone was spying on our unit. Hell—we were the only Army nuclear unit in Europe—and everyone knew it. The 56th was a challenging place to be—we had a real world mission and when we woke each morning we knew we had a job to do. In the 56th you either stayed leaning forward in your foxhole ... or you were eaten alive. My boss, the Battalion S-3, always looked after me and was concerned that I would form a negative opinion about the Army based on what I saw in the 56th. One day he grabbed me and told me "Bill, the 56th eats its young ... please don't form your opinion about the Army based on this place. This place is like no other place in the Army. Wait till you go somewhere else before you decide if the Army's for you." "Damn!" I thought. What does a Lieutenant have to do to find the *real Army*?

After 25 challenging and rewarding months as a Battalion S-2 I returned to Fort Huachuca to attend the MI Officers Advanced Course. It was there, again, that I heard talk of the Intel Center and School "not being the *real Army*." At that point I started seriously asking career soldiers "Please if you can, tell me what the *real Army* is and where it's located." My effort to find out where this *real Army* was uncovered some very interesting and provocative answers. I suspect that many of the soldiers I asked this question to had never been asked this particular question before. I continued to ask soldiers this question even after leaving Fort Huachuca. Asking soldiers I served with in the 2nd Infantry Division in Korea and soldiers from my Dad's Vietnam unit, the 4th Infantry Division with whom I also served with at Fort Carson CO, some 23 years later, I was able to validate and refine the answer. After several years of telling the story and thorough analysis, I am now able to clearly articulate the answer. So here it is:

The *real Army* is everywhere. The *real Army* is your "personal Grid Square," that 3-foot-by-3-foot square of ground that you call your own. You, your soldiers, your unit, your unit's mission are an extension of your personal grid square. When all these personal grid squares fit together, an effective fighting force is formed. Your personal grid square is everywhere you are, regardless of your unit, your boss, or situations in the Army. Here are a few more bits to the answer:

1. Every soldier has a personal grid square.

2. Every soldier I ever led or followed received my full commitment, honesty, and loyalty—they expected and deserved nothing less.

3. For every day I wore the uniform, *I* was the *real Army*. I was not "in" the Army, I *was* the Army, and every soldier around me was the *real Army* as well. All of our collective efforts, represented by the concept of personal grid squares, were the *real Army*. There were times when I was disillusioned, times when I was elated, times when I questioned my role and worth; but I know now in hindsight that all of my jobs were important, and all of the soldiers I worked with had important jobs in the *real Army* as well.

4. Everyone in the Army today is also in the *real Army* ... *everyone*. No one can wish this fact away. It is true, whether one cares to believe it or not. To not believe this underestimates the importance of your job, assigned mission, and the soldiers of your unit.

5. The notions that distance lends enchantment and glory's on the horizon are fallacious. Glory is here today—and for all the soldiers "on point" in today's Army, all I have to say to you is "Welcome to the *real Army*, you've arrived—no matter where you are. These are truly the good old days. Make the most of them." If you don't believe this now, wait a few years after you ETS and look back on those great days in the Army, the camaraderie, the excitement, the challenges met and exceeded, the great soldiers (America's finest!), the sacrifices of brow sweat, emotional energy and elbow grease deposited for values we hold near and dear to our hearts.

Yes, truly my years in the Army were "good old days." I cherish them and would not trade them for anything. I wish all the soldiers in today's Army could consciously know and emotionally feel the importance of their personal grid square and the important role they play in supporting and defending everything this country stands for.

Today in my office here in Colorado Springs, I have but two photos on display from my Army days. They are the two photos I am most proud of. One is of my soldiers and me standing inside the "1K (Kilometer) Zone" on the Inter-German Border near Bad Herdsfeld, Germany. The second photo is of my soldiers and me standing in a trench on the DMZ in Korea, near Radar Site #7 and the Sibion-Ni approach. Those days, with my soldiers, literally on the frontiers of freedom, fighting the "Cold War," were to me the best of the *real Army*. Today there are many frontiers of freedom where American soldiers walk point—in Kosovo, Bosnia, Korea, Kuwait, throughout dozens of other countries, and as well as throughout CONUS-based units. Today there are nearly 500,000 *real* personal grid squares in the *real* Active Army alone. All of these soldiers, all of their grid squares, and all of their units are the *real Army*. Period.

I have taken the time to put pen to this story because I believe this story represents one of the greatest lessons I have learned. There are many stories and lessons out there to be taught and learned, and I suspect the only unique aspect of my story is the fact that it is mine to tell and the one I feel it is most important to share.

William T. Coffey, Jr.
MAJ (USAR)
Citizen and Soldier

[A version of this story appeared in the September 2000 issue of *ARMY Magazine*, published by the Association of the U.S. Army.]

POINT, COUNTERPOINT

The below paragraph was printed in the *US News and World Report* (USN&WR, October 4, 1999), and offers some opinions of the military Reserve Officer Training Corps (ROTC). Following the USN&WR Letter to the Editor are some responses to this article which provide opposing views of ROTC and the military at large. Such exchanges of ideas and opinions are what continue to make America worth fighting for ... freedom of speech.

HOW DISTURBED I WAS TO SEE YOUR article in the September 6 issue about ROTC scholarships as a means of providing funds for a college education. The education associated with ROTC is a contradiction to the academic freedom enjoyed at university campuses; military training on college campuses, in fact, makes a mockery of education. Far from taking a global view of learning, ROTC encourages narrow patriotism and a philosophy of any means (killing people and polluting environments) to the end. The institutionalized mistreatment of gays and lesbians in the military and sexual harassment of women are par for the course.

KATHERINE VAN WORMER
Professor of Social Work
University of Northern Iowa
Cedar Falls, Iowa

Response 1:

Dear Professor Van Wormer,

I just finished reading your letter to the editor in U.S. News & World Report magazine (4 Oct) and was compelled to address your shockingly prejudiced, obviously uninformed and frankly laughable viewpoint on ROTC and the military in general. Your unenlightened perspective belies a reckless if not tragic ignorance that brings disrepute upon the institution that employs you. It is a shame you felt obliged to comment on something you apparently know so little about. I wonder if in your extensive research in "Social Work" you ever encountered someone who's actually served in the armed forces? The answer goes without saying. Allow me to be your first.

It troubles me that you must be reminded that the academic freedom you enjoy and cherish so dearly was purchased with the precious lives and blood of many a noble soldier on wretched battlefields here and abroad over the past 223 years. Do you honestly believe freedom of any sort comes without tremendous cost? Are you so willfully naive to think you'd enjoy the same license if you were a professor in China, Iran, North Korea, or the Sudan?

How many young men and women have you talked to lately who spent their Christmas holiday patrolling some godforsaken minefield like Bosnia, or their 5th wedding anniversary in a row at sea, or the birthday of their first daughter stopping a madman from achieving his goal of ethnic cleansing? Tell me. Do you really think we acknowledge a call to the profession of arms so we can "kill people and pollute environments"? To believe such sophomoric rubbish demands some fairly sophisticated cerebral blinders.

I have served in the U.S. Air Force for 11 years now, flying long hours over countless global hot spots, and I have not once encountered a fellow solider, sailor, or airman who subscribes to a "narrow patriotism and a philosophy of any means." Not one. Rather, they are ladies and gentlemen of highest caliber, selfless devotion to the cause of freedom, and tireless service to an often-thankless nation. Your mischaracterization is so off base it borders on unforgivable.

It would seem to me that your Department of Social Work would have whole syllabi devoted to the role of the military in the field of social work. I can think of no greater social service than an institution committed to risking the lives of its members to preserve and defend the very citizenry from which it hails. How many oppressed refugees, disaster victims, and starving children have been mercifully delivered from their plight by the military in just the last decade? Need we reflect on the fact that the whole of Western Europe owes its freedom from Nazi fascism to a valiant few in olive drab and khaki? Perhaps you should invite a concentration camp survivor or a Kosovar Albanian to give a guest lecture extolling the magnificent "social services" they've benefited from at the hands of the military.

Finally, I find it humorous that academics like yourselves who indoctrinate our youth with the dogma of "positive tolerance" for every aberrant lifestyle cannot find it within yourselves to tolerate an institution to which you owe your very peace, comfort, and well being. It is an amusing double standard.

My exhortation to you is to get out of the rarified air in your office, walk over to your ROTC detachment in Lang Hall and interact with the men and women in uniform and those aspiring to wear it. Perhaps then you will wake up from your slumber of conscious ignorance, join the ranks of the enlightened, and offer a prayer of thanksgiving to God for the freedoms you take for granted and those who sacrifice daily on your behalf to secure it.

In Service To You,
Capt. Jonathan Clough

Response 2:

Dr. Van Wormer,

Greetings from Bosnia-Herzegovina.

Coming from a military family, and having spent 15+ years serving my country—half overseas (82 months), I find your comments in USN&WR laughable. I am sure by now you either regret your decision to write such dribble, or are trying to defend your views with some pathetic academic rationalization. The irony is your academic freedom is borne on the backs of the servicemen and women who gave their last full measure in conflict and war, and so-called peacekeeping ventures around the world.

I would love to hear your views on patriotism, as clearly they must be more worldly than mine. While you can sip your coffee and read your academic journals snug and comfy in your office, the folks who received their college degrees through the ROTC programs you so disdain are at this very moment performing dangerous duty all over the world. Underpaid, overworked, and in some dangerous environments you would never wish upon your worst enemy, they are laboring to provide you the security and freedoms you take for granted. These fine women and men rarely complain. Why, you might ask? Are they programmed automatons brainwashed by narrow patriotism? Of course not. However, they are far more global and perhaps understand patriotism more than you will ever realize.

Let me give you some testimony to the "globalism" you cannot understand from your perch in life:

I've seen the generosity of the American soldier in Desert Storm—under fire, sleepless, hungry, hot and miserable, the soldiers gave up their own bottled water and rations to feed the prisoners of war and displaced persons throughout the ground offensive and its aftermath.

In Bosnia during the war, I witnessed countless crews fly their precious aid cargos in and out of Sarajevo Airport, at great risk from small arms fire and occasional shelling. I watched the same crews airdrop food, medicine and blankets to Bosnian refugees encircled in the tiny remote villages of Zepa and Gorazde.

In Northern Iraq, I witnessed aircrews brilliantly perform the Symphony from Mars as they daily patrolled the skies over the Northern No Fly Zone to protect the Kurds, a nationality without a nation from the barbarity of Saddam Hussein.

In these and countless other places, I've seen the destitute faces of folks who look to the United States as the great experiment they wish to emulate. By the way, soldiers abhor war more than anyone, as they have seen its ugly face first hand. While it may seem trite to you, "Freedom isn't free." I have friends that have died to protect your academic freedom, including some great civilians. While you have doubtlessly enjoyed your holidays, I've spent Christmas, New Year's and Easter in harms way on more than one occasion. And my experience is probably not unlike any of the folks who have been in the service during the same timeframe. The next time you question the global views and patriotism of today's ROTC programs, keep in mind that these folks are ready and willing to lay their lives down for you. Your blanket statements about mistreatment of gays and sexual harassment of women are eloquent displays of your prejudice.

Think about us in Bosnia when you sit down at your Thanksgiving table this year. Say a prayer for the soldiers, sailors and airmen who will be doing their duty, so you can enjoy your wonderful dinner. Better yet, sit down and compose a letter of gratitude next time you get the urge to write USN&WR.

I'd write more, but frankly ... duty calls.

> Most Sincerely,
> MAJ Jim Stockmoe
> Eagle Base
> Bosnia-Herzegovina

Response 3:

Dr. Van Wormer,

I would like to tell you that in my opinion there is no greater pacifist on this earth than the young man or woman who has to fight and bleed and die. Those soldiers, and I was one of them for 10 years, hate and fear war and violence more than you could possibly imagine. When I was an 8-year-old child, my Dad was almost killed on two separate occasions in Vietnam—as a young boy I learned to hate war. As a Captain in the Army I was called up during Operation Desert Shield and told to be "ready to go in 48 hours"—I hated that call and feared the unknown. Now, as a father of two young children, I fear that they too may be called upon one day to serve this nation, and I know full well that this is their duty, and it may require them to fight and bleed and die—and this prospect makes me detest war and violence like only a parent can hate. Maybe a close analogy is the citizen who states "I have nothing against policemen, I just hate crime, domestic violence, gang riots, rape, and murder." It is important to recognize that the real comparison between a policeman and a soldier is that the policeman protects us and our neighborhoods and the soldier protects us and our country.

William Coffey

The greatest social service which a nation can provide for its people is to keep them alive and to keep them free.

General Bernard W. Rogers
Former Army Chief of Staff and
Supreme Allied Commander, Europe (SACEUR)

AMERICA: THE GOOD NEIGHBOR

Widespread but only partial news coverage was given recently to a remarkable editorial broadcast from Toronto by Gordon Sinclair, a Canadian television commentator. What follows is the full text of his trenchant remarks as printed in the congressional record:

This Canadian thinks it is time to speak up for the Americans as the most generous and possibly the least appreciated people on all the earth. Germany, Japan and, to a lesser extent, Britain and Italy were lifted out of the debris of war by the Americans who poured in billions of dollars and forgave other billions in debts. None of these countries is today paying even the interest on its remaining debts to the United States.

When the franc was in danger of collapsing in 1956, it was the Americans who propped it up, and their reward was to be insulted and swindled on the streets of Paris. I was there. I saw it. When distant cities are hit by earthquakes, it is the United States that hurries in to help. This spring, 59 American communities were flattened by tornadoes. Nobody helped.

The Marshall Plan and the Truman Policy pumped billions of dollars into discouraged countries. Now newspapers in those countries are writing about the decadent, warmongering Americans. I'd like to see just one of those countries that is gloating over the erosion of the United States Dollar build its own airplane. Does any other country in the world have a plane to equal the Boeing Jumbo Jet, the Lockheed Tristar, or the Douglas 10? If so, why don't they fly them? Why do all the International lines except Russia fly American Planes? Why does no other land on earth even consider putting a man or woman on the moon? You talk about Japanese technocracy, and you get radios. You talk about German technocracy, and you get automobiles. You talk about American technocracy, and you find men on the moon—not once, but several times—and safely home again.

You talk about scandals, and the Americans put theirs right in the store window for everybody to look at. Even their draft-dodgers are not pursued and hounded. They are here on our streets, and most of them, unless they are breaking Canadian laws, are getting American dollars from ma and pa at home to spend here.

When the railways of France, Germany and India were breaking down through age, it was the Americans who rebuilt them. When the Pennsylvania Railroad and the New York Central went broke, nobody loaned them an old caboose. Both are still broke. I can name you 5000 times when the Americans raced to the help of other people in trouble. Can you name me even one time when someone else raced to the Americans in trouble?

I don't think there was outside help even during the San Francisco earthquake. Our neighbors have faced it alone, and I'm one Canadian who is damned tired of hearing them get kicked around. They will come out of this thing with their flag high. And when they do, they are entitled to thumb their noses at the lands that are gloating over their present troubles. I hope Canada is not one of those.

A CONTRIBUTION TO EVERY CITIZEN

Speech (excerpts) by GEN (RET) Bernard W. Rogers upon being awarded the George C. Marshall Medal on 13 October 1999, at the Association of the United States Army (AUSA) Convention, Washington, D.C.

I should like to turn to some other matters, which I believe are of major importance to our Army. As the old sarge once said: "The Army ain't like it used to be, and it never was." But there are constants in our business, which remain sacred throughout time:

First, we should never forget: the mission of our Army is to fight and win the nation's battles on land. Victory is our mission. I shall never forget watching my boss, Gen. Mark Clark, then the UN/Far East Commander—when I was his executive officer—in Panmunjon on 27 July 1953 as he signed the Korean Armistice agreement with anguish on his face and tears in his eyes—victory had not been achieved.

Second, there are values, qualities and principles which must remain inviolable in our profession. No matter how they may be viewed in other professions—or on the political scene—we must protect them in our Army today, tomorrow, and in the 3rd Millennium. You see, the ethos of our profession is constructed around three factors:

1. A high level of professional competence—knowing the business of our profession;

2. Inviolate honor—the faithful adherence to moral and ethical principles;

3. Absolute integrity—the incorruptible moral character displayed in fulfilling trusts; integrity, the foundation of one's credibility.

Why is such a strict and rigid ethos required of our profession? Two key reasons:

First, we serve the common good of the American public, which places its trust in our profession to discharge our responsibilities in the competent and honorable manner they have grown to expect of us.

Second, military leaders are entrusted with God's greatest gift, the lives of their troops. In the terrible stress of combat, there must be trust and loyalty upwards, downwards, sideways. So in our profession, from the most junior to the most senior member in our chain of command: character matters; high moral standards matter; honesty matters; integrity matters; serving our country matters. With respect to the latter, Matthew Miller, in his review of Josiah Bunting's book, *An Education for Our Time*, reminds us: "It is difficult to escape the conclusion that America's best and brightest no longer feel the call to duty, and that the only service they feel is personal, the only affiliation is the cult of the individual."

Third, in our business there are other matters, which I have always deemed important:

- The NCO Corps is the backbone of our Army, something I learned in 1943 on the barracks floor at Camp Adair as my platoon sergeant taught me everything he knew about the heavy machine gun. We must support and enhance the corps at every opportunity by whatever means we can.

- In our business, there is no place for "spin control," which is nothing more than misleading at best and lying at worst. Competent leaders should want their subordinates to "stand up and be counted," "tell it like it is," to speak out until a decision is made and then implement that decision to the best of their ability. (After all, "yes men" come a dime a dozen.) This requires that superiors create an environment in which candor can flourish, with all concerned understanding that disagreement does not equate to disloyalty.

- In our business, we must not be afraid of change; we should welcome it, exploit it, and always think new, think different, think better. We must not accept as justification for actions such phrases as: "We've always done it this way," "It's so because I say it's so," or, "Just believe me it's true." Seldom are actions relevant when based solely on custom, authority or faith.

- Competent leaders should search for ways to get feedback about their daily operations so they might improve them. And they must not be "frightened leaders," afraid of what they might learn. Leaders must strive to take the molasses out of the system and to remove the harassments and the burrs from under soldier's saddles. Leaders must make decisions to take actions based—not on what they believe is best for their careers—but on what is best and right for soldiers.

- The greatest moral imperative for leaders is to take proper care of their troops and their families. Thus, they must balance strict discipline, tough training and enforcement of the authority-obedience hierarchy with preserving the dignity and worth of the individual soldiers. Compassion, respect, caring and equality all play a role.

- Finally, all of us must understand and appreciate the media and Congress and the roles they play. Bashing them or ignoring them makes no sense: They'll always be there, fulfilling their roles as they perceive them to be. Our challenge is to understand these roles, take them into account and learn how to get along with and influence these two important institutions, as we seek their support.

Well, I've given you an earful this evening, delving into nostalgia, talking about questions which must be faced and underscoring some of the important characteristics, values, and qualities which I believe are so important in our Army. AUSA has not only paid me the high honor of recognizing my family and me with the Marshall Medal—for which I shall forever be grateful—it has also given me the chance to raise these matters. And why did I want to do so? Because, I love our Army, and have for over six decades, and I wish to "undergird" our leaders in their efforts to retain the high standards and principles which have been the Army's strength for two centuries.

We must never allow them to be eroded. We must never permit ourselves to board the train, which is heading toward the lowest common denominator for standards and quality. And always remember: Our profession is unique among all others. A doctor contributes to his patients; a priest to the members of his parish; a lawyer contributes to his clients; a politician to his constituents. But those privileged to wear our nation's uniforms belong to a profession in which every member, every day, makes a contribution—no matter how small—to every citizen of this great land. And in the end, isn't that why so many of us wear the uniform for so long, just to be able to make that kind of contribution?

Do your duty in all things,
you cannot do more,
you should never wish to do less.

Duty is the most sublime word
in the English language.

General Robert E. Lee

The consideration that human happiness and
moral duty are inseparably connected,
will always continue to prompt me to
promote the former by inculcating the
practice of the latter.

George Washington

I am only an average man, but I work
harder at it than the average man.

Theodore Roosevelt

I believe that every right implies a responsibility;
every opportunity, an obligation;
every possession, a duty.

John D. Rockefeller, Jr.
1839–1937
Founder of Standard Oil Company,
Philanthropist

THE VERY BEST I KNOW HOW

Abraham Lincoln

If I were to try to read, much less answer, all the attacks made on me, this shop might as well be closed for any other business. I do the very best I know how—the very best I can, and I mean to keep doing so until the end. If the end brings me out all right, what is said against me won't amount to anything. If the end brings me out wrong, ten angels swearing I was right would make no difference.

*Do what you can, with what you have,
where you are.*

Theodore Roosevelt
1858–1919
25th President of the United States
(1901–1909)

*We are not to expect to be translated from
despotism to liberty in a featherbed.*

Thomas Jefferson
in a letter to LaFayette
1743–1826
3rd President of the United States
(1801–1809)

*Let us have faith that right makes might; and in that
faith let us dare to do our duty as we understand it.*

Abraham Lincoln

IN THE HOUR OF THIS COUNTRY'S PERIL

*No matter how humble the positions we were destined
to fill after the Civil War, we were always to derive
infinite satisfaction from the thought that in the hour
of the country's peril we had not been found wanting,
but had cheerfully rendered what little service we
could, to defend its honor and preserve its life.*

Theodore Gerrish
20th Maine Volunteers, Civil War
from his book, *Rank and File*

Scouts and Guides for the Army of the Potomac   Photographed at Berlin,
Maryland, October 1862, by Alexander Gardner.
© National Archives.

Private Robert H. Lister

27th Infantry Division
Office of the Commanding General
Fort Ord, California

27 February 1942

The Honorable Clinton P. Anderson, M.C.
House of Representatives

Dear Mr. Anderson:

Your letter of February 17, to the Adjutant General, concerning Private
Robert H. Lister, Company A, 165th Infantry, has been sent to me.
You state:

"I am wondering if there has been some mistake in his assignment to
Fort Ord.

Robert Lister, has had a fine education, has a Master's Degree, is about ready for a Doctor's Degree, is an expert Spanish student, a skilled archeologist, and has been an instructor at the University of New Mexico."

In this division of 22,000 men, I receive many letters similar to yours from parents, relatives, friends and sweethearts. They do not understand why the man who had a good law practice at home cannot be in the Judge Advocate Generals Department, why the drug store manager cannot work in the post hospital, why the school teacher cannot be used in educational work. They are willing for someone else to do the hard, dirty work of the fighting man so long as the one they are interested in can be spared that duty.

If doctors in the future are to have the privilege of practicing their profession, if archeologists are to investigate antiquity, if students are to have the privilege of taking degrees, and professors the privilege of teaching in their own way, somebody must march and fight and bleed and die and I know no reason why students, doctors, professors, and archeologists shouldn't do their share of it.

You say, "It strikes me as too bad to take that type of education and bury it in a rifle squad," as though there were something low or mean or servile being a member of a rifle squad and only morons and ditch diggers should be given such duty. I know of no place red blooded men of intelligence and initiative are more needed than in the rifle or weapons squad.

In this capacity, full recognition is given to the placing of men so that they may do the work most beneficial to the unit of which they are a part. Whenever men are needed for a particular duty, the records of all men having the required skills and qualifications are considered. I have examined the records of Private Lister and it is fairly complete. I know he holds the 100-yard dash and broad jump records in the Border Conference; that he was president of his fraternity; that his mother was born in Alabama and his father in Michigan; that his father lives at the Burlington Hotel in Washington and I suspect asked you to do what you could to get his son on other duty.

It is desirable that all men, regardless of their specialty, shall learn by doing; how hard it is to march with a pack for 20 miles; how to hold their own in bayonet combat; and how to respect the man who really takes it, namely the private in the rifle squad.

If Private Lister has special qualifications for intelligence duty, he will be considered when a vacancy occurs in the regimental, brigade, or division intelligence section. You can't keep a good man down in the Army for long. Every commander is anxious to get hold of men with imagination, intelligence, initiative, and drive.

Because you may think I'm a pretty good distance from a rifle squad, I should like to tell you I have a son on Bataan peninsula. All I know of him is that he was wounded on January 19. I hope he is back by now where the rifle squads are taking it, and I wish I were beside him there.

I have written you this long letter because in your high position you exercise a large influence on what people think and the way they regard the Army. It is necessary for them to understand men must do that which best helps to win the war and often that is not the same as what they do best.

Sincerely yours,

Ralph T. McPernell
Brig Gen, USA
Commanding

PEARL HARBOR

At 7:55 on Sunday morning, December 7, 1941, Imperial Japan launched a surprise attack on American forces at Pearl Harbor, thrusting the United States into the crucible of World War II.

Attacking in two waves, Japanese aircraft killed or wounded almost 3,600 Americans (over 1,000 of them aboard the battleship Arizona) sank or badly damaged most of our Pacific Fleet, and destroyed or damaged almost all U.S. aircraft in the area. In his historic speech to the Congress on the following day, President Franklin Roosevelt requested and the Congress approved a declaration of war against Japan. With characteristic optimism and confidence in the spirit of the American people, he provided the following speech:

Mr. Vice President, Mr. Speaker, members of the Senate and the House of Representatives ... yesterday, December 7th, 1941, [was] *a date which will live in infamy.* The United States of America was suddenly and deliberately attacked by naval and air forces of the Empire of Japan. The United States was at peace with that nation, and at the solicitation of Japan then still in conversation with its government and its emperor, looking toward the maintenance of peace in the Pacific. Indeed, one hour after Japanese air squadrons had commenced bombing in the American island of Oahu, the Japanese Ambassador to the United States, and his colleague, delivered to our Secretary of State a formal reply to a recent American message. And while this reply stated that it seemed useless to continue the existing diplomatic negotiations, it contained no threat or hint of war of armed attack. It will be recorded that the distance of Hawaii from Japan makes it obvious that the attack was deliberately planned many days or even weeks ago. During the intervening time, the Japanese government has deliberately sought to deceive the United States by false statements and expressions of hope for continued peace. The attack yesterday on the Hawaiian Islands has caused severe damage to American naval and military forces. I regret to tell you that very many American lives have been lost. In addition, American ships have been reported torpedoed on the high seas between San Francisco and Honolulu. Yesterday, the Japanese government also launched an attack against Malaya, last night Japanese forces attacked Hong Kong, last night Japanese forces attacked Guam, last night Japanese forces attacked the Philippine Islands, last night the Japanese attacked Wake Island, and this morning the Japanese attacked Midway Island. Japan has therefore undertaken a surprise offensive extending throughout the Pacific area. The facts of yesterday and today speak for themselves. The people of the United States have already formed their opinions and well understand the implications to the very life and safety of our nation. As Commander and Chief of the Army and Navy, I have directed that all measures be taken for our defense, that always will our whole nation remember the character of the onslaught against us.

No matter how long it may take us to overcome this premeditated invasion the American people in their righteous might will win through to absolute victory.

I believe that I interpret the will of the Congress and of the people when I assert that we will not only defend ourselves to the uttermost, but will make it very certain that this form of treachery shall never again endanger us. Hostilities exist, there is no blinking at the fact that our people, our territory, and our interest are in grave danger. With confidence in our armed forces, with the unbounding determination of our people, we will gain the inevitable triumph, so help us God. I ask that the Congress declare, that since the unprovoked and dastardly attack by Japan on Sunday, December 7th, 1941, a state of war has existed between the United States and the Japanese Empire.

President Franklin Delano Roosevelt
Address to Congress and the Nation
December 8, 1941

*Confidence is contagious.
So is lack of confidence.*

Vince Lombardi
1913–1970
Coach of the Green Bay Packers

Three thousand miles from home, an American Army is fighting for you. Everything you hold worthwhile is at stake. Only the hardest blows can win against the enemy we are fighting. Invoking the spirits of our forefathers the Army asks your unflinching support to the end with the high ideals for which America's stand may endure upon the earth.

General John Joseph "Blackjack" Pershing
1860–1948
Army General
Mexican Civil War and World War I

We must be the great arsenal of democracy.

Franklin Delano Roosevelt
1882–1945
32nd President of the United States
(1933–1945)

DUTIES OF AN OFFICER

The safety, honor, and welfare of your country come first ... always and every time.

The honor, welfare, and comfort of the men you command come next.

Your own ease, comfort, and safety come last ... always and every time.

General George S. Patton, Jr.

General George S. Patton, Jr.

Commander, Third Army
World War II
1885–1945

Mediterranean Theater of Operations
LTC Lyle Bernard, Commanding Officer, 30th Infantry Regiment and LTG George S. Patton, Jr. discuss military strategy near Brolo, Sicily, 1943.
©National Archives.

If you can't get them to salute when they should salute, and wear the clothes you tell them to wear, how are you going to get them to die for their country?

Any commander who fails to obtain his objective, and who is not dead or severely wounded, has not done his full duty.

General George S. Patton, Jr.

NOBILITY AND DIGNITY

Look at an infantryman's eyes and you can tell how much war he has seen … . I don't make the infantryman look noble, because he couldn't look noble even if he tried. Still there is a certain nobility and dignity in combat soldiers and medical aid men with dirt in their ears. They are rough and their language gets coarse because they live a life stripped of convention and niceties. Their nobility and dignity come from the way they live unselfishly and risk their lives to help each other. They are normal people who have been put where they are, and whose actions and feelings have been molded by their circumstances … there are gentlemen and boors; intelligent ones and stupid ones; talented ones and inefficient ones. But when they are all together and they are fighting, despite their bitching and griping and goldbricking and mortal fear, they are facing cold steel and screaming lead and hard enemies, and they are advancing and beating the hell out of the opposition.

SGT Bill Mauldin
from his book, *Up Front*, 1945
*U.S. Army Sergeant, Cartoonist, and
War Correspondent for "Stars & Stripes" during World War II*

Medics helping an injured soldier   France, 1944. World War II.
©National Archives.

WORDS BEFORE D-DAY

From: Supreme Headquarters Allied Expeditionary Force

Soldiers, Sailors and Airmen of the Allied Expeditionary Force!

You are about to embark upon the Great Crusade, toward which we have striven these many months. The eyes of the world are upon you. The hopes and prayers of liberty-loving people everywhere march with you. In company with our brave Allies and brothers-in-arms on other fronts, you will bring about the destruction of the German war machine, the elimination of Nazi tyranny over the oppressed peoples of Europe, and security for ourselves in a free world.

Your task will not be an easy one. Your enemy is well trained, well equipped and battle hardened. He will fight savagely.

**General Dwight David
"Ike" Eisenhower**
1890–1969
34th President of the United States
(1953–1961)

But this is the year 1944! Much has happened since the Nazi triumphs of 1940–41. The United Nations have inflicted upon the Germans great defeats, in open battle, man-to-man. Our air offensive has seriously reduced their strength in the air and their capacity to wage war on the ground. Our Home Fronts have given us an overwhelming superiority in weapons and munitions of war, and placed at our disposal great reserves of trained fighting men. The tide has turned! The free men of the world are marching together to Victory!

I have full confidence in your courage, devotion to duty and skill in battle. We will accept nothing less than full Victory!

Good luck! And let us all beseech the blessing of Almighty God upon this great and noble undertaking.

A Son-of-a-Goddamned-Bitch Named George Patton

Below is the full uncensored text of General Patton's speech to the Third Army just before the Normandy invasion, somewhere in England, June 5, 1944.

The Corps Chaplain gave the invocation while the men stood with bowed heads, asking divine guidance for the great Third Army so that they might speed victory to enslaved Europe. Major General Cook then introduced Lieutenant General Simpson, whose Army was still preparing for their part in the war.

"We are here," said General Simpson, "to listen to the words of a great man. A man who will lead you into whatever you might face, with heroism, ability, and foresight. A man who has proved himself amid shot and shell. My greatest hope is that someday soon, I will have my own great army fighting with him, side by side."

General Patton arose and strode swiftly to the microphone; the men snapped to their feet and stood silently. Patton surveyed them grimly. "Be seated," he said. The words were not a request but a command. The General's voice rose high and clear.

Men, this stuff that some sources sling around about America wanting out of this war, not wanting to fight, is a crock of bullshit. Americans love to fight, traditionally. All real Americans love the sting and clash of battle. You are here today for three reasons. First, because you are here to defend your homes and your loved ones. Second, you are here for your own self respect, because you would not want to be anywhere else. Third, you are here because you are real men and all real men like to fight. When you, here, everyone of you, were kids, you all admired the champion marble player, the fastest runner, the toughest boxer, the big league ball players, and the All-American football players. Americans love a winner. Americans will not tolerate a loser. Americans despise cowards. Americans play to win all of the time. I wouldn't give a hoot in hell for a man who lost and laughed. That's why Americans have never lost nor will ever lose a war; for the very idea of losing is hateful to an American. You are not all going to die. Only two percent of you right here today would die in a major battle. Death must not be feared. Death, in time, comes to all men. Yes, every man is scared in his first battle. If he says he's not, he's a liar. Some men are cowards but they fight the same as the brave men or they get the hell slammed out of them watching men fight who are just as scared as they are. The real hero is the man who fights even though he is scared. Some men get over their fright in a minute under fire. For some, it takes an hour. For some, it takes days. But a real man will never let his fear of death overpower his honor, his sense of duty to his country, and his innate manhood. Battle is the most magnificent competition in which a human being can indulge. It brings out all that is best and it removes all that is bad. Americans pride themselves on being He Men and they ARE He Men. Remember that the enemy is just as frightened as you are, and probably more so. They are not supermen. All through your Army careers, you men have bitched about what you call "chicken shit drilling." That, like everything else in this Army, has a definite purpose. That purpose is alertness. Alertness must be bred into every soldier. I don't give a fuck for a man who's not always on his toes. You men are veterans or you wouldn't be here. You are ready for what's to come. A man must be alert at all times if he expects to stay alive. If you're not alert, sometime, a German son-of-an-asshole-bitch is going to sneak up behind you and beat you to death with a sockful of shit! There are four hundred neatly marked graves somewhere in Sicily, all because one man went to sleep on the job. But they are German graves, because we caught the bastard asleep before they did.

An Army is a team. It lives, sleeps, eats, and fights as a team. This individual heroic stuff is pure horse shit. The bilious bastards who write that kind of stuff for the Saturday Evening Post don't know any more about real fighting under fire than they know about fucking!

We have the finest food, the finest equipment, the best spirit, and the best men in the world. Why, by God, I actually pity those poor sons-of-bitches we're going up against. By God, I do. My men don't surrender, and I don't want to hear of any soldier under my command being captured unless he has been hit. Even if you are hit, you can still fight back. That's not just bull shit either. The kind of man that I want in my command is just like the lieutenant in Libya, who, with a Luger against his chest, jerked off his helmet, swept the gun aside with one hand, and busted the hell out of the Kraut with his helmet. Then he jumped on the gun and went out and killed another German before they knew what the hell was coming off. And, all of that time, this man had a bullet through a lung. There was a real man! All of the real heroes are not storybook combat fighters, either.

Every single man in this Army plays a vital role. Don't ever let up. Don't ever think that your job is unimportant. Every man has a job to do and he must do it. Every man is a vital link in the great chain. What if every truck driver suddenly decided that he didn't like the whine of those shells overhead, turned yellow, and jumped headlong into a ditch? The cowardly bastard could say, "Hell, they won't miss me, just one man in thousands." But, what if every man thought that way? Where in the hell would we be now? What would our country, our loved ones, our homes, even the world, be like? No, Goddamnit, Americans don't think like that. Every man does his job. Every man serves the whole. Every department, every unit, is important in the vast scheme of this war. The ordnance men are needed to supply the guns and machinery of war to keep us rolling. The Quartermaster is needed to bring up food and clothes because where we are going there isn't a hell of a lot to steal. Every last man on K.P. has a job to do, even the one who heats our water to keep us from getting the "G.I. Shits." Each man must not think only of himself, but also of his buddy fighting beside him.

We don't want yellow cowards in this Army. They should be killed off like rats. If not, they will go home after this war and breed more cowards. The brave men will breed more brave men. Kill off the Goddamned cowards and we will have a nation of brave men. One of the bravest men that I ever saw was a fellow on top of a telegraph pole in the midst of a furious fire fight in Tunisia. I stopped and asked what the hell he was doing up there at a time like that. He answered, "Fixing the wire, Sir." I asked, "Isn't that a little unhealthy right about now?" He answered, "Yes Sir, but the Goddamned wire has to be fixed." I asked, "Don't those planes strafing the road bother you?" And he answered, "No, Sir, but you sure as hell do!" Now, there was a real man. A real soldier. There was a man who devoted all he had to his duty, no matter how seemingly insignificant his duty might appear at the time, no matter how great the odds. And you should have seen those trucks on the rode to Tunisia.

Those drivers were magnificent. All day and all night they rolled over those son-of-a-bitching roads, never stopping, never faltering from their course, with shells bursting all around them all of the time. We got through on good old American guts. Many of those men drove for over forty consecutive hours. These men weren't combat men, but they were soldiers with a job to do. They did it, and in one hell of a way they did it. They were part of a team. Without team effort, without them, the fight would have been lost. All of the links in the chain pulled together and the chain became unbreakable.

Don't forget, you men don't know that I'm here. No mention of that fact is to be made in any letters. The world is not supposed to know what the hell happened to me. I'm not supposed to be commanding this Army. I'm not even supposed to be here in England. Let the first bastards to find out be the Goddamned Germans. Some day I want to see them raise up on their piss-soaked hind legs and howl, "Jesus Christ, it's the Goddamned Third Army again and that son-of-a-fucking-bitch Patton." We want to get the hell over there. The quicker we clean up this Goddamned mess, the quicker we can take a little jaunt against the purple pissing Japs and clean out their nest, too, before the Goddamned Marines get all of the credit. Sure, we want to go home. We want this war over with. The quickest way to get it over with is to go get the bastards who started it. The quicker they are whipped, the quicker we can go home. The shortest way home is through Berlin and Tokyo. And when we get to Berlin, I am personally going to shoot that paper hanging son-of-a-bitch Hitler. Just like I'd shoot a snake!

When a man is lying in a shell hole, if he just stays there all day, a German will get to him eventually. The hell with that idea. The hell with taking it. My men don't dig foxholes. I don't want them to. Foxholes only slow up an offensive. Keep moving. And don't give the enemy time to dig one either. We'll win this war, but we'll win it only by fighting and by showing the Germans that we've got more guts than they have; or ever will have. We're not going to just shoot the sons-of-bitches, we're going to rip out their living Goddamned guts and use them to grease the treads of our tanks. We're going to murder those lousy Hun cock suckers by the bushel-fucking-basket. War is a bloody, killing business. You've got to spill their blood, or they will spill yours. Rip them up the belly. Shoot them in the guts. When shells are hitting all around you and you wipe the dirt off your face and realize that instead of dirt it's the blood and guts of what once was your best friend beside you, you'll know what to do! I don't want to get any messages saying, "I am holding my position." We are not holding a Goddamned thing. Let the Germans do that. We are advancing constantly and we are not interested in holding onto anything, except the enemy's balls. We are going to twist his balls and kick the living shit out of him all of the time. Our basic plan of operation is to advance and to keep on advancing regardless of whether we have to go over, under, or through the enemy. We are going to go through him like crap through a goose; like shit through a tin horn! From time to time there will be some complaints that we are pushing our people too hard. I don't give a good Goddamn about such complaints. I believe in the old and sound rule that an ounce of sweat will save a gallon of blood. The harder WE push, the more Germans we will kill. The more Germans we kill, the fewer of our men will be killed. Pushing means fewer casualties. I want you all to remember that.

There is one great thing that you men will all be able to say after this war is over and you are home once again. You may be thankful that twenty years from now when you are sitting by the fireplace with your grandson on your knee and he asks you what you did in the great World War II, you WON'T have to cough, shift him to the other knee and say, "Well, your Granddaddy shoveled shit in Louisiana." No, Sir, you can look him straight in the eye and say, "Son, your Granddaddy rode with the Great Third Army and a Son-of-a-Goddamned-Bitch named George Patton!"

That is all.

When I want my men to remember something important, to really make it stick, I give it to them double dirty. It may not sound nice to some bunch of little old ladies at an afternoon tea party, but it helps my soldiers to remember. You can't run an army without profanity; and it has to be eloquent profanity. An army without profanity couldn't fight it's way out of a piss-soaked paper bag. As for the types of comments I make, sometimes I just, by God, get carried away with my own eloquence.

General George S. Patton, Jr.

WW II POSTER

This poster was created in the early 1940s, when we were only forty-eight states, to appeal to our honor and patriotic spirit in the face of adversity. It captures the essence of duty in the U.S. military—teamwork, unity, and strength in numbers.

TO HELL AND BACK

I ... believe in ... all the men who stood up against the enemy, taking their beatings without whimper and their triumphs without boasting. The men who went and would go again to hell and back to preserve what our country thinks right and decent.

Audie Murphy
from his book, *To Hell and Back*
1949

Lieutenant Audie Murphy

Medal of Honor recipient; most decorated American soldier in WW II. Author, Actor, Soldier

The duty of a soldier in time of war is to fight and if need be to die.

T. R. Fehrenbach
from his book, *This Kind of War*

American Infantrymen   Korean War

LIFE AMONG THE INDIANS

In 1954 Lieutenant General W. B. Palmer wrote the article "Life Among the Indians" about the importance of quality staff work, gathering complete facts and employing common sense, patience and good temper.

The General Staff is a corporate tribe with a few chiefs and many Indians. The latter do the work and expend the sweat all in the interests of the United States Army.

The General Staff is no place for glamour boys, self-seekers, and glory-hunters. It requires officers who are thorough, painstaking and sound. General Staff work is mostly hard digging to establish the facts. Our biggest concern is to be sure we know what we are talking about. That is the hardest thing in the world, to know what you are talking about. First and last we must have facts: real, verified facts; complete facts.

So what we look for first is common sense, just plain horse sense. Second, patience. And, most important of all, good temper.

You also need the ability, which you must develop, to show one or two essential facts on a piece of paper no bigger than the palm of my hand.

An Army exists for only one purpose: action. The staff exists only to produce action. We call you an "action officer" because we want action. All you are here for is to get something done. Any paper, any word you write, is wasted effort unless it directly contributes to getting something done. You may have a long hard task, a lot of research, a lot of conferences, a lot of concurrences; but all the time your mission is to find that solution and get something done.

Now the first thing is to gather all the pertinent facts; but the hardest part of that is to be sure that they are in truth factual. I cannot warn you too solemnly that this is very hard, this being sure you have right and true facts. The most awe-inspiring people sometimes make important assertions that are not facts at all.

In London, one day in February 1944, one of our greatest generals told me that for the invasion of France our M4 tanks must have half of their ammunition in the form of white phosphorus shells. He said our tanks had burned up lots of German tanks with white phosphorus shells in Sicily, and anybody in the 2d Armored Division could tell me about it. I think we were then manufacturing about five percent white phosphorus shells for the M4 tank, so he was making a hair-raising demand. I went at once to the 2d Armored Division to get the story. The commanders all assured me that it was quite true—white phosphorus had really paid off in Sicily, destroying many German tanks with fire.

I then asked them for detailed, exact accounts of some actions in which this had occurred. Ten days later, I was told that they had been unable to find a single soldier or officer who would claim to have set a German tank on fire with white phosphorus shells fired from an M4 tank.

They did find one case in which a self-propelled 75mm mountain howitzer of low muzzle velocity had been shooting white phosphorus at a German tank which broke into flames. The gunner said very honestly that everybody had been firing at the German tank and he did not know whether he had fired the shot that did it. There was no discoverable basis of truth in the very positive assertions which made one of the greatest tank experts in the world want to change the whole production of tank ammunition. This incident certainly taught me a profound lesson about getting the facts.

Now that man honestly thought he was sure of his facts. But you are going to find a whole lot of people, of high rank and low, who will try to brush you off or give you a snow job. The most usual reason is pure laziness. But sometimes you are sniffing around a man's pet hobby or even his private racket. Whatever the reason, a whole lot of people are going to give you inaccurate information, airy assurances, vague promises, and useless generalities. None of these substitutes for facts is acceptable.

I cannot say this too brutally: You are no good on the General Staff if you accept inaccurate information. It is your business to verify facts. We can't tolerate people who try to hand the General Staff a snow job. I won't tolerate General Staff officers who let themselves be put off with snow jobs.

When you write your report you probably start out like most other people including me. You grope around sorting out your ideas, and you get better ideas as you go along, and it always works out that in the first part of the paper you say poorly what you repeat more clearly in the second part and finally state well in the third part. The secret is to throw away the first and second parts and save the last paragraph in which you stated it all (for the third time) very clearly. You will be a third-rater so long as you treasure your big words and fancy phrases and can't bear to boil your paper down to bare facts simply stated. Just lay out the facts, and tabulate them if you can so we can see quickly what you are talking about with the maximum economy of words.

One way I can spot an amateur is by the word furthermore. Probably one third of all the papers I look at begin with a fairly clear presentation and then comes that word furthermore; and then a lot of wild swinging. You will never find anything after furthermore but argument.

Now let's summarize what I have said so far. Your sole purpose is to produce action. First, persist in and insist on obtaining and verifying facts. Second, marshal those facts in logical order and cut away all the fancy phrases that obscure the facts. Then you are ready to seek the concurrences of all agencies whose responsibilities are affected by what you propose to do. When you get all that done you have a solution.

A word about non-concurrences: suppose some other Indian comes around to you with his project and you look at it and you think it's terrible. Well that's too bad, but the only ground on which you can non-concur is that it will be unworkable in the area for which you are the responsible General Staff man. You are not entitled to non-concur because you personally don't like that solution. I give concurrences quite regularly to schemes which I personally dislike: if the logistic operations of the Army will not be adversely affected by the proposed action, I have no right to obstruct G1, G2, or G3 just because my private views are different.

Staffs exist to produce action. You have worked hard at getting the facts, writing them up and getting the concurrences. Now the directive is issued. You have created it and you read it proudly. But my question now is: having produced that directive, have you produced any action?

Not one bit. You haven't produced anything but the distribution of a piece of paper by the Adjutant General (AG). It is just going to pile up on a lot of desks, lost, buried, ignored. Nobody is going to read it. If anyone does, he'll misinterpret it. So up to now, you have accomplished nothing at all.

Every directive must be accomplished by positive provisions for follow-up, to insure that it is obeyed. A staff that thinks its whole business is to keep the mimeograph machine smoking all day long doesn't accomplish a thing. It issues ten times as many orders as it should and doesn't enforce any of them; then issues more orders saying that others will be obeyed.

I have tried all my life to follow this rule: Never issue an order that you don't intend to enforce.

It is easy. You set target dates in the directive. You call for periodic progress reports. You make staff visits. You make command inspections. You take official notice of inadequate performance, in three stages of severity. The first is a polite note, calling attention. The second is an official letter mentioning the basic directive and the polite note, and directing immediate attention. The third lists all prior actions and calls for an explanation. Down comes the boom. If you show you mean business from the beginning, things almost never reach that last unpleasant stage.

Whenever anybody gives me a date when something will be accomplished, I put it in a special drawer I keep for that purpose; and when the date comes around I ask if the promise has been kept. People think I am merciless and perhaps I am, but when I am given a promise I want to know if it was dependable or just another snow job. People know it and don't trifle with me. That is follow-up.

We have to work out many solutions with the people in Defense, Navy, and Air Force. They are sincere, they are trying to serve their country, just as we are. When you work at this national level, so many factors come in that no one man can begin to see the whole problem. Everybody finds it exasperating as unsuspected difficulties keep rising. Just keep a tight hold on your good temper, your sense of humor and your plain common sense. That is the essence of the whole business.

There are no envies and jealousies among my colleagues, the other Gs. We are all on the same team and we are all friends. We never raise our voices in talking to each other. I think each of us is likely to be more impressed by the judgement of the others than he is by his own. What I know of those men from a lifetime of association has won them that sort of respect from me. They are sound men, and they are only interested in serving the Army well.

In conclusion, the thing that is essential is to know what we are talking about. When you have the facts right, you will soon have a well organized, well coordinated, workable solution. We want to have a good Army and we'll buy any solution that is good for the Service. We are not here to worry about the importance of our staff position.

We sometimes talk about feeling frustrated. We push a solution up and get it thrown back. There's always somebody we can't get it past. Every one of those people is bringing mature judgement to bear; he may be a nuisance to you but he has a good point just the same.

The pay-off, after this struggle and turmoil, is that what finally gets out to the troops causes the absolute minimum of confusion and disorder. The hard grinding out of the solution up here means that you won't issue a poor order, half-baked, not properly coordinated, that has to be followed with a string of amendments and afterthoughts, all driving the people in the field crazy. It is the extra effort up here that pays off.

The General Staff is a corporate brain. Only the Chief of Staff and two or three other people are entitled to speak for it, but each Indian on the General Staff, however obscure, overworked and beset by darkness, is a very important member of the U.S. Army.

From *Combat Forces Journal*
February, 1954

People are not in the Army, they are the Army.

General Creighton William Abrams, Jr.

**General
Creighton William Abrams, Jr.**
1914–1974
Army Chief of Staff
(1972–1974)

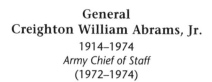

*Battles are won by the infantry, the armor,
and artillery and air teams, by soldiers living in
the rain and huddling in the snow. But wars are won
by the great strength of a nation—the soldier and the
civilian working together.*

General Omar Nelson Bradley
"The GI General"
1893–1981
Army General, World War II

DUTY, HONOR, COUNTRY

Douglas MacArthur, General of the Army
Farewell Address to the US Military Academy
at West Point, May 12, 1962

"Duty," "honor," "country"—those three hallowed words reverently dictate what you want to be, what you can be, what you will be. They are your rallying point to build courage when courage seems to fail, to regain faith when there seems to be little cause for faith, to create hope when hope becomes forlorn.

Unhappily, I possess neither that eloquence of diction, that poetry of imagination, nor that brilliance of metaphor to tell you all that they mean.

The unbelievers will say they are but words, but a slogan, but a flamboyant phrase. Every pedant, every demagogue, every cynic, every hypocrite, every troublemaker, and, I am sorry to say, some others of an entirely different character, will try to downgrade them even to the extent of mockery and ridicule.

But these are some of the things they build. They build your basic character. They mold you for your future roles as the custodians of the nation's defense. They make you strong enough to know when you are weak, and brave enough to face yourself when you are afraid.

They teach you to be proud and unbending in honest failure, but humble and gentle in success, not to substitute words for action, not to seek the path of comfort, but to face the stress and spur of difficulty and challenge; to learn to stand up in the storm, but to have compassion on those who fall; to master yourself before you seek to master others; to have a heart that is clean, a goal that is high; to learn to laugh, yet never forget how to weep; to reach into the future, yet never neglect the past; to be serious, yet never take yourself too seriously; to be modest so that you will remember the simplicity of true greatness; the open mind of true wisdom, the meekness of true strength.

They give you a temperate will, a quality of imagination, a vigor of the emotions, a freshness of the deep springs of life, a temperamental predominance of courage over timidity, an appetite for adventure over love of ease.

They create in your heart the sense of wonder, the unfailing hope of what next, and the joy and inspiration of life. They teach you in this way to be an officer and a gentleman.

And what sort of soldiers are those you are to lead? Are they reliable? Are they brave? Are they capable of victory?

Their story is known to all of you. It is the story of the American man at arms. My estimate of him was formed on the battlefields many, many years ago, and has never changed. I regarded him then, as I regard him now, as one of the world's noblest figures; not only as one of the finest military characters, but also as one of the most stainless.

His name and fame are the birthright of every American citizen. In his youth and strength, his love and loyalty, he gave all that mortality can give. He needs no eulogy from me, or from any other man. He has written his own history and written it in red on his enemy's breast.

In 20 campaigns, on a hundred battlefields, around a thousand campfires, I have witnessed that enduring fortitude, that patriotic self-abnegation, and that invincible determination which have carved his statue in the hearts of his people.

From one end of the world to the other, he has drained deep the chalice of courage. As I listened to those songs in memory's eye I could see those staggering columns of the First World War, bending under soggy packs on many a weary march from dripping dusk to drizzling dawn, slogging ankle deep through mire of shell-pocked roads; to form grimly for the attack, blue-lipped, covered with sludge and mud, chilled by the wind and rain, driving home to their objective, and for many, to the judgment seat of God.

I do not know the dignity of their birth, but I do know the glory of their death. They died unquestioning, uncomplaining, with faith in their hearts, and on their lips the hope that we would go on to victory.

Always for them: duty, honor, country. Always their blood, and sweat, and tears, as they saw the way and the light. And 20 years after, on the other side of the globe, against the filth of dirty foxholes, the stench of ghostly trenches, the slime of dripping dugouts, those boiling suns of the relentless heat, those torrential rains of devastating storms, the loneliness and utter desolation of jungle trails, the bitterness of long separation of those they loved and cherished, the deadly pestilence of tropic disease, the horror of stricken areas of war.

Their resolute and determined defense, their swift and sure attack, their indomitable purpose, their complete and decisive victory—always victory, always through the bloody haze of their last reverberating shot, the vision of gaunt, ghastly men, reverently following your password of duty, honor, country.

You now face a new world, a world of change. The thrust into outer space of the satellite spheres and missiles marks a beginning of another epoch in the long story of mankind. In the five or more billions of years the scientists tell us it has taken to form the earth, in the three or more billion years of development of the human race, there has never been a more abrupt or staggering evolution.

We deal now, not with things of this world alone, but with the illimitable distances and yet unfathomed mysteries of the universe. We are reaching out for a new and boundless frontier. We speak in strange terms of harnessing the cosmic energy, of making winds and tides work for us . . . of the primary target in war, no longer limited to the armed forces of an enemy, but instead to include his civil population; of ultimate conflict between a united human race and the sinister forces of some other planetary galaxy; such dreams and fantasies as to make life the most exciting of all times.

And through all this welter of change and development your mission remains fixed, determined, inviolable. It is to win our wars. Everything else in your professional career is but corollary to this vital dedication. All other public purpose, all other public projects, all other public needs, great or small, will find others for their accomplishments; but you are the ones who are trained to fight.

Yours is the profession of arms, the will to win, the sure knowledge that in war there is no substitute for victory, that if you lose, the Nation will be destroyed, that the very obsession of your public service must be duty, honor, country.

Others will debate the controversial issues, national and international, which divide men's minds. But serene, calm, aloof, you stand as the Nation's war guardians, as its lifeguards from the raging tides of international conflict, as its gladiators in the arena of battle. For a century and a half you have defended, guarded and protected its hallowed traditions of liberty and freedom, of right and justice.

Let civilian voices argue the merits or demerits of our processes of government: Whether our strength is being sapped by deficit financing indulged in too long, by federal paternalism grown too mighty, by power groups grown too arrogant, by politics grown too corrupt, by crime grown too rampant, by morals grown too low, by taxes grown too high, by extremists grown too violent; whether our personal liberties are as firm and complete as they should be. These great national problems are not for your professional participation or military solution. Your guidepost stands out like a tenfold beacon in the night: duty, honor, country.

You are the leaven which binds together the entire fabric of our national system of defense. From your ranks come the great captains who hold the Nation's destiny in their hands the moment the war tocsin sounds.

The long gray line has never failed us. Were you to do so, a million ghosts in olive drab, in brown khaki, in blue and gray would rise from their white crosses, thundering those magic words: duty, honor, country.

This does not mean that you are warmongers. On the contrary, the soldier above all other people prays for peace, for he must suffer and bear the deepest wounds and scars of war. But always in our ears ring the ominous words of Plato, that wisest of all philosophers: "Only the dead have seen the end of war." The shadows are lengthening for me. The twilight is here. My days of old have vanished—tone and tints. They have gone glimmering through the dreams of things that were. Their memory is one of wondrous beauty, watered by tears and coaxed and caressed by the smiles of yesterday. I listen then, but with thirsty ear, for the witching melody of faint bugles blowing reveille, of far drums beating the long roll.

In my dreams I hear again the crash of guns, the rattle of musketry, the strange, mournful mutter of the battlefield. But in the evening of my memory I come back to West Point. Always there echoes and reechoes: duty, honor, country.

Today marks my final roll call with you. But I want you to know that when I cross the river, my last conscious thoughts will be of the corps, and the corps, and the corps. I bid you farewell.

General Douglas MacArthur
1880–1964
*General in World Wars I and II and
the Korean War*

Simple Answers

They say the world has become too complex for simple answers. They are wrong. There are no easy answers, but there are simple answers. We must have the courage to do what we know is morally right. Winston Churchill said that: "The destiny of man is not measured by material computation. When great forces are on the move in the world, we learn we are spirits—not animals. There is something going on in time and space, and beyond time and space, which, whether we like it or not, spells duty."

Ronald Reagan
October 27, 1964

I Have Held a Job

May 3,1974 Ohio Senate Democratic primary; Howard Metzenbaum and John Glenn are competing for the Senate seat. Howard Metzenbaum remarks to John Glenn: "How can you run for Senate when you've never held a **job**?".
John Glenn responds:

I served 23 years in the United States Marine Corps. I was through two wars. I flew 149 missions. My plane was hit by antiaircraft fire on 12 different occasions.

I was in the space program. It wasn't my checkbook, it was my life that was on the line. This was not a 9 to 5 job where I took time off to take the daily cash receipts to the bank. I ask you to go with me ... as I went the other day to a Veterans Hospital and look those men with their mangled bodies in the eye and tell them they didn't hold a job. You go with me to any Gold Star mother, and you look her in the eye and tell her that her son did not hold a job.

You go with me to the space program, and you go as I have gone to the widows and the orphans of Ed White and Gus Grissom and Roger Chaffee, and you look those kids in the eye and tell them that their dad didn't hold a job.

You go with me on Memorial Day coming up, and you stand on Arlington National Cemetery—where I have more friends than I like to remember—and you watch those waving flags, and you stand there, and you think about this nation, and you tell me that those people didn't have a job.

I tell you, Howard Metzenbaum, you should be on your knees every day of your life thanking God that there were some men—**some men**—who held a job. And they required a dedication to purpose and a love of country and a dedication to duty that was more important than life itself. And their self-sacrifice is what has made this country possible ... .

I HAVE HELD A JOB, HOWARD!

CHAPTER TWO
Selflessness and Sacrifice

The selflessness and sacrifices displayed by all Americans, especially those who took up arms in defense of our liberties, is the focus of this important chapter. The greatest price any country must pay for its freedoms is the loss of its citizens' lives. This chapter also discusses the selflessness and suffering our military and its soldiers demonstrate and experience in their service to us.

I only regret that I have but one life to lose for my country.

Captain Nathan Hale
Continental Army, September 22, 1776
Long Island, New York

Captain Nathan Hale being prepared for his hanging by the British Army.
©National Archives.

ONE HEART AND ONE MIND

On Dec. 17th 1777, Washington wrote as follows:

The General ardently wishes it were now in his power to conduct the troops into the best winter quarters; but where are they to be found? Should we retire to the interior of the State, we would find it crowded with virtuous citizens, who, sacrificing their all, have left Philadelphia and fled hither for protection; to their distress humanity forbids us to add. This is not all. We should leave a vast extent of country to be despoiled and ravaged by the enemy, from which they would draw vast supplies, and where many of our firm friends would be exposed to all the miseries of an insulting and wanton depredation. A train of evils might be enumerated, but these will suffice. These considerations make it indispensably necessary for the army to take such a position as will enable it most effectually to prevent distress, and give the most extensive security; and in that position we must make ourselves the best shelter in our power.

These urgent reasons have determined the General to take post in the neighborhood of this camp, and influenced by them, he persuades himself that the officers and soldiers, with one heart and one mind, will resolve to surmount every difficulty with a fortitude and patience becoming their profession, and the sacred cause in which they are engaged.

General George Washington
Continental Army
1732–1799
1st President of the United States
(1789–1797)

LETTER WRITTEN BY GENERAL GEORGE WASHINGTON AT VALLEY FORGE

To Governor George Clinton,

Head Quarters, Valley Forge, February 16, 1778

Dear Sir:

It is with great reluctance, I trouble you on a subject, which does not fall within your province; but it is a subject that occasions me more distress, than I have felt, since the commencement of the war; and which loudly demands the most zealous exertions of every person of weight and authority, who is interested in the success of our affairs. I mean the present dreadful situation of the army for want of provisions, and the miserable prospects before us, with respect to futurity. It is more alarming than you will probably conceive, for, to form a just idea, it were necessary to be on the spot. For some days past, there has been little less, than a famine in camp. A part of the army has been a week, without any kind of flesh, and the rest for three or four days. Naked and starving as they are, we cannot enough admire the incomparable patience and fidelity of the soldiery, that they have not been ere this excited by their sufferings, to a general mutiny or dispersion. Strong symptoms, however, discontent have appeared in particular instances; and nothing but the most active efforts every where can long avert so shocking a catastrophe.

Our present sufferings are not all. There is no foundation laid for any adequate relief hereafter. All the magazines provided in the States of New Jersey, Pennsylvania, Delaware and Maryland, and all the immediate additional supplies they seem capable of affording, will not be sufficient to support the army more than a month longer, if so long. Very little has been done to the Eastward, and as little to the Southward; and whatever we have a right to expect from those quarters, must necessarily be very remote; and is indeed more precarious, than could be wished. When the forementioned supplies are exhausted, what a terrible crisis must ensue, unless all the energy of the Continent is exerted to provide a timely remedy?

Impressed with this idea, I am, on my part, putting every engine to work, that I can possibly think of, to prevent the fatal consequences, we have so great a reason to apprehend. I am calling upon all those, whose stations and influence enable them to contribute their aid upon so important an occasion; and from your well known zeal, I expect every thing within the compass of your power, and that the abilities and resources of the state over which you preside, will admit. I am sensible of the disadvantages it labours under, from having been so long the scene of war, and that it must be exceedingly drained by the great demands to which it has been subject. But, tho' you may not be able to contribute materially to our relief, you can perhaps do something towards it; and any assistance, however trifling in itself, will be of great moment at so critical a juncture, and will conduce to keeping the army together till the Commissary's department can be put upon a better footing, and effectual measures concerted to secure a permanent and competent supply. What methods you can take, you will be the best judge of; but, if you can devise any means to procure a quantity of cattle, or other kind of flesh, for the use of this army, to be at camp in the course of a month, you will render a most essential service to the common cause. I have the honor etc.

General George Washington

MY OWN OBITUARY

On 7 July, 1970, an Army Captain was strapped into a helicopter that was caught up in a tropical storm and slammed into a hillside in a remote mountain area of Vietnam. Shortly before, while commanding a company of the 1st Cavalry Division, he had written a sealed letter to his wife, which began:

I am writing my own obituary ... because I am quite simply the last authority on my own death.

I loved the Army: it reared me, it nurtured me, and it gave me the most satisfying years of my life. Thanks to it I have lived an entire lifetime in 26 years. It is only fitting that I should die in its service. We all have but one death to spend, and insofar as it can have any meaning it finds it in the service of comrades in arms.

And yet, I deny that I died *for* anything—not my Country, not my Army, not my fellow man, none of these things. I *lived* for these things, and the manner in which I chose to do it involved the very real chance that I would die in the execution of my duties. I knew this and accepted it, but my love for West Point and the Army was great enough—and the promise that I would someday be able to serve all the ideals that meant anything to me though it was great enough—for me to accept this possibility as part of the price which must be paid for all things of great value. If there is nothing worth dying for—in this sense—there is nothing worth living for.

The Army let me live in Japan, Germany, and England, with experiences in all of these places that others only dream about ... I have climbed Mount Fuji, visited the ruins of Athens, Ephesus, and Rome ... and earned a master's degree in a foreign university. I have known what it is like to be married to a fine and wonderful woman and to love her beyond bearing with the sure knowledge that she loves me; I have commanded a company and been a father, priest, income-tax advisor, confessor, and judge to 200 men at a time; I have played college football and rugby, won the British National Diving Championship two years in a row, boxed for Oxford against Cambridge only to be knocked out in the first round ... I have been an exchange student at the German Military Academy, and gone to the German Jumpmaster School. I have made thirty parachute jumps from everything from a balloon in England to a jet at Fort Bragg. I have written an article for *ARMY Magazine*, and I have studied philosophy.

I have experienced all these things because I was in the Army and because I was an Army brat. The Army is my life, it is such a part of what I was that what happened is the logical outcome of the life I have lived. I never knew what it was to fail, I never knew what it is to be too old or too tired to do anything. I lived a full life in the Army, and it has exacted the price. It is only just.

ON COMRADESHIP

When a soldier was injured and could not get back to safety, his buddy went out to get him, against his officer's orders. He returned mortally wounded and his friend, whom he had carried back, was dead.

The officer was angry. "I told you not to go," he said. "Now I've lost both of you. It was not worth it."

The dying man replied, "But it was, sir, because when I got to him he said, 'Jim, I knew you'd come'."

Leslie D. Weatherhead

I hold it to be one of the simplest truths of war that the thing which enables an infantry soldier to keep going with his weapons is the near presence of a comrade.

S.L.A. Marshall, from *Men Against Fire*

Then darkness enveloped the whole American armada.
Not a pinpoint of light showed from those hundreds
of ships as they surged on through the night toward
their destiny, carrying across the ageless and
indifferent sea tens of thousands of young
men, fighting for ... for ... well,
at least for each other.

Ernest "Ernie" Taylor Pyle, from his book, *Brave Men*,
describing the Normandy invasion
1900–1945
WW II War Correspondent, Pulitzer Prize Winner,
American Folk Hero

NOT FOR SELF, BUT FOR COUNTRY

The following speech was delivered by General Charles C. Krulak, USMC, Commandant of the Marine Corps, at the 19th Commencement Remarks for the Uniformed Services University at the DAR Constitution Hall, Washington DC, 16 May 1998.

First let me say what a pleasure and an honor it is for me to be here this morning. Like most of you in the audience, I too have a loved one that is graduating today ... And, I too feel that overwhelming sense of pride from seeing a person I cherish garner such a high achievement.

I am also honored to address the future leaders, researchers, and healers of the medical profession ... the graduates of the (F. Edward) Hebert School of Medicine, the Graduate School of Nursing, and the Graduate School of Medicine. And, it is to these men and women that I would like to speak for the next few minutes.

Last month, I had the opportunity to visit the island of Iwo Jima. Known to the Japanese as Sulfur Island, it is a hot, bubbling, volcanic atoll that to this day, still has active sulfur vents. During February and March 1945, it was the scene of one of the most horrific battles of World War II.

During the 36 day campaign to take that Island, a Marine fell to Japanese fire every two minutes ... every two minutes for 36 days ... a Marine was killed or wounded. It was the only battle, in the history of our Corps, where Marines suffered more casualties than the enemy.

Today, the island still bears the scars of the titanic struggle ... It is a place heavy with history and along-on memories ... The winds that constantly blow

Two KIA Marines, Iwo Jima   Marines died on the beaches of
Iwo Jima for two weeks.

across the black sands of the Iwo Jima beaches seem, at times, to carry the
voices of the warriors that fought there so long ago.

It is a mournful and reverent place. Joining me on that tortured ground
was the family of the late John Bradley. They had never been there before, and
they wanted to see where their husband and their father had fought. John
Bradley, who survived the battle, rarely spoke to his family about his experiences on Iwo Jima.

When pressed, he would gloss over and downplay how he had won the
Nation's second highest award for bravery—the Navy Cross. He earned that
decoration by rushing to the aid of two wounded Marines, and then shielding
them with his body while he tended to their wounds. When Bradley hurried
to their aid, he didn't exactly rush ... he crawled ... crawled, because he had
been shot through both legs just a few minutes before. Another reason the
Bradley family wanted to visit Iwo Jima was because they wanted to see
the site of the most famous battle photograph ever taken ... the raising of the
American flag on Mount Suribachi.

That memorable event ... captured in a bronze and granite sculpture ... is
known today as the Marine Corps War Memorial. Five Marines and one Navy
Corpsman took part in that flag raising—three did not survive the battle. The
Navy Corpsman did ... and as you have probably guessed ... his name
was Pharmacist Mate 2 John Bradley. Let me encourage you to visit the War
Memorial one day ... run your hands across the cool granite ... step back
and read the engraved words: "Where Uncommon Valor Was a Common
Virtue"... and then, let your eyes travel up to the sculptured figures ... young
men ... forever captured in bronze ... Look for Corpsman John Bradley,
you'll recognize him ... he's the one with the empty canteen pouch. You
see, prior to climbing Mount Suribachi, he gave the last of his water to a dying

Pictured here are the five Marines and one Navy Corpsman, John Bradley, raising the flag on Mount Suribachi, Iwo Jima, February 23, 1945.

Marine … on hot … bubbling … Sulfur Island, John Bradley would go the next 24 hours without water… .

What I want to talk to you about today goes beyond bravery … goes beyond sacrifice … I want to talk to you about selflessness … John Bradley was a brave man and he sacrificed greatly, but most of all, he was selfless. His brave acts were not done for any reward … nor were they intended to be captured by NewsCam 4 or CNN … there was no public glory in what he did.

In fact, men under fire rarely speak of glory … instead … they speak of: "who can be counted upon and who cannot." Above all, they speak about and remember the small individual acts of selflessness. When Felix de Weldon, the sculptor of the Marine Corps War Memorial, asked John Bradley what had happened to his canteen— John couldn't even remember … in the heat of battle, he had completely forgotten. But, the surviving Marines of Bradley's unit knew … and they remembered … and they told de Weldon the story of his sharing his water.

Selflessness is unforgettable … even small acts of selflessness are unforgettable.

Today, when you leave here, you will find yourselves placed into positions of great responsibility. You will be men and women of letters and possess a special and unique educational experience. That alone, will cause the mantle of responsibility to be thrust upon you. And because of who and what you are, you must don that mantle of responsibility. With responsibility comes many challenges. These challenges normally are translated into choices.

A choice to operate … a choice for therapy … a choice to do nothing. But of all choices you will face, there is none greater than the choice between self … or selflessness.

Is the benefit for you ... Or, is it for your team?... Or your patient?... Or your clinic?... Or your family?...

Over the chapel doors at the United States Naval Academy is a simple Latin inscription—*Non Sibi Sed Patriae*—"Not for self, but for country."

Simple, but powerful ... Selflessness takes time to develop.

Rarely does a man or woman suddenly grow a brain and a spine in the middle of an operating room or on a battlefield. Likewise, rarely does a person develop a sense of selflessness in a single moment in time. Spontaneous selfless acts rarely happen. Instead, they are built on a strong moral foundation and then carefully layered by doing the right thing ... time and time again.

All of you possess a strong character ... strong morals ... and a strong sense of duty. Let me encourage you to add to those strengths a spirit of selflessness. That spirit is within you now ... draw from it ... use it ... and encourage it from others. Use it to lead ... to build your team ... and to serve those you know and those you know not. John Bradley gave the last of his water to a wounded Marine on 23 February 1945. That afternoon, he was struggling to climb the fire swept heights of Mount Suribachi. The next day, he braved enemy fire to aid two wounded Marines and just a few days later, though wounded himself, he again braved enemy fire to aid two more Marines. It was not for sense of self that he performed those brave deeds. It was for others ... for those he

Empty canteen pouch

knew and for those he knew not … Deep within his soul, John Bradley instinctively understood that: *Non Sibi Sed Patriae*, is contagious.

After aiding those final two wounded Marines, Corpsman John Bradley … badly wounded … lost consciousness. He awoke 36 hours later aboard the hospital ship USS *Solace*. How he arrived there is unknown. The names of those Marines and Sailors that carried him off the fire swept field of battle … who placed him on the small boat … who carried him to the ship … have been lost to history … only their selfless deed remains … even small acts of selflessness are unforgettable.

Thank you and Godspeed … *Non Sibi Sed Patriae*—Not for self, but for country!

They Don't Wear Purple Hearts in Heaven

I lost my brother to a foreign land;
I was too young to even understand.
There was a knock at the front door,
then Momma wasn't smiling anymore.

The man at the door was a Marine;
the first I've ever seen.
Momma told me to go out and play,
then the preacher came and they started to pray.

Tears ran down Momma's eyes,
and I heard her say, "Why, Lord, Why"?
Father stood there seemingly mindless,
all he said was, "We've lost another
of America's finest."

The Marine handed Momma a small velvet case,
inside was a Purple Ribbon, attached to a
gold heart with Washington's face.
I asked Momma if it were mine,
but she said, "It's your brother's, Sunshine."
"Momma can we send it to Kevin?"
She answered, "They don't wear Purple Hearts in Heaven."

Author Unknown

FIGHTING FOR MY FLAG

This article was submitted by Tom Tanney, John Tanney's brother. Tom is the National Director of "Operation: Arlington Ridge,"an organization of tens of thousands of active and veteran Marines, Navy Corpsmen, and their families commemorating the 225-year history of the United States Marine Corps. Dedicated to the memory of John Tanney, and all those who served God and Country in the name of freedom, their website can be found at <http://www. OperationArlingtonRidge.com>.

John Tanney enlisted in 1967 as he always felt it was his duty to serve his country. He was a true patriot in every sense of the word. While at Khe Sahn at the age of 18, John wrote a letter to my baby brother Bob, who was only seven months old at the time. It was written just before the 26th Marines launched their assault on Hill 881 North. The letter was only to be opened in the event of John's death. John was wounded by mortar fire at the siege of Khe Sahn in April of 1968, where he received his first Purple Heart.

After his death in September, the letter was opened by my parents. Our Congressman, Alexander Pirnie, read it and asked permission to read it in a Congressional session,

John Tanney, USMC

where it is now a permanent part of the Congressional record. It was also run on the front page of our newspaper, *The Rome Sentinel*, whereupon the author Alex Haley (*Roots*) called us and said that it touched him deeply that such thoughts could come from the mind of such a young boy. The letter and an article about John were again run on the front page of the newspaper on Veteran's Day in 1984. Here is the text of that letter exactly as he wrote it.

Dear Brother Bob,

I know that you won't be able to read this for awhile, but I just felt a compulsion to write to you anyway. I'm waiting to be picked up by helicopter with the rest of my buddies to push on to Hills 861, 881, 881 North, and 689. My platoon is spearheading the assault up Hill 881 North. The enemy has many soldiers up top and they are dug in as well as we are at Khe Sahn (a Viet Cong siege of U.S. Marines). It will be a hard and bitter struggle, but as always, we Marines will take the objective.

You are little now and haven't the slightest idea of what is going on in the world, but what we are doing here concerns all. It is important for you to remember that we are fighting for freedom for Viet Nam. The Bible says "I am my brother's keeper." This is also true for our Viet Nam brothers.

Someday, when you come of age, you too will render your services to your country. You do not have to join the Marine Corps because I did. Just fulfill your duty—your privilege. Yes, it is a privilege to fight for a noble cause. War is far, far worse than hell.

Men are torn apart like a worn-out rag doll. War has a smell to it. It is the smell of charred flesh. War has sounds. They are the sounds of men dying. Bob—I hope that you will never have to go to war. I hope that we can stop this thing from spreading. I hope that the men of peace will sit down and discuss living in peace—but, alas, I hope in vain.

I am nearly going crazy thinking about assaulting that hill. But, I am a Marine and I shall not falter. I will be confident in the Lord and in my training as a Marine. Bob—if anything should happen, remember this: I am fighting for what I believe in—you, Mom, Dad, Tom and Cindy. I am fighting for the right to chose my own religion, make my own decisions, and to be my own man. And yes, I am fighting for my flag. My country means a lot to me and I am proud to fight for it. I know that you will be, too.

You know, I am over 18 years older than you and I have spent so little time with you. But, you are near to me not so much in my mind as in my heart.

I hope that your generation of people will respect what we are doing here. I hope that they will understand that we, too, love life. We have lost many friends and now it is time for the enemy to lose some.

We are United States Marines. We are the best troops in the world. We fight odds that are heavily against us—and win! Our spirit is indomitable, our courage unexcelled, and our loyalty is unquestionable.

I felt like writing to you. Perhaps it sounds foolish. Perhaps it is. But you can never imagine what it is like—not knowing if I'm coming back down that hill. I wanted you to have something from me to you. I love you, Bob, but you are too young to know it.

Someday you will know.

I will leave now—time is short.

Love to you,

Brother John

One More Time

Sergeant Christopher Reid ... had been wounded in action ... when fighting had erupted in Mogadishu. He told me his squad and members of his platoon had fought through three city blocks to reach a downed U.S. Army helicopter. The last thing he remembered was the heat of the helicopter burning and everything turning red.
When he woke up, he was in a hospital, missing a leg and part of an arm. Chris told me his story in a strong, unwavering voice. He did not have to be there that cold, winter morning, but he wanted to be with his squad, with his friends, one more time. He then looked into my eyes and with great determination said, "You know, sir, knowing what I know now, I would do it again."

GEN Gordon R. Sullivan
from his book, *Hope Is Not a Method*
1996

HERO QUALITY

From Camp Bondsteel, Kosovo, Army News Service, Sept. 3, 1999

Soldiers with the 67th Combat Support Hospital here recently demonstrated their hero quality with a 6-year-old child. Emergency room personnel received the child with a gunshot wound to the abdomen, according to Maj. Lonnie Imlay, general surgeon, who performed surgery on the child. Second Lt. Amanda Eli, ground ambulance platoon leader, helped unload the child from a MEDEVAC helicopter to bring him into the ER. She said she was very shocked by his condition, despite what she has already seen since being here. "He was blue; I mean literally blue. It really struck me so we hurried to get him into the ER. It is always a tad more overwhelming when a child is involved," Eli said. "We received him in very bad shape. He had almost bled to death by the time we took him. He was not breathing but had a very faint pulse," Imlay said. "We managed to get him breathing again, but our biggest difficulty was that his blood was not clotting like it should. Initially, we used stored blood but it was not enough." According to Imlay, the child required a whole blood transfusion to make up for the massive blood loss he suffered and the damage done to his liver. But, whole blood is stored broken into three components: red blood cells, plasma and platelets, and all the components were needed to restore the child's blood clotting ability. The only way to get the whole blood that was needed was through direct transfusion from one person to another. According to Imlay, whole blood transfusions are not something normally done, since there are risks of it being rejected by the host or disease transfer due to the inability to test the blood during an emergency. In fact, they are almost never done in the United States or Germany, yet here it has been necessary twice. "This was the fourth (patient) we have received who had such massive injuries we had to use extreme measures. When this happened with this child and we called for volunteers to give blood. We had so many; we had to turn all but eight away. Some were doctors and surgeons working the case," Col. Russell Taylor, 67th CSH commander, said Specialist Gary Escoffery, a surgical technician, was one of the soldiers who donated his blood to help save the child's life. "When Col. Taylor asked for volunteers to give blood, it wasn't really very hard to make a decision. I did it because this may very well be the finest moment in my life. I wanted to do this," Escoffery said. "It is very gratifying. Sometimes you help people and it doesn't go the best way possible. This time I was happy because it had a good ending." Imlay said over a 24-hour period, the amount of blood given to the child was, for his size, equivalent to replacing his blood three times. The child received three to four units of red blood cells, several more units of plasma and eight units of whole blood from donors, he added. "We first applied a patch directly to his liver and then closed him up to allow his body to begin the clotting process.

However, the massive transfusion caused his body temperature to drop, inter-fering with the blood's ability to clot," Imlay said. "The patch was to help him begin to warm up, but it was still not enough. We ended up repeating the transfusion procedure ... and his blood started clotting." The child, known by his first name, Arlind, lived through his injury and surgery. He remained in the care of the hospital staff for approximately 10 to 12 days before being transferred to a hospital in Skopje, Macedonia. The Skopje hospital is better suited for his medical needs, according to Imlay. According to Maj. Jimmie Keenan, chief nurse for the ER, she received word recently from Arlind's par-ents that he was doing better and off his medication. "It all comes back to why we are here. We're here to do a job. I try to do mine to the best of my ability. I am certainly grateful to the people who gave blood. It is a true gift, with noth-ing expected in return and totally selfless. Without them, the boy may be dead regardless of anything I did," Imlay said. "They are heroes in the truest sense of the word."

Sergeant Christopher DeHart

THE WORDS OF COLONEL HAROLD KUSHNER

This is the story of Doctor Hal Kushner, his service in Vietnam, and his horrible ordeals: extreme pain and suffering and unflinching loyalty and honor to the United States Army and our country. This is an account of the speech he gave to a reunion of the 1-9th at Ft. Hood, Texas.

I want you to know that I don't do this often. I was captured 2 December, 1967, and returned to American control on 16 March, 1973. For those of you good at arithmetic, that is 1931 days. Thus it has been 32 years since capture and 26 years since my return. I have given a lot of talks ... about medicine, about ophthalmology, even about the D-day invasion ... as I was privileged to go to Normandy and witness the 50th anniversary of the invasion in June, 1994. But not about my captivity. I don't ride in parades; I don't open shop-ping centers; I don't give interviews and talks about it. I have tried very hard **not** to be a professional PW. My philosophy has always been to look forward, not backward, to consider the future rather than the past. That's a helluva thing to say at a reunion, I guess. In 26 years, I've given only two interviews and two talks. One to my home town newspaper ... which my dad made me give ... one to the *Washington Post* in 1973 ... which the Army PIO made me give, and a talk at Ft. Benning in '91 ... which COL Ted Chilcotte made me give ... and to the Military Flight Surgeons in '93 ... which they made me give. I've refused about 1000 invitations to speak about my experiences. But you don't say no to the 1st of the 9th, and you don't say no to your commander. COL Bob Nevins and COL Pete Booth asked me to do this, and so I said "yes sir," and prepared the talk. It will probably be my last one.

I was a 26-year-old young doctor, just finished 9 years of education, college at the University of North Carolina, med school at Medical College of VA, a young wife and 3-year-old daughter. I interned at the hospital in which I was born, Tripler Army Med Center in Honolulu, HI. While there, I was removed from my internship and spent most of my time doing orthopedic operations on wounded soldiers and marines. We were getting hundreds of wounded GIs there, and filled the hospital. After the hospital was filled, we erected tents on the grounds and continued receiving air evac patients. So I knew what was happening in Vietnam. I decided that I wanted to be a flight surgeon. ... I had a private pilot's license and was interested in aviation. After my internship at Tripler, I went to Ft. Rucker and to Pensacola and through the Army and Navy's aviation medicine program and then deployed to Vietnam. While in basic training and my "e and e" course, they told us that as doctors, we didn't have to worry about being captured. Doctors and nurses they said were not PWs, they were "Detained Personnel" under the Geneva Convention. If they treated us as PWs, we should show our Geneva Convention cards and leave. It was supposed to be a joke ... and it was pretty funny at the time.

I arrived in Vietnam in August '67 and went to An Khe, the HQ of the 1st Cavalry Division. I was told that the division needed two flight surgeons ... one to be the division flight surgeon at An Khe in the rear, and the other to be surgeon for 1/9th a unit actively involved with the enemy. I volunteered for 1/9th. The man before me, CPT Claire Shenep had been killed and the dispensary was named the Claire Shenep Memorial Dispensary. Like many flight surgeons, I flew on combat missions in helicopters ... enough to earn three air medals ... and one of my medics, S/Sgt Jim Zeiler, used to warn me: "Doc, you better be careful: we'll be renaming that dispensary, the K & S Memorial Dispensary."

I was captured on 2 December, 1967 and held for 5-1/2 years until 16 March, 1973. I have never regretted the decision that I made that August to be the 1/9th's flight surgeon. Such is the honor and esteem that I hold the squadron. I am proud of the time I was the squadron's flight surgeon.

On 30 November, 1967, I went to Chu Lai w/MAJ Steve Porcella, WO-1 Mr. Giff Bedworth, and SGT McKeckney, the crew chief of our UH-1H. I gave a talk to a troop at Chu Lai on the dangers of night flying. The weather was horrible, rainy and windy, and I asked MAJ Porcella, the A/C commander, if we could spend the night and wait out the weather. He said: "Our mission is not so important but we have to get the A/C back." I'll never forget the devotion to duty of this young officer ... it cost him his life.

While flying from Chu Lai to LZ Two Bits, I thought we had flown west of Highway 1, which would be off course. I asked Steve if we had drifted west. He called the ATC at Duc Pho and asked them to find him. The operator at Duc

Pho said that he had turned his radar off at 2100. He said, "Do you want me to turn it on and find you?" MAJ Porcella replied, "roj" and that was the last thing he ever said. The next thing I knew, I was recovering from unconsciousness in a burning helicopter which seemed to be upside down. I tried to unbuckle my seat belt and couldn't use my left arm. I finally managed to get unbuckled and immediately dropped and almost broke my neck. My helmet was plugged into commo and the wire held me as I dropped out of the seat which was inverted. The helicopter was burning. Poor MAJ Porcella was crushed against the instrument panel and either unconscious or dead. Bedworth was thrown, still strapped in his seat, out of the chopper. His right ankle bones were fractured and sticking through the nylon of his boot. SGT Mac was unhurt ... but thrown clear and unconscious. I tried to free Porcella by cutting his seatbelt and moving him. However, I was unable to. The chopper burned up and I suffered burns on my hands and buttocks and had my pants burned off. While trying to free Porcella, some of the M-60 rounds cooked off and I took a round through the left shoulder and neck. My left wrist and left collarbone were broken in the crash, and I lost or broke 7 upper teeth.

We assessed the situation ... we had no food or water ... no flares ... no first aid kit or survival gear. We had two thirty-eight pistols and 12 rounds, one seriously wounded WO co-pilot, a moderately wounded doctor, and an unhurt crew chief. We thought we were close to Duc Pho and Hwy. 1 and close to friendlies. Bedworth and I decided to send Mac for help at first light. We never saw him again.

Later, ... 6 long years later, COL Nevins told me that SGT Mac had been found about 10 miles from the crash site, shot and submerged in a rice paddy. So on that night of 30 November, 1967, I splinted Bedworth's leg, with tree branches, made a lean-to from the door of the chopper, and we sat in the rain for three days and nights. We just sat there. We drank rain water. On the third morning, he died. We could hear choppers hovering over our crash site and I fired most of the rounds from our 38s trying to signal them, but the cloud cover was so heavy and the weather so bad, they never found us.

I took the compass from the burned out helicopter and tried to go down the mountain toward the east and I believed friendlies. My glasses had been broken or lost in the crash and I couldn't see well, the trail was slippery, and I fell on rocks in a creek bed and cracked a couple of ribs. I had my left arm splinted to my body with my army belt. My pants were in tatters and burned, I had broken teeth and a wound in my shoulder ... I hadn't eaten or drunk anything but rainwater for three days ... I looked and felt like hell.

One of the cruel ironies of my life ... you know how we all play the what if games ... what if I hadn't done this or that...Well, when I finally reached the bottom of the mountain, I estimated 4 hours after first light, the weather cleared and I saw choppers hovering over the top. I knew I couldn't make it up the mountain, and had to take my chances. But if I had only waited another 4 hours.

I started walking up the trail and saw a man working in a rice paddy. He came over and said, "Dai-wi, Bac-si"... CPT Doctor. He took me to a little hooch, sat me down and gave me a can of sweetened condensed milk and a C ration can opener and spoon. This stuff was like pudding and it billowed out of the can and was the best tasting stuff I had ever had. I felt very safe at that point. One minute later, my host led a squad of 14 VC with two women and 12 rifles upon me. The squad leader said, "surrenda no kill." He put his hands in the air and I couldn't because my left arm was tied to my body. He shot at me with an M2 carbine and wounded me, again in the neck. After I was apprehended, I showed my captors my Geneva Convention card ... white with a red cross. He tore it up. He took my dogtags and a medallion which had a St. Christoper's on one side and a Star of David on the other, which my dad had given me before leaving. They tied me with commo wire in a duck wing position, took my boots and marched me mostly at night for about 30 days. The first day they took me to a cave, stripped my fatigue jacket off my back, tied me to a door, and a teenage boy beat me with a bamboo rod. I was told his parents were killed by American bombs. We rested by day, and marched by night. I walked on rice paddy dikes, and couldn't see a thing. They would strike these little homemade lighters and by the sparks they made, see four or five steps. I was always falling off the dikes into the rice paddy water, and had to be pulled back up by my bonds. It was rough. On the way, I saw men, women and kids in tiger cages, and bamboo jails. I was taken to a camp, which must have been like a medical facility as my wound was festering, and full of maggots and I was sick. A woman heated up a rifle-cleaning rod and gave me a bamboo stick to bite on. She cauterized my through-and-through wound with the cleaning rod and I almost passed out with pain. She then dressed the wound with Mercurochrome and gave me two aspirin. I thought, what else can they do to me? I was to find out.

After walking for about a month through plains, then jungle and mountains, always west, they took me to a camp. I had been expecting a PW camp like a stalag w/Hogan's heroes, barbed wire, search lights, nice guards and red cross packages ... and a hospital where I could work as a doctor. They took me to a darkened hut with an oriental prisoner who was not American. I didn't know whether he was Vietnamese, Cambodian, Laotion or Chinese. He spoke no English and was dying of TB. He was emaciated, weak, sick and coughed all day and night. I spent two days there and an English speaking Vietnamese officer came with a portable tape recorder and asked me to make a statement against the war. I told him that I would rather die than speak against my country. He said words which were unforgettable, and if I ever write a book, will be the title. He said, "You will find that dying is very easy; living, living is the difficult thing."

A few days later, in a driving rain, we started the final trek to camp. I was tied again, w/no boots, and we ascended higher and higher in the mountains. I was weak and asked to stop often to rest. We ate a little rice, which the guards cooked, and actually needed ropes to traverse some of the steep rocks. Finally, we got to PW Camp One. There were four American servicemen there ... two from the mainland U.S. and two from Puerto Rico. Three were Marines, and one in the Army. These guys looked horrible ... they wore black PJs, were scrawny with bad skin and teeth and beards and matted hair. The camp also had about 15 ARVNs [Army of the Republic of Vietnam ... our allies], who were held separately, across a bamboo fence. The camp was just a row of hooches made of bamboo with elephant grass roofs [situated] around a creek, with a hole in the ground for a latrine. This was the first of five camps we lived in in the South ... all depressingly similar, although sometimes we had a separate building for a kitchen and sometimes we were able to pipe in water thru bamboo pipes from the nearby stream.

I asked one of the Marines, the man captured longest and the leader, if escape was possible. He told me that he and a Special Forces CPT had tried to escape the year before, and the CPT had been beaten to death, while he had been put in stocks for 90 days, having to defecate in his hands and throw it away from him or lie in it. The next day I was called before the camp commander and chastised and yelled at for suggesting escape. My fellow PW then told me never to say anything to him that I didn't want revealed, because the Vietnamese controlled his mind. I threatened to kill him for informing on me. He just smiled and said I would learn.

Our captors promised us that if we made progress and understood the evils of the war they would release us. And the next week, they released the two Puerto Ricans and 14 ARVN PWs. The people released wore red sashes and gave anti-war speeches. I was deeply shocked and shaken by the event. Just before the release, they brought in another 7 American PWs from the 196th Light Brigade who were captured in the TET offensive of '68. I managed to write our names, ranks and serial numbers on a piece of paper (ironically, that was the only time during three and a half years in the jungle that we had paper and pencil) and slip it to one of the PRs who was released. They transported the information home, and in March '68 our families learned we had been captured alive. I still have a photocopy of that paper scrap, by which my dad identified my handwriting and confirmed that I was captured alive.

We were held in a series of jungle camps from January, 1968 to February, 1971. At this time, conditions were so bad, and we were doing so poorly, that they decided to move us to NVN. They moved 12 of us. In all, twenty-seven Americans had come through the camp. Five had been released and ten had died. They died of their wounds, disease, malnutrition, and starvation. One was shot while trying to escape. All but one died in my arms after a lingering, terrible illness. Five West German nurses in a neutral nursing organization, called the Knights of Malta, similar to the Red Cross, had been picked up (I always thought by mistake) by the VC in the spring of '69. Three of them died and the other two were taken to NVN in 1969 and held until the end of the war.

The twelve who made it were moved to NVN on foot. The fastest group, of which I was one, made it in 57 days. The slowest group took about 180 days. It was about 900 km. We walked thru Laos and Cambodia to the Ho Chi Minh trail and then up the trail across the DMZ until Vinh. At Vinh, we took a train 180 miles to Hanoi in about 18 hours. We traveled on the train with thousands of ARVN PWs who had been captured in Lam Song 719, an ARVN incursion into Laos in 1971.

Once in Hanoi, we stayed in an old French prison called The Citadel or as we said, "The Plantation," until Christmas of '72, when the Xmas bombing destroyed Hanoi. Then we were moved to the Hoa Lo or Hanoi Hilton for about three months. The peace was signed in January '73, and I came home on March 16th with the fourth group.

In the north, we were in a rough jail. There was a bucket in the windowless, cement room used as a latrine. An electric bulb was on 24 hours. We got a piece of bread and a cup of pumpkin soup twice each day and three cups of hot water. We slept on pallets of wood and wore PJs and sandals and got three tailor-made cigarettes per day. We dry shaved and bathed with a bucket from a well twice per week, and got out of the cell to carry our latrine bucket daily. Toward the end, they let us exercise. There were no letters or packages for us from the south, but I understand some of the pilots who had been there a while got some things. In the summer it was 120°F in the cell and they gave us these little bamboo fans ... the kind funeral homes in the South used to give out at funerals. During the summer, we all had heat rash, and sweated as if in a steam bath 24 hours per day. In the winter, it was cool and damp.

But there were officers and a rank structure and commo done through a tap code on the walls. No one died. It was hard duty, but not the grim struggle for survival which characterized daily life in the camp in the south. In the north, I knew I would survive.

In the south, we often wanted to die. I knew that when they ordered us north, I would make it. In the south, each day was a struggle for survival. There were between three and twenty-four PWs at all times. We ate three coffee cups of rice per day. In the rainy season, the ration was cut to two cups. I'm not talking about nice, white, Uncle Ben's. I'm talking about rice that was red, rotten and eaten out by bugs and rats, cached for years, shot through with rat feces and weevils. We arose at 4, cooked rice on wood ovens made of mud. We couldn't burn a fire in the daytime or at night unless the flames and smoke were hidden, so we had these ovens constructed of mud that covered the fire, and tunnels that carried the smoke away. We did slave labor during the day, gathering wood, carrying rice, building hooches, or going for manioc, a starchy tuberous plant like a potato. The Vietnamese had chickens and canned food. We never got supplements unless we were close to dying, then maybe some canned sardines or milk. We died from lack of protein and calories. We swelled up with what is called hungry edema and beriberi. We had terrible skin disease, dysentery, malaria. Our compound was littered with piles of human excrement because people were just too sick or weak to make it to the latrine.

We slept on one large pallet of bamboo. So the sick vomited and defecated and urinated on the bed and his neighbor. For the first two years, we had no shoes, clothes, mosquito nets or blankets. Later, in late '69, we got sandals, rice sacks for blankets, and a set of black pajamas. We nursed each other and helped each other, but we also fought and bickered. In a PW situation the best and the worst come out. Any little flaw transforms itself into a glaring lack. The strong can rule the weak. There is no law and no threat of retribution. I can report to you that the majority of the time, the Americans stuck together, helped each other, and the strong helped the weak. But there were exceptions … and sometimes the stronger took advantage of the weaker ones. There was no organization, no rank structure. The VC forbid the men from calling me Doc, and made me the latrine orderly to break down rank structure and humiliate me. I was offically forbidden from practicing medicine. But I hoarded medicine, had the men fake malaria attacks and dysentery so we could acquire medicine and keep it until we needed it. Otherwise, it might not come. I tried to advise the men about sanitary conditions, about nutrition and to keep clean, active, and eat everything we could … rats, bugs, leaves, etc. We had some old rusty, razor blades, and I did minor surgery, lancing boils, removing foreign bodies, etc. with them … but nothing major.

At one time, in the summer of '68, I was offered the chance to work in a VC hospital and receive a higher ration. The NVA political officer who made the offer and was there to indoctrinate us, said it had been done in WW II. I didn't believe him and didn't want to do it anyway, so I refused and took my chances. Later, upon return, I learned that American Army doctors in Europe in WW II, particularly those captured in the Battle of the Bulge, had indeed worked in hospitals treating German soldiers. But I'm glad now I did what I did.

We had a 1st Sergeant who had been in Korea and in WW II. He died in the fall of '68, and we were forbidden from calling him Top. He was experienced and courageous, and a potential leader. The VC broke him fast. He had a terribly wounded hand. He was reduced from a proud and tough noncom to just a little old man. I was not allowed to practice medicine unless a man was 30 minutes away from dying, then they came down with their little bottles of medicine and said "Cure him." At one point we were all dying of dysentery, and I agreed to sign a propaganda statement in return for chloromycetin, a strong antibiotic, to treat our sick. Most of us were seriously ill, although, a few never got sick, maintained their health and their weight. I never figured it out.

When a man died, we buried him in a bamboo coffin and I usually eulogized him with some words over his grave and marked it with a pile of rocks. Sometimes we had Mercurochrome to mark the rocks or we built a cross of bamboo. I was forced to sign a death certificate in Vietnamese. I did this thirteen times. The worst period was the fall of '68. We lost five men between September and Christmas. Shortly before the end of November, I thought I was going to lose my mind. All of these fine young strong men were dying. It would have been so easy to live ... just nutrition, fluids, and antibiotics. I knew what to do, but had no means to help them. I was depressed and didn't care whether I lived or died myself. At this time, we were simply starving to death. As an example of how crazy we were, we decided to kill the camp commander's cat. Several of us killed it, and skinned it. We cut off its head and paws and it dressed out to about 3 lbs. We were preparing to boil it when one of the guards came down and asked what was going on. We told him we had killed a weasel by throwing a rock. The guards raised chickens and the chickens were always being attacked by weasels. Well the guard, who was a Montagnard, an aborigine, found the feet, and knew it was the cat. The situation became very serious. The guards and cadre were mustered ... it was bout 3 A.M. The prisoners were lined up and a Marine and I were singled out to be beaten. He was almost beaten to death. I was beaten badly, tied up with commo wire very tightly (I thought my hands would fall off, and knew I would never do surgery again) for over a day. I had to bury the cat. ... And I was disappointed I didn't get to eat it. That's how crazy I was.

About a month later, the Marine who had been beaten so badly died. He didn't have to. He simply gave up, like so many. They said, "Doc, I just can't hack it anymore. I don't want to live"... and they didn't. Marty Seligman, a professor of psychology at University of Pennsylvania has written a book about these feelings called *Learned Helplessness and Death*. This Marine simply lay on his bamboo bed, refused to eat, wash or get up, and died. So many did this. We tried to force them to eat, and be active, but nothing worked. It was just too hard and they were too weary. This Marine wavered in and out of coma for about two weeks. It was around Thanksgiving, the end of November. The rains had been monstrous and our compound was a muddy morass littered with piles of feces. Sgt. David Harker of Lynchburg VA and I sat up with him all night. He hadn't spoken coherently for over a week. Suddenly, he opened his eyes and looked right at me. He said, "Mom, dad, sis, I love you very much. Box 10, Dubberly, Louisiana." That was in November '68.

We all escaped the camp in the south. Five were released as propaganda gestures. Ten Americans and three Germans died, and twelve Americans and two Germans made it back. I am the only PW who was captured before 1968 to survive that camp. I came back March 16, 1973 and stayed in the hospital in Valley Forge, PA for a month getting fixed up with several operations, and then went on convalescent leave. The first thing I did was go to Dubberly, LA and see that Marine's father. His parents had divorced while he was captured. I went to see five of the families of those that died and called the others on the phone. Every family but one was extremely grateful for the call or visit. One mother didn't want to talk to me.

It was a terrible experience, but there is some good to come from it. I learned a lot. I learned about the human spirit. I learned about confidence in oneself. I learned about loyalty to your country and its ideals and to your friends and comrades. No task would ever be too hard again. I had renewed respect for what we have and swore to learn my country's history in depth

(I have done it) and to try to contribute to my community and set an example for my children and employees.

I stayed on active duty until 1977 when I was honorably discharged and entered the reserve from which I retired as an O-6 in 1986. If I live another year and there is any money, I'm supposed to get a pension. I have had a busy medical practice down in Florida and have been remarkably successful. I am active in my community in a number of ways and despite being drenched with Agent Orange a number of times, and having some organs removed, have enjoyed great health. Except for some arthritis and prostate trouble, I'm doing great. So I was lucky ... very lucky and I'm so thankful for that. I'm thankful for my life and I have no bitterness. I feel so fortunate to have survived and flourished when so many braver, stronger and better-trained men did not.

Thank you for your attention ... Garry Owen.

F. Harold Kushner, M.D., F.A.C.S.
COL(ret)   MC   US Army

CHAPTER THREE
Integrity & Discipline

Integrity is an element of personal discipline that provides individuals a foundation from which to make the right choice time and time again, especially when facing difficult, and sometimes, life and death situations. This chapter provides examples and discussion on the importance of integrity and discipline in our individual lives and in the military.

No nation can safely trust its martial honor to leaders who do not maintain the universal code which distinguishes between those things that are right and those things that are wrong.

Douglas MacArthur
1880–1964
General, WW I, WW II, Korean War

General Dwight D. Eisenhower
1890–1969
34th President of the United States
(1953–1961)

Responsible citizenship in a free country means what it says. It means conducting one's self responsibly, in the interest of others as well as self.

General Dwight D. Eisenhower

COOLNESS AND VIGOR

Let officers and men be made to feel that they will most effectively secure their safety by remaining steadily at their posts, preserving order, and fighting with coolness and vigor.

General Robert E. Lee

The purpose of discipline is to make men fight in spite of themselves.

Ardant Du Picq

THE RIGHT THING

It is the eternal struggle between these two principles—right and wrong—throughout the world. They are the two principles that have stood face to face from the beginning of time.

President Abraham Lincoln

Discipline is the soul of an Army. It makes small numbers formidable; procures success to the weak and esteem to all.

General George Washington

*The American people rightly look to their
military leaders not only to be skilled in
the technical aspects of the profession of
arms, but to be men of integrity.*

General Joseph L. Collins
1896–1987
Division and Corps Commander, WW II

*Do the right thing because it is the right thing to do.
Live with honor. Let integrity be your hallmark. ...
If your soldiers see you lie or "fudge the truth,"
then they will assume that it is all right
to lie to you, too. ...
Remember the movie,* An Officer and a Gentleman.
*In that movie, we have the case of a drill sergeant
working with a very selfish flight cadet who
wanted everything for himself, nothing
for the good of the organization.
Finally, the drill sergeant in exasperation ...
jerks him up by the shirt, looks him in the eye,
says, "Now, look here son, around here
we're not talking about flying airplanes,
around here we're talking about character."*

General Gordon Sullivan

*T*he Army needs soldiers who do not have a price
at which they can be bought; who willingly put
in a 14-hour day for an 8-hour paycheck;
who do not borrow from integrity to pay for expediency;
whose handshake is an ironclad contract;
who are honest in small matters as they are in large
ones; whose ambitions are big enough to include
others; who do not believe that shrewdness,
cunning, and ruthlessness are the three keys
to success; who are occasionally wrong
and always willing to admit it.

Anonymous

BUTCH AND EDDIE

During World War II, many people gained fame in one way or another. Butch O'Hare was a fighter pilot assigned to an American aircraft carrier in the Pacific. One day his entire squadron was assigned to fly a particular mission. Once airborne, he looked at his fuel gauge and realized that someone forgot to top off his fuel tank. He knew there was not enough fuel to complete his mission and return to his ship. His flight leader told him to leave formation and return.

As he was returning to the mothership, he saw a squadron of Japanese Zeroes heading toward the fleet. With all the fighter planes gone, the fleet was almost defenseless. His was the only opportunity to distract and divert them. Single-handedly, he dove into the formation of planes and attacked them. The American fighter planes were rigged with cameras so, as they flew and fought, pictures were taken so pilots could learn more about the terrain, enemy maneuvers, etc.

Butch dove at them and shot until all his ammunition was gone. He then dove trying to clip off a wing or tail so the enemy planes could not fly. His goal—keep the Japanese Zeroes from reaching the American ships. Finally, the Japanese squadron took off in another direction. Butch O'Hare and his fighter plane, both badly shot up, managed to limp back to the carrier.

He told his story, but not until the film from the camera was developed did they realize the extent he really went to, to protect his fleet. He was recognized as a hero and given America's highest military honor, the Medal of Honor. Chicago's O'Hare International Airport is named after him.

Prior to WW II, there was a man named Easy Eddie, who worked for Al Capone. Capone was notorious for the murders he'd committed and the

Avengers Flying in Formation
September, 1942
©National Archives.

illegal things he'd done. Easy Eddie was Al Capone's very talented lawyer who was able to keep Capone out of jail. To show his appreciation, Capone paid Eddie very well and gave him extra things, like a residence that filled an entire Chicago city block. The house was fenced and he had live-in help along with all of the conveniences of the day.

Easy Eddie had a son whom he loved deeply and Eddie gave him all the best things while he was growing up; clothes, cars, and a good education. Because he loved his son he tried to teach him right from wrong. But one thing he couldn't give his son was a good name, and a good example. Easy Eddie decided a good name was much more important than all the riches. So, he went to the authorities in order to rectify the wrongs he had done. In order to tell the truth, it meant he must testify against Capone, and Eddie knew Capone would do his best to have him killed.

Most of all, Eddie wanted to be an example and to do the best he could to give a good name back to his son. He testified. Within the year, he was shot and killed on a lonely street in Chicago.

Two unrelated stories? Butch O'Hare was Easy Eddie's son.

Author Unknown

*When one is loyal to the truth,
we say he/she is a person of integrity.
When one is loyal to the truth under
intense opposition, we say he/she
is a person of great integrity.*

Anonymous

*During the Gulf War, one of the hundreds of
thousands of soldiers General Frederick Franks
(VII Corps Commander) had touched said
to him before the attack into Iraq,
"Don't worry, General. We trust you." ...
What greater thing could a soldier say to a leader?*

General Gordon Sullivan

TODAY'S YOUTH SHARE DESIRE FOR STRICTER RULES

Richmond Times-Dispatch
June 20, 1999

by Gen. Charles Krulak

On April 20, the nation watched in horror as the carnage created by two student gunmen at Columbine High School flashed across their television screens. It was the 14th time in just over three years that a student had killed at least one person by opening fire in a school. Sadly, we didn't have to watch the violence on the evening news; we could have seen the same cold-blooded killing in shows designed to garner ratings for their entertainment value. This is the society in which today's youth are being raised. It is a culture where our standards, values, and principles have been under constant attack.

I am convinced that the vast majority of parents, teachers, and clergy are struggling mightily to counter the many negative influences so prevalent in today's society and to build young men and women of character. The Marine Corps sees the results of their Herculean efforts in the individuals who accept the challenge and enter our recruit depots each year. Many of them arrive with solid value systems. But being a person of character is not an easy task. To be a man or woman of character means a life-long battle to live by the highest moral and ethical standards. The Marine Corps has made a solemn pledge to join in that battle; to build upon and reinforce the values that were cultivated so carefully in the homes, schools, and churches of our new recruits.

To engage in this fight we needed to understand today's youth—how they view the world and what motivates them. After consultation with psychiatrists, psychologists, and other experts, we found that among the characteristics common to young people is a desire for standards—something to be measured against. They want to know the limits of acceptable conduct and they want to be held accountable. Generation "X" and Generation "Next" do not want to be "babied." These young Americans are looking for a real challenge. They desperately want to be part of a winning team and are willing to sacrifice to reach that goal.

The Marines Raised Standards

So at a time when the trend was to ease standards and expectations in order to attract new recruits, the Marine Corps did just the opposite. We raised our quality standards for enlistment beyond those required by the Department of Defense. We increased the length of our recruit training allowing for additional instruction on values, integrity, personal accountability, and individual responsibility. We added a 54-hour final "defining moment" at the end of boot camp called the Crucible that challenges each recruit physically, mentally, and morally. Finally, we re-energized all of our leadership to ensure that we set the highest standards for our Marines.

What we have discovered is that the youth of our nation are rising to the challenge. The United States Marine Corps has experienced 47 months of unbroken success in recruiting. More important, the young men and women who are joining our Corps are exceeding every standard. They are tough and smart—more than 97 percent are high school graduates. They know that while technology is a great enabler, when it comes down to winning, nothing takes the place of the individual Marine. They are not concerned with operational tempo and frequent deployments; they understand that their duties require that they sacrifice to serve this great nation. They are dedicated patriots who know they must uphold our core values of honor, courage, and commitment.

While these young Marines understand the need for high standards, others believe that our emphasis on traditional values is outdated and that the military is at odds with the public it is sworn to protect. Critics point to our standards and values and urge that we change them to reflect more closely those of the rest of America. Some even go so far as to imply that the military culture is somehow a threat to our democratic way of life.

Military Culture Is Needed

Our unique military culture is not a reason for concern, but rather a significant source of strength for our nation—vital to our continued security and prosperity. We should not attempt to close the cultural divide that separates the military and civilian communities, but to understand why it exists and why America is stronger because of it.

There is no great mystery as to why people question our military culture today. It is a lack of understanding. During the early part of this century, you would be hard-pressed to find anyone in a community who had not served in the military, tried to serve in the military, or had family and friends who served. Many of those who served went on to become the leaders of this nation in business and government. They had experienced military training firsthand. They knew what it took, not only to build successful warriors, but also to keep them finely tuned and trained for the next conflict.

Fifty years later, only 9 percent of the people in this country have had military experience. The customs, traditions, and requirements we must levy on our men and women are an unknown commodity to many Americans, including some who are in positions to influence the policies and legislation that govern our armed forces. As a result, various efforts have been made during the past decade to "help" the military get in line with the public it serves. In some cases these moves have resulted in new policies; in other situations, reviews have been mandated to evaluate the merits of such policies as integrated vs. segregated recruit training or the military's stance on fraternization and adultery. Fortunately, these efforts have not yet seriously eroded the foundation upon which our military rests.

Americans need to understand that our nation's Marines, like our sister services, exist to fight and win her wars. It is our heritage, the ultimate nature of our business today, and our dominant priority as we prepare for the future. It is the requirement to focus on life-and-death matters, on war-fighting and the preparations for success on the battlefield, which distinguish the military so dramatically from the society that we serve. Anything that detracts from that focus is not only counterproductive, but also destructive to the nation.

The Need for Military Rigor

History shows that on those occasions when various segments of our society have forgotten the virtue of military rigor—when shrill voices have succeeded in closing the gap between the civilian and military cultures—our nation, our armed services, and America's families have paid a horrible price. Such was the case with the Doolittle Commission in 1946. The erosion of the authority of junior officers and NCOs between 1946 and 1950 so weakened the fighting spirit of some U.S. units that the North Korean Peoples' Army nearly succeeded in drowning Korean democracy in the Sea of Japan. The mortgage on military readiness was not paid with discipline and training, but with American lives during the first three months of that war.

Today, the discipline and fortitude of the individual Marine remain the most vital components of Marine combat readiness. Modern warfare will be conducted with units operating across the spectrum of crisis and conflict with incredibly lethal weapons at their disposal. It will require complex decision-making at lower levels and place greater stress on the individual Marine than ever before. To accomplish our assigned missions in a manner consistent with the expectations of the American public, Marines must be proficient at making morally sound tactical judgments about the use of force. They must possess an uncompromising integrity that dominates their every decision. To friend and foe alike, Marines represent our nation ... therefore, they must project the best qualities and highest standards. And they do.

As I write this, there are more than 25,000 Marines forward deployed, literally around the globe. They are participating in Operation Allied Force, maintaining peace and stability in the Asia-Pacific region, and conducting military-to-military exchanges with our allies around the world. They are gone for six months at a time, away from hearth and home, family and friends. They live every day with uncertainty and danger ... ready to answer the nation's call to action at a moment's notice. They are sustained by the qualities instilled in them since their first minutes at boot camp—discipline, selfless devotion to their duties and their fellow Marines, subordination of their personal desires to the demands of their unit, and willing obedience to the orders of their seniors. Without these qualities, which are at the heart of our warrior culture, the readiness of our military would quickly disappear.

Finally, as we transform the youth of America into United States Marines, I believe that we are not merely assuring the quality of our fighting force, but also building better citizens for our nation: men and women characterized by integrity, moral courage, and a selfless devotion to duty. When they return to civilian society—be it after a single enlistment or a 30-year career—they will be better for having served and having learned the valuable lessons taught so effectively by immersion in our military culture.

A Positive Influence on Society

Those of us who are privileged to serve are obliged to uphold the high standards that have long distinguished the profession of arms. In doing so, we honor our past and preserve the hard-won and sacred trust bestowed upon us by our fellow citizens. By doing so we can, in fact, set the standard and through our example positively influence society. Americans should preserve and even treasure our military's culture. While public appreciation of the military may waver on occasion, American respect for core values—for honor, courage, and commitment—never does. They are the American ideal, the bedrock of our society, and the reason that America's youth will rise above the recent school tragedies to lead this great nation into the future.

Semper Fi

SCHOFIELD'S DEFINITION OF DISCIPLINE

The discipline which makes the soldiers of a free country reliable in battle is not to be gained by harsh or tyrannical treatment. On the contrary, such treatment is far more likely to destroy than to make an army. It is possible to impart instruction and to give commands in such a manner and such a tone of voice to inspire in the solider no feeling but an intense desire to obey, while the opposite manner and tone of voice cannot fail to excite strong resentment and a desire to disobey.

The one mode or the other dealing with subordinates springs from the corresponding spirit in the breast of the commander. He who feels the respect which is due to others will inspire in them regard for himself, while he who feels and hence manifests disrespect toward others, especially his inferiors, cannot fail to inspire hatred against himself.

General John McAllister Schofield
in his address to cadets of the United States Military
Academy, August 11, 1879
1831–1906

A USMA graduate and served under General Sherman during the
Civil War. After the war he served as Superintendent of the USMA and
later as General of the Army from 1888 to 1895.

INTEGER

B elow is the keynote speech presented by GEN (ret) Charles C. Krulak at the annual Joint Services Conference on Professional Ethics (JSCOPE) on 28 January, 2000.

We study and we discuss ethical principles because it serves to strengthen and validate our own inner value system ... It gives direction to what I call our moral compass. It is the understanding of ethics that becomes the foundation upon which we can deliberately commit to inviolate principles.

It becomes the basis of what we are ... Of what we include in our character.

Based on it, we commit to doing what is right. We expect such commitment from our leaders. But most importantly, we must demand it of ourselves.

Sound morals and ethical behavior cannot be established or created in a day or a semester ... Or a year. They must be institutionalized within our character over time ... They must become a way of life. They go beyond our individual services and beyond our ranks or positions; they cut to the heart and to the soul of who we are and what we are and what we must be ... men and women of character. They arm us for the challenges to come and they impart to us a sense of wholeness. They unite us in the calling we now know as the profession of arms.

Of all the moral and ethical guideposts that we have been brought up to recognize, the one that, for me, stands above the rest ... The one that I have kept in the forefront of my mind ... Is integrity. It is my ethical and personal touchstone.

Integrity as we know it today, stands for soundness of moral principle and character—uprightness—honesty. Yet there is more. Integrity is also an ideal ... A goal to strive for ... And for a man or woman to "walk in their integrity" is to require constant discipline and usage.

The word integrity itself is a martial word that comes to us from an ancient Roman army tradition.

During the time of the 12 Caesars, the Roman army would conduct morning inspections. As the inspecting centurion would come in front of each legionnaire, the soldier would strike with his right fist the armor breastplate that covered his heart. The armor had to be strongest there in order to protect the heart from the sword thrusts and from arrow strikes.

As the soldier struck his armor, he would shout "integritas" (in-teg'-ri-tas), which in Latin means material wholeness, completeness, and entirety. The inspecting centurion would listen closely for this affirmation and also for the ring that well-kept armor would give off. Satisfied that the armor was sound and that the soldier beneath it was protected, he would then move on to the next man.

At about the same time, the praetorians or imperial bodyguard were ascending into power and influence. Drawn from the best "politically correct" soldiers of the legions, they received the finest equipment and armor. They no longer had to shout "integritas" to signify that their armor was sound. Instead, as they struck their breastplate, they would shout "hail Caesar," to signify that their heart belonged to the imperial personage—not to their unit—not to an institution—not to a code of ideals. They armored themselves to serve the cause of a single man.

A century passed and the rift between the legion and the imperial bodyguard and its excesses grew larger. To signify the difference between the two organizations, the legionnaire, upon striking his armor would no longer shout "integritas" (in-teg'-ri-tas), but instead would shout "integer" (in-te-ger).

Integer (in-te-ger) means undiminished—complete—perfect. It not only indicated that the armor was sound, it also indicated that the soldier wearing the armor was sound of character. He was complete in his integrity ... His heart was in the right place ... His standards and morals were high.

He was not associated with the immoral conduct that was rapidly becoming the signature of the praetorian guards.

The armor of integrity continued to serve the legion well. For over four centuries they held the line against the marauding Goths and Vandals but by 383 A.D., the social decline that infected the republic and the praetorian guard had its effects upon the legion. As a 4th century Roman general wrote, "when, because of negligence and laziness, parade ground drills were abandoned, the customary armor began to feel heavy since the soldiers rarely, if ever, wore it."

Therefore, they first asked the emperor to set aside the breastplates and mail and then the helmets. So our soldiers fought the Goths without any protection for the heart and head and were often beaten by archers.

Although there were many disasters, which lead to the loss of great cities, no one tried to restore the armor to the infantry. They took their armor off, and when the armor came off—so too came their integrity.

It was only a matter of a few years until the legion rotted from within and was unable to hold the frontiers ... the barbarians were at the gates.

Integrity ... It is a combination of the words, "integritas" (in-teg'-ri-tas) and "integer" (in-te-ger). It refers to the putting on of armor, of building a completeness ... a wholeness ... a wholeness in character. How appropriate that the word integrity is a derivative of two words describing the character of a member of the profession of arms.

The military has a tradition of producing great leaders that possess the highest ethical standards and integrity. It produces men and women of character ... character that allows them to deal ethically with the challenges of today and to make conscious decisions about how they will approach tomorrow.

However, as I mentioned earlier, this is not done instantly. It requires that integrity becomes a way of life ... it must be woven into the very fabric of our soul. Just as was true in the days of imperial Rome, you either walk in your integrity daily, or you take off the armor of the "integer" and leave your heart and soul exposed ... open to attack.

My challenge to you is simple but often very difficult ... Wear your armor of integrity ... Take full measure of its weight ... Find comfort in its protection ... Do not become lax. And always, always, remember that no one can take your integrity from you ... You and only you can give it away!

The biblical book of practical ethics—better known as the book of proverbs—sums it up very nicely: "the integrity of the upright shall guide them: but the perverseness of transgressors shall destroy them." (Prov. 11:3)

Thank you.

To be trusted is a greater compliment than to be loved.

George MacDonald

THE IMPORTANCE OF ETHICS AND INTEGRITY

Statement Submitted to the Committee on Judiciary,
United States House of Representatives.

By Leon A. Edney, Admiral USN (Retired), December 01, 1998

Mr. Chairman, I appear before your distinguished Committee today to participate in a panel discussion addressing leadership and ethics as they relate to the current issues before this committee and the nation. In view of my particular experience as a career military officer serving this nation's defense needs for over 37 years, I will focus my remarks on the importance of ethics and integrity in the military leadership of this great Country of ours.

For the past two years, I have been the full time occupant of the Distinguished Leadership Chair at the United States Naval Academy. This Chair is endowed by the private donation of one the Academy's alumni and therefore my remuneration is not paid for with government or taxpayers dollars. I spend my time teaching ethics three days a week, leadership two days a week and participate in a Brigade-wide Integrity Development Program once a month. This is an indicator of the relevance and importance placed on these subjects by those charged with developing the ethical-based leadership required by our officer corps. While I provide this information as background,

I appear before you today and make this statement as a concerned individual citizen and retired military officer; not as a representative of any organization with which I am currently affiliated.

We live in a society that more and more is transmitting a confused message on the subject of ethics and integrity, which makes one wonder if we are losing our way. In our last Presidential election, both candidates emphasized family values, one wanted two parents to be the center of the family responsibilities. The other felt it takes a village of caring people to raise our children; it seems to me both were right. When we look in the window of the American society to see how we are doing, the picture is not too comforting. Approximately 1 out of 4 babies born today is illegitimate and 25% of all children are being raised by a single parent. Even in the declining base of our more traditional two parent families, both parents routinely work full-time jobs. It often appears we are more interested in raising wealth than our children. Consequently, TV viewing is up 60% among our children and scanning the Internet, not reading the classics, is a close second. Those interested in leadership and ethics development must ask this question. What ethical messages are our children getting from many afternoon TV talk shows as well as the prime time violence and comic titillation on TV in the evening? Now this same material is easily available on the Internet. Recent surveys indicate 70% of college students admit cheating at least once. You can buy books on How to Cheat and Succeed in most off-campus book stores. The suicide rate among teens is up 11% in the last 5 years. Crime and drugs remain dominant factors in our cities. More interesting is the fact, 50% of our crime involves employees stealing from employers. These are values and lessons of life that are getting transmitted to our youth. It is often a message that subtly implies, "so what if it is wrong, everyone is doing it." This is the background from which our entry level enlisted and officers are coming from. Faced with this reality, the armed forces have concluded, all personnel must be inculcated repeatedly with the requirement and expectation that military leadership must evolve from a foundation of trust and confidence. The ethics and integrity of our military leadership must be much higher than the society at large and even the elected officials that serve that society. Success in combat, which is our business, depends on trust and confidence in our leaders and each other. Ethics and integrity are the basic elements of trust and confidence in our military leadership, both from above and more importantly from below. While the requirements for successful military leadership are clear, it is also clear we do not always meet these standards.

At the end of the Gulf War, just 7 years ago, our military and its leaders stood at the pinnacle of professional performance and public esteem following the dramatic successes in the Gulf War. We led everyone's list of those for whom the public had trust and confidence. Since then we have had Tailhook as a watershed event. There have been serious sexual harassment and ethical behavior charges in all the services, many involving very senior leadership that have resulted in more than a dozen flag officers being removed from office for violations of integrity and ethics. The issue of chemical weapons exposure in the Gulf War raises questions concerning straight talk if not the integrity of the leadership with regards to our troops and the public. Leadership within the Army has been tarnished by Skin Head racial incidents at Fort Bragg, the revelations at Aberdeen and the alleged abuses of the former Sergeant Major of the Army. The tragic shoot down of friendly helos in Northern Iraq as well as several Navy and Marine air accidents also raised questions of confidence and integrity in the military training process. The Naval Academy had the EE [Electrical Engineering] Cheating Scandal in 1993–1994 plus a few highly publicized incidents of drug use and car thefts by members of the Brigade. The Marine Corps had cheating on exams at their Officers Basic School, the publicized tradition of blood pinning and the recent relief of a commander in the field for apparently advocating the destruction of any films documenting routine failures in flight discipline.

Unfortunately, I could list more examples but the message is: our house does not look in order on the issue of ethics and integrity, no matter where you look from the White House to the house next door. Whenever these disconnects between our standards of behavior and our actions occur, the solution is not to lower our standards. Rather we must maintain the standards and improve our performance while holding those who fail accountable.

In the military profession, a breach of your integrity, ethics or honor is always accompanied by a leadership failure. The bottom line for our military leadership requirements is that integrity and ethics cannot be taken for granted or treated lightly at any level of training or interaction. All our personnel must be inculcated repeatedly with the requirement that military leadership must evolve from a foundation of trust and confidence in our ethics and core values of honor, courage and commitment to do what is right. Today we are asking our people, What is right? Why do what is right? The moralist answer is: because it is the right thing to do. Our answer is: because the trust and confidence required of our profession demands it. Doing what is right based on the whole truth must be natural and automatic for the American military officer. We need to clearly identify our core values and repeatedly re-enforce them among all members of the armed forces so that they become second nature.

Whenever one reflects on the need for ethics within the military profession, as executed by those who have the privilege of leading the American Soldier, Sailor, Airman, Marine and Coast Guardsman in the duty of defending our national security interests, I believe it is necessary to reflect on the roots of our nation. For it is there where the higher calling of this nation, some call it a moral purpose that we serve today, began. Some current day thinking would have us believe that those who espouse a bridge to the past have no vision. I submit, if the vision of the present is missing the values that this nation was founded on, we should strengthen that bridge to the past for it is built on the lives of those who fought and gave the ultimate sacrifice for those principles and beliefs.

While there are many effective styles of leadership, two essential ingredients of successful military leadership are integrity and ethics. Rank and high positions do not confer privileges; they entail unavoidable responsibilities and accountability. Young Americans in our military place their leadership on a pedestal of trust and confidence when we earn it. They have the right to expect unfailing professional performance and integrity from each level of leadership. Military leaders at all levels need to consistently display that match between words and deeds, between rules and compliance, between institutional values and behavior. The catch is this match must take place 24 hours a day—there is no duty and then off time where you can let your hair down and not represent these core values. There can be no compromise on this issue in a profession where the ultimate you can demand of a subordinate is that they lay their life on the line in the execution of your orders.

When all is said and done, military leadership must have a moral base, a set of ethical values, to keep us true to the high ideals of our forebearers who provided us the cherished inheritance of freedom. The integrity of an officer's word, signature, commitment to truth, discerning what is right and acting to correct what is wrong; must be natural, involved and rise to the forefront of any decision or issue. Leadership by example must come from the top, it must be consistently of the highest standards and it must be visible for all to see. "Do as I say and not as I do" just won't hack it!

This country is firmly entrenched in the principle of civilian leadership of our military in the authority of the President. Therefore, those who hold that leadership position, to be credible, must meet the same standards. America and her Armed Forces have always stood on the side of right and human decency. You do not throw these core values away in the process of defending them. You also do not lower the bar of ethical standards and integrity when individuals fail to live up to them. We must continue to remove those who fall short and seek those who meet and exceed the requirements. Dual standards and less accountability at the top will undermine the trust and confidence so essential to good order and discipline as well as mission success. The fact is, core values for military leaders and their civilian Commander in Chief remain in effect no matter where they are or what you are doing 24 hours a day. When observed by anyone, they must reflect the institution's core values of respect for decency, human dignity, morality and doing what is right, in or out of uniform, on or off duty.

I believe that ethical men and women have a conscience that warns you when you are about to cross the line from right to wrong. The true test of integrity for the ethical leader is doing what is right when no one is watching. He or she knows and that is all that is required to do what is right. Unfortunately those few senior military and civilian officials that bring shame on themselves, their families and their country by ethical indiscretions were probably doing the same thing as more junior officials. It was not newsworthy then, but it was just as wrong. If in these cases the leader chooses to lie or otherwise avoid his/her responsibilities, the continuation of that military leadership is adverse to morale, good order and discipline and eventually combat effectiveness. As has been said on many occasions: "Habit is the daily battleground of character." I agree with Stephen Crater's three requirements for ethical action on issues of integrity. First, discern what is right and what is wrong based on all the facts and the truth. This takes proactive involvement—not selective avoidance. Second—Then you must act on what you discern to be wrong, even at personal cost and I might add the corrective action must be effective. And finally third—openly justify your actions as required to meet the test of right and wrong. Under this clear definition, whenever an individual or collective breakdown in our core values is observed, immediate corrective action must be taken. There are any number of courses of action available and the best one will depend on the circumstances at the time. What is never acceptable, is the toleration of observed wrong actions or the acceptance of an environment that allows wrong actions to occur. To allow this is a fundamental breakdown in the integrity of the leadership responsibilities and trust placed in the acceptance of one's oath of office.

Above all else, military leadership is a commitment to seek out responsibility, to understand and accept accountability, to care, to get involved, to motivate, to get the job done right the first time, through our people. Mistakes will happen and can be corrected, usually with a positive learning curve. The cover-up of mistakes and responsibility by lying or obfuscation cannot be tolerated. The leadership of our Armed Forces must be based on principle— not litigious double talk. Thus the leadership traits of our military as well as the civilian leadership of the military must demonstrate, above all else, a commitment to integrity and ethics on a daily basis. This must be most visible at the top, if we as a nation are to meet our constitutional responsibilities to "Provide for the Common Defense" now burdened with the mantle of world leadership.

In closing, I offer the following summary observations: On Ethics and Military Leadership:

- We must learn from our past mistakes, but we must get on with the business at hand and focus on the future not our wake. We have a cadre of young leadership in our armed services that makes me confident for the future

- Ethics and Integrity essential for successful military leadership start at the top. In our country the top military leadership is subject to duly elected civilian authority specifically empowered in the office of the President of the United States

- Military readiness and mission accomplishment depends on trust and confidence in the integrity of the leader

- Actions of the leader are more important than words. It is important for those you lead to know what you stand for and equally important what you won't stand for

- Loyalty down is just as important as loyalty up

- Regardless of what the exit polls imply, the character of a nation and its leaders does matter and it matters most to those who are prepared to lay down their lives for that nation. Those entrusted with the defense of our nation are in a risk-taking business. If we ever become risk-adverse because the integrity of our leadership is in question or even perceived to be in question, we all lose

- Finally, our leaders must "Eschew Obfuscation" in all we do. Our national leaders must talk straight and with integrity on every issue. If we lie to ourselves as an institution or as individuals within that institution, we are laying the seeds of our own individual and national destruction.

Thank you for the privilege of addressing this Committee on these important issues.

HE COULD GIVE NO MORE

Army Tech-Sergeant Leland Wendling sent the following verbatim letter to his parents after being injured in WW II and before he went back into battle where he was eventually killed.

November 14, 1944

Dear Folks,

I never did tell you exactly how I was hit because I was afraid it would worry you too much. So now since I am coming along good I will explain the whole thing in detail. If some of this happens to be censored think nothing of it because it will only be something of a definite nature and wouldn't interest you.

The 15th of Sept. was one of those droopy dreary days you know what I mean—damp, foggy and heavy woods. We had just busted the first row of pill boxes on the Siegfried line—but the Germans were still launching severe counter-attacks. It so happened that our platoon caught the brunt of several of them. About 4:30 in the afternoon I was called up to the C.P. The Lt. Said "We have a little mission to perform." A German machine gun supported by approximately 8 or 10 riflemen had cut around to our rear and have a large group of us isolated. Also, they had been harassing fire on us for several hours. We were to take 1 squad out of the 3rd platoon and 1 out of the 2nd platoon and wipe out the enemy machine gun. One thing we did not account for was their visibility and the fact that they could contact their own artillery. As soon as I heard the details of the mission, I said, "Let's go before it gets too dark." So we took off. We had passed the last outpost and were well on our way and started to go across a small open space. Here is where they saw us. The Germans laid down an artillery barrage that would be hard to match. I distinctly remember the first shell because it was the one that got me. I thought it was going high but it hit just in the treetops. The next thing I knew I was lying on the ground with terrible pains around my heart—also I was paralyzed. Finally the Medic got there (shelling continued all the time)—he lifted me up and I began to cough blood and suck air in and out of my neck. The rest I remember very little of except I was given a shot of morphine to ease the pain. In a few minutes I began to sweat—and then I passed out.

The last thing I remember saying was "Doc—my rosary—put it in my right hand." Then, I was taken back to the aid station and given plasma, from there on to the Evacuation Hospital and then more blood plasma—8 pints in all.

One piece went into my neck and down into my left lung. That was why I coughed blood and breathed thru the wound. It was removed thru my left side and now my lung is O.K.—no fluid or anything.

My left leg was hit 3 places. 2 very small and 1 not as big as a dime. It does not bother me now. One piece went thru my right leg. It is O.K. now. They took 8 stitches. There are still 11 pieces of shrapnel in it.

Another piece hit my right forefinger and split the knuckles length ways. It is a little crooked but in good shape. Another piece hit the loose skin between my right thumb and forefinger—tearing it all out. It is all right now because I worked it a lot—practically no scar. Another piece hit my right side and is still there but does not bother. Two more pieces hit my head and cut down toward my forehead. They are all healed up one leaving only a small scar. Now, I am giving exercises in this ward and my chest does not bother me.

I think I was awfully lucky that I didn't get hurt worse. Perhaps I shouldn't have told you all this but I knew you were wondering and since I wasn't hurt any worse and am coming along good you might want to know that whole story. About all I am doing now is convalescing, so will close for today hoping to hear from you soon.

Love
Leland.

p.s.   Disregard all rumors you have heard about me coming back to the
        U.S. The war is not over. Remember!

[end of letter]

Near the end of T-SGT Wendling's fifth month of recuperation, he learned that his brother, Donald A. Wendling, was captured by the Germans and was in a group of prisoners being marched to the southern part of Germany toward Italy.

His unit, the 22 Infantry Regiment, 4th Infantry Division was chosen to try to rescue these prisoners. He begged to return to his unit and was mortally wounded on this march. As he lay wounded he did not ask for his rosary to be placed in his hand, instead, because of his wounds, he asked the medic to place the rosary in his mouth. Moving the beads with his tongue and teeth he said his dying prayers. The day was March 5th, 1945. He was twenty-four years old. With his last breath, he gave his life to his country and his soul to God. He could give no more.

CHAPTER FOUR
Courage and Bravery

Physical and moral courage, bravery, heroism, and valor are the focus of this chapter. These qualities have proven to be a standard for the men and women of our military. Time and again, our soldiers have put aside their fears and concern for their own well being to serve the greater cause, specifically, the defense of our freedoms.

Our Army love their General very much, but they have one thing against him, which is the little care he takes of himself in any action. His personal bravery, and the desire he has of animating his troops by example, make him fearless of danger. This occasions us much uneasiness. But Heaven, which has hitherto been his shield, I hope will still continue to guard so valuable a life.

From One of General Washington's Officers

VICTORY OR DEATH!

The Alamo San Antonio, Texas

LTC W. Barret Travis

Alamo
24 February 1836

To the people of Texas and all Americans in the world. Fellow citizens and compatriots:

I am besieged by a thousand or more of the Mexicans under Santa Anna. I have sustained a continued bombardment for twenty-four hours and have not lost a man. The enemy have demanded a surrender at discretion; otherwise the garrison is to be put to the sword if the place is taken. I have answered the summons with a cannon shot and our flag still waves proudly from the walls.

I shall never surrender or retreat.

Then I call on you in the name of liberty, of patriotism, and everything dear to the American character to come to our aid with all dispatch. The enemy are receiving reinforcements daily and will no doubt increase to three or four thousand in four or five days. Though this call may be neglected, I am determined to sustain myself as long as possible and die like a soldier who never forgets what is due to his own honor and that of his country. *Victory or Death!*

W. Barret Travis
Lieutenant Colonel, Commanding

P.S. The lord is on our side. When the enemy appeared in sight, we had not three bushels of corn. We have since found in deserted houses, 80 or 90, bushels and get in the walls 20 or 30 head of beeves [cattle].

*Physical bravery is an animal instinct;
moral bravery is a much higher and truer courage.*

Wendell Phillips
1811–1884
American Orator and Reformer

*General George Marshall epitomized the attributes of
character required of all officers. He persevered—he was
a lieutenant for 15 years. He learned that some days are better
than others. He stuck with his profession. He had courage
to disagree with superiors, to stand up for his beliefs.
In 1917, during a visit of training in France, General Pershing
was dissatisfied and let the division commander know it in
very clear terms. Marshall, a junior staff officer, witnessed
the event and thought Pershing's appraisal was unfair.
As Pershing was leaving, Marshall caught up to him and
in a flurry of facts he refuted the General's assessment.
Pershing later made Marshall his aide. The lesson:
disagreement is not disrespect. Have the courage
to stand up for your convictions.*

General Gordon Sullivan

*You gain strength, courage,
and confidence by every experience
in which you really stop to
look fear in the face.
You must do the thing which
you think you cannot do.*

Eleanor Roosevelt
1884–1962
*First Lady,
American Humanitarian,
and Writer*

Eleanor Roosevelt

Conquer or Die

The time is now near at hand which must probably determine whether Americans are to be freemen or slaves; whether they are to have any property they can call their own; whether their houses and farms are to be pillaged and destroyed, and themselves consigned to a state of wretchedness from which no human efforts will deliver them.

The fate of unborn millions will now depend, under God, on the courage of this army. Our cruel and unrelenting enemy leaves us only the choice of brave resistance, or the most abject submission. We have, therefore to resolve to conquer or die.

General George Washington
an order issued to his troops
from his Headquarters in New York
July 2, 1776

SERGEANT JOSEPH SADOWSKI

In the midst of WW II there occurred an episode that GEN Creighton Abrams would remember, and speak of with reverence, for the rest of his life. At Valhey tanks from his Company A rolled into the center of town, led by the company commander, Captain William Spencer, in the first tank. Commanding the second tank in the column was Sergeant Joseph Sadowski. The lead tank swung north around a corner as Sadowski clattered into the village square. There a German armor-piercing round from an 88 mm antitank gun scored a direct hit on his tank, catching it in the flank and setting it afire. The doomed vehicle lurched to a halt next to the town's water trough as the flames built in intensity. Sadowski ordered his crew to dismount and got them to shelter against a nearby building, dodging a hail of machine-gun and small-arms fire as they ran across the square. Then, taking a count, he discovered that the tank's bow gunner was not with him. Looking at the crippled tank, Sadowski saw that the man's hatch was still shut tight.

What happened next is indelibly inscribed in the division's history: "The sergeant ran back to his tank, clambered up the smoking front slope plate and tried to pry open the bow gunner's hatch with his bare hands. He stood on the smoking tank and strained at the hatch until he had been hit so many times he could no longer stand. He slid from his medium and died in the mud beside its tracks. Altogether eight antitank guns and some three hundred German infantry had been defending Valhey. After the town was cleared the attacking force swirled on east toward Moncourt, and it was four days before anyone could be sent back to Valhey to recover Sadowski's body. There they found that the local townspeople had buried him in their local cemetery, his grave heaped with flowers. The next day, under a pouring rain, the entire population of the village stood in a silent tribute as the fallen tanker's body was removed for transfer to a military cemetery." Abrams never forgot Sadowski, or the selfless actions that won him the Medal of Honor that day. Often he would speak of him as an exemplar of a leader's devotion to his men. He could never do so without a husky throat and a catch in his voice, communicating more eloquently than his words how he felt about such a soldier.

Later, taking over a battalion on occupation duty in Germany that needed some bucking up, Abrams assembled the whole outfit in the post theater. There he explained to them about how Sergeant Sadowski had won the Medal of Honor in World War II, winding up with a charge to these soldiers of the postwar Army. ... "You people are in the same Army, with the same traditions. Remember when you walk through the streets of Chemnitz and Grafenwoehr that you walk with Sergeant Sadowski."

Lewis Sorley
from his book, *Thunderbolt: General Creighton Abrams
and the Army of His Times*

RETURN TO BAYONET HILL

From the Army News Service, Osan Air Base, South Korea, February 23, 1998

The words "legend" and "hero" are so often misused today in the context of sports and music superstars that these words tend to lose their impact. But, when it comes to retired Col. Lewis L. Millett, who received a Medal of Honor for his exploits during the Korean War, the same words fail to do him justice.

In late January 1951, Hill 180, as it was called in those days, lay between the Chinese augmenting North Korean forces and Gen. Matthew Ridgeway and the Eighth U.S. Army. Ridgeway sent the 27th Infantry "Wolfhounds" north toward Osan. Easy Company, part of the Wolfhounds, was commanded by then-Capt. Millett, a tough World War II hardened soldier.

Company E was moving through a frozen rice paddy in their tanks Feb. 5, when the enemy attacked and pinned down the first platoon. Millett rose up and shouted for the second platoon to fix bayonets and follow him. As the soldiers appeared at the top of the hill with Millett leading the charge, the enemy jumped out of their foxholes and scurried down the other side. Millett and his troops quickly dispatched the ones that remained. Millett was nominated for a Distinguished Service Cross for his actions. No one knew at the time that this was just a rehearsal for what was to follow 48 hours later. With tanks, Millett and two of his platoons approached Hill 180 fully expecting to bypass it. Then one of his men noticed movement above them. Once notified of the situation, Millett deployed his men along the paddy dike. They were already under heavy machine-gun fire from the enemy and taking casualties. Millett jumped aboard the nearest tank, grabbed its .50-caliber machine gun and sent a stream of tracers toward the enemy position. He told the gunner to keep the fire directed in that region and then jumped off the tank and prepared to get the counterattack underway.

Millett didn't want the enemy to get away like they had on the previous occasion, but another Chinese machine gun opened fire before Millett could plan an attack. As gunfire tore into the first platoon, casualties mounted. Their .50-caliber machine gun jammed with a ruptured cartridge.

The attack was crumbling even before it had a chance to begin.

Millett ran across the bullet-strewn ground and shouted to his platoon sergeant, "Get ready to move out; we're going up the hill. Fix Bayonets! Everyone goes with me. Charge!"

He raised his rifle and took off across the open field. The platoon sergeant led about a dozen or so soldiers behind Millett; those that didn't follow were cut down by enemy machine-gun fire.

Millett dodged bullets and natural obstacles on the ground as he raced across the icy field and up the hill. Shouting Chinese phrases, Millett and his men tore into the enemy with their bayonet-tipped rifles.

Millett was so far ahead of his troops, he had to avoid grenades thrown by both sides. Millett avoided a cluster of grenades thrown by the enemy— dodging around the detonation of eight grenades—but the ninth one got him. With blood pouring from the wound, Millett continued the charge, not caring about his intense pain. With their bayonets ripping and tearing into the enemy, Millett and his men continued the bloody charge until the enemy was routed. When it was all over, Millett stopped at the top of the ridge and pumped his bloody rifle up and down, signaling to those below that the hill was conquered. To the men of Easy Company, and in the records of U.S. military history, the hill will forever be known as "Bayonet Hill."

After the battle, 47 enemy were dead on the forward slope—30 had died of bayonet wounds. On the back slope lay another 50 enemy, dead of either gun- shot or bayonet wounds. About 100 enemy were estimated to have escaped.

Millett was evacuated due to the seriousness of his wounds. His Medal of Honor was presented to him at the White House on July 5, 1951.

Millett revisited the site of the deadly battle Feb. 6 [1998] to commemorate the Hill 180 Memorial. During an emotional speech, which had more than half the audience in tears, Millett praised the bravery of those who died here during the battle. The speech, which lasted about 30 minutes, was delivered seamlessly without notes.

> "The men who died here would be very proud and understanding of the sacrifice they made if they could return and see this beautiful country—just fly over and see the condominiums that didn't exist 50 years ago. They would also be very proud to have been associated with the United States and South Korean military," Millett said.
>
> "I have fought in three wars in seven different countries, visited with kings and commoners, soldiers and strangers. Of all the people I've met, civilians or soldiers, through all these wars, they have all only wanted one thing—to be free and to live in peace. But, the price of freedom comes very high. We've lost Soldiers, Sailors, Airmen and Marines, not only fighting for their own country but for the freedom of other people. I hope all of these young people standing here today realize that the freedom they enjoy was paid for by the high price of blood, sweat and tears of people who died on the battlefields. The troops who died not only here, but also on the other battlefields did not die in vain. They died so you and I could live in freedom, the Korean people could live in freedom."

He said that ethnicity or the color of one's skin should not stop people from enjoying the same freedom Americans enjoy.

Millett defended land mines along the Demilitarized Zone and said, "Think of all those poor soldiers on the border, without the land mines, they would be overrun easily by North Korean tanks. Don't tell me I don't know anything about being overrun, I've been overrun by both German and North Korean tanks."

Millett fought back tears as he spoke about his family, especially his youngest son who died coming home from a peacekeeping mission in the Sinai. The irony of that situation was not lost on those in attendance. Here is a man who spent nine continuous years in combat, a hero of many battles, a man who fought with reckless abandon, and a son who died on a peacekeeping mission.

Millett praised the soldiers he met, both U.S. and South Korean, and thanked them for their dedication. He quoted a Marine priest, Father Desmond O'Brien, to give emphasis to his praise. "It's the soldier not a reporter who gives us the freedom of press. It's the soldier not the court that gives us freedom of speech. It's the soldier not the campus agitator who gives us the right to demonstrate. It's the soldier who salutes the flag and whose coffin is covered by the flag who gives the asinine agitator the opportunity to burn that flag." It's soldiers like Washington, Lincoln, Bush and Reagan and a host of others who laid down the sword and became our president, and brought to the civil service the ideas they learned in the field of battle—duty, honor, country.

Millett ended his commemoration speech with a poignant poem, entitled "A Soldiers Prayer," which again had the audience wiping away tears. Millett said that he had written the poem for all those who laid down their lives but particularly for the 347 men and his youngest son who died returning from the peacekeeping mission.

After the commemoration ceremony, Millett attended a reception in his honor. He met and talked with Junior Reserve Officer Training Course cadets, and young scouts. He also reenlisted two active-duty soldiers.

He later met with the press and said that he felt very emotional at being back here again. He said that though his body is now "old and decrepit," his heart was still of a warrior, and he liked to be around other warriors. He said that he had been born 300 years too late and would loved to have been around during the time of Braveheart. Millett praised military spouses and said they do a "hell of a job" keeping the house together in the soldiers' many absences from home. He once again praised the soldiers of today and said he had no doubt that when faced with a situation similar to his, today's soldier, who is better trained and is supported by better technology, would be more effective.

Recalling the battle, Millett said, "I wasn't thinking about my safety. I just wanted to defeat the enemy and protect my troops. After the bayonet charge, I was so weak from fighting that I could barely stand up. That is when good leadership is the key, because when the troops are fatigued from fighting they might not be able to carry on without somebody reorganizing and regrouping them."

He said that nine of the soldiers who charged the hill were killed and maybe twice as many were wounded. Only ten soldiers from that battle are still alive today.

To fight for what he believed in, Millett deserted the U.S. Army to join the Canadian Army at the start of World War II.

> "Inherent in every man or woman's soul, there is a desire to be free, and if you really believe in that and see people who are subjugated by tyranny, you ought to go fight for them. That is the reason I deserted the Army once, not to get out of the war but to get into one."

by Sergeant Antony M.C. Joseph

No arsenal or no weapon in the arsenals of the world is so formidable as the will and moral courage of free men and women. It is a weapon our adversaries in today's world do not have. It is a weapon that we as Americans do have.

President Ronald Reagan
First Inaugural Address
January 20, 1981
40th President of the United States
(1981–1989)

Keep your fears to yourself; share your courage with others.

Robert Louis Stevenson
1850–1894

Courage is doing what you're afraid to do. There can be no courage unless you're scared.

Eddie Rickenbacker
1890–1973
American Aviator

But first of all, let me assert my firm belief, that the only thing we have to fear, is fear itself. Nameless, unreasoning, unjustified terror, which paralyzes needed effort to convert retreat into advance.

Franklin Delano Roosevelt

THE DIFFERENCE

There are no monuments on Hill 402—
like at Bunker Hill, Gettysburg, or Normandy,
—but there is no difference in the valor
displayed by American fighting men there and
in a thousand other forgotten locations.
The difference lies only in that most
Americans choose to forget.

Author Unknown

Wounded U.S. Soldiers   A forgotten location in Vietnam.

WHERE IS YOUR MORAL COMPASS POINTING?

Draft Remarks for: The Lighthouse Project '99, Central High School, North Carolina, 29 January 1999, by Gen. Charles C. Krulak, Commandant, US Marine Corps.

I am honored to be here today before such a prestigious audience. Before the leadership of tomorrow ... the leaders that will advance our Nation into the 21st Century. I cannot help but be excited when I think of what lies before you ... the adventure and excitement ... and oh, how I envy you! You will be the ones to take us to new heights and new accomplishments. You will be making the breakthrough discoveries and finding solutions to the problems that previous generations, to include my own, simply could not solve. And it will be you who will have to stand up to the new challenges that will arise tomorrow ... and there will be challenges ... there always are.

How will you prepare yourself for this exciting, yet challenging future? How will you make yourself ready, so that you may be found worthy of the mantle of leadership that will surely be placed upon your shoulders?

Perhaps the best way for me to illustrate these concepts is to relate to you some examples from my experience in Vietnam. It was 0600, the third of June, 1966. I was in command of "G" Company, Second Battalion, First Marine Regiment. I was a First Lieutenant at the time, and had been given this command because the previous commander had been killed about one week earlier.

My Company had been given a simple mission that began with a helicopter assault. We would land in a series of dried-up rice paddies about six football fields in length, and three football fields in width. These paddies were surrounded by jungle-covered mountains, with a dry stream bed running along one side. We were supposed to land, put on our packs, and do what all Marines do: find the largest mountain, and climb to the top. There we would put ourselves in a defensive perimeter to act as the blocking force for an offensive sweep conducted by two battalions.

The helicopters landed, unloaded my company of Marines, and had just started to leave when the world collapsed. Automatic weapons, mortar fire, artillery—it was hell on earth. Fortunately, a good portion of my Company had managed to move into the dry stream bed where they were protected from most of the fire. However, one platoon had landed too far west to move immediately to the cover of the stream bed. As they tried to move in that direction, the fires on them became so heavy they had no alternative but to hit the deck. One particular squad found itself directly in the line of fire of a North Vietnamese 12.7 mm heavy machine gun. In a matter of seconds, two Marines were killed and three were seriously wounded.

As I watched what was happening from my position in the stream bed, I knew that it was just a matter of time before that machine gun would systematically "take out" that whole platoon—squad by squad. If I didn't act immediately, they would be lost in just a matter of minutes.

I made a call to the commander of the first platoon that had made its way into the stream bed, directing him to move up the stream bed so he could attack across the flank of the gun position—not having to assault it directly from the front. At the same time, I directed another platoon to provide suppressive fire that might diminish the volume of fire coming from the machine gun position. All this was happening in the midst of smoke, multiple explosions, heavy small arms fire, and people yelling to be heard over the din of battle.

Suddenly, my radio operator grabbed me by the sleeve and pointed toward the middle of the rice paddy where a black Marine, a Lance Corporal by the name of Grable, had gotten to his feet, placed his M-14 rifle on his hip, and charged the machine gun—firing as fast as he could possibly fire. He ran about 40 meters directly toward the machine gun and then cut to the side, much like a running back might do during a football game. Sure enough, the machine gun, which had been delivering heavy fire on his squad, picked up off of the squad and began firing at Grable.

Seeing the fire shift away from them, the squad moved immediately to the cover of a small rice paddy dike—thick ground, about a foot high separating each paddy from the other. Both they, and the other two squads were able to drag their casualties and gear to the position of safety behind this dike. Grable didn't look back. He didn't see what happened. He kept on fighting. He dodged back and forth across these paddies, firing continuously. He would run out of ammunition, reload on the run, and continue forward, dodging back and forth as he ran. BAM! Suddenly he was picked up like a dishrag and thrown backward—hit by at least one round.

The rest of the platoon charged. My radio operator grabbed me again, but saying nothing, he just pointed to the middle of the rice paddy. That young Marine, Lance Corporal Grable, had gotten to his feet. As he stood, he didn't put the rifle to his hip; he locked the weapon into his shoulder ... took steady aim—good sight picture, good sight alignment, and walked straight down the line of fire into that machine gun.

About four minutes later, my command group and the rest of the unit finally arrived at the now-silent machine gun position. There were nine dead enemy soldiers around the gun ... Lance Corporal Grable was draped over the gun itself. As only Marines can do, these battle-hardened young men tenderly picked up Grable and laid him on the ground. When they opened his "flak jacket" he had five massive wounds from that machine gun. **Five** ...

About seven months later, I traveled back to Headquarters Marine Corps in Washington and watched the Commandant of the Marine Corps present Lance Corporal Grable's widow with the nation's second highest decoration for valor—the Navy Cross. In this woman's arms was the baby boy that Grable had only seen in a Polaroid picture.

Grable displayed great physical courage. Somewhere in his character was another kind of courage as well—moral courage—the courage to do the right thing. When he had the chance to do something else, he chose to do the right thing. His squad was in mortal danger. He had a choice to make, and he did what was right, at the cost of his life. Let me remind you, this was 1966. Grable was a black Marine from Tennessee, who couldn't even buy a hamburger at the McDonald's in his hometown.

So, what of your character? Who are you? No, not the physical and superficial image ... but who are you really? What do you stand for? What is the essence of your character? Where is your moral compass pointing?

Which course do you follow?

Everyday we have to make decisions. It is through this decision-making process that we show those around us the quality of our character. The majority of the decisions we have to make are "no brainers." Deciding what we are going to have for breakfast is not going to test your character, judgment maybe, but not character.

The true test of character comes when the stakes are high ... when the chips are down ... when your gut starts to turn ... when the sweat starts to form on your brow ... when you know the decision you are about to make may not be popular ... but it must be made. That is when your true character is exposed. The associations you keep, the peers you choose, the mentors you seek, the organizations you affiliate with, all help to define your character. But, in the end, you will be judged as an individual, not as part of a group.

Success in life, like in combat, has always demanded a depth of character.

Those who can reach deep inside themselves—and draw upon an inner strength, fortified by strong values—always carry the day against those of lesser character. Moral cowards never win in war. Moral cowards never win in life. They might believe that they are winning a few battles here and there, but their victories are never sweet ... they never stand the test of time ... and they never serve to inspire others. In fact, each and every one of a moral coward's "supposed victories" ultimately leads them to failure.

Those who have the courage to face up to ethical challenges in their daily lives will find that same courage can be drawn upon in times of great stress ... in times of great controversy ... in times of the never ending battle between good and evil.

All around our society you see immoral behavior ... lying, cheating, stealing, drug use and alcohol abuse, prejudice, and a lack of respect for human dignity and the law. In the not too distant future, each of you are going to be confronted with situations where you will have to deal straight-up [with] these issues. The question is ... what will you do when that happens? What action will you take? You will know what you should do ... the issue is ... will you **do** what you know is right? It takes moral courage to hold your ideals above yourself. It is the **defining** aspect of your character.

So, when the test of your character, of your moral courage comes, regardless of the noise and confusion around you, there will be a moment of inner silence in which you must decide what to do. Your character will be defined by your decision ... and it is yours and yours alone to make. When that moment of silence comes and you are wrestling with your decision, consider this poem:

The Eagle and The Wolf

There is a great battle that rages inside me.
One side is a soaring eagle
Everything the eagle stands for is good and true and beautiful.
It soars above the clouds.
Even though it dips down into the valleys,
it lays its eggs on the mountain tops.

The other side of me is a howling wolf.
And that raging, howling wolf represents the worst that is in me.
He eats upon my downfalls and justifies himself
by his presence in the pack.
Who wins this great battle? ...
The one I feed.
The one I feed.

I challenge you all to feed the eagle. Remember, your Nation depends upon it.

God bless you all and Semper Fidelis.

Let us act in the spirit of Thucydides that "the bravest are surely those who have the clearest vision of what is before them, glory and danger alike, and yet notwithstanding go out to meet it."

Henry Alfred Kissinger
1923–
Secretary of State
(1973–1977)

*All men are frightened. The more intelligent
they are, the more they are frightened.
The courageous man is the man who forces
himself, in spite of his fear, to carry on.*

General George S. Patton, Jr.

*Courage consists, not in blindly overlooking danger,
but in seeing and conquering it.*

Richter

*Courage that grows from constitution, often forsakes a
man when he has occasion for it, courage which arises
from a sense of duty, acts in a uniform manner.*

Joseph Addison
1672–1719

Courage is grace under pressure.

Ernest Hemingway
1899–1961
Author

*On the field of fire it is the touch of human nature
which gives men courage and enables them to
make proper use of their weapons.*

S.L.A. Marshall, 1947

God has fixed the time for my death. I do not concern myself about that, but to be always ready, no matter when it may overtake me. That is the way all men should live, and then all would be equally brave.

General Thomas Jonathon "Stonewall" Jackson
1824–1863
Confederate General, Civil War

THE COURAGE OF SAM BIRD

by B.T. Collins

Reprinted with permission from May 1989 *Reader's Digest*
Copyright © 1989 by The Reader's Digest Assn., Inc.

I met Capt. Samuel R. Bird on a dusty road near An Khe, South Vietnam, one hot July day in 1966. I was an artillery forward observer with Bravo Company, 2nd/12th Cavalry, 1st Cavalry Division, and I looked it. I was filthy, sweaty, and jaded by war, and I thought "Oh, brother, get a load of this." Dressed in crisply starched fatigues, Captain Bird was what we called "squared away"—ramrod straight, eyes on the horizon. Hell, you could still see the shine on his boot tips beneath the road dust. After graduation from Officer Candidate School, I had sought adventure by volunteering for Vietnam. But by that hot and dangerous July, I was overdosed on "adventure," keenly interested in survival and very fond of large rocks and deep holes. Bird was my fourth company commander, and my expectations were somewhat cynical when he called all his officers and sergeants together.

"I understand this company has been in Vietnam almost a year and has never had a party," he said.

Now we officers and sergeants had our little clubs to which we repaired. So we stole bewildered looks at one another, cleared our throats and wondered what this wiry newcomer was talking about. "The men are going to have a party," he announced, "and they're not going to pay for it. Do I make myself clear?" A party for the "grunts" was the first order of business! Sam Bird had indeed made himself clear. We all chipped in to get food and beer for about 160 men. The troops were surprised almost to the point of suspicion—who, after all, had ever done anything for them? But that little beer and bull session was exactly what those war-weary men needed. Its effect on morale was profound. I began to watch our new captain more closely.

Bird and I were the same age, 26, but eons apart in everything else. He was from the sunny heartland of Kansas, I from the suburbs of New York City. He prayed every day and was close to his God. My faith had evaporated some-where this side of altar boy. I was a college dropout who had wandered into the Army with the words "discipline problem" close on my heels. He had grad-uated from The Citadel, South Carolina's proud old military school. If ever a man looked like a leader, it was Sam Bird. He was tall and lean, with penetrat-ing blue eyes. But the tedium and terror of a combat zone take far sterner qual-ities than mere appearance.

Our outfit was helicoptered to a mountain outpost one day for the thank-less task of preparing a position for others to occupy. We dug trenches, filled sandbags, strung wire under a blistering sun. It was hard work, and Sam was everywhere, pitching in with the men. A colonel who was supposed to oversee the operation remained at a shelter, doing paperwork. Sam looked at what his troops had accomplished, then, red-faced, strode over to the colonel's sanctu-ary. We couldn't hear what he was saying to his superior, but we had the un-mistakable sense that Sam was uncoiling a bit. The colonel suddenly found time to inspect the fortifications and thank the men for a job well done. An-other day, this time on the front lines after weeks of awful chow, we were given something called "coffee cake" that had the look and texture of asphalt paving. Furious, Sam got on the radio phone to headquarters. He reached the colonel and said, "Sir, you and the supply officer need to come out here and taste the food, because this rifle company is not taking one step further." "Not a good way to move up in the Army," I thought. But the colonel came out, and the food improved from that moment. Such incidents were not lost on the men of Bravo Company. During the monsoon season we had to occupy a landing zone. The torrential, wind-driven rains had been falling for weeks. Like everyone else I sat under my poncho in a stupor, wondering how much of the wetness was rainwater and how much was sweat. Nobody cared that the position was becoming flooded. We had all just crawled inside ourselves. Then I saw Sam, Mr. Spit and Polish, with nothing on but his olive-drab un-dershorts and his boots. He was digging a drainage ditch down the center of the camp. He didn't say anything, just dug away, mud spattering his chest, steam rising from his back and shoulders. Slowly and sheepishly we emerged from under our ponchos, and shovels in hand, we began helping "the old man" get the ditch dug. We got the camp tolerably dried out and with that one simple act transformed our morale. Sam deeply loved the U.S. Army and traditions. Few of the men knew it, but he had been in charge of a special honors unit of the Old Guard, which serves the Tomb of the Unknown Soldier in Arlington National Cemetery and participates in the Army's most solemn ceremonies. He was the kind of guy whose eyes would mist during the singing of the National Anthem. Sam figured patriotism was just a natural part of be-ing an American. But he knew that morale was a function not so much of in-spiration as of good boots, dry socks, extra ammo and hot meals. Sam's philosophy was to put his troops first. On that foundation he built respect a brick at a time. His men ate first; he ate last. Instead of merely learning their names, he made it a point to know the men. A lot of the soldiers were high school dropouts and would-be tough guys just a few years younger than himself. Some were scared, and a few were still in partial shock at being in a shooting war. Sam patiently worked on their pride and self-confidence. Yet there was never any doubt who was in charge. I had been around enough to know what a delicate accomplishment that was. Half in wonder, an officer once told me, "Sam can dress a man down till his ears burn, and the next minute that same guy is eager to follow him into hell." But he never chewed out a man in front of his subordinates. Sam wouldn't ask his men to do anything he wasn't willing to do himself. He dug his own foxholes. He never gave lectures on appearance, but even at God-forsaken outposts in the Central Highlands, he would set aside a few ounces of water from his canteen to shave. His uniform, even if it was jungle fatigues, would be as clean and neat as he could make it. Soon all of Bravo Company had a reputation for looking sharp. One sultry and miserable day on a dirt road at the base camp, Sam gathered the men together and began talking about how tough the infantryman's job is, how proud he was of them, how they should always look out for each other. He took out a bunch of Combat Infantryman's Badges, signifying that a soldier has paid his dues under fire, and he presented one to each of the men. There wasn't a soldier there who would have traded that moment on the road for some parade-ground ceremony. That was the way Sam Bird taught me leadership. He packed a lot of lessons into the six months we were together. Put the troops first. Know that morale often depends on small things. Respect every person's dignity. Always be ready to fight for your people. Lead by example. Reward performance. But Sam had another lesson to teach, one that would take long and painful years, a lesson in courage. I left Bravo Company in December 1966 to return to the States for a month before joining a Special Forces unit. Being a big, tough paratrooper, I didn't tell Sam what his example had meant to me. But I made a point of visiting his parents and sister in Wichita, Kan., just before Christmas to tell them how much he'd affected my life, and how his troops would walk off a cliff for him. His family was relieved when I told them that his tour of combat was almost over and he'd be moving to a safe job in the rear. Two months later, in a thatched hut in the Mekong Delta, I got a letter from Sam's sister, saying that he had conned his commanding officer into letting him stay an extra month with his beloved Bravo Company. On his last day, January 27, 1967—his 27th birthday—the men had secretly planned a party, even arranging to have a cake flown in. They were going to "pay back the old man." But orders came down for Bravo to lead an airborne assault on a North Vietnamese regimental headquarters. Sam's helicopter was about to touch down at the attack point when it was ripped by enemy fire. Slugs shattered his left ankle and right leg. Another struck the left side of his head, carrying off almost a quarter of his skull. His executive officer, Lt. Dean Parker, scooped Sam's brains back into the gaping wound. Reading the letter, I felt as if I'd been kicked in the stomach. I began querying every hospital in Vietnam to find out if Sam was still alive. But in June, before I could discover his fate, I was in a fire fight in an enemy-controlled zone. I had thrown four grenades.

The fifth one exploded in my hand. I lost an arm and a leg. Nearly a year later, in March 1968, I finally caught up with Sam. I was just getting the hang of walking with an artificial leg when I visited him at the VA Medical Center in Memphis, Tenn. Seeing him, I had to fight back the tears. The wiry, smiling soldier's soldier was blind in the left eye and partially so in the right. Surgeons had removed metal shards and damaged tissue from deep within his brain, and he had been left with a marked depression on the left side of his head. The circles under his eyes told of sleepless hours and great pain. The old clear voice of command was slower now, labored and with an odd, high pitch. I saw his brow knit as he looked through his one good eye, trying to remember. He recognized me, but believed I had served with him in Korea, his first tour of duty. Slowly, Sam rebuilt his ability to converse. But while he could recall things from long ago, he couldn't remember what he had eaten for breakfast. Headaches came on him like terrible firestorms. There was pain, too, in his legs. He had only partial use of one arm, with which he'd raise himself in front of the mirror to brush his teeth and shave. He had the support of a wonderful family, and once he was home in Wichita, his sister brought his old school sweetheart, Annette Blazier, to see him. A courtship began, and in 1972 they were married. They built a house like Sam had dreamed of—red brick, with a flagpole out front. He had developed the habit of addressing God as "Sir" and spoke to him often. He never asked to be healed. At every table grace, he thanked God for sending him Annette and for "making it possible for me to live at home in a free country." In 1976, Sam and Annette traveled to The Citadel for his 15th class reunion. World War II hero Gen. Mark Clark, the school's president emeritus, asked about his wounds and said, "On behalf of your country, I want to thank you for all you did." With pride, Sam answered "Sir, it was the least I could do." Later Annette chided him gently for understating the case. After all, he had sacrificed his health and career in Vietnam. Sam gave her an incredulous look. "I had friends who didn't come back," he said. "I'm enjoying the freedoms they died for." I visited Sam in Wichita and phoned him regularly. You would not have guessed that he lived with pain every day. Once, speaking of me to his sister, he said, "I should never complain about the pain in my leg, because B.T. doesn't have a leg." I'd seen a lot of men with lesser wounds reduced to anger and self-pity. Never a hint of that passed Sam's lips, though I knew that, every waking moment, he was fighting to live. On October 18, 1984, after 17 years, Sam's body couldn't take any more. When we received the news of his death, a number of us from Bravo Company flew to Wichita, where Sam was to be buried with his forebears. The day before the burial, his old exec, Dean Parker, and I went to the funeral home to make sure everything was in order. As Dean straightened the brass on Sam's uniform, I held my captain's hand and looked into his face, a face no longer filled with pain. I thought about how unashamed Sam always was to express his love for his country, how sunny and unaffected he was in his devotion to his men. I ached that I had never told him what a fine soldier and man he was. But in my deep sadness I felt a glow of pride for having served with him, and for having learned the lessons of leadership that would serve me all my life. That is why I am telling you about Samuel R. Bird and these things that happened so long ago. Chances are, you have seen Sam Bird. He was the tall officer in charge of the casket detail at the funeral of President John F. Kennedy. Historian William Manchester described him as "a lean, sinewy Kansan, the kind of American youth whom Congressmen dutifully praise each Fourth of July and whose existence many, grown jaded by years on the Hill, secretly doubt." There can be no doubt about Sam, about who he was, how he lived and how he led. We buried him that fall afternoon, as they say, "with honors." But as I walked from that grave, I knew I was the honored one, for having known him.

[Note: At the time that this article was written, Mr. B.T. Collins had recovered from severe war wounds to become the highly acclaimed director of the California Conservation Corps and later chief of staff to the governor of California. He later became California's deputy state treasurer. He is now deceased.]

CHAPTER FIVE

Combat Voices and the Warrior Spirit

Throughout our nation's history our soldiers have displayed a warrior's spirit and level of esprit that has provided the motivation for a sustained commitment to total victory. This chapter provides the spoken and written words from many a battlefield where our soldiers displayed initiative, determination, will, tactics, and unit cohesion.

Being shelled is the main work of an infantry soldier, which no one talks about. Everybody has his own way of going about it. In general, it means lying face down and contracting your body into as small a space as possible.

Louis Simpson
from his book,
Air and Armed Men
1972

THE MILITARY FAMILY

*… my first wish would be that my Military Family,
and the whole Army, should consider themselves as a
band of brothers, willing and ready, to die for each other.*

George Washington
to Henry Knox
October 21, 1798

*We must, indeed, all hang together,
or most assuredly we shall all hang separately.*

Benjamin Franklin
In the Continental Congress just before signing the
Declaration of Independence
July 4, 1776

Benjamin Franklin
1706–1790
*Statesman, Printer,
Scientist, and Writer*

A Dash About Them

*This body of men moving along with no order, their guns
carried in every fashion, no two dressed alike,
the officers barely distinguishable from the privates,
were these the men who had driven back, again and
again, our splendid legions? They were the dirtiest men I
ever saw, the most ragged, lean and hungry set
of wolves ... Yet there was a dash about them
that the northern men lacked.*

A Northern woman
watching General Robert E. Lee's army
pass by on its invasion of Maryland

*I shall come out of this fight a line major
general or a dead brigadier.*

Brigadier General Abner Perrin
who was killed at the Battle of Bloody Angle
Spotsylvania, Virginia

Confederate soldiers
Civil War
© National Archives.

Artillery unit drilling c. 1863 © National Archives.

Look at Jackson's Brigade!
It stands there like a stone wall!

General Bernard E. Bee
of South Carolina,
at the Battle of Bull Run, July 1861

To move swiftly, strike vigorously, and secure all the
fruits of victory, is the secret of successful war.

General Stonewall Jackson

ONE TACTICAL PRINCIPAL

There is only one tactical principle which is not
subject to change. It is to use the means
at hand to inflict the maximum amount of
wounds, death, and destruction on the
enemy in the minimum amount of time.

General George S. Patton, Jr.

**American howitzers
shell German forces**
Near Carentan, France,
July 11, 1944
© National Archives.

Thirty Minutes

*We have talked the matter over, and could have
settled the war in thirty minutes had it been left to us.*

An anonymous Confederate private
after he and a Union soldier had conversed between the lines

Confederate Soldier   **Union Soldier**

HE WHO CONTINUES

General Ulysses S. Grant
1822–1885
Union General, Civil War
18th President of the United States
(1869–1877)

*In every battle there comes a time when
both sides consider themselves beaten,
then he who continues the attack wins.*

*The art of war is simple enough. Find out where your
enemy is. Get at him as soon as you can,
and strike him as hard as you can,
and keep moving on!*

General Grant

Any blow, to be successful, must be sudden and hard.

General Robert E. Lee

It is well that war is so terrible, else we would grow too fond of it.

General Lee
viewing the ill-fated Union
advance at Fredericksburg
December 1862

General Robert E. Lee
1807–1870
Confederate Army, U.S. Civil War

A SEA OF BLOOD

*To be a good soldier, you must love the army.
To be a good commander, you must be willing to order the death of the thing you love. We do not fear our own death, you and I, but there comes a time, we are never quite prepared for so many to die. We do expect the occasional empty chair, a salute to fallen comrades. But this war goes on and on, and men die, and the price gets ever high. We are prepared to lose some of us, but we are never prepared to lose all of us. And there is the great trap, General. When you attack you must hold nothing back, you must commit yourself totally. We are adrift here in a sea of blood, and I want it to end. I want this to be the final battle.*

General Lee
to General Longstreet, Battle of Gettysburg, July 2, 1863

General Robert E. Lee

*Come on, you sons of bitches—
do you want to live forever!*

Gunnery Sergeant Dan Daly, USMC
Belleau Wood, France
June 1918

... This war is flooded with human nature.

From an unknown U.S. Soldier
in a letter home, WW I

It is fatal to enter a war without the will to win it.

General Douglas MacArthur

Our country won't go on forever, if we stay soft as we are now. There won't be any America— because some foreign soldiery will invade us and take our women and breed a hardier race!

General Lewis "Chesty" Puller, USMC

Your job is to point that rifle into the other guy's face and shoot him dead.

General Matthew Ridgway

SIX RULES

Early in his military career, General Washington formulated a set of six rules for military guidance, by which he measured and directed the actions of his Army and followed to the letter himself. They are:

1. Never attack a position in front which you can gain by turning.

2. Charges of Cavalry should be made if possible on the flanks of infantry.

Battle of Bunker Hill   Engraving from a painting by John Trumbull
© National Archives.

3. The first qualification of a soldier is fortitude under fatigue and privation. Courage is only the second. Hardship, poverty and actual want are the soldier's best school.

4. Nothing is so important in war as an undivided command.

5. Never do what the enemy wishes you to do.

6. A General of ordinary talent, occupying a bad position and surprised by superior force, seeks safety in retreat; but a great captain supplies all deficiencies by his courage and marches boldly to meet the attack.

You must acquire the Warrior's soul.

*Wars may be fought by weapons,
but they are won by men.*

*No bastard ever won a war by dying for his country ...
he won it by making the other poor dumb bastard die for his.*

General George S. Patton, Jr.

*The 82nd Airborne Division provides the enemy the
maximum opportunity to die for his country ... day or night.*

Text on an 82nd Airborne Division Recruiting Poster

**WW II
German infantry soldier**
Mortally wounded,
taking his last breath.

A RIBBON

African-American "Doughfoots"   The 92nd Infantry (Buffalo) Division pursues the retreating Germans through the Po Valley, Italy, WW II. c. May 1945

A man wouldn't sell his life to you,
but he will give it to you for a
piece of colored ribbon.

William Manchester
while describing his WW II experience as a foot soldier,
on the importance of recognition

General George S. Patton

*In the Army the ribbon has replaced
the knightly spur and belt and at
a greatly reduced cost.*

*It's possession (ribbon) gives
differentiation, distinction, fame.*

*For the privilege of wearing a dime's
worth of taffeta, many will do
deeds which all the treasures
of the Incas were impotent to
cause him to attempt.*

*We must have more decorations
and we must give them with
no stingy hand ... .*

General George S. Patton, Jr.

THE SOLDIER'S HEART

**American Soldiers,
WW I**

*The soldier's heart, the
soldier's spirit, the soldier's
soul, are everything.
Unless the soldier's soul
sustains him, he cannot be
relied on and will fail himself
and his command and his
country in the end.*

*It is not enough to fight.
It is the spirit which we
bring to the fight that decides
the issue. It is morale that
wins the victory.*

Morale is a state of mind. It is steadfastness, and courage, and hope. It is confidence and zeal and loyalty. It is elan, esprit de corps, determination.

It is staying power, the spirit which endures in the end ... the will to win.

With it, all things are possible; without it everything else, planning, preparation, and production, count for naught.

General George C. Marshall
Secretary of State
(1947–1949)
Recipient of Nobel Peace Prize
(1953)

Dwight David Eisenhower

What counts is not necessarily the size of the dog in the fight— it's the size of the fight in the dog.

Dwight David Eisenhower
General of the Army

PFC Angelo B. Reina   391st Infantry Regiment guards a
lonely Oahu beach position. Kahuka, Oahu. March 1945

Forging the Warrior Spirit

At a lonely post somewhere, soldiers are watching.

They wait for the storm that they are trained to battle ...

The storm they surely hope never comes.

The night encroaching,
they are our final vestige of democracy.

They will sacrifice their comfort, their needs,
and their very lives,
for love of our great nation.

They are ready, tense, hard, and confident in duty and task.

They are spouses,
They are siblings,
They are parents,
They are friends,
They are timeless,
They are warriors.

Author Unknown

RULES TO LIVE BY

Get up front.
Any man who thinks he is indispensable ain't.
Always be alert to the source of trouble.
Always do everything you ask of those you command.
Punishment for mistakes must be immediate.
Keep moving and pain will never hit you.
To gain strength, always go beyond exhaustion.
Never fear failure.
Man is the only war machine.
No good decision was ever made in a swivel chair.
Talk with the troops.
Never make a decision too early or too late.
Success is how you bounce when you hit bottom.
Never let the enemy pick the battle site.
Better to fight for something than live for nothing.
Always keep something in reserve.
Fear kills more people than death.
When at war we must kill people.
The way to win is to never lose.
Never take counsel of your fears.

General George S. Patton, Jr.

Soldiers of the 55th Armored Infantry Battalion and the 22nd Tank Battalion move through a smoke filled street in Wernberg, Germany.
WW II photo by Private Joseph Scippens, April 22, 1945

My Credentials

Yanks of the 60th Infantry Regiment   advance into a Belgian town under the protection of a tank. September 9, 1944   © National Archives.

In September 1944, on the Crozan Peninsula, the Assistant Division Commander for the U.S. 8th Infantry Division, Brigadier General Canham, prepared to take the surrender of General Hermann Ramcke. As the two generals faced each other, American troops crowded behind the American General to watch the proceedings. As the moment approached, General Ramcke, speaking through an interpreter, questioned General Canham's credentials for accepting the surrender. Canham looked at his counterpart directly and jerked his thumb behind him at the assembled troops, and said gruffly, **"They are my credentials."**

Author Unknown

More Than Nuts

During the Battle of the Bulge, December, 1944, Hitler ordered a last gasp offensive designed to split the Allied Armies in two and destroy all Allied forces north of the line from Antwerp to Bastogne. To succeed, the attack required an initial breakthrough, subsequent widening of the gap, and seizure of fuel supplies and road networks at St.Vith and Bastogne. Despite reservations, the German commander, Field Marshal Karl von Rundstedt, followed his orders and launched the attack on December 16 while fog, rain, and snow inhibited Allied air support. With the assault, the 101st Airborne Division rushed to protect the vital road junction at Bastogne only to find itself completely surrounded and heavily outnumbered by German panzer forces. The German drive continued, forming a massive bulge in the Allied line, until the attack was blunted by the 2nd Armored Division. With the assault halted, the 4th Armored Division began punching a narrow relief corridor that finally reached Bastogne on December 26.

When General Troy Middleton dispatched the 101st Airborne on December 18, the only standing order that he issued to its commander, Major General Anthony McAuliffe, was "Hold Bastogne." This McAulliffe did despite a severe shortage of ammunition and ever increasing enemy pressure that continuously shrank his defensive perimeter.

On December 22, the Germans realized the 101st Airborne Division's dire straits. A group of two officers and two soldiers approached the lines of the 2nd Battalion, 327th Infantry under a white flag. They issued an ultimatum, signed by "The German Commander," that described the success of the German spearheads in the west and demanded the Americans to honorably surrender the encircled town within two hours or be annihilated by German artillery. The message was quickly forwarded to division where General McAuliffe was just leaving the headquarters to congratulate the defenders of a roadblock who had beaten back a German attack. He read the message, said "Nuts," threw it to the floor, and left. Upon returning, he was reminded about the ultimatum. After giving it some thought, he asked his staff how they thought he should reply. The senior operations officer commented that "That first remark of yours would be hard to beat." "What did I say?" asked McAuliffe. When he was told, McAuliffe had a formal response typed on bond paper that read: "To the German Commander: Nuts! From the American Commander." The note was then delivered to the German officers waiting at the 327th under the command of Colonel Joseph Harper. Of course, the Germans were unfamiliar with the American slang and arrogantly demanded Harper explain the note's meaning. He did, and told them:

"If you don't understand what 'Nuts' means, in plain English it is the same as 'Go to hell.' I will tell you something else. If you continue to attack, we will kill every goddamn German that tries to break into this city."

Upon learning of the initial German success, Lieutenant Colonel Creighton Abrams, then a tank battalion commander in the 4th Armored Division, made the second most famous remark of the battle as his unit prepared to launch its counter-offensive, *"They've got us surrounded again, the poor bastards."*

Author Unknown

Men Who Will Fight

[General MacArthur's Order to General Eichelberger, WW II, as told by General Eichelberger]

General MacArthur
Leaving the U.S.S. *Nashville,*
his command ship

"Bob," said MacArthur in a grim voice, "I'm putting you in command at Buna. Relieve Harding. I am sending you in, Bob, and I want you to remove all officers who won't fight. Relieve regimental and battalion commanders; if necessary, put sergeants in charge of battalions and corporals in charge of companies—anyone who will fight. Time is of the essence. The Japanese may land regiments any night."

General MacArthur strode down the breezy veranda again. He said he had reports that American soldiers were throwing away their weapons and running from the enemy. Then he stopped short and spoke with emphasis. He wanted no misunderstandings about my assignment.

"Bob," he said, "I want you to take Buna, or not come back alive." He paused a moment and then, without looking at Byers, pointed a finger. "And that goes for your Chief of Staff too. Do you understand?" "Yes sir," I said.

IN YOUR COFFIN

If the enemy gets into Taegu you will find me resisting him in the streets and I'll have some of my trusted people with me and you had better be prepared to do likewise. Now get back to your division and fight it! I don't want to see you back from the front again unless it's in your coffin.

LTG Walton Walker
Commander, Eighth US Army (EUSA)
September, 1950

*I love the infantry because
they are the underdogs.
They are the
mud-rain-frost-and-wind boys.
They have no comforts,
and they even learn to live
without the necessities.
And in the end they are the guys
that wars can't be won without.*

Ernie Pyle

Ernie Pyle

*There are really two wars and they haven't much to
do with each other. There is the war of maps and logistics,
of campaigns, of ballistics, armies, divisions and
regiments—and that is General George Marshall's war.
Then there is the war of the homesick, weary, funny,
violent, common men who wash their socks in their
helmets, complain about the food, whistle at the
Arab girls, or any girls for that matter, and bring
themselves through as dirty a business as the world
has ever seen and do it with humor and dignity
and courage—and that is Ernie Pyle's war.*

John Steinbeck
Nobel Prize-Winning Author

Last Night's Artillery Battle

One night during the Korean War, Private First Class (PFC) Minelli, a trumpeter assigned as a Division Artillery (DIVARTY) night duty clerk, single-handedly directed a successful artillery battle. The duty officer was exhausted, and PFC Minelli did not want to wake him, so at 0100, when the battle began with the receipt of the first reports of incoming mortar shell attacks, he responded to each requirement. By 0330 the 54 guns of the division artillery were all in action and the corps artillery with four battalions was well into its counterbattery plan. More than 3,000 artillerymen were hard at work ... . The subdued thunder of artillery fire was … constant and omnidirectional. The sky was lighted by gun flashes from three quadrants.

During all this the division artillery commander and his staff slept on. Any artilleryman worth his salt can sleep through a fire mission with his cot 50 yards from the gun position, and unless he is purposely awakened will never know that the guns have fired. After the battle, Minelli completed the duty log, and when the duty officer woke, Minelli told him that everything was fine, though he added that he had managed to keep busy all night. By this time the day crew had begun to straggle into the bunker and the duty officer went off to shave … . A few minutes later … the DIVARTY commander came in and said, "Can anyone here inform me concerning an artillery battle fought last night? … The division commander … complimented me on the conduct of this division artillery during the engagement."

It took some time to pry the whole story out of Minelli, and after the DIVARTY Commander had been briefed he drummed his fingers on the desk top and dictated two short memos. The first consisted of additional instructions to the night duty officer … "The officer in charge will take such steps as are necessary to prevent Private First Class (to be promoted to Corporal) Minelli from assuming command of the division and corps artillery." … The second was a directive to the adjutant ordering Minelli's promotion to corporal.

COL Daniel T. Chapman
from the periodical,
Front and Center, 1991

In the Korean War … I was a 2nd Lieutenant, commanding a company. I had a corporal as a platoon leader, a sergeant as a platoon leader and one other sergeant in the company. That's not the way you want to go to war, but that's the way you may have to go to war. So we have to train our people the best we can so we're able to perform in whatever manner we're called upon. I've always been amazed at what individuals can do when they have to when called upon, particularly in combat.

Understrength units, properly trained, can fight like hell.

General Edward C. Meyer

Three-Square-Feet of Ground

And out there, a few hundred yards away, they were fighting: staring at the fitful dark, crouching hip-deep in water, shoulders hunched under their helmets, checking by feel for grenades, flare cartridges, alarm cords, power phones, struggling to hear sounds of human movement against the lashing fury of the rain. The focal point of what Washington was pleased to call The War Effort.

The private in his concealed outpost, soaked to the very marrow of his bones, hungry, shaking with malaria, a jungle ulcer suppurating on his neck, his guts griping and burning with dysentery spasms, straining to hear, alone with his fear of the shadow darker-than-darker, the near flurry of movement, the knife, the cataclysmic flash of the grenade: held together by loyalty to his squad mates, pride in his company, grinding hatred of the enemy who had killed and mangled the bodies of his friends, fugitive dreams of that hometown whose inhabitants now worried about B-cards and points for roast beef and shoes and liquor, who cursed the ration boards and cheered and clapped at the newsreels between the feature film. ...

American machine-gunner   World War I

There, in that outpost, on that three-square-feet of ground, was where the real war was being fought, no matter who denied it; and how that private did tonight—whether he had the hardihood and the craft to resist exhaustion and debility and slumber and kill the weary, sick, resourceful enemy who sought his life—would decide who would win this war, and nothing else.

Anton Myrer
Excerpt from *Once An Eagle*

Infantrymen win or lose all wars in the final analysis.

Colonel Stevenson
Brigade Commander
1st Cavalry Division

Goddamn it, get back up on that hill! You'll die down here anyway— you might as well go up on that hill and die there!

Lieutenant Thomas Heath
G Company, 23rd Infantry
Chipyong-Ni, Korea, Korean War

Do Like The Romans Do

You may fly over a land forever; you may bomb it, atomize it, and wipe it clean of life—but if you desire to defend it, protect it, and keep it for civilization, you must do this on the ground, the way the Roman Legions did—by putting your soldiers in the mud.

T. R. Fehrenbach
from his book, *This Kind of War*

The Man With The Rifle Knows

Men might argue forever on what wins their wars
And welter in cons and pros,
And seek for their answer at history's doors,
But the man with the rifle knows.

He must stand on the ground on his own two feet,
And he's never in doubt when it's won,
If it's won he's there; if he's not, it's defeat,
That's his test, when the fighting is done.

When he carries the fight, it's not with a roar
Of armored wings spitting death.
It's creep and crawl on the earthen floor,
Butt down and holding his breath.

Saving his strength for the last low rush,
Grenade throw and bayonet thrust;
And the whispered prayer, before he goes in,
Of a man who does what he must.

And when he's attacked, he can't zoom away,
When the shells fill the world with their sound,
He stays where he is, loosens his spade,
And digs his defense in the ground.

That ground isn't ours till he's there in the flesh,
Not a gadget or bomb but a man.
He's the answer to theories which start afresh,
With each peace since war began.

So let the circle of argument rage
On what wins, as war comes and goes.
Many new theories may hold the stage
But the man with the rifle knows.

Author Unknown

*There must be, within our army,
a sense of purpose and a
dedication to that purpose.
There must be a willingness to
march a little farther,
to carry a heavier load,
to step out into the dark and
the unknown for the safety
and well-being of others.*

General Abrams

**General
Creighton Abrams**

DYING WORDS

The following are the last words spoken by U.S. soldiers and Marines on the field of battle, Vietnam.

*No sweat, sir. You can count on me.
We'll stop them.*

Last words of SP4 James K. Stoddard as he
lay bleeding out, and he knew it, Hill 614, Vietnam
26 February 1968

THE ULTIMATE DETERMINANT

The ultimate determinant in war is a man on the scene with a gun. This man is the final power in war. He is control, he determines who wins. There are those who would dispute this as an absolute, but it is my belief that while other means may critically influence war today, after whatever devastation and destruction may be inflicted on an enemy, if the strategist is forced to strive for final and ultimate control, he must establish, or must present as an inevitable prospect, a man on the scene with a gun. This is the soldier.

Rear Admiral Wylie, U.S. Navy

It don't mean nothin.

Last words of SP4 Henry Lawrence when
told his unit was surrounded by 66th and
174th NVA Regiments, Hill 614, Vietnam
26 February 1968

Red Hat Six, this is Ghost Rider Two-Seven.
I'm sorry I won't be able to help you any more today.
I'm gut shot. I'll have to leave you now.
Hang on and good luck.

Last words and radio transmission from
helicopter pilot to an army captain and his
unit fighting the 174th and 66th NVA
Regiments, Hill 614, Vietnam
27 February 1968

I'm dying, ain't I Sarge;
I'm dying, ain't I Sarge?

Last words of radio operator SP5 Paul
Sperry, spoken to SFC Herbert Lloyd,
near the Village of Bau Tron, Vietnam
17 September 1962

Look out, they're coming.

Last words of CPT Don J. York, after 33rd
Vietnamese Airborne Rifle Company was
caught in a vehicle ambush near Ben Suc, Vietnam
14 July 1962

This is Red Hat Eight-One,
we need a medevac bad,
three soldiers are hurt bad by a mine
and my legs are blown off.
Tell them to hurry!

Last words of 1st LT "Chuck" Hemingway,
Vietnam
09 June 1967

I know, I'll be careful, but they need
this machine gun up front.

Last words of 1st LT Bob Arvin
(as a Cadet was First Captain at West Point),
Vietnam
05 September1967

I can see you, you are coming up on our left.
Be careful, they have a 57MM recoilless
in the brown building.

Last words of CPT Terry Sage, killed by
57MM recoilless fire in JGS Compound,
Saigon, Vietnam
02 February 1968

Don't forget to tell my Momma I love her.

Last words of 20-year-old, Lance Corporal
Freddie Bivens, of H Company, USMC,
to his buddy as he lay gut shot in a ravine on
Hill 881 near KhaSahn, Vietnam

WHO PACKS YOUR PARACHUTE?

Charles Plumb, a U.S. Naval Academy graduate, was a jet fighter pilot in Vietnam. After 75 combat missions, his plane was destroyed by a surface-to-air missile. Plumb ejected and parachuted into enemy hands. He was captured and spent six years in a North Vietnamese prison. He survived that ordeal and now lectures about lessons learned from that experience.

One day, when Plumb and his wife were sitting in a restaurant, a man at another table came up and said, "You're Plumb! You flew jet fighters in Vietnam from the aircraft carrier Kitty Hawk. You were shot down!"

"How in the world did you know that?" asked Plumb.

"I packed your parachute," the man replied.

Plumb gasped in surprise and gratitude. The man pumped his hand and said, "I guess it worked!"

Plumb assured him, "It sure did—if your chute hadn't worked, I wouldn't be here today."

Plumb couldn't sleep that night, thinking about that man. Plumb says, "I kept wondering what he might have looked like in a Navy uniform—a Dixie cup hat, a bib in the back, and bell-bottom trousers.

I wondered how many times I might have passed him on the *Kitty Hawk*. I wondered how many times I might have seen him and not even said good morning, how are you or anything because, you see, I was a fighter pilot and he was just a sailor."

Plumb thought of the many hours the sailor had spent on a long wooden table in the bowels of the ship carefully weaving the shrouds and folding the silks of each chute, holding in his hands each time the fate of someone he didn't know.

Now, Plumb asks his audience, "Who's packing your parachute?"

Everyone has someone who provides what they need to make it through the day. Plumb also points out that he needed many kinds of parachutes when his plane was shot down over enemy territory—he needed his physical parachute, his mental parachute, his emotional parachute, and his spiritual parachute.

He called on all these supports before reaching safety. His experience reminds us all to prepare ourselves to weather whatever storms lie ahead.

Suggestion: Recognize people who pack your parachute and strengthen yourself to prevail through tough times.

Reprinted with permission of Mr. Charles Plumb.

Because They Went To War

In World War II, he whispered, I was wounded by a blast.
As he began his story, Reminiscing of his past.

I was just a boy back then, I lied about my age.
To get into the Army, And fight for the USA.

I love this country very much, It's still the very best.
And I would fight to keep it free, And safe from a foreign pest.

We won that war, and I came home, My wounds had healed enough,
To reenlist with other men. The Army made us tough.

Then a little flare up, In Korea called us out.
A threat against our freedom, Spreading fear without a doubt.

There I caught a bullet, When I tried to save a friend.
Another wound for Uncle Sam, They sent me home to mend.

"Soldier have you had enough?" My Sergeant said to me.
"Or do you want another tour, If ever there's to be?"

We would train and fight again, If ever it need be,
Because we love America, We'll fight to keep it free.

It didn't take too long, Before my boys were off again.
We were shipped off to a war, We thought would never end.

I didn't understand it much, If it was wrong or right.
But, I was a US soldier, And my country said, "Go fight."

I never questioned orders, That were sent from up above.
I did it for America, The country, that I love.

I fought to keep my country safe, Again, in Viet Nam.
Then, wounded I came home again, A victim of napalm.

My fighting days were over now, And, I had given all.
But, some had given more than me, Their names are on a wall.

I am now well up in years, A soldier old and worn.
I could only sit and pray, As I watched Desert Storm.

So proud of our boys over there, Who stand for what is right.
Freedom is the battle cry, The reason why they fight.

Young soldiers fight for liberty, Protecting freedom's bliss.
Old soldiers dream of by-gone-days, While fighting loneliness.

We were heroes in our day, He said, and then he sighed.
Forgotten in some VA home, And all my friends have died.

I never ask for anything, Just wanted to live free.
But, if you read this story, There are many just like me.

Who fought to keep our country, Safe and free from every foe.
Only to come home again, And have no place to go.

Sadly, when the limelight fails, Heroes fade away.
Some men fight the silent battles, Till their dying day.

Please remember what it took, And what we had to pay.
And join with us remembering, On this Memorial Day.

Memorial Day is special, It is not just summer's start.
The reason that we have this day, Should be etched on your heart.

Lives were lost, and young men died, To keep this country free.
So, take a moment on that day, To meditate with me.

Remember all those valiant men, And women who fought for,
The lifestyle that you now enjoy, Because they went to war.

Author Unknown

*The cohesion that matters on the battlefield
is that which is developed at the company,
platoon and squad levels.*

General Edward C. Meyer

*The nature of modern war indicates
that mall-unit cohesion is the only force
capable of causing soldiers to expose
themselves consistently to enemy fire
in pursuit of an army's goals.*

Colonel W. D. Henderson

WHAT IS A VIETNAM VETERAN?

A couple years ago, just before Veterans' Day, a college student named Adam wrote to an internet e-mail discussion list. He was working on a school assignment in which he was supposed to obtain original narratives from "people old enough to have actually been there in person." I asked how I could help, and he asked me to respond to the question "what is a Vietnam veteran?" This is what I wrote.

Vietnam veterans are men and women. We are dead or alive, whole or maimed, sane or haunted. We grew from our experiences or we were destroyed by them or we struggle to find someplace in between. We lived through hell or we had a pleasant, if scary, adventure. We were Army, Navy, Marines, Air Force, Red Cross, and civilians of all sorts. Some of us enlisted to fight for God and Country, and some were drafted. Some were gung-ho, and some went kicking and screaming.

Like veterans of all wars, we lived a tad bit—or a great bit—closer to death than most people like to think about. If Vietnam vets differ from others, perhaps it is primarily in the fact that many of us never saw the enemy or recognized him or her. We heard gunfire and mortar fire but rarely looked into enemy eyes. Those who did, like folks who encounter close combat anywhere and anytime, are often haunted for life by those eyes, those sounds, those electric fears that ran between ourselves, our enemies, and the likelihood of death for one of us. Or we get hard, calloused, tough. All in a day's work. Life's a bitch then you die. But most of us remember and get twitchy, worried, sad.

We are crazies dressed in cammo, wide-eyed, wary, homeless, and drunk. We are Brooks Brothers suit wearers, doing deals downtown. We are housewives, grandmothers, and church deacons. We are college professors engaged in the rational pursuit of the truth about the history or politics or culture of the Vietnam experience. And we are sleepless. Often sleepless.

We pushed paper; we pushed shovels. We drove jeeps, operated bulldozers, built bridges; we toted machine guns through dense brush, deep paddy, and thorn scrub. We lived on buffalo milk, fish heads and rice. Or C-rations. Or steaks and Budweiser. We did our time in high mountains drenched by endless monsoon rains or on the dry plains or on muddy rivers or at the most beautiful beaches in the world.

We wore berets, bandanas, flop hats, and steel pots. Flak jackets, canvas, rash and rot. We ate cloroquine and got malaria anyway. We got shots constantly but have diseases nobody can diagnose.

We spent our nights on cots or shivering in foxholes filled with waist-high water or lying still on cold wet ground, our eyes imagining Charlie behind every bamboo blade. Or we slept in hotel beds in Saigon or barracks in Thailand or in cramped ships' berths at sea.

We feared we would die or we feared we would kill. We simply feared, and often we still do. We hate the war or believe it was the best thing that ever happened to us. We blame Uncle Sam or Uncle Ho and their minions and secretaries and apologists for every wart or cough or tic of an eye. We wonder if Agent Orange got us.

Mostly, we wish we had not been so alone. Some of us went with units; but many, probably most of us, were civilians one day, jerked up out of "the world," shaved, barked at, insulted, humiliated, de-egoized and taught to kill, to fix radios, to drive trucks. We went, put in our time, and were equally ungraciously plucked out of the morass and placed back in the real world. But now we smoked dope or drank heavily. Our wives or husbands seemed distant and strange. Our friends wanted to know if we shot anybody.

And life went on, had been going on, as if we hadn't been there, as if Vietnam was a topic of political conversation or college protest or news copy, not a matter of life and death for tens of thousands.

Vietnam vets are people just like you. We served our country, proudly or reluctantly or ambivalently. What makes us different—what makes us Vietnam vets—is something we understand, but we are afraid nobody else will. But we appreciate your asking.

Vietnam veterans are white, black, beige and shades of gray. Our ancestors came from Africa, from Europe, and Asia. Or they crossed the Bering Sea Land Bridge in the last Ice Age and formed the nations of American Indians, built pyramids in Mexico, or farmed acres of corn on the banks of Chesapeake Bay. We had names like Rodriguez and Stein and Smith and Kowalski. We were Americans, Australians, Canadians, and Koreans; most Vietnam veterans are Vietnamese.

We were farmers, students, mechanics, steelworkers, nurses, and priests when the call came that changed us all forever. We had dreams and plans, and they all had to change ... or wait. We were daughters and sons, lovers and poets, beatniks and philosophers, convicts and lawyers. We were rich and poor but mostly poor. We were educated or not, mostly not. We grew up in slums, in shacks, in duplexes, and bungalows and houseboats and hooches and ranchers. We were cowards and heroes. Sometimes we were cowards one moment and heroes the next.

Many of us have never seen Vietnam. We waited at home for those we loved. And for some of us, our worst fears were realized. For others, our loved ones came back but never would be the same.

We came home and marched in protest marches, sucked in tear gas, and shrieked our anger and horror for all to hear. Or we sat alone in small rooms, in VA hospital wards, in places where only the crazy ever go. We are Republicans, Democrats, Socialists, and Confucians and Buddhists and Atheists—though as usually is the case, even the atheists among us sometimes prayed to get out of there alive.

We are hungry, and we are sated, full of life or clinging to death. We are injured, and we are healers, despairing and hopeful, loved or lost. We got too old too quickly, but some of us have never grown up. We want, desperately, to go back, to heal wounds, revisit the sites of our horror. Or we want never to see that place again, to bury it, its memories, its meaning. We want to forget, and we wish we could remember.

Despite our differences, we have so much in common. There are few of us who don't know how to cry, though we often do it alone when nobody will ask "what's wrong?" We're afraid we might have to answer.

Adam, if you want to know what a Vietnam veteran is, get in your car next weekend or cage a friend with a car to drive you. Go to Washington. Go to the Wall. It's going to be Veterans Day weekend. There will be hundreds there ... no, thousands. Watch them. Listen to them. I'll be there. Come touch the Wall with us. Rejoice a bit. Cry a bit. No, cry a lot. I will. I'm a Vietnam Veteran; and, after 30 years, I think I am just beginning to understand what that means.

Dan Mouer

DESERT SHIELD AND DESERT STORM

*M*uch *of what we did from August 1990 through February 1991 had not even been dreamed of in July 1990.*

Author Unknown

I have seen in your eyes a fire of determination to get this war job done quickly. My confidence in you is total, our cause is just. Now you must be the thunder and lighting of Desert Storm.

General Norman Schwarzkopf

*The quality of our Army stands out in stark relief
in the Arabian desert. Everywhere I went, our soldiers
demonstrated high standards of discipline and an
impressive commitment to what our nation has asked
of them. They have great faith in their training,
in their weapons, and in their leaders. There is no idle
chest thumping or empty boasting among our soldiers;
rather, each of them is soberly and quietly confident.
"If he wants a fight," several soldiers told me,
"he's come to the right place."*

General Carl E. Vuono
October 12, 1990

TO THE SOLDIERS OF DESERT STORM

Spring, 1991

To the men and women of Desert Storm; On the behalf of the entire army and a grateful nation, WELCOME HOME. For each of you, this day marks the end of an operation of historic significance—an operation that will help define the very soul of the community of nations for decades to come.

Under some of the most demanding conditions ever faced by America's army, you have won a monumental victory—victory that will be honored for as long as Americans remember their past. You have restored freedom to a nation brutalized by a ruthless dictator, have brought peace to a region that is vital to the health of the entire world; and you have rekindled a deep sense of national pride that wells in the hearts of the American people. This pride is evident in all the flags and yellow ribbons that cover our landscape from coast to coast. It also shines in the eyes of your sons and daughters, your husbands and wives, and your friends and neighbors who now welcome you back with open arms.

Equally important, you have shown to a watching world what the trained and ready army of the United States can accomplish. The magnificent victory in the desert will give a powerful lesson to the renegade regimes of the world that might be foolish enough to contemplate aggression. Above all, you have shown the character and the mettle of the American people: Courageous in war, compassionate in peace, and committed to the service of the nation. Even as we celebrate your triumphant homecoming, let us never forget those soldiers who will never return, the valiant men and women who have given their lives in the name of freedom. They now join the sacred roll call of brave

Americans who have fallen in battle in the defense of this nation and our way of life over the past two centuries. Their sacrifice—and yours—have not been in vain. For in a land thousands of miles away, the children of Kuwait are now awakening to a new day, a day free from repression and fear, a day bright with renewed hope for the future. Your mission is now over; your task is complete. As you now rejoin your friends and families, you should each carry with you great pride in the contributions you have made to a peaceful world. Where ever you go in the years ahead, and whatever course your life may take, you will forever be known as a soldier of Desert Storm.

Welcome Home,

Carl E. Vuono
General
U.S. Army Chief of Staff

A FOND FAREWELL

The following is a farewell letter from Gen. H. Norman Schwarzkopf, Allied Commander of Operation Desert Storm and Commander of U.S. Central Command, MacDill Air Force Base, Florida. The letter was written on August 30, 1991, his last day in uniform.

To The Soldiers:

As some of you may have heard, at the end of this month I am retiring from the United States Army. Today is my last day in uniform. The Department of the Army very graciously offered to have a retirement parade in my honor in Washington; however, I asked them not to for the following reasons.

First, I wanted to leave the Army the same way I entered, without fanfare or pageantry, simply proud to be serving my country. Secondly, to have a parade at the end of August would have meant that many fine soldiers would have had to stand another formation in the hot sun. It seemed to me that enough soldiers have stood in the hot sun for me in the last year to give me a lifetime of memories.

Somehow it did not seem right for me to leave the Army without saying goodbye to you. I have often said that if the Army did not have soldiers, I would not be in the Army. I have so many things to thank you for, all of you—officers, noncommissioned officers, and magnificent young men and women in the ranks. I shall never forget your loyalty, your respect, your mentoring, your sacrifice, your bravery both in and out of battle, and most of all your selfless sense of duty that drives you to serve your country with great dignity and little reward.

I have loved you as only a soldier loves another soldier, but now I must say goodbye, for that is the Army way and it is the right way. Someone once said that you can take the soldier out of the Army, but you can't take the Army out of the soldier. In my case that will most certainly be true. Until that day when I will be taken across the river and into the trees, I will always proudly consider myself the only thing I ever wanted to be, a soldier.

Goodbye and thank you for the great privilege I have had to serve in your ranks as a commander, but most of all as one of you soldiers of the United States Army.

> Gen H. Norman Schwarzkopf
> Commander
> U.S. Central Command
> MacDill Air Force Base, Florida

There are only two types of warriors in this world. Those that serve tyrants and those that serve free men.

Special Forces NCO Stefan Mazak

The clash of infantry in close quarters is the pinnacle of violence and brutality.

An Infantryman

Soldiering is still an outdoor sport.

U.S. Army General in Bosnia

*I was at Andrews Air Force Base one night when
some wounded soldiers returned from Mogadishu.
Private Ly ... lay on a stretcher.
On his Army T-shirt, I pinned a Purple Heart.
I said to him,
"Ly, I see you're an engineer in the 41st Engineers."
He looked up ... and he said to me,
"Sir, I'm not an engineer. I'm a sapper!" ...
That's the warrior spirit talking.*

General Gordon R. Sullivan
from his book,
Hope Is Not a Method, 1996

*When you're in the Army, you can be in the
infantry at any given moment.*

SGT Michael Davis
in "Sergeants on Training" *Sergeants' Business*
July–August 1988

*The fact is that younger leaders [not generals]
are the ones who really make history.
They earn the medals for valor and achievement.
They are the ones who get things done and
make the Army great.*

General John A. Wickham, Jr.
Army Chief of Staff
(1983–1987)

A conglomerate mass of Americans gathered from all walks of life who had been shaped into a cohesive organization for the purpose of performing certain military tasks, the unit was ... not simply the place where members lived and worked, ate and slept, the unit was the soldier's family.

A description of the squads, platoons,
and companies of the
291st Engineer Combat Battalion in WW II

MY PERSONAL TRADEMARK

During World War II while in the Sicilian Campaign, General Omar N. Bradley was confronted by his 9th Infantry Division Commander, Major General Manton S. Eddy, with the problem of finding a colonel to command the 39th Infantry Regiment. According to General Eddy, the 39th had been doing poorly, and was "showing signs of sluggishness." It was just not carrying its load compared to the other regiments. "What we need in the 39th is a character," General Eddy said.

General Bradley sent Colonel Harry A. Flint to the 39th. Shortly after "Paddy" Flint arrived in the 39th, he began showing up in the forward combat areas stripped to the waist (for easy identification), wearing a black scarf, carrying a rifle, and wearing a helmet with **AAA-O** stenciled on both sides. He would snarl at the enemy, and, while single-handedly rolling a cigarette, he would talk to the troops huddled in their foxholes, telling them, "The Krauts couldn't shoot in the last war and they can't shoot in this one." Not many days passed before his officers and men of the 39th began inquiring as to what this **AAA-O** on his helmet was supposed to mean. "My personal trademark," was his reply. He went on to tell the officers that it meant **"Anything, Anytime, Anywhere, Bar Nothing,"** but a person had to live up to it and mean it. His officers asked, "Can we stencil it on our helmets?" But Paddy Flint was reluctant. He told them that it was a sort of sacred thing to him and he didn't want to see it plastered all over. "If a man means it, he can use it," was Paddy Flint's standard.

Not long thereafter, **AAA-O** began popping up on other helmets, on jeeps, rifles, howitzers, and soon it was everywhere in the 39th. It became the symbol of the 39th Infantry. It ignited a spark in the troops and gave them an identification unique in the U.S. Army. The spirit that ensued lasted throughout the war and resulted in the 39th becoming one of the fightingest regiments in the European Theater.

Paddy Flint died of a sniper's bullet in Normandy. But his spirit lived on. Even today, the 39th Infantry introduces its new recruits to Paddy Flint, and to the meaning of **AAA-O**. They wear it everywhere, for he gave them the identity that they so sorely needed.

From the book, *Bradley*
1951

★

*It is better to have lived one day as a lion
than one thousand days as a sheep.*

Inscription on the stone of
Lieutenant Colonel Charles G. Clinger
U.S. Army, Section 8, Arlington National Cemetery

★

*If my nose had been a shovel I'd have been speaking
Chinese in another five minutes.*

SGT R. C. Billington
after being shelled during WW II
The G.I. Journal of Sergeant Giles, p. 39.

JUST PEOPLE, AND FEELINGS, AND SOUNDS

by Brigadier General Mark A. Welsh, III, Commandant of Cadets
United States Air Force Academy (USAFA)
Speech and Slide Presentation to Air Force Academy Cadets

August 26, 1999

Not long ago I was asked to give a presentation on personal lessons learned from my experiences in combat during Operation DESERT STORM. So, I sat down and spent about an hour and a half just thinking and thinking and thinking ... what can I put on this list—what great lessons have I learned and want to pass on to future generations? When I finished, I only had about 15 items, and I realized that none of them were lessons learned, not one of them. Every one of them was a person, or an event, or just a feeling I had. But

I've never forgotten them and never will. And those are the things I want to talk to you about today. It's important, before I start, for you to remember that every kind of combat is different. Aerial combat happens at about a thousand miles an hour of closure. It's hot fire and cold steel; it's instant death and big destruction; it happens like this (snaps fingers) and it's over. Ground combat's not that way, as you can imagine. Those of you who've heard infantry soldiers talk about it know it's kinda endless time, and soaking fear, and big noises and darkness. It's a different game. And you need different training to do it, and different types of people to handle it well and to provide leadership in that environment. But it doesn't matter how many people you have standing beside you in the trenches, or how many people you have flying beside you in formation—combat, especially your first combat, is an intensely personal experience. Today, I'll tell you some of the things I remember.

You don't have to see this picture very well—it's an F-16 parked on a ramp with a helmet on the canopy rail. One week before the DESERT STORM air campaign actually started we were flying missions to northern Saudi Arabia to practice dropping simulated bombs at night on targets in the desert, so those of us who didn't routinely fly night missions would be ready if the war started. On this particular night, after we'd "destroyed" our target, we hit a post-strike tanker and headed back to our base almost 400 miles away. We climbed up to about 42,000 feet, put the autopilot on and I leaned back in that 30° tilt-back seat and just kinda stared at nature. It was a gorgeous night. The moon was big and full and directly overhead, and I remember thinking, "I can't believe how bright the desert moon is." And out around the horizon, something I'd never seen before and haven't seen again to this day, was a halo. A beautiful, huge white halo that went all the way around the moon, completely unbroken. I talked to my wingman later, and he said he did the same thing I did—we just stared at that thing all the way home, thinking, "I can't believe how beautiful this is." It's one of those moments you have flying airplanes. I'll never forget that halo … .

I also won't forget that when I landed that night my assistant operations officer met me at the bottom of the ladder and said, "Boss, we lost an airplane."

The name on the canopy rail in that picture belongs to a young captain named Mike, who'd joined us in the desert only two weeks earlier because he'd stayed back in Utah to get married. He and his wife had been married for two weeks when he told her that he had to go to war and join the boys. He'd just finished his three-ride local checkout and was on his second night ride. We think that somehow he got a light on the ground confused with his flight lead's rotating beacon and tried to rejoin on it as he headed for the tanker. Mike hit the ground going over 600 miles an hour, 60° nose-low, inverted and in full afterburner. He died relaxed. You know, I don't think "dying relaxed" was good news to his wife when I called and spoke to her after we'd confirmed he was in that smoking hole, or to his Mom and Dad when I called them. I won't forget those phone calls … or that great young American who, like so many before him, died in the company of warriors, in a place where warriors were called, at a time when warriors were needed most. I'll **never** forget Mike … .

And I'll never forget sitting at his memorial service two days later, looking at **this** airplane with his name on the canopy rail, the helmet with his name on the visor cover, his spare G-suit hanging under the wing, and his crew chief saluting the jet, while bagpipes played "Amazing Grace" in the background. Every fighter pilot on base was wearing these big stupid sunglasses so nobody would know they were bawlin' their eyes out. I won't forget staring at that airplane thinking, "How many more of these are we going to have when the war starts?"

The night before the war actually did start, our wing commander told the squadron commanders that we were "kicking it off tomorrow morning." So we gathered our squadrons together at about 5 o'clock in the afternoon and gave most of them the first briefing they'd seen on our previously-classified Day 1 mission. Then I did what I thought was a real "commanderly" thing. I told them all to go back to their rooms and write a letter to their family. And I told them that before I gave them their aircraft tail number in the morning, they had to hand me their letter, so I could ensure it was delivered if they didn't come back. In that letter, I wanted them to shed all of the emotional baggage you take with you into combat—I didn't tell my wife this; I didn't do that; I didn't hug my daughter; I didn't tell my son I loved him; I didn't call my parents … . I told them they didn't fly until I got that letter. Which shut 'em all up for the first time since I'd known them! They headed out the door, and I was feeling pretty proud of myself and patting myself on the back when my ops officer came up to me and said, "What a great idea!" I nodded knowingly, and he added, "By the way, you can give me your letter before I give you **your** tail number in the morning." Now, if you haven't had the pleasure of sitting down and thinking about your family the night before you think you may die; if you haven't tried to tell your children that you're sorry you won't be there to see their next ballet recital or watch them play little league baseball, or high school football, or graduate from college, or meet their future spouse, or get to know your grandkids; or if you haven't had the pleasure of telling your parents and brothers and sisters what they mean to you; or tried to tell your wife how the sun rises and sets in her eyes; and tried to do it all on a piece of paper, at midnight, 9,000 miles away from home, then you haven't lived. I'd recommend it. I won't forget writing that letter … .

This is a picture of the base where we were stationed. The whole thing is about two miles long and about a mile wide. You can see the main runway, a parallel taxiway, and on the left side of the picture there's a road that ran the whole length of the base. In the upper left corner is where the tents and hooches were for the officers, and about halfway down the field is where the tent city was. That next morning we got up about 1:30 A.M., because we had a 2:15 briefing. All my guys met in the chow hall and we had breakfast, then we jumped in cars to drive to our mass briefing, which was down here at the lower left-hand corner of this slide. As we drove down that parallel road, two things happened. The first was that the night fighters from the 421st Fighter Squadron lit their afterburners as part of the first launch of the Gulf War. And at 20-second intervals, as we traveled down that road, they lifted off going the other way, one at a time. They each accelerated to about 400 miles an hour, pulled the nose straight up and climbed to avoid possible SAMs at the end of the runway; pulled the engine out of afterburner, and disappeared. And I suddenly realized that this was the first time I'd ever seen airplanes take off with no lights on—they were "blacked out" for combat. It was pretty sobering. And then halfway down this road, one of the guys in the car with me says, "Boss, look at this," and he points out the right side of the car. And on the right side of that road were thousands of people. The entire population of our tent city had come out of their tents when that first afterburner lit, and they were standing along this road. They were in uniforms, they had just gotten off work; they were wearing jeans; they were wearing cutoffs; they were wearing underwear, pajamas—everything. Not one of them was talking. They were just watching those airplanes take off; they knew what was going on. The other thing that I noticed immediately was that all of them were somehow in contact with the person next to them … every single one of them. They were holding hands, or holding an arm, or had their arm around someone's shoulders or their hand on someone's back, or they were just leaning on each other. These were people who didn't even know each other. But they were all Americans; they were all warriors; and they were all part of the cause. I will never, ever forget their faces coming into those headlights, then fading out. They're burned into my memory.

Later that morning, after our mission briefing, we went to the life support trailer where my squadron kept all our flying gear. All 24 airplanes were flying, so 24 of my guys were going, and I was lucky enough to be the mission commander for this first one. Now, anybody who's been in a fighter squadron, or any kind of flying squadron, knows that Life Support, as you're getting ready to go, is a pretty raucous place. You're giving people grief; you're arguing about who's better at whatever—something's going on all the time. It's fun. This morning, there wasn't a sound. I got dressed listening to nothing but the whisper of zippers as people pulled on flight gear. I walked out of the trailer and left the door open so the light from inside shined out in a little pool around the trailer steps. The rest of the base was blacked out, and we were under camouflaged netting and couldn't see anything outside this trailer. As my guys came down the steps I shook each one of their hands and just nodded at 'em; nobody said anything. I watched as, one by one, they turned and disappeared into the black. And as each one left, I wondered if he'd be coming back that afternoon … we didn't really know what to expect from this war. When the last one had gone, Master Sergeant Ray Uris, who ran my life support shop and had been standing in the doorway watching this act, walked to the bottom of the steps, shook **my** hand, and watched **me** disappear. I'll never forget watching their backs disappear in the dark … .

One of those backs belonged to an incredibly talented young weapons officer named Scott, probably the best fighter pilot in our wing at the time. About the second week of the war we flew a mission against the nuclear power plant south of Baghdad. Scott was one of the flight leads that day. It was easily the toughest mission my squadron flew during the war because the Iraqis defended the area south of Baghdad, and they **really** defended the nuclear power plant. From about 25 miles to the target, till we got to the power plant, the pilots on that mission will tell you they saw 50 to 100 SAMs in the air. I remember screaming and cussing to myself all the way to the target, until it came time to roll in—at which point your training takes over and you kinda go quiet—until you drop your bombs, and you start screaming and cussing again. This was scary. Scott's wingman got hit as we came off target. An SA-3 exploded underneath his airplane and blew off his fuel tanks. It put about 100 holes in the airplane—70 of them through the engine and engine compartment, which isn't good in a single engine F-16. For the next 2½ hours Scott escorted him to several different emergency bases because the weather had rolled in and closed some of them and they couldn't get him on the ground. While his wingman struggled with the crippled jet, Scott worked emergency tanker diverts to get them gas; coordinated with AWACS for clearance to the next divert field; arranged safe passage through air base defenses; and kept assuring his wingman that he was gonna make it. He was phenomenal; he helped save this guy's life. So he landed about two hours after the rest of us did. When I heard he was on the ground, I left my debrief to see how things had gone with his wingman. It was dark by this time. And as I walked out to the life support trailer, I came around a corner under that darkened out camouflage netting and ran into something. And then realized it was Scott. He was leaning against a bunch of sandbags, just holding onto them with both hands, and shaking. He couldn't walk, he couldn't talk, he couldn't do anything. All he could do was stand there and shake. The guy had nothing left. All his adrenaline was gone. He'd given everything he had to give that day. As I'm trying to figure out what the heck to do with Scott, the door to the life support trailer opened and a young, 19-year-old life support technician named Shawn walked out, looked at what was going on, and said, "Boss, I know you've got stuff to do. I'll take care of him." And I said, "Well, let me help you get him inside." And he said, "Boss, you've got stuff to do. **I'll** take care of him." So I left. I saw Shawn helping Scott up the steps to the life support trailer as I went around the corner. About five hours later, I left the next day's mission planning cell and went to see how Scott was doing. When I came around the corner of his tent there was Shawn, sitting in the sand in front of the tent shakin' like a leaf, 'cause he's still wearing just the BDU pants and T-shirt he had on in life support. This was January in the desert, folks; it was **cold** outside! I said, "Shawn, what are you doing here?" and he said, "Sir, the major finally got to sleep. I was afraid that he might wake up, and if he does, I wanna make sure I let him know everything's okay." You'll meet lots of Shawns in the Air Force; I'll never forget this one … .

This is a Catholic priest—Father John. Father John was our squadron chaplain. The first day of DESERT STORM, I got to my jet and standing right in front of the nose of the jet was Father John. At first I thought he was a crew chief until I got close enough to see who he was. Now, Father John was popular with us because he was the first guy to buy you a whiskey; the first guy to light up a cigar; the first guy to start a party; and the last guy to leave. He also would've been the first one to wade into Hell in his BVDs to pull you out, if he had to. We knew Father John real well; he fit in great with a fighter squadron. Anyway, as I got to the airplane, Father John just said, "Hey, I thought you might like a blessing before you go." I immediately hated myself, because I consider myself fairly comfortable in my religion, and I'd never thought of that—too many other, wrong priorities on my mind at the time. So I knelt down on the cement right there in front of the jet, and Father John gave me a blessing. And then I finished the preflight on my airplane. As I'm getting ready to climb up the ladder I noticed all these guys running toward me out of the darkness. They were all my other pilots who had seen this and were coming over to get Father John to bless **them**. So he did. And when everybody came back safe from the first sortie we kinda decided "That's it, Father John has to bless everybody ... can't change that." It didn't matter if you were Jewish or Baptist or Islamic—it just didn't matter. Father John gave the blessing for the 4th Fighter Squadron. The amazing thing was that it didn't matter whether you flew at two in the afternoon or two in the morning—Father John was there. Later on, talking to Colonel Tom Rackley, the commander of the 421st Fighter Squadron, I found out that Father John did the same for his guys. I don't know how he did it, but he did. Every time I landed from a combat sortie—every single time—my canopy would open, I'd shake hands with my hero and crew chief, TSgt Manny Villa, then I'd climb down the ladder; and at the bottom of the ladder was Father John, to bless me and welcome me home.

When I came back from DESERT STORM I ended up alone—different story—but I ended up as a single ship returning to Hill AFB. And when I pulled into the parking spot there, these are the folks who were waiting for me. Now, my squadron had been home for three days before I got there, and down at the far end you'll recognize Father John. That's my wife Betty, and a couple of my kids, and a couple of friends who were with them. I'd written Betty and told her about Father John and his blessings. You want to know how cool she is? When the airplane stopped and the canopy came up, Manny Villa climbed the ladder and shook my hand, and I climbed down to the bottom of the ladder, and Betty told Father John, "You first." Father John walked over and blessed me and welcomed me home ... then Betty and I did some serious groping!

A year and a half later, Father John dropped dead of a massive heart attack. Too much whiskey, too many cigars, too many parties, I guess. By the week after he died, 16 of the 28 pilots who flew in my squadron during DESERT STORM had contacted his family in Stockton, California. They called from Korea; they called from Europe; they called from Australia; they called from all over the United States—to tell his family about Father John, and to bless him, and ask God to welcome him home. I'll never forget Father John … .

This is a picture of ammunition storage bunkers in northwestern Iraq. They're not real significant, except there's a guy I want to tell you about who had something to do with the holes in them. His name's Ed. Ed left for the desert with his wife Jill pregnant with their first child. This was a story repeated throughout DESERT STORM in all the services and throughout history in the military. Obviously he couldn't go home for the birth. Late one night, my exec woke me up in my hooch and told me I had a phone call in the command post. So I got dressed and sprinted over there. It was my wife, and she said, "Mark, I'm at the hospital with Jill. She's in labor and is having problems. Is there any way we can get Ed on the phone with her?" So we went and rousted Ed and brought him down to the command center. My wife had worked out an arrangement with the hospital so that when Ed walked in and sat down, I handed him the phone and he was talking to Jill, who's in the middle of a really bad labor. As he held the phone with one hand and talked to his wife, I sat in a chair in front of him and held his other hand (which is something neither of us has ever admitted publicly before). I could see the happiness in his eyes every time she spoke to him. And I could see the worry and pain in his eyes every time another contraction started and he heard her gasp. And I felt him squeeze my hand every time he could hear her scream. And … I saw him smile when he heard his son Nate cry for the first time, from 9,000 miles away. I'll never forget that smile … .

Twelve hours after Ed hung up that phone, he was part of an F-16 strike package that hit those ammunition storage bunkers. It was the best battle damage assessment we had in our squadron during the war. They hit every target, and a lot of them, as you saw on that photo, dang near dead center. Ed went from caring, concerned, loving father and husband, to intense, indomitable warrior in just 12 hours. Only in combat folks. I'll never forget watching the transformation … .

One of the most important things about combat is sound. Anybody who's been there will tell you that things you hear are the things you remember the longest. I want to tell you about two things I heard that I'll never forget. The first one was during one of our missions up north in the Baghdad area. An F-16 from another unit was hit by a surface-to-air missile. We listened to him and his flight lead talk about his airplane falling apart as he tried to make it to the border so rescue forces could get to him. He'd come on the radio every now and then and talk about the oil pressure dropping, and vibrations increasing … and his flight lead would encourage him to stick with it, "We can get there, we can get there." This went on for about 12–14 minutes. Until finally he said, "Oil pressure just went to zero," and then, "My engine quit," then, "That's all I got—I'm outta here." Now, we couldn't see him. I'm not exactly sure where they were. But I am sure there wasn't another sound on that radio … and the silence was deafening. I'll never forget those 14 minutes … .

The other unforgettable thing I heard came after the ground war had started. An F-16 was shot down in the middle of the retreating Republican Guard, and I mean right in the middle of them. A call went out from AWACS for any aircraft with ordnance remaining and the fuel to get to where the pilot was down, in case they needed 'em for SARCAP. A lot of people responded, but the first one I really paid attention to was an Army Chinook helicopter pilot, who came on the radio and said, "Look, I've got this much gas, here's my location, I can be there in that many minutes, give me his coordinates—I can pick him up." Now, everybody knew where the Republican Guard was, and everybody knew the downed pilot was right in the middle of them. You gotta remember a Chinook is about the size of a double-decker London bus with props on it. And it doesn't have guns! We kid around a lot about interservice rivalries, but I guarantee you I would follow **that** Army helicopter pilot into combat ... and I'll never forget **her** voice ... .

This is the Highway of Death. You guys have seen pictures of it before. This road leads north out of Basra; it was the main retreat route for the Republican Guard and they got cut off, right about where the black smoke from the oil well fires went over the Euphrates River Valley. Everywhere south of there it looked like this. It's not a new picture, but I'll tell you what's significant about it. I killed people here. **Me.** This combat is an intensely personal thing, folks; I think I mentioned that. I'm sure I'd killed people before during the war, but this time I saw 'em. I saw the vehicles moving before the bombs hit. I saw soldiers firing up at me, then running as I dropped my bombs to make sure they wouldn't get away. War is a horrible, horrible, horrible thing. There is nothing good about it. But it is sometimes necessary. And so **somebody** better be good at it. I am. You better be. I won't forget the Highway of Death ... .

On my trip home from the Gulf, I flew with the 421st Squadron on the way to the east coast of the United States. The first U.S. air traffic control site that we talked to was Boston Center. Tom Rackley's check-in with them was something along the lines of, "Boston Center, Widow Flight, 24 F-16s comin' home." And the air traffic controller responded, "Welcome home, Widow." And then at regular intervals for the next five or six minutes, every airliner on that frequency checked in and said something. "Welcome back." "Good job." "Great to have you home." "God bless you, Widow."

About 10 minutes after that, I got my first glimpse of the U.S. coastline—it was the coast of Massachusetts. And I sat in my cockpit and I sang "America the Beautiful" to myself. I'll never forget how bad it sounded ... or how proud I was when it was over ... .

Take a look at this flag, folks. Those white stripes represent the integrity that you cherish here at the Air Force Academy and that you better carry with you into our Air Force. Those stars carry the courage of all the people who have gone before you; they belong to you now. And that red is for Mike, and for Father John, and for the millions more like 'em who died serving this great country. In the not too distant future, one of you is going to be standing up here talking about your experiences in combat to the Classes of 2015, or '16, or '17. And you're going to be talking about the USAFA Classes of 2000, 2001, 2002, and 2003. This is who you are. And this is what you face in the United States Air Force. If you're not ready for it, let me know and I'll help you find another line of work. You are damn good ... you need to get better. All these people I just talked about are counting on it.

SHANKS BOOTEES

It was during the dark days of the December retreat when I first saw them. They were hanging from the cold muzzle of an old, battered, Springfield rifle—a pair of tiny blue baby bootees. Their pale silk ribbons ended in a neat bow behind the front sight, and each little boot hung down separately, one slightly above the other, swinging silently in the wind. They reminded me of tiny bells, and even though one had a smudge of dirt on its soft surface, and part of the ribbon that touched the barrel had lost color from scorching heat, they seemed to me to be the freshest, cleanest objects in all of drab Korea.

At first the bootees had fixed my attention, but after the surprise of seeing these symbols of home in such an incongruous place had worn off, I let my eyes drift, unobserved, to their owner. He was a lieutenant, young, I could see, and tired; not so much from the exertion of the trudging march, but with the wear of long days and nights in combat. He was talking to men from his platoon, all of them together watching the core of a little blaze in their center, and I could tell that he was answering some of their disturbing questions about the war. There was a tone of hopelessness in the men's voices, but the lieutenant sounded cheerful; there was a glint in his eye, and a squint that melted into an easy smile when he spoke. As my companions moved on, I glanced back briefly to the blue bootees still fresh, still swinging. Often in the next few weeks I saw the lieutenant and his bootees while we moved southward before the Chinese armies. Around the ever-present warming fires I heard the simple story of the officer and his boots. The lieutenant was named Shank, and he, twenty-two years old, led a rifle platoon. He had come over from Okinawa while the Army was clamped in the vise of the Pusan perimeter, short on manpower. Shank had his baptism of fire on the hills outside Taegu. His youth and fire helped keep his decimated platoon intact, while the North Koreans frantically tried to crack the American lines. Then came the breakthrough, and Shank's company rode on the record-breaking tank and truck dash northward. He picked up the Springfield rifle then, and kept it because of its renowned accuracy and apparent immunity to the cold weather. A violent day south of Pyongyang won Shank a Silver Star for gallantry, as he led his flesh-and-blood infantrymen against T-34 tanks and destroyed three of them.

The Chinese intervention and beginning of the American retreat brought him up to where I met him, south of Kunari.

The bootees? That was simple. He was an expectant father, and the little boots sent by his young wife in the States reflected his whole optimistic attitude while the battle was the darkest. I also learned that when the baby came it would be announced by a new piece of ribbon on the boots—blue for a boy, pink for a girl. Then I forgot about him as we prepared to defend Seoul from above the frozen Han River. We were hit hard by the Chinese. They streamed down from the hills and charged the barbed wire. They charged again and again, piling up before our smoking guns. The days were but frantic preparation for the nights. Companies dwindled, and my platoon was almost halved as cold, sickness, and the enemy took their toll. I neared the end of my mental reserves. Names of casualties were rumored, and I heard Shank's among them. I wondered where Shank's bootees were now. Then the endless night of the retreat from Seoul came. When we got the word my few men were too dulled to show any emotion at the announcement. Most were too miserable to want to retreat again for twenty-five miles, Chinese or no. But we did, and the temperature dropped to 30 degrees below zero as our silent column stumbled along the hard ground. It was the most depressing night I had ever endured—pushed by the uncompromising cold, the pursuing enemy and the chaotic memory of the bloody nights before. I, as a leader, was close to that mental chasm. Only the numbness prevented thinking myself into mute depression. We plodded across the cracking ice of the Han River at four-thirty in the morning, and marched on south at an ever-slowing pace. Finally the last five mile stretch was ahead. We rested briefly, and as the men dropped to the roadside they fell asleep immediately. I wondered if I could get them going again. Worse yet, I didn't think I could go myself—so tired, numb, and raw was my body. Then in the black despair of uselessness in a second-page war I looked up as a passing figure brushed against my inert shoe pacs. There walked young Lieutenant Shank up the Korean Road, whistling softly, while every waking eye followed him to see the muzzle of his battered Springfield rifle. Swinging gaily in the first rays of the morning sun were Shank's bootees, and fluttering below them was the brightest, bluest, piece of ribbon I have ever seen.

> Lt David Hughes
> Company K, 7th United States
> Cavalry
> Seoul, Korea, December, 1950

A FEW GOOD WORDS FOR
A FEW GOOD MEN

*The deadliest weapon in the world
is a Marine and his rifle!*

General John Pershing, *US Army*

---★---

Marines of the 51st Marine Division   Korea,
August 1950.

*T*he more Marines I have around the better I like it!

General Mark Clark, *US Army*

———————⭐———————

*C*asualties many; Percentage of dead not known;
Combat efficiency: we are winning!

Colonel David M. Shoup, *USMC*

———————⭐———————

I can never again see a United States Marine
without experiencing a feeling of reverence.

General Johnson, *US Army*

———————⭐———————

*T*he raising of that flag on Suribachi means
a Marine Corps for the next 500 years.

James Forrestal, *Secretary of the Navy*

———————⭐———————

*W*e're not retreating, Hell!
We're just attacking in a different direction!

General Oliver Smith, *USMC*

———————⭐———————

I have just returned from visiting the Marines
at the front, and there is not a finer fighting
organization in the world!

General Douglas MacArthur, *US Army*

———————⭐———————

So they've got us surrounded, good!
Now we can fire in any direction,
those bastards won't get away this time!

General Lewis "Chesty" Puller, USMC

———————⭐———————

We have two companies of Marines running
all over this island and thousands of
Army troops doing nothing!

General John Vessey, *Chairman of the Joint Chiefs*

———————⭐———————

Retreat hell! We just got here!

Captain Lloyd Williams, USMC

———————⭐———————

The safest place in Korea was right behind a platoon
of Marines. Lord, how they could fight!

Major General Frank Lowe, US Army

———————⭐———————

Panic sweeps my men when they are
facing the American Marines.

Captured North Korean Major

———————⭐———————

Some people spend an entire lifetime wondering if they
made a difference. The Marines don't have that problem.

President Ronald Reagan, 1985

———————⭐———————

The Will to Win

*The poor devil in the Army marches tremendous
distances; he is in the mud; he's filthy dirty;
he hasn't had a full meal ... and he fights in a place
he has never seen before. It is morale that wins the
victory. It is steadfastness and courage. It is
confidence and zeal and loyalty and determination ...
Above all, it is staying power, the spirit which
endures to the end ... the will to win.*

General George C. Marshall

One More Round

*Fight one more round. When your feet are so tired that
you have to shuffle back to the center of the ring,
fight one more round. When your arms are so tired
that you can hardly lift your hands to come on guard,
fight one more round. When your nose is bleeding and
your eyes are black and you are so tired that you wish
your opponent would crack you on the jaw and put you
to sleep, fight one more round—remember that the man
who always
fights one more round is never whipped.*

James J. Corbett
Heavyweight Boxing Champion

*Tell the men to fire faster and not to give up the ship;
fight her till she sinks.*

Commander James Lawrence, U.S.N.
On board the Chesapeake
June 1, 1813

War is cruel and you cannot refine it.

William Tecumseh Sherman
in his reply to the protest of the Atlanta, Georgia, city
government on his planned invasion of Atlanta in 1864
1820–1891
Union General, Civil War

In war, the only sure defense is offense, and the efficiency of offense depends on the war-like souls of those conducting it.

General George S. Patton, Jr.

I am tired and sick of war. Its glory is all moonshine. It is only those who have neither fired a shot nor heard the shrieks and groans of the wounded who cry aloud for blood, more vengeance, more desolation. War is hell.

William Tecumseh Sherman
attributed to an address
before the graduating class
Michigan Military Academy
June 19, 1879

General William Tecumseh Sherman
© National Archives.

Each Player

Omar Bradley

But it [Pearl Harbor], and the subsequent lessons we learned, day by day, until September 1945, should have taught all military men that our military forces are one team—in the game to win regardless of who carries the ball. This is no time for "fancy dans" who won't hit the line with all they have on every play, unless they can call the signals. Each player on this team—whether he shines in the spotlight of the backfield or eats dirt in the line—must be an all-American.

Omar Bradley
Testimony, Hearings before the Committee on Armed Services
House of Representatives
October 19, 1949

IF YOU REALLY WANT TO KNOW

If you really want to know what it might be like to be an Infantryman in combat, consider this following description:

Dig a hole in your back yard while it is raining. Sit in the hole until the water climbs up around your ankles. Pour cold mud down your shirt collar. Sit there for forty-eight hours, and, so there is no danger of your dozing off, imagine that a guy is sneaking around waiting for a chance to club you on the head or set your house on fire.

Get out of the hole, fill a suitcase full of rocks, pick it up, put a shotgun in your other hand, and walk on the muddiest road you can find. Fall flat on your face every few minutes as you imagine a big meteor streaking down to sock you.

After ten or twelve miles (remember—you are still carrying the shotgun and suitcase) start sneaking through the wet brush. Imagine that somebody has booby-trapped your route with rattlesnakes which will bite you if you step on them. Give some friend a rifle and have him blast in your direction once in a while.

Snoop around until you find a bull. Try to figure out a way to sneak around him without letting him see you. When he does see you, run like hell all the way back to your hole in the back yard, drop the suitcase and shotgun, and get in.

If you repeat this performance every three days for several months you may begin to understand why an infantryman sometimes gets out of breath. But you still won't understand how he feels when things get tough.

Sergeant Bill Mauldin
from his book,
Up Front
1945

Sergeant Bill Mauldin

When Bullets Are Whacking Against Tree Trunks … Antietam

**Union General
Ulysses S. Grant, Civil War**

We lay there till dusk, … when the fighting ceased. During that hour, while the bullets snipped the leaves from a young locust-tree growing at the edge of the hollowing and powdered us with the fragments, we had time to speculate on many things—among others, on the impatience with which men clamor, in dull times, to be led into a fight. We heard all through the war that the army 'was eager to be led against the enemy.' It must have been so, for truthful correspondents said so, and editors confirmed it. But when you came to hunt for this particular itch, it was always the next regiment that had it. The truth is, when bullets are whacking against tree trunks and solid shot are cracking skulls like egg-shells, the consuming passion in the breast of the average man is to get out of the way. Between the physical fear of going forward and the moral fear of turning back, there is a predicament of exceptional awkwardness from which a hidden hole in the ground would be a wonderfully welcome outlet.

David L. Thompson
Company G, 9th New York Volunteer Infantry
1st Brigade, Third Division, Ninth Corps
(Burnside's corps)
[From *Battles and Leaders of the Civil War,*
Volume II, p. 662]

CHAPTER SIX

Faith and Religion on the Battlefield

Founded on Christian values, our nation has always found strength, purpose, and inspiration from our varied religions and denominations. For America's soldiers, sailors, airmen, and marines, faith and religion have always provided this strength and inspiration during both peace and war. I believe America's religious convictions have served this nation well, they have served our soldiers well, and they have served to provide future generations an equally solid foundation on which to build values and character.

This chapter provides poems, prayers, stories and examples of how our nation's military finds strength and purpose and how these qualities allow each warrior to remain with the task at hand.

A Navy chaplain holds Mass for Marines at Saipan. The service was held in memory of brave buddies who lost their lives in the initial landings. WW II, June 1944
© National Archives.

Young Warriors; Should fate find you on the battlefield, may your cause be a just one. May your courage not falter. May you show mercy to your enemies. May your efforts bring the blessings of peace. May you be triumphant and earn victory. May your sacrifice be always appreciated. May you endure the conflict unharmed. Should you be harmed, may your wounds heal. Should you perish in the struggle, may God embrace you and find a place for you in His kingdom

Scott A. Tackett, Sr.

We Humbly Beseech Thee

Each day of his eight years of the Presidency, and every day thereafter until his death, President Thomas Jefferson recited this prayer:

Almighty God, who has given us this good land for our heritage, we humbly beseech Thee that we may always prove ourselves a people mindful of Thy favor and glad to do Thy will. Bless our land with honorable industry, sound learning, and pure manners.

Save us from violence, discord and confusion; from pride and arrogance, and from every evil way. Defend our liberties, and fashion into one united people the multitude brought hither out of many kindreds and tongues.

Endow with the spirit of wisdom those to whom in Thy name we entrust the authority of government, that there may be justice and peace at home, and that thorough obedience to Thy law, we may show forth Thy praise among the nations of the earth.

In time of prosperity, fill our hearts with thankfulness, and, in the day of trouble, suffer not our Trust in Thee to fail; all of which we ask through Jesus Christ our Lord,

Amen.

Democracy is itself a religious faith. For some it comes close to being the only formal religion they have.

E. B. White
The New Yorker, February 18, 1956

My religious convictions teach me to feel as safe in battle as if I were safe asleep in bed. The time of my death is fixed. I do not concern myself about that, but to be always ready no matter when it may overtake me. That is the way all men should live, and then all would be equally brave.

General Stonewall Jackson

*America is another name
for opportunity.
Our whole history appears
like a last effort of
divine Providence in behalf
of the human race.*

Ralph Waldo Emerson
1830–1882
Author and Philosopher

THE PARADE GROUND OF ETERNITY

In a street near the arsenal we stacked our guns, and upon their bayonets we hung for the last time our equipment. It was a sad moment; we had not realized before how it would seem to separate. … Eyes grew moist, cheeks that had been unblanched amid the horrors of the battlefield became pale and sad in those moments of separation. The ties that bound us together were of the most sacred nature; they had been begotten in hardships and baptized in blood. Men who lived together in the little shelter tent, slept beneath the same blanket, had divided the scanty rations, and "drank from the same canteen" were now to be separated forever. The last good-bye was said, our ranks were broken for the last time, and we turned our faces homeward. … Many of us have never met each other since; I presume we never shall in this world; but in that day when the reveille of God shall awaken the slumbering hosts of humanity, may we reform our ranks upon the parade ground of eternity, as the soldiers of the great Prince of Peace.

Theodore Gerrish
20th Maine Volunteers, Civil War
from his book, *Rank and File*

*The chaplain, like the artillery,
is never held in reserve.*

General Edward C. Meyer

*Then I heard the voice of the Lord saying,
"Whom shall I send? Who will go for us?"
"Here I am," I said; "send me!"*

The words of the Prophet Isaiah 6:8–9

*I saw a Catholic chaplain at Salerno gather up his white
robes and beat a Focke-Wulf's tracer into a muddy ditch
by a split second, then return and carry on the service as
if nothing had happened. I have a lot of respect for those
chaplains who keep up the spirits of the combat guys.
They often give the troops a pretty firm anchor to hang onto.*

SGT Bill Mauldin
from his book, *Up Front*
1945

**Private Paul Oglesby,
30th Infantry**
standing in reverence before
an altar in a damaged
Catholic church,
Acerno, Italy. WW II,
September 23, 1943
© National Archives.

Two American soldiers   stripped of all equipment, lie dead, face down in the slush of a crossroads somewhere on the Western Front. WW II. Captured German photograph. Belgium. c. December 1944

© National Archives.

Greater love has no man than this, that a man lay down his life for his friends.

The Gospel according to John 15:13

The Marine's Prayer

Almighty Father, whose command is over all and whose love never fails, make me aware of Thy presence and obedient to Thy will. Keep me true to my best self, guarding me against dishonesty in purpose and deed and helping me to live so that I can face my fellow Marines, my loved ones and Thee without shame or fear. Protect my family, Give me the will to do the work of a Marine and to accept my share of responsibilities with rigor and enthusiasm. Grant me the courage to be proficient in my daily performance. Keep me loyal and faithful to my superiors and to the duties my country and the Marine Corps have entrusted to me. Make me considerate of those committed to my leadership. Help me to wear my uniform with dignity and let it remind me daily of the traditions which I must uphold.

If I am inclined to doubt, steady my faith; if I am tempted, make me strong to resist; if I should miss the mark, give me courage to try again.

Guide me with the light of truth and grant me wisdom by which I may understand the answer to my prayer.

Amen.

Author Unknown

Prayer for Those in Command

Heavenly Father,

I am in need of Your guidance so very, very much for the job I have been commissioned to do. Lead me, Lord, so I can lead the men in my command properly and wisely.

I long for their friendship—I guess everyone wants most of all to be liked—But I know that I need most of all their respect and their obedience. I know that sometimes they resent the ground I walk on and the air I breathe and that at times they feel I am most unfair and completely unreasonable. For there are times, almost every day at first, when they feel ready to drop of exhaustion and I push them even harder; and times when I seem to magnify and pick on the slightest weakness or disorder and impose the severest penalty.

Father, sometimes I want to get right out there and carry their load and take the brunt of the punishment I prescribed. But I know they have to learn to take it. Someday their very lives may depend on it.

But, Lord, make me a good leader—that I can push my men without pushing them too far; that I can maintain discipline without being unfair; that I can instill the strict obedience of respect rather than of hate-filled fear.

Help me ever to respect each man as a valued human being, remembering that Jesus cared enough for him to live and die for him. And make it possible for each of my men to see the spirit of Christ in me.

I ask one more thing, heavenly Father; Watch over my men! Protect them! Keep them unharmed in spirit as well as in body. And let me, Father, regard the life of each one of these men as highly as my own.

Author Unknown

Sergeant William Post, U.S. Army.   Zegra, Kosovo, 1999

*Blessed are the peacemakers:
for they shall be called the children of God.*

The Gospel according to Matthew 5:9

My Rock to Cling to

*I carried a Testament with me. I have the Testament
I carried with me during all my fighting at home now.
I read it through five times during my stay in the army.
I read it everywhere. I read it in dugouts, in fox holes, and
on the front line. It was my rock to cling to. It and my
diary. I didn't do any cursing, no, not even in the front line.
I cut all of that out long ago, at the time I was saved.*

Sergeant Alvin Cullum York
from his wartime diary, WW I
1887–1964

A HIGHER POWER THAN MAN

At the battle of the Argonne Forest in the fall of 1918, as a member of the American 82nd Division, SGT York killed 25 Germans, knocked out 35 machine guns, and captured 132 prisoners almost single-handedly. After this battle SGT York was invited back to the scene of his heroics with officers from his chain of command. This is his account of the visit.

After the Armistice was signed, I was ordered to go back to the scene of my fight with the machine guns. General Lindsey and some other generals went with me. We went over the ground carefully. The officers spent a right smart amount of time examining the hill and the trenches where the machine guns were, and measuring and discussing everything. And then General Lindsey asked me to describe the fight to him. And I did. And then he asked me to march him out just like I marched the German major out, over the same ground and back to the American lines.

Our general was very popular. He was a natural born fighter and he could swear just as awful as he could fight. He could swear most awful bad. And when I marched him back to our old lines he said to me, "York, how did you do it?" And I answered him, "Sir, it is not man power. A higher power than man power guided and watched over me and told me what to do." And the general bowed his head and put his hand on my shoulder and solemnly said, "York, you are right."

Sergeant Alvin York

Back Home, Thanks to God

We stayed there around Bordeaux [France] for several weeks before our time to go across the waters. I wanted all the time to get back to the mountains where I belonged. I wanted to live the quiet life again and escape from the mad rush of the world. It was all over. We had done the job we set out to do, and now, like all of the other American soldiers, I wanted to get back home.

I came on home to Pall Mall, Tennessee, on the 29th of May. My people from all over the mountains, thousands of them, were there to meet me. And my big red-headed brothers were there. And we all had a right smart time. And then I lit out for the old log cabin and the little old mother. And then I went to see Gracie [wife to be]—

I didn't do any hunting for a few days. I'm telling you I went hunting Gracie first.

And then, when it was all over and I had taken off the old uniform of the All American Division and got back into the overalls, I got out with the hounds and the old muzzle loader; and I got to thinking and wondering what it was all about.

And I went back to the place on the mountain where I prayed before the war, and received my assurance from God that I would go and come back. And I just stayed out there and thanked that same God who had taken me through the war.

Sergeant York

Sergeant York
1887–1964
American Soldier, WWI

I have fought a good fight, I have finished my course, I have kept the faith.

From the Letters of Paul, in II Timothy 4:7

The Nobel Ruins of Men

Alone and far removed from earthly care
The noble ruins of men lie buried here.
You were strong men, good men endowed with youth
and much the will to live
I hear no protest from the mute lips of the dead.
They rest; there is no more to give.
So long my comrades,
Sleep ye where you fell upon the field.
But tread softly please
March o'er my heart with ease
March on and on,
But to God alone we kneel.

Audie Murphy

The Final Inspection

The soldier stood and faced his God
Which must always come to pass
He hoped his shoes were shining bright
Just as brightly as his brass.

"Step forward now, soldier,
How shall I deal with you?
Have you turned the other cheek?
To my Church have you been true?"

The soldier squared his shoulders and said,
"No Lord I guess I ain't
Because those of us who carry guns
can't always be a saint.

I've had to work most Sundays
and at times my talk was tough,
But, I never took a thing
That wasn't mine to keep ...
Though I worked a lot of overtime
When the bills got just too steep,

And I never passed a cry for help,
Though at times I shook with fear,
And sometimes, God forgive me,
I've wept unmanly tears.

I know I don't deserve a place
Among the people here,
They never wanted me around
Except to calm their fears.

If you've a place for me here, Lord,
It needn't be so grand,
I never expected or had too much,
But if you don't I'll understand."

There was a silence all around the throne
Where the saints often trod
As the soldier waited quietly,
for the judgment of his God,

"Step forward now, soldier,
You've borne your burdens well,
Come walk peacefully on Heaven's streets,
You've done your time in HELL."

Author Unknown

GOD WAS WITH US

One of the key decisions of General Schwarzkopf during Desert Storm was a flanking maneuver, nicknamed the "Hail Mary," which used the 101st Airborne to cut off the retreating Iraqi Republican Guard. Shortly after this maneuver he commented:

"I began to believe that, when my forward commander radioed that they had reached the Euphrates River ahead of schedule. I waited for the other shoe to fall. 'General,' he said, 'I've got to tell you about the casualties.' I braced myself. 'One man was slightly wounded.' That's when I knew God was with us."

General H. Norman Schwarzkopf
in an interview with David Frost, 1991

A Commander's Prayer

Well, it's been a long time since we talked, Lord.
Guess you'd just about given up on me.
I think it was at Go Dau Ha, wasn't it?
I sure prayed a lot that day…
He was so young.
I was young too, I guess.

Now I wouldn't blame you
If you don't want to hear me out.
But I want you to know
I'm not asking anything for myself.
I'll play my hand the way it's dealt.

It's the soldiers, Lord.
I need your help taking care of them.
I find I can't handle this one by myself.
Just look at 'em—young and earnest.
They work hard and do anything I ask.
And our business is so dangerous.

If we fight on my watch,
It's gonna be as hard and fast
As I can make us go.
I pray our cause be just.
We must train to be ready now.
They'll be safer that way.
They need to be hard and fast in peacetime too.

But I worry for them so,
And can't bear to see them hurt.
Help me see and check and teach
The things that might go wrong.
I need your help tonight.
As we prepare to roll.
Please keep these men safe.

Author Unknown

An Army Chaplain posted the following sign on the door of his quarters.

*If you have troubles, come and tell us about them.
If not, come in and tell us how you do it.*

Author Unknown

*Whatever makes men good Christians,
makes them good citizens.*

Daniel Webster
Speech at Plymouth, Massachusetts
December 22, 1820

*The character of our countrymen, moreover,
was sober, moral, and religious; and there was,
little in the change to shock their feelings of justice
and humanity, or even to disturb an honest prejudice.
We had no domestic throne to overturn,
no privileged orders to cast down,
no violent changes of property to encounter.
In the American Revolution, no man sought or wished
for more than to defend and enjoy his own.*

*None hoped for plunder or for spoil. Rapacity was
unknown to it; the axe was not among the
instruments of its accomplishment; and we all know
that it could not have lived a single day under any
well-founded imputation of possessing a tendency
adverse to the Christian religion.*

Daniel Webster
at the celebration of the Bunker Hill Monument
June 17, 1825

TO SET FREE A SUFFERING HUMANITY

The day after the Normandy D-Day, June 6, 1944, President Franklin Roosevelt led the nation in a National prayer. The text of this prayer is reprinted as follows:

My fellow Americans, last night when I spoke with you about the fall of Rome, I knew at that moment the troops of the United States and our Allies were crossing the Channel in another and greater operation. It has come to pass for success thus far. And so, in this poignant hour, I ask you to join with me in prayer.

All mighty God, our sons, pride of our nation, this day has set upon a mighty endeavor, a struggle to preserve our republic, our religion, and our civilization, and to set free a suffering humanity. Lead them straight and true, give strength to their arms, selflessness to their hearts, steadfastness in their faith, they will need Thy blessings, their road will be long and hard. For the enemy is strong, he may hurl back our forces, success may not come with rushing speed, but we shall return again and again, and we know that by Thy grace, and by the righteousness of our cause our sons will triumph. They will be forth tried, by night and by day, without rest, until the victory is won. The darkness will be rent by noise and flame, men's souls will be shaken with the violences of war. For these men, uniquely drawn from the waves of peace. They fight not for the lust of conquest, they fight to end conquest. They fight to liberate. They fight to let justice to arise, and tolerance and goodwill among all Thy people. They yearn but for the end of battle, for their return to the haven of home. Some will never return. Embrace these Father, and receive them thy heroic servants, into Thy kingdom. And for us at home, fathers, mothers, children, wives, sisters, and brothers of brave men overseas, whose thoughts and prayers are ever with them, help us almighty God, to rededicate ourselves in renewed faith in Thee, in this hour of great sacrifice. Many people have urged that I call the nation into a single day of special prayer. But because the road is long, and the desire is great, I ask that our people devote themselves in a continuance of prayer, that they rise to each new day, and again when each day is spent, let lords of prayer be on our list, invoking Thy help to our efforts. Give us strength too, strength in our daily tasks, redouble the contributions we make in the physical and the materiel support of our armed forces. And let our hearts be stoked, to weed out the long trial, to bear sorrows that may come, to impart our courage unto our sons, wherefore thou may be. And oh Lord, give us faith, give us faith in Thee, faith in our sons, faith in each other, faith in our united crusade. Let not the keenness of our spirit ever be dull, let not the impact of temporary events, of temporal matters of fleeting moments, let not these deter us in our unconquerable purpose. With Thy blessing, we shall prevail, over the unholy forces of our enemy. Help us to conquer the apostles of greed and racial arrogances. Lead us to the saving our country, and with our sister nations into a world unity, that will spell a sure peace. A peace invulnerable to the steamings of unworthy men, and a peace that will let all men live in freedom, reaping the just rewards of their honest toils. Thy will be done, almighty God, Amen.

by President Franklin D. Roosevelt

CHAPTER SEVEN
The American Warrior

Americans warriors have mostly been volunteers while some were draftees. Yet, regardless of their reasons for serving, there remains something unique about American warriors: soldiers serving free men, soldiers whose love of country provides a unique inspiration. This chapter attempts to shed some light on who the American warriors are and what it is that permits them to excel over soldiers from other countries.

The American soldier has been much the same, probably, from the Revolutionary War to the present day. He reflects the national character, and the national character has not changed a great deal. Weapons, tactics, strategic concepts, equipment—all these have changed enormously; yet the human material of which American armies are made is today very much as it was generations ago. As the battle record of many wars attests, this material has uniformly been pretty good. If there is one thing in America we can be sure of, it is that there is a value in our loose, easy-going, good-natured society here that is worth everything anyone can sacrifice for it. The American soldier usually plays it by ear. He never really becomes very military; for better or worse, he remains to the end a citizen in arms.

U.S. Marines gathered in front of a Japanese dugout on Cape Totkina on Bougainville, Solomon Islands, which they helped to take. January 1944 © National Archives.

By author-historian, Bruce Canton, in his book *America Goes to War*, 1958, summing up the G.I.

HOMESPUN GALLANTRY

To the New York Legislature, June 26, 1775:

General Washington

... When we assumed the soldier, we did not lay aside the citizen; and we shall most sincerely rejoice with you in that happy hour when the establishment of American liberty, upon the most firm and solid foundations, shall enable us to return to our private stations in the bosom of a free, peaceful and happy country.

**General
George Washington**

Letter from a Navy Pilot
Battle of Midway, WW II

The Fates have been kind to me. When you hear people saying harsh things about American youth, you will know how wrong they all are. So many times that now they have become commonplace, I've seen incidents that make me know that we were never soft, never weak.

Many of my friends are now dead. To a man, each died with a nonchalance that each would have denied was courage, but simply called a lack of fear and forgot the triumph. If anything great or good has been born of this war, it should be valued in the youth of our country, who were never trained for war, who almost never believed in war, but who have, from some hidden source, brought forth a gallantry which is homespun, it is so real.

Out here between the spaceless sea and sky, American youth has found itself, and given of itself, so that a spark may catch, burst into flame, and burn high. If our country takes these sacrifices with indifference it will be the cruelest ingratitude the world has ever known.

You will, I know, do all in your power to help others keep the faith. My luck can't last much longer. But the flame goes on and only that is important.

Anonymous

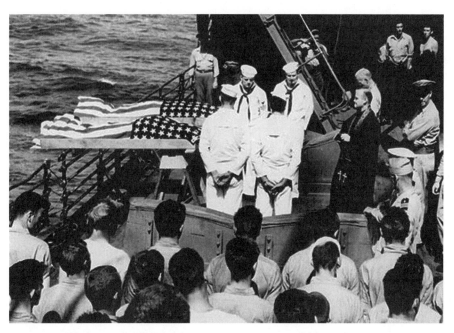

Burial at Sea   Two enlisted men of the ill-fated U.S. Navy aircraft carrier *Liscome Bay*, which was torpedoed by a Japanese submarine off the Gilbert Islands, are buried at sea from the deck of a Coast Guard-manned assault transport. November 1943

© National Archives.

A PROUD ONE

The American soldier is a proud one and he demands
professional competence in his leaders.
In battle, he wants to know that the job is going to be
done right, with no unnecessary casualties.
The noncommissioned officer wearing the
chevron is supposed to be the best soldier
in the platoon and he is supposed to know
how to perform all the duties expected of him.
The American soldier expects his sergeant
to be able to teach him how to do his job.
And he expects even more from his officers.

General Omar Bradley

THERE STANDS AMERICA

*S*oldiers ... make us all proud. You represent America.
You remind us of our roots and of the strength of this
nation—the willingness of America's best to step
forward to serve their nation. ... American soldiers
represent a proud, glorious history of service to nation.
... Where our troops stand, there stands America.

General Gordon Sullivan

*T*he soldier is a representative of everything
that our nation stands for.

Richard A. Kidd
Sergeant Major of the Army (SMA)
in "SMA Kidd Defines Roles"
Sentinel, March 12, 1993

*T*he American soldier ... is unbeatable in war. ...
We cannot give the American soldier too much credit. ...
He deserves everything we can do for him and he
deserves all the respect we can show him. ...
Whether or not a war is popular among the nation's people,
and whether or not it is supported by the legislators,
has no bearing on what the soldiers do and think.
They perform their duties magnificently and bravely.

They don't make the policies, and they don't declare war.
But they fight, they bleed, and they die.
And they do it unhesitatingly.
They should be appreciated and recognized for it,
without regard for the political aspects of the war.

George W. Dunaway
Sergeant Major of the Army (SMA)
from an interview given at the
Center of Military History, 1990

Die On Our Feet

*We, too, born to freedom, and believing in freedom,
are willing to fight to maintain freedom.
We, and all others who believe as deeply as we do,
would rather die on our feet than live on our knees.*

Franklin Delano Roosevelt
June 19, 1941

WHY WE SERVE

The title of that short but very profound piece of tape is "Why We Serve," and it is meant as a declaration, a strong, positive statement to all those who see it, soldiers or civilians: "Hey, this is why we serve." I sent a copy to my parents several years ago after I first saw it, just before heading off to the unknown—again—in Haiti. I wanted them to understand why I serve—but, for all of us in uniform, and for those spouses who serve beside and with us, it can also be a question, "why, indeed?". Why do I serve? Each one of us in our most private moments, especially in times of great frustration, has asked—why indeed? Why am I doing this? Well, I can't speak for you. I can only speak for me, why I serve?— why, indeed!

Graduating from high school in 1964—fully one year before the first major battle of the Vietnam War, the first battle for the Ia Drang Valley, described in LTG Hal Moore and Joe Galloway's brilliant book, *We Were Soldiers Once and Young*—I had appointments to the Naval and Air Force Academies, but at the last minute decided that I didn't want anything to do with military life. So off I went to Trinity University in San Antonio, sight unseen, where much to my surprise there was mandatory Army ROTC. Vietnam looming on the horizon, I stayed in after two years, went to ROTC summer camp, and found I kind of liked the camaraderie, the challenge. I chose Infantry on commissioning in 1968, thinking that I liked what I thought was the Army and might even make it a career, but if I was going off to war, I might as well find out what real war was about and go as an infantryman. And, I confess, I was 21, and like many youths, a naive idealist, a romantic. I believed there was glory in war, a chance to test my courage. I know now that there is no glory in war, in its suffering and agony and tragedy, but there can be honor in war, honor found in the soldier's creed of selfless service, service to a people, and a group of soldiers, and a country, and an army, and an imperfect process called democracy.

I joined and served a draftee army in Vietnam—a very good army. I was a rifle platoon leader, a recon platoon leader, and a company commander in combat—honored to lead American soldiers in combat. To this very day I hold that service, command of an infantry rifle company in combat, as my greatest privilege—my Combat Infantryman's Badge, my highest award. I served in a disciplined force, saw nothing of the horror stories of indiscipline shown in movies like "Platoon." I did not serve in Oliver Stone's Vietnam. I remember young men of courage, good humored, and good-natured, under some terrible and frightening conditions, longing to return to the "world" as we called it. And we all did return, some on freedom birds to an uncaring, unsympathetic society, and some in body bags, to grieving families, alone in their sorrow because we didn't go as units, and therefore family support groups—God bless family support groups—weren't there to help. Another word on family support groups. I'm going to read a segment from the epilogue of *We Were Soldiers Once and Young*. The words are Betty Mapson's whose father died in the Ia Drang Valley. If after hearing it if you still don't understand the absolute necessity for family support groups and pledge yourself to be more helpful to families—that is the calling I spoke of earlier—then I say you just don't get it and probably won't. So, at the end of your tour of duty, go on back home, let someone more caring take your place. We lead and serve people, not personnel.

> After the initial shock of receiving the telegram announcing daddy's death, we kids had to go back to school because it would be two weeks or more before his body would arrive home. It seemed everyone was looking at us and whispering, not really knowing what to say except how bad it was our daddy died over there. They mostly left us alone. There were no support groups or any of that to help us cope. Our family was left alone in our grief. My brothers did not talk about their feelings at all. My mother was devastated. She and daddy were sweethearts in school but each went on to marry other people. When both were divorced around the same time they met again and were married. Daddy and I used to take trips together on the Greyhound bus, mostly home to Savannah. Whenever he and my mother went out, he would not be ready until he sat in a chair and had me comb and brush his hair. It was cut real close but he made it seem like I had really done something special.
>
> I remember when he first told us he had to go to Vietnam. We drove him to Fort Benning. I remember the army trucks filled with soldiers and hearing daddy say he might not come back. I was young and didn't really see the seriousness of it. He was a good, strict father and my brothers and I thought his being away for so long meant we would be able to stay out later and have more fun. I blamed myself for daddy being killed because

of those selfish feelings when he left. My daddy was a good man, a preacher's son. His given name is Jeremiah. Two weeks after the initial telegram, we got another one stating when to meet the body at the train station. The hearse was already there when we got to the station and soon a wooden cart with a long gray box was being pulled toward us. My daddy! This is how he came back to us. And the pain started all over again for us, only more so because now he was home. You could have heard me screaming three states away. At the funeral home I remember looking at him closely and for a long time to make sure it was really him. Then I saw that little mole on his cheek—and I knew.

I am so proud of my father and wished that somehow he could know that and know that he is still very much alive with us. For a long time it seemed to me that he was just away like he usually was on Army duty, and one day he would come home. For a lot of years I waited and watched our driveway because I wanted so much for him to come home for my momma and my brothers and me. I would like to visit the Ia Drang. It is something I have to do for my own sake. I have to know, have to see that this place really exists. I need to see and to be where my daddy died. Then maybe this will all somehow be complete for me. I just wish with all my heart that we had not been so alone to deal with such a monumental tragedy back then. We needed someone to reach out to us, to explain for us, to help us see why. My mother has passed away now. She never remarried. She loved daddy so.

There is a plaque on the right wall, just as you enter the Tropic Lightning Soldier's Chapel. It is dedicated to the dead of Vietnam, but I believe also dedicated to the survivors. It reads, "not for fame or reward, not goaded by ambition or lured by necessity, but in simple obedience to discipline as they understood it, these men dared all, suffered, and died." You ask why I serve— why, indeed! I found out something about myself in the jungles of Vietnam. I loved the Infantry and the Army ... and I was pretty good at it. I stayed, applied for and received a regular army commission. But, the army that emerged from the jungles of Vietnam was a shell of its former self, the old NCO corps—the sergeants of World War II and Korea that led the Army into Vietnam—had either retired or been killed. The American people, through their congress, decided we needed a volunteer army, not an army of conscripts, and ended the draft.

We entered into a new age—and the birth pains were agonizing. It was the '70s, the period I call the "Awful Army" ... where in the 25th Infantry Division of the mid-seventies you could not go to the field without losing one or two weapons ... when, as a company commander, if you only had 5–6 AWOLs a week in your company, you were a great leader and people asked you how you did it ... where sergeants feared to go into the barracks when they were charge of quarters, and staff duty officers wore side arms. And I do not exaggerate to make a point. It was that way, and not only in Hawaii, but throughout the Army. There were three involuntary officer reductions-in-force in the seventies: the first got bums, the second and third took good officers, and other good officers were bailing out right and left. As a young captain, I signed my resignation papers twice, but just could not go through with it. I told my wife, Toni, that I simply could not walk away and leave it—my Army, my soldiers—in the hands of others.

Who will lead? I asked her. Who will lead? Why I serve? Why, indeed. Well, we survived the '70s and began to thrive in the '80s. We hit rock bottom as an army, and maybe as a nation, in the desert of Iran as we failed ignominiously trying to rescue our 53 hostages in the embassy in Tehran. We weren't trained, and we weren't ready, and as a result, we failed the Nation. It's so vivid to me, the sixties and the seventies, just like it all happened yesterday, yet I know that it is alien to all of you here—and throughout the 25th Infantry Division, that is true. Neither of my assistant division commanders served in Vietnam, and of all my brigade level, 0-6 commanders and staff, only the Chief of Staff, served in Vietnam. Very few of our CSMs served in Vietnam, only two leap to mind. And while the colonels know the '70s, even most of my battalion commanders, entered the Army in 1980 and afterwards. So, how did we survive the '70s to thrive in the '80s? I believe it's because we shared a common set of values: honor, duty, courage, loyalty, integrity, respect, and selfless service. Even in the darkest hour, when it appeared that the inmates were running the asylum, the leadership, steeled in the jungles of Vietnam, didn't quit on the American dream, though for a time we thought the American ideal had quit on us. We stayed the course, believed in ourselves and in our values—duty, honor, courage, loyalty, integrity, respect, and most importantly, selfless service—and we did not lower ourselves to the lesser standard. We were guided by the visionaries of the day—Chiefs of Staff of the Army like General Shy Meyer who had the guts to call it "hollow" like it was then, but not today, and General John Wickham who almost single-handedly reminded us that we had to respect each other, to be our brother's and sister's keeper, to make a difference in the lives of soldiers and their families, and thereby readiness. They gave us the tools to reclaim the Army; urinalysis, higher recruiting standards—high school graduates became the norm not the exception—the Combat Training Centers (CTC), a new training management system and ethos, and "Be All You Can Be." None of you will remember the original recruiting slogan of the volunteer army—"the U.S. Army wants to join you"—join you? No way I want to join you; I want you to join us—be all you can be, a challenge to leader and led alike.

So, for the most part, it was my generation who rebuilt the "Awful Army," rebuilt it with discipline and hard work and Ronald Reagan dollars and vision, rebuilt it into a trained and ready force, the best army the world has ever seen, took it to the desert and proved it to be so. It wasn't easy—it took sacrifice and courage and hard work by some of the very best men and women in this nation—but it was worth it.

Today, the American people respect, not revile you; you are a revered group of professionals—as it should be and will be, or I'm out of here. I will not go back. You ask why I serve? Why, indeed. We have endured as an army of professionals because we were, are, and will remain a values-based army, an army made up of folks who live and understand the values of honor, duty, courage, loyalty, integrity, respect and, mostly, selfless service. We all come at selfless service from different perspectives, but we all come to it knowing that we serve a greater good, a greater cause and we do it as I said earlier, not for fame or reward, not goaded by ambition or lured by necessity. And, so it must always be.

We won the cold war, yet there is no peace. There are still forces, evil forces, at work in the world today that would take away our freedom, destroy our way of living. We must, you and I, continue to stand in the breach, to serve, to protect and defend our country and our people. And it requires the best men and women among us, men and women dedicated to selfless service, bolstered by duty, honor, courage, loyalty, integrity, and respect. Those values got us through the '70s, and they will guide us as we continue to be a trained and ready Army, as we overcome the troubles of today just as we did in the past. Why I serve? Why, indeed.

I am reminded at gatherings with young professionals like you, like this. I am reminded every day. I am reminded every time I run with soldiers and hear their cadence and the sound of their feet striking the pavement. I am reminded every time I hear of a family support group picking up the pieces after tragedy strikes in a unit. I'm reminded every time I see Army family volunteers giving freely of themselves for the greater good of the community. I'm reminded every time I hear Reveille, To the Colors, and Retreat, and especially Taps at night. I am reminded every time I look into the face of my son who is the future of this magnificent country. And, yes, I'm reminded by the faces and voices of the past, who call out to me at odd times—faces and voices with names unfortunately long forgotten, I'm embarrassed to confess; soldiers who asked for little except to be well led, treated with dignity and respect—and honored. It seems to me that sometimes I can feel and touch their spirits as if they were still here, soldiers forever young. For as the poem goes, "they shall not grow old as you and I are left to grow old, age shall not weary them nor the years condemn." I deeply believe that you and I, the very best men and women our nation can produce, serve in a noble, honorable profession—the profession of arms. And, I don't know about you but, as for me, when this life ends, as it certainly will, I will be content if my tombstone reads: "He served. He was there." You ask why I serve? Why, indeed. God bless you. God bless our great Army and Nation.

by Major General James T. Hill
Commanding General, U.S. Army
25th Infantry Division (Light)

It Is the Soldier

It is the soldier, not the reporter,
who has given us freedom of the press.
It is the soldier, not the poet,
who has given us freedom of speech.
It is the soldier, not the campus organizer,
who has given us the freedom to demonstrate.
It is the soldier,
who salutes the flag, who
serves beneath the flag, and whose coffin is
draped by the flag, who allows the
protester to burn the flag.

Father Edward O'Brian, *USMC*

THE REASON I LIKE MARINES

Excerpts from a speech by RADM J. Stark, USN, made in Newport, RI on
10 November 1995.

The first reason I like Marines. They set high standards—for themselves
and those around them—and will accept nothing less. I like the way Marines
march. I like the way Marines do their basic training whether it's Quantico,
Parris Island, or San Diego. I like the idea that Marines cultivate an ethos con-
ducive of producing hard people in a soft age. I like the fact that Marines stay

in shape. I like the fact that the Marines only have one boss—the Commandant. And

- I like the directness of the Commandant.

- I like the fact that Marines are stubborn.

- I like the way Marines obey orders.

- I like the way the Marines make the most of the press.

- I like the wholehearted professionalism of the Marines.

... it occurred to me that the services could be characterized by different breeds of dogs ...

The Air Force reminded me of a French Poodle. The poodle always looks perfect ... sometimes seems a bit pampered ... always travels first class. But don't ever forget that the poodle was bred as a hunting dog and in a fight it's very dangerous.

The Army is kind of like a St. Bernard. It's big and heavy and sometimes seems a bit clumsy. But it's very powerful and has lots of stamina. So you want it for the long haul.

The Navy, God bless us, is a Golden Retriever. They're good natured and great around the house. The kids love 'em. Sometimes their hair is a bit long ... they go wandering off for long periods of time, and they love water.

... Marines I see as two breeds, Rottweilers or Dobermans, because Marines come in two varieties, big and mean, or skinny and mean. ... They're aggressive on the attack and tenacious on defense. They've got really short hair and they always go for the throat. That sounds like a Marine to me!

So what I really like about Marines is that "first to fight" isn't just a motto, it's a way of life. From the day they were formed at Tun Tavern 221 years ago, Marines have distinguished themselves on battlefields around the world. From the fighting tops of the *Bonhomme Richard*, to the sands of the Barbary coast, from the swamps of New Orleans to the halls of Montezuma, from Belleau Wood, to the Argonne Forest, to Guadalcanal, and Iwo Jima, and Okinawa and Inchon, and Chosin Reservoir and Hue City and Quang Tri and Dong Ha, and Beirut, and Grenada, and Panama, and Somalia and Bosnia and a thousand unnamed battlefields in godforsaken corners of the globe, Marines have distinguished themselves by their bravery, and stubbornness and aggressive spirit, and sacrifice, and love of country, and loyalty to one another.

They've done it for you and me, and this Country we all love so dearly.

And they asked for nothing more than the honor of being a United States Marine.

And that's why I like Marines!

THE AMERICAN SOLDIER

Excerpts from General Dennis Reimer's address at the
Dwight David Eisenhower Luncheon,
Annual Meeting of the Association of the United States Army (AUSA),
Washington, D.C., October 13, 1998

First of all let me thank you. Thanks to the Association of the United States Army [AUSA] for what you do. You know the Army is indeed fortunate in a lot of things, but I think it is most fortunate in having an association like AUSA to back us—helping us take care of our soldiers. And—I'm not only talking about the national chapter which all of your represent, but also all those individual chapters that are scattered around America. Thank you for all you do every day in your own special way to take care of our soldiers. Thank you very much.

Welcome to distinguished guests—and you're all distinguished guests as far as I'm concerned—friends of America's Army—allies and partners from around the world, congressional leaders, leaders from the Department of Defense, our veterans—our alumni, our partners in industry—and flanking the room from one end to the other—truly the world's best soldiers. What a great team! Thank you all so very much for all you do for America's Army. I also want to recognize the Army's senior leaders sitting up here with me. On any given day thousands of our men and women are deployed around the world—our soldiers continue to do the heavy lifting for our nation. The fact that we've done it so successfully—that we've accomplished mission after mission—that we've brought our soldiers home—and trained them up again for

General Reimer speaking with a soldier from Fort Bliss, Texas.

the next mission—and taken care of them and their families—and at the same time kept our eye on the future—that is no small feat.

It didn't just happen. None of that Herculean effort would be possible without the leadership you see here.

Whatever we do—wherever we go—we must never forget it is all about the American soldier. It is an honor to be making my fourth address to you. Every year in the life of the United States Army is precious—year by year we gather here to review one more chapter in our glorious history. If there has been one theme in my remarks to you over the last four years it has been—the challenge of change—change has been our constant companion, our battle buddy—it is one of the few constants in the world today. Dealing with change is terribly important—it's also terribly difficult.

And now, today, as every year, for the past 223 years, we add another chapter ... Where does the Army stand today? What did this year 1998 represent—and what can we look forward to in 1999? First, I think you, all of you, all of you, and indeed all Americans should be immensely proud of our Army. What you the Army team have accomplished in the last decade is unprecedented. The Army has undergone its greatest transformation since World War II—and you have done that transformation better than any army in history—and that's no boast. History is a great teacher. It teaches us who we are by reminding us of who we were. Remember that five years after the end of World War II, when the first American soldiers were sent into combat during the Korean War, they were insufficiently trained, poorly equipped and totally unprepared for the mission. We must never forget what the system did to the brave Americans of Task Force Smith. Remember, five years after Vietnam, we had an army, that didn't train to standard ... that didn't understand the importance of standards. We had an army full of broken, obsolete equipment.

An army with empty units. And even more onerous—it was an army that had lost its spirit and misplaced its soul. We labeled it hollow. Nine years after the fall of the Berlin wall—nine years after the end of the Cold War, we have the best equipped, best trained army on earth. That's not my opinion—results speak volumes. Just look around the world. We have over 30,000 soldiers deployed to 80 different countries, keeping the peace, providing stability. Just look around this room. We are surrounded by the reason for that unprecedented accomplishment—American soldiers. In Bosnia, you can, and people do, argue about whether we should be there—but you cannot argue about what our soldiers have done. There are children there that are a year older. There are families that have celebrated another year of holidays and anniversaries together. What a wonderful contribution.

American soldiers did that. At the same time, when we needed a show of force in Southwest Asia, within 72 hours we had the most modernized, best trained brigade combat team in the history of warfare on the ground in the desert.

American soldiers did that.

And every day the Army is deployed around the world in almost a hundred countries—training, helping, keeping the peace. At home our army responded to everything from forest fires to hurricanes—helping our neighbors, saving lives, saving property, serving the nation, protecting our communities. American soldiers did that. Five years after WW II we could not do that. Five years after Vietnam we could not do that. Today, there is no other army in the world that could do that. Only American soldiers. We know we have a great army, but we also recognize keeping it great is no easy task—it requires tough, difficult choices—one of the most difficult is how to balance requirements with resources. We have to do the best job with the resources we have. We owe that to the American taxpayer.

America's Army is cost effective. Our Army receives less than 25% of the total Department of Defense budget, less than Americans spend on beer and pizza every year. Spending on the entire Army accounts for less than 1% of GDP—the lowest level of spending since Pearl Harbor. Our reduced resourcing reflects both the change in the nation's national security needs since the end of the Cold War, and the priority given to balancing the federal budget in order to maintain the health of our economy. And this shift has had a profound effect on our nation. Reduced defense expenditures have amounted in a "peace dividend" of $700 billion over the last decade. And this year for the first year in almost thirty years we have a balanced budget, a budget surplus and a thriving economy. This should not be surprising, for during the same time, the Army has helped maintain peace and stability around the world, stability that has added almost two million jobs to the American economy. We have kept the force trained and ready while implementing the most fundamental change since World War II and we have done all that despite 14 straight years of declining buying power. American soldiers did that. American servicemen and women have unselfishly carried a heavy load for the nation, but it has required us to make tough choices, and to balance current and future readiness. But we must ask—ready for what? The measures of Cold War readiness no longer apply—we now have a new military strategy—a strategy based on three pillars—shape, respond and prepare. We must prepare now for the future—shape the international environment, pushing the possibility of war to the right—and respond to crisis when needed. It's a good strategy, the right strategy—and we must manage readiness to support each of these pillars. In particular, to ensure our ability to prepare for the future now, we have had to shift some of the risk to near-term readiness and there has been a price associated with that shift. The readiness concerns that you hear from commanders and soldiers in the field are a fair and honest reflection of this shift in risk. The pace of operations is higher. The time and resources to train are less. The entry level of units at combat training centers is lower. The ability to balance investment in training, our installations and quality of life is becoming more difficult. In short we have too few resources chasing too many requirements—and we must fix that. And our number one concern for continuing to balance current and future readiness ... is as it has always been, the American soldier. We cannot sacrifice quality. Global reach requires a professional career force. We must recognize that our post cold war strategy is leadership intensive—requiring a higher leader-to-led ratio in both the institutional and tactical army. The heart of our force is experienced, highly trained soldier-leaders, both officers and non-commissioned officers. Today these soldiers are smart and dedicated. They are also overworked. Our principal readiness concerns are continuing to recruit, retain and take care of our soldiers and their families. We must counter the growing concerns of our soldiers over the disparity between military and civilian pay and declining military benefits such as retirement, health care, adequate housing and aging facilities. We will continue to carry that message to our national leadership and to the American people. Still, I stand in front of you enormously proud, optimistic and hopeful. Proud of all that the Army has accomplished. Optimistic that we can approach all our challenges from a Total Army perspective. And hopeful that we can continue to get the balance of our investments right and the support we need to serve the nation. Today we have the best army on earth—there is no potential enemy—anywhere that thinks they can take on the American Army in battle and win. We are going to make sure they understand that until the day they die. That is how I read this chapter in our history. But our story never ends.

And I want to close, as I started, by talking about the American soldier. Douglas MacArthur introduced me to them in May 1962 when he spoke for the last time to the cadets at West Point. General MacArthur called them "one of the world's noblest figures, not only as one of the finest military characters, but also as one of the most stainless. His name and fame is the birthright of every American. In his youth and strength, his love and loyalty he gave—all that mortality can give. He needs no eulogy from me or from any other man. He has written his own history and has written it in red on his enemy's breast.

But when I think of his patience under adversity, of his courage under fire, and of his modesty in victory, I am filled with an emotion of admiration I cannot put into words. He belongs to history." Wherever I have been in the last 36 years I have seen those soldiers of whom MacArthur spoke so eloquently—and passionately. They have done the nation's bidding. They have accomplished every mission. "They have drained deep the chalice of courage." They truly belong to history. Recently Steven Spielberg captured part of that history for all to see in a film—"Saving Private Ryan." For me the most profound moment was when Private James Francis Ryan from Iowa was standing on the windswept cliffs of Normandy, by the sweeping fields of crosses and stars of David—the youth long gone, the war and the terror of Normandy many years in his past—and he turned to his wife and said "tell me I'm a good man. Tell me I did a good job." He had to know if saving him had been worth the sacrifice of Captain John Miller and a handful of brave men. But, "Saving Private Ryan" was not about saving one man—it was about a generation who saved the world—who gave us the priceless gift of freedom. For me it brought home what General MacArthur had said 36 years ago to me and my fellow cadets at West Point. "Yours is the profession of arms, the will to win, the sure knowledge that in war there is no substitute for victory, that if you lose the nation will be destroyed." The soldiers who fought World War II did not lose—thank God. What a magnificent story Steven Spielberg tells. But, I will tell you what is even more magnificent. For every fictional story of courage—there are thousands, hundreds of thousands of real stories of courage—in our history, in our Army today. They are called, simply, American soldiers. Each year I ask a handful of them to join me here on the stage. I do that because I can think of no better way to recognize the contributions of each and every individual soldier, who has ever served, past and present. There are thousands of monuments to the American soldier from the battle of bronze and marble rising monuments on the fields of Gettysburg to the simple crosses in Arlington just a few miles away. Each speaks to a special moment of service and sacrifice. Each reminds us of the men and women of America's Army ... working at a refugee center in Bosnia, standing guard at the DMZ in Korea, sitting next to you in the audience today, America's sons and daughters—our most precious asset. It is in their eyes, in their hearts, and through their deeds that we answer James Francis Ryan. Yes, the American soldier has led a good life. It is now my very, very great honor, for the last time as your Chief of Staff, to introduce to you America's soldiers ... Staff Sergeant Kim Dionne from Auburn, Maine; Staff Sergeant Jason Wolfe from Springfield, Illinois; and Sergeant First Class Greg Seibert from Philadelphia, Pennsylvania. They are the Army Reserve, National Guard and Active recruiters of the year. They are where the Army begins. Every year these noncommissioned officers and thousands like them work harder, put in longer hours, spend more time away from home—to make sure we have quality soldiers for the Total Army. Staff Sergeant Bradley Houston from Nashport, Ohio and Sergeant First Class Timothy Graves from Mount Vernon, Kentucky. They are the Active and

Reserve Drill Sergeants of the year. Every day they accomplish minor miracles by taking young Americans and making them proud soldiers in a remarkably short time. They teach them what the motto "this we'll defend" really means. They teach them how to be steely eyed killers—but also how to treat others with dignity and respect. They teach them how to act—they teach them how to be—American soldiers. And because the efforts of recruiters and trainers we have great soldiers like ... Sergeant Lisa Weisbeck from Sturgis, South Dakota, an assistant squad leader from the 411th Base Support Battalion in the US Army Europe. Airborne qualified, she is a veteran of operations in Somalia, Bosnia and Macedonia. She is a recognized leader in her unit and her community. Specialist Mamie Jenkins from Red Bank, New Jersey, fulfilling a lifelong dream of becoming a soldier, as a member of the elite 101st Airborne Division, she successfully completed air assault training. Currently deployed on a one-year hardship tour to Korea, she was the runner-up for the command's soldier of the year. And Sergeant Jose Marengo from Lindenwood, New Jersey and Sergeant First Class Greg Valcin from Port Arthur, Texas. Ranger Marango, is a squad leader in A Company, 2d Battalion, 504th Parachute Infantry Regiment—a highly skilled infantrymen who has trained in every theater in the world from Asia to Germany to Saudi Arabia. He also participated in Operation Uphold Democracy in Haiti. Platoon Sergeant Valcin is a decorated veteran of Just Cause and Operation Desert Storm. He holds the combat infantry badge and master rated combat parachutist badge. American soldiers all. They need no eulogy from me—but they deserve the very best support we can give them. Ladies and gentlemen standing before you are our credentials ... They suffered at Valley Forge. They were the "first wavers" at Omaha beach. They walked point in Ia Drang. They crushed the Iraqi army. They separated warring factions in Bosnia. When it is all over for me ... this is what I will always remember. It is a great honor to ask you to join me in recognizing one of the noblest figures in history ... the American soldier.

ARMY VALUES

In 1998 the Army formally approved seven Army values. These values constitute the foundation of soldiering in today's army. The truth is, the American Army has always been considered "a values-based Army." This is true. The following verbatim message formalized this truth.

February 17, 1998

On 13 January 1998, the Chief of Staff of the Army (CSA) approved the seven Army values and their definitions. CSA also approved that the values be listed, and displayed, in specific order (Loyalty, Duty, Respect, Selfless-service, Honor, Integrity, and Personal courage) to form the acronym—LDRSHIP—(pronounced LEADERSHIP) using the first letter of each value. The approved definitions are:

1. Loyalty: Bear true faith and allegiance to the U.S. Constitution, the Army, and other soldiers.

2. Duty: Fulfill your obligations.

3. Respect: Treat people as they should be treated.

4. Selfless-service: Put the welfare of the nation, the Army and your subordinates before your own.

5. Honor: Live up to all the Army values.

6. Integrity: Do what's right, legally and morally.

7. Personal courage: Face fear, danger, or adversity (physical and moral).

The Army's
Values poster

Your Troops Are Better

People are our greatest strength.
Time and time again, visitors from all over
the world come to the United States.
They see soldiers, sailors, airmen, marines,
and members of the Coast Guard.
Inevitably, on their way home from
their visit, they will tell one of the
Joint Chiefs, or the Chairman,
or the civilian political leadership:
"You have great equipment,
but your troops are better."

General Gordon Sullivan

America's Army

This is America's Army. It is filled with great
soldiers with lots of enthusiasm and energy.
We must harness that energy and spirit and
shape an Army that is ready for the challenges of
today and the opportunities of the next century. ...

*Each year, the armed forces bring in almost
250,000 people, a fifth of our entire force.
This turnover refreshes our links to the American
people, and ensures that when they look in our
faces, they see brothers, sisters, sons, daughters,
husbands, and wives. They see themselves.
They see America.*

General Gordon Sullivan

*Your relationship with your soldiers will motivate and
sustain you. ... You will learn from them ...
You will be inspired by them. ... You are entering an
Army that is the best in the world because it has the
best soldiers and the best leaders in the world.*

General Gordon Sullivan

*We came American. We shall remain American
and go into battle with Old Glory over our heads.
I will not parcel out American boys.*

General Pershing
on keeping the American Expeditionary Force (AEF)
together as a fighting force

SOLDIER

A guy pinned me right to the wall the other day. I was giving a talk to some basic and advance course officers out at Fort Benning. I'd just finished raising all sorts of hell about the pernicious nature of the "civilian equivalency" theme, and about the uniqueness of the soldier. The question period began. This young 2d lieutenant stood up, and, sort of slow and careful like, he said, "Sir, would you please give us your definition of a 'soldier'?"

Well, at first, I thought he was a smart ass, but then I looked more carefully at his eyes, and I saw that he was sincere, and concerned, and serious ... and it was really me who was the smart ass for thinking that he was. At any rate, I tried to wing it and define "soldier" then and there. I didn't do worth a damn. I know. I watched his eyes.

Some days later, back at the [US Army] War College, there came a letter from the lieutenant—his name is Tom—and he said, "Sir, when I asked you what is a soldier, I didn't mean to stump you or embarrass you. The thought and response you gave to the question was good, and yet you still weren't able to put your finger on what is a soldier. This is the same way I feel, but I'm just starting out (like you once were) and I need to learn what a 'soldier' is."

Well, young Tom, many people, many times have tried to define "soldier." General C.T. Lanham did a real fine job with a short, beautiful poem called "Soldier" in *Infantry Journal*, way back in 1936. You got to read that. Another guy, named Herbert, I think, did a sorry job with a long, sick book called *Soldier*, just a few years ago. Some people define a soldier as a "summer chimney." And here lately, various Congresspersons have been defining a soldier as simply a "civilian equivalent."

I suppose only a fool would try to sit down and actually write out a definition of "soldier," so, I'm going to have at it—in one, sometimes-dated, often-maudlin, sentimental sentence. Here we go. A soldier is

... a boy now a man, telling his ma, and his father, and his brothers and sisters, and his girl, and his friends that he's "going in" ... a line of silent young men sitting on benches in the recruiting station ... promises of a boundless future, of stripes and bars, and education, and retirement, and medical care, and PXs and commissaries ... many forms, of many shapes and several colors, signed (right by the recruiter's "x") with little comprehension and a world of faith ... the long ride on the Greyhound, and the loud, boastful, hollow, pitiful tales of touchdowns scored, and money made, and women conquered ... a long and sleepless night in a strange hotel, in a strange town, with six men to a room, and a government-paid breakfast, and more dieselly Greyhound ... .

... the initial silence and uneasy jokes when the MP waves the bus through the gates of the first Army post ... loud sergeants with clipboards and lists of names ("You people git over there!") ... young men with special problems, trying to get an audience with authority ... the first, shattering look in the mirror after the barbers, smirking, have done their deed ... the fast flight of the "Flying $20" ... uniforms that will "shrink," or "you'll grow into" ... the consolidated mess and a new buddy on detail, scraping trays ... the first, clumsy attempts to spit-shine a boot ... the impossibility of carrying a duffle bag with the shoulder strap ... the break-up of newly-established, desperately-needed friendships ... the first ride in a covered "deuce-and-a-half," with dust rolling in over the tailgate ... .

... the company area, and "The Man," the first awkward and ragged formation, the countless and incomprehensible rules, and the fear, and the insignificance ... long rooms with posts down the center, and lined-up rows of lockers, and lined-up double-decked steel bunks with bare webs of wire springs, and lined-up, side-by-side commodes ... the schemes, arguments, threats and bargains about the relative merits of upper and lower bunks ... the cold, impersonability of supply corporals ... the haughtiness of cooks behind serving tables in the mess hall ... chronic, epidemic, unadmitted, and unmanly constipation ... sad, lonely, aching, hot and wet-eyed homesickness, and the probing flashlight of the CQ, searching for the white towels on the bed foots of the KP detail ... the quick flicker of time between Lights Out and Reveille ... the pre-dawn formation, dimly lit by 40-watt firelights, and dark shapes of men numbly silent except for shuffling feet, and sniffles, and coughs, and the hard, flat, unquestionable barks of the First Sergeant ("Not so fast there, Rodriguez!"), clipboard at the chest and pencil making checks ... .

... thighs sore from "High Jumper" ... heels and tendons aching from new boots, shoulders black and blue from the KD range ... lickin' and stickin', and Maggie's Drawers and cold, sour, smelly target paste, and constant threats, and break time pushups, and the strange, new sound—snap!—of rifle rounds passing close by overhead ... exploring the first intriguing mysteries of C-rations ... lips burnt on a hot canteen cup, sweetened with sugar dipped from a torn paper sack with a great, sticky spoon ... the search for brass in the grass, and the droning voice in the tower, and the sergeants' shiny boots, and the shiny helmets, and cleaning rods ... and raking sand, and painting rocks, and signs: "FIGHTING FIRST", "SECOND TO NONE", "DIRTY THIRD", "FEARLESS FOURTH" ... .

... the wonder, magic, and confusion of Army weapons and equipment ("Good morning, men. GOOD MORNING, SERGEANT! Today we will cover the nomenclature of the M1A1.") ... huge mock-ups, and great charts, and scratchy movies of frostbite horrors and things venereal, and sergeants' names on podiums, and officers standing in the rear by Herman Nelson ... the downright haunting beauty of Jody, sung by unseen troopers moving somewhere out in the dawn ... ("Jody's got your gal and gone") ... the joy and strength and oneness of boots pounding the pavement at a steady 180 per ... a young recruit with all his teeth pulled, and the tears in his eyes not from the pain ... sleeping on the springs with the mattress rolled, late on a Friday night ... empty boots standing side-by-side, laces tied ... unneeded razors and toothbrushes and bars of soap, all alike, lined up with a string ... stenciled names put on clothing, backwards, with too much ink ... the clink and rattle of dog tags as a thin youngster tosses in his sleep ... the thunk of a major's polished "tanker" boot striking the tailbone of a terrified trainee, crying and crawling under barbed wire and bullets ... the clenched fist and gritted teeth and animal urge to smash a fist into the face of authority ... cold, grey, November wind whipping coal smoke around the mess hall ... cold, grey fingers cleaning cold, grey grease from the mess hall sump late at night ... a box of stale and tasteless cornflakes stolen from the mess hall, smuggled under a field jacket, and devoured, symbolically, by buddies after Taps ... .

... the PX and milkshakes, and cokes, and Snicker bars ... thin stationary with black and gold Army eagles, and air mail envelopes ... long lines of young troopers by the pay phones outside ... the sissies at the Service Club ... proficiency tests, and M-1 pencils, and parades, and the silliness and impotence of pistol belts and .45s hung under too-fat officer bellies ... pictures for the family with uniform, and American flag, and a too-big hat ... the company photo with cadre in the front row, CO in the center, and the guidon ... the yearbook, the dufflebag, the AWOL bag, the spit-shined shoes, and the first leave form—signed ... .

... the strength of a mother's hug ... the wide-eyed and unashamed admiration of little brothers and sisters ... the dog, excited, peeing on the rug ... Dad, a fellow man ... home-cooking, too-much, and force-fed ... a contrived meaning for "S.O.S." ... outrageous lies, and war stories of mean sergeants, and physical agony, and special buddies ... the smooth escape of an errant four-letter adjective ... the strange feel of driving a car again ... excitement and anticipation at the sweetheart's front door ... the warmth, the wonder, the fragrance, and the dizzy feeling of the first kiss... .

... pride in the uniform, and visits to the recruiter, and favorite teachers, and coaches, and buddies, and old hangouts, and the main street ... the careful nonchalance in response to friends ("How you've changed!") ... the inexorable, too-fast passage of squares on the kitchen calendar ... the last supper, the manilla envelope with records, and orders, and last name first ... that goddamn unmanageable, awkward, sonofabitchin' dufflebag ... the late-night and last possible Greyhound ... the darkness, the sadness, the loneliness ... and the Big Dog movin' thru a rainy night ... .

... sergeants with clipboards ... classrooms and more equipment, and more charts, and officer instructors ("Remember the life you save may be your own!") and more tests ... a pay-day night on the Neon Strip, and country music, and tough women with hard eyes, and sateen skirts, and tiny, tattooed butterflies ... a fight with civilians in a parking lot ("Man, I ran away from home when I found out my mother was a civilian!") ... stompin', and kicking and slashing with antennas torn off cars, and not being able to hit a guy hard enough ... a broken nose, a black eye, a cracked tooth, scraped knuckles, and a morning hangover, and a headache, and braggin' and lying, and the melancholy of Sunday night horse cuts and beans ... .

... bulletin boards with three sections, and little lettered label signs, done by the company "artist," found by the First Sergeant ... papers posted in perfect alignment, and lined-up lists of names, and "by orders of," and fancy, affected, unreadable signatures ... and the strange mathematics of detail rosters ... morning agonies at the urinal, and disbelief, and a pre-reveille formation in raincoats only, and arms inspections and "non-specific urethritis" ... the company commander, and the First Sergeant, and the section NCO ... and the curious, ambivalent mixture of personal shame and manly pride ... loud talk, feigned unconcern, and penicillin ... .

... a Post theater graduation ceremony, with flags and "chairs, steel, folding, OD" on the stage ... a colonel reading a "speech" ... the pumping adrenaline and thundering heart of standing in line to shake hands with a general ...

the agony of trying to remember: shake with the right above (or below?); take with the left (or right?) below (or above?) ... the smile and glittering stars coming closer ... a little diploma ... an MOS, another stripe, another set of orders, and the unfathomable, omnipotent mysteries of EDCSA, and TDN, and WPOA and RPTNLT-NET, and 2172020 57-1021 P810000-2190 S36004 (812783.12001) ... .

... and again, the damnable dufflebag ... and home, and sweetheart, and time passing, and good-byes and a new Army post ... the loss of identity and significance and personal worth at the replacement depot ... the insecurity, the boredom, the telephone bargaining for "good deals" by NCOs and officers ... the new unit, and the company sign with a smaller sign beneath ("NO AWOLS IN 43 DAYS") and a brass-tip-brassoed guidon ... and outside the Orderly Room, the full length mirror with a sign on the glass ("SOLDIER, CHECK YOURSELF!") which gives the soldier personal significance and a gift of trust and confidence ... and inside the Orderly Room, another sign which takes it all away ("A UNIT DOES WELL ONLY THOSE THINGS THE BOSS CHECKS!") ... .

... reveilles, and classes, and details ... guard mounts, and guard posts, and guard paddles, and trying to surprise the O.D. on his 0300 inspection tour ... "bitch sessions" with the C.O., who calls them something else ... IG inspections, and pre-IGs, and pre-pre IGs ... officers and NCOs with endless checklists ... paint, paint, paint ... and clean, new paperwork ... and the trading value of acetate, green tape, and sheets of plywood ... long, weary hours of cleaning and shining, and extra equipment hidden in ventilator shafts ... a last-minute, high speed, tip-toe trip to a stringed-off latrine reeking with pine oil, and a quick swipe with a handkerchief at a wet dab of overlooked scouring powder ... the disappointing, anti-climatic, one simple-assed question ("Where are you from, son?") and cursory glance of the inspector ... the critique in the dayroom, and numbers, and decimals, and adjectives, and rationalizations ... and the wet handkerchief mixing company in the pocket with the broomstraw, the piece of lint, the burnt match, and the tiny paper balls of field-stripped cigarettes ... .

... convoys rolling out past the Motor Pool gates, past NCOs with clipboards, past officer jeeps with long antennae ... steady speeds, and equal distances, and lieutenants with strip maps and compasses and march tables, and hesitancy, and "route conferences" with their NCOs ... dispersed vehicles and camouflaged nets, and eyes and lips burning from grease sticks, green/brown, M1A2 ... the smell of the inside of a tent on a hot afternoon ... the whoosh and thump of immersion heaters lit off wrong by scared KPs ... lister bags and iodine water and tactical feeding ("Spread out, goddamit!") ... mermite cans with containers empty except for the yellow-green juice of now-departed peas and spinach ... the rattle of mess kits sluiced in boiling water ... NCOs checking for grease and the "hot clean" rinse ... .

... man-holes in the ground (" ... two by two by you") ... and grenade sumps, and firing steps of sand, and the strange, secret smell of deep earth ...

and little, wiggly, inch-long things with a thousand legs and pinchers ... the artful camouflage of yesterday wilted by the hot sun of today ... the difference between a straddle trench and a slit trench ... long marches at night, and red flashlights, and the unrelievable bite of shoulder straps, and feet up on packs at breaks ... and foot powder, and NCOs checking, and dark platoon leaders whispering encouragement ... the mystery, authority, and unseen strength of a jeep approaching quietly with cat-eyes ... tense, last-minute checks, and green star-clusters, and leaders shouting and cursing in the fog and half-light of dawn ... the acrid, gagging smoke of smoke grenades, the crack of M-80s ... and the whistle and boom of artillery simulators ... strange "enemy" with crests on their helmets and green uniforms with no buttons on the shirt-sleeves, running from the hill ... and "victory," and critiques, and camouflage, and range cards and marches, and rain, and wet holes ... .

... more of the same, and the passage of time, and more schools, and more promotions ... and the sweetheart now a wife, and kids, and a puppy, and fur-niture from "Sears and Rawbutt," on time ... more orders, more posts, and long moves across the land in middle-aged, middle-priced Fords and Chevys with loaded roof racks, wrapped in torn plastic, whipped by the wind ... econ-omy motels, and hamburgers, and sticky, face-down, grape-red jelly bread, and wet, smelly diapers and awful fusses, and smacked kids, and threats of divorce neither meant nor believed ... rents too high, and quarters too small, and sofa legs broken, and treasures lost, and movers anxious to leave and full of assurances ("Just sign right here") ... .

... orders to a combat zone, a move to "home," and a leave filled with sad-ness, and seriousness, and love ... good-byes at the airport, the sweet-heart wife trying to smile ... the dad, now grey, with eyes cast down, and breaking voice, and a little tremble in his chin ... the Delta bird, winging west in the late afternoon ... the sadness, the loneliness, the thoughts of little children ... and a certain thing they once said, and a certain way they once looked ... final pro-cessing at the POE, and shot records, and dog tags, and equipment checks, and the awful agony of the last stateside phone call, collect, to the kids and the sweetheart-wife ("I love you, darlin' ") ... .

... the mighty surge of the Starlifter, nose-up and tail-down from Califor-nia and west toward the sun ... a familiar face in a nearby seat, and the old, of-ten-played games of "where in the hell did we serve together?" and "did you ever know 'ole whatsisname'?" ... box lunches with boiled eggs and apples and Milky Ways, the steady drone of the big jet engines ... watch hands changed forward (or backward?) ... callous, calloused stewardesses ... and the gift shop and snack bar and men's room at Midway ... .

... a bright green land with great V-shaped fish nets in the river mouths, the blazing white of salt pans, and the curving contours of tiny rice paddies stepping down the sides of the hills ... shell craters, and bomb craters, and tracks of tracked vehicles, and grass huts, and villages, and dirt roads, and ears popping, and paved roads, and jeeps, and a helicopter, and an airfield, and the skronk! of wheels down on the Pleiku strip ... .

... the heat and the dazzle and the newness of an alien land as the door opens ... the long line of home-bound troops waiting to fill the still-warm and still-littered seats of the still-whining Starlifter ... a waiting truck, and another replacement center, and more of those phone calls (" ... but General So-and-so told me I would be assigned to ... "), and cold, impersonal briefings, and insignificance ... a long, long letter home, telling of the newness of this land, and of the loneliness, and of the love of a husband and father ... a morning formation, a list of names, a check on a roster, and a dusty road to an infantry division's base ... .

... orientations ("Don't ever pat one on the head!"), and classes, and confusion, and bewilderment, and war stories (" ... and the damned NVA cut off the lieutenant's head!"), and anticipation, and clothing and equipment issued and stored, and moves by truck, jeep, and helicopter to the forward bases of the combat units ... the battalion fire base, and the battalion commander, and the company commanders tanned, tough, and thin ... apple-cheeked lieutenants with little blond moustaches, and grizzly NCOs, and scruffy troopers laughing, joking, competent ... barbed wire, and sand bags, and artillery pieces, and radio antennae, and holes, and trenches, and bunkers ... and great, gaunt, mahogany trees torn and blasted and chain-sawed ... rucksacks, and rifles, and steel helmets and troopers reading pocket books, poorly printed ... the awe, and bewilderment, and confusion, and frustrating inability to rapidly assimilate and adapt ... .

... the chopper with no doors and no seats, on the battalion pad ... door gunners and black machine guns ... frightening speed across the roof of the jungle canopy, with tree tops blurring by ... tight, canted circles, and the whop! whop! whop! of rotor blades as the bird eases down an open shaft in the jungle ... troops on the ground, looking up, serious, busy, with longer hair, and beard stubble, and fatigue trousers split open at the rear, and no drawers ... a company commander with old-man eyes, and maturity, and authority, and strength ... a radio operator with the quick, alert look of a "college kid" ...
.

... Claymore mines, and machetes chopping brush, and troopers digging, and fresh holes in the ground, covered over with saplings and sandbags ... C-ration beans, with C-ration cheese and "Loosiana" hot sauce, warmed with heat tabs ... a coffee cup made from a partially opened can, lid bent back for a handle ... nighttime, and animal sounds, and whispers, and distant artillery, and the cold of the Central Highlands pouring down unseen into the bunkers ... fitful sleep, and soft-grey light, and dawn, and sore muscles, and cleared throats, and broken wind, and wry commentary ("Salute! Awake! Arise! And behold the birthing of a bright new day, you scroungy rat-bastards!") ... and cigarettes, and malaria pills, and hot coffee, and yawning, and scratching, and bitching ... short briefings, and Claymores packed, and sandbags emptied, and weapons checked, and a dirty column of dirty men moving out through the jungle along a mountain ridge, bent over under heavy rucksacks, eyes peering forward under the rim of steel helmets, green towel around the neck to wipe the sweat and ease the bite of shoulder straps ... fingernails black and split, sleeves rolled up, and old, nasty, dirty bandages put on by "Doc," and patches of swollen, red-brown jungle rot ... and around the trooper's neck, things hanging and swinging: dog tags and rosaries, beads and can openers, crosses and bandoliers ... and on his head, the steel, with its camouflage cover the billboard whereon he proclaims his individuality, with names and words of wisdom and wit, and fear, and hope, and love ... JESUS ... JANET ... MOM AND POP ... FTA ... HO CHI MIN IS A ROTTEN BASTARD ... SHORTIMER ... COLOR ME GONE ... GOD MUST LOVE ENLISTED MEN 'CAUSE HE MADE SO MANY OF 'EM ... .

... the column moving forward along the ridge ... near the rear, a shortimer, afraid to be up where contacts are made, afraid to be back where folks get left, and lost ... near the center, the CO and his shadow and bunkermate, the radio operator, both mindful of the stories of snipers in trees, and CO's shot square between the eyes, falling, staring, without a word ... and up front and out alone, all by himself, the pointman, moving down the ridge with raw courage, and the sure knowledge that sooner or later some pointman would be in the sights of an NVA weapon ... and the young, lanky, flat-nosed, white-eyed black whose skill and courage as point was legendary ("Man, 'day calls 'dat cat 'de 'Cat'!"), and who time and again volunteered to walk in other men's boots ... .

... and late afternoon with a final halt, and bunkers dug, and trip flares out, and trees blown down to let choppers in ... the distant throb of a gas-turbined Huey, the vulnerable belly now overhead, and the whop! whop! whop! and the whap! whap! whap! of careful descent as the bird settles and squats among the holes and splintered stumps ... dirt, and paper, and maps, and leaves, and ponchos, and green t-shirts whirling everywhere, and the angry, nervous voice of the pilot ("6, this is Ghostrider ... will you clean that goddamn crap off the pad?") ... a trooper with all his gear jumping from the skids and running to the edge of the pad, bent low with one hand on his steel ... boxes of banded C's with half-moons on the side, and demolitions, and chain saws, and rope, and a case of beer, and a box of grenades, and great, big, orange bags of ... mail! ... and letters, and longing, and a little boy in an Easter suit ... .

... and another night, and another day, and many more just the same— curious blends of monotony and tension and physical exertion and a special sort of discipline marked not by shined shoes and short hair and salutes, but by proficiency and dependability and automatic habits of combat never learned in school ... .

... the moving column, and the noonday break, the cold C's lunch, and the CO with his boots off and his feet in the sun ... the powerful, pungent, scrungy, skanky smell of feet and socks too long together ... and rucks up once again on bent, young backs, and jungle boots and jungle fatigues down a jungle trail ... and way up front, the sounds of contact ... at first, tentative, like firecrackers on the 4th ... and then the staccato bursts, and the thumps of

grenades, and the building crescendo ... excited voices on the radio ("John, get the hell up here!") ... men dropping to their knees, rolling out of their rucksacks, and moving forward behind NCOs ... a helicopter overhead, suddenly on the scene, whopping and circling ... the gradual fade of the fire to the front, and troops squatted down, looking around, alert and afraid and big-eyed and ready ... the CO on the radio ("Ranger, this is 6 ... 3 NVA in a bunker ... killed 2 ... we got one KIA ... request Dust-off to take him out.") ... .

... dead little men in khaki clothes, and entrenching tools with whittled handles, and short black hair, and too-big helmets and too-long belts ... troopers searching for pistols, and papers, and insignia, and souvenirs ... splotches of fresh red blood on the ground, and on the bushes, leading down the hill ... a Dust-off bird hovering up above the jungle canopy, with its winch cable hanging down to the ground ... the lifeless body of the young black pointman, lifting and turning slowly up into the bird, web straps under arms, head hanging down, feet together ... .

... a spooky night, and deeper holes, and more flares, and more alertness, and the deafening, splitting crack of protective artillery registering nearby ... and briefings, and patrols, and excited reports of fresh tracks, and new commo wire, and recently-emptied enemy holes, and seven NVA seen running down a trail ... another company comin' in, and more trip flares, and Claymores and concertina, and artillery pieces slung under big, fat, bug-eyed Hookbirds, and helicopters, and colonels, and conferences on stumps and ammo boxes ... and all night long, the rumbling thunder of the great Arclights out across the valley, ripping life and limbs and sap from trees and men ... .

... a huge, jolting explosion close by, then more, then the firecracker sounds, and flashes everywhere in the pre-dawn dark ... all around, the snap! snap! snapsnapsnap! and the whir and whack of frags ... men running, and yelling, and some already groaning, and flares popping up above ... the blue fireballs of NVA tracers, moving slowly at first, then zipping by ... small dark figures coming forward, in ones and twos, up the hill, outside the wire ... and into the wire, and through the wire, and into the bunkers ... and fire, and explosions, and the trembling earth, and dust, and great geysers of dirt, and boards, and boxes, and bodies, flying through the air ... .

... and on the radios, the fear and the fire and the fury ("Ranger! Ranger! My eyes ... I'm hit ... I can't see! ... please ... somebody help ... I can't see") ... ("This is 6 ... the little sonofabitches are up on the artillery bunkers ... beehive the bastards!") ... ("Grenadier, we got an awful fight going ... I need all available air strikes ... right now ... get me nape and CBU") ... ("81, 6, get that damn company moving and get up here ... we got 'em in our bunkers!") ... ("Jesus Christ! They're coming up behind us! ... they're goin' to cut us off!") ... ("John, the CO's hit bad ... send a medic and ammo ... over by my bunker") ... ("Where in the hell is that rocket fire coming from?") ... ("Ranger ... we got to pull back from our bunkers ... I've still got some wounded there, but the little bastards are all over us ... I can't hold on here.") ... ("81, 6, goddamnit, where are you?") ... ("Ranger ... whop! whop! whop! ... this is Big Daddy ... whop! whop! whop! ... what is your present situation?") ... ("3, I *know* we've got wounded in there—now put the goddamn Redleg right on the goddamn bunkerline! VT ... *Now*, goddamnit!") ... ("This is Tonto ... I can't see your firebase ... it's all fire and smoke and dust ... Jesus!") ... ("82, 6! 82, 6!") ... ("Hummingbird, can you run that air right across the end of the gun-target line? ... that's where the little bastards are.") ... ("This is Grenadier ... we've got two companies airborne and proceeding to your location ... where can we put them in?") ... ("26 Alpha, we got to have ammo! ASAP!") ... ("Pete, see if you can move those wounded up behind the CP") ... ("Jesus Christ! They got a flame thrower!") ... ("81, 6, I moved the Redleg ... now work your way down the bunker line ... lot of 'em in there ... be careful!") ... ("6! 6! They're right in the next bunker! ... they killed Jackson!") ... ("3, Alpha's hit in the belly, but he's still sitting there running air strikes ... ") ... ("Ghostrider, goddamn you got guts ... if you can't see the pad, can you see our flag? ... drop the ammo right on it!") ... ("Well, kill the little bastard if he's in there!") ... ("Ranger, they're pullin' back!") ... .

... and on and on through the grim hours, with the noise, and the snaps, and the whirs, and the whacks, and the yelling, and the thunder, and the fire, and the smoke, and the dust, and the troopers darting and crawling, and throwing; the shooting, and cussing, and dying, and bleeding ... and the big Phantom birds screaming down behind the hill to lay their nape ... and the artillery pounding steady ... and the fingers of a dead trooper slowly growing stiff as his hoping, hoping buddy holds his hand ... .

... and dawn at last, and exhaustion, and relief, and "victory" ... and the grotesque, everywhere clusters of ragged dead enemy outside and inside the wire ... and big Tiny crushed under fallen timbers in a bunker ... and 'ole Smitty, who honestly enlisted to fight a second time for his country, lying there trembling, with one eye gone and his hand reaching out ... and the handsome recon platoon leader, "Steve the Stud," blown to hell by a rocket ... him and his Doc, too, when the final reserve of medics and radio operators and the headquarters guys had gone, without question, to help Company D ... and the strange smell of belly wounds, and all the bloody bandages ... and all the dead troopers silent and still under ponchos, lined up—for the last time—on a ragged line of litters by the pad ... .

... and shot-up companies dragging their weary, wore-out asses aboard the birds ... and the rear area, the rest and refit ... and more of the same ... jungle and rain, and mines, and ambushed convoys, and the red dust and tall bamboo of Pleiku, and Dak Pek, and Dak To ... assault helicopters on short final, the artillery shifted, the firecracker sounds down below on a hot LZ, the gunships making their staccato runs, and scared, grim troopers, weapons ready, beads dangling, sitting in the open doors of another chopper flying right alongside ... .

... and still more, day after day with time growing short, and odds running out, and buddies dead or med-evacked ... and night patrols, and fire bases, and combat assaults, and the always-dreaded shout ("Incoming!") ... and captured NVA with *Time* magazine articles ... and the splendid victory of Tet, with hundreds of NVA lying scattered in heaps and wide rows outside Kontum, where the deadly gunships had caught them coming, uncharacteristically, across open rice paddies in broad daylight (" ... they was all doped up and goin' to a party ... musta been ... crazy little bastards ...") ... and the victory strangely, puzzlingly, lost, somehow, somewhere, up in the air waves of the ten thousand miles between Kontum and home ... .

... and "the Day," suddenly here, and the quick good-byes, and shucked equipment, and that 'ole steel helmet, and the beat-up, never failing submachine gun ... the relief, the peace, the sense of completion ... the fire base, the base camp, the strange feel of pavement ... and the hot, hot shower with gallons and gallons and gallons of water ... and great, long, deep hours of untroubled, buck-naked, spread-eagled, flat-backed, mouth-agoggled sleep ... .

... a dusty, mildewed, khaki uniform, unworn for a year and still starched, drawers, *white* ones, and a too-big belt ... a handful of treasures from the PX, a black-faced Seiko, a footlocker, that damned dufflebag, and a set of orders ... .

... Nha Trang, and the Starlifter once more, and blue water down below, and great thunderheads up above, and a hundred quiet sleeping men, and Midway, and Stateside, and cars, and neon lights ... the worry about not enough seats on the eastbound plane, the ticket, the lift-off, the shunting aside of attempted conversations, the building anticipation and excitement, the ache in the loins, the pictures and thoughts running thru a dozing mind, trained to stay half-awake ... .

... Kansas City, and St. Louis, and Atlanta ("Man, if you die and go to hell, you gotta change in Atlanta!") ... and the skronk, and the bags, and the cab, and the street, and the house... .

... shrieking, flying, socks-down children, and screen doors banging, and khaki knees in the grass, and somehow, four little, precious people held close and tight and fiercely and long ... and a tired head, with a little grey, pressed into soft tummies, and filled with nothing but boundless joy ... and big brown eyes, with tears ... and once again, as years ago, the warmth, the wonder, the softness, the fragrance, the dizzy feeling of the first kiss ... .

... unintelligible, excited, simultaneously-jabbered stories of school, and scouts, and drum majorettes, and the neighbor's dog ... the treasures from the distant PX ... a supper of who knows who cares what, and more talk, and bedtime, and kids asleep, and an endless night of soft talk, and moonlight, and touches, and sweet tears of thankfulness, and the pent-up love of a thousand thoughts and dreams ... .

... a clear blue morning, and a bright yellow school bus, and an apple-green housecoat, and hot black coffee ... elbows up on the kitchen table, and the first, tentative plans for the next duty station and the next move ... and ... and if all these wondrous things, which thousands of us share in whole or in part, can—by some mindless "logic" of a soul-less computer programmed by a witless pissant ignorant of affect—be called "just another job," then I'm a sorry, suck-egg mule.

Tom, my friend, that's the best I can do ... .

by Colonel Dandridge M. Malone

G.I.s

As Chairman of the Joint Chiefs of Staff, I referred to the men and women of the armed forces as "G.I.s." It got me in trouble with some of my colleagues at the time. Several years earlier, the Army had officially excised the term as an unfavorable characterization derived from the designation "government issue."

Sailors and Marines wanted to be known as sailors and Marines. Airmen, notwithstanding their origins as a rib of the Army, wished to be called simply airmen. Collectively, they were blandly referred to as "service members."

I persisted in using G.I.s and found I was in good company. Newspapers and television shows used it all the time. The most famous and successful government education program was known as the G.I. Bill, and it still uses that title for a newer generation of veterans. When you added one of the most common boy's names to it, you got G.I. Joe, and the name of the most popular boy's toy ever, the G.I. Joe action figure. And let's not forget G.I. Jane. G.I. is a World War II term that two generations later continues to conjure up the warmest and proudest memories of a noble war that pitted pure good against pure evil and good triumphed.

The victors in that war were the American G.I.s, the Willies and Joes, the farmer from Iowa and the steelworker from Pittsburgh who stepped off a landing craft into the hell of Omaha Beach. The G.I. was the wisecracking kid Marine from Brooklyn who clawed his way up a deadly hill on a Pacific island.

He was a black fighter pilot escorting white bomber pilots over Italy and Germany, proving that skin color had nothing to do with skill or courage. He was a native Japanese-American infantryman released from his own country's concentration camp to join the fight. She was a nurse relieving the agony of a dying teenager. He was a petty officer standing on the edge of a heaving aircraft carrier with two signal paddles in his hands, helping guide a dive-bomber pilot back onto the deck. They were America.

They reflected our diverse origins. They were the embodiment of the American spirit of courage and dedication. They were truly a "people's army," going forth on a crusade to save democracy and freedom, to defeat tyrants, to save oppressed peoples and to make their families proud of them. They were the Private Ryans, and they stood firm in the thin red line. For most of those G.I.s, World War II was the adventure of their lifetime. Nothing they would ever do in the future would match their experiences as the warriors of democracy, saving the world from its own insanity. You can still see them in every Fourth of July color guard, their gait faltering but ever proud.

Their forebears went by other names: doughboys, Yanks, buffalo soldiers, Johnny Reb, Rough Riders. But "G.I." will be forever lodged in the consciousness of our nation to apply to them all. The G.I. carried the value system of the American people. The G.I.s were the surest guarantee of America's commitment. For more than 200 years, they answered the call to fight the nation's battles. They never went forth as mercenaries on the road to conquest. They went forth as reluctant warriors, as citizen soldiers. They were as gentle in victory as they were vicious in battle.

I've had survivors of Nazi concentration camps tell me of the joy they experienced as the G.I.s liberated them: America had arrived! I've had a wealthy Japanese businessman come into my office and tell me what it was like for him as a child in 1945 to await the arrival of the dreaded American beasts, and instead meet a smiling G.I. who gave him a Hershey bar. In thanks, the businessman was donating a large sum of money to the USO. After thanking him, I gave him as a souvenir a Hershey bar I had autographed. He took it and began to cry. The 20th century can be called many things, but it was most certainly a century of war. The American G.I.s helped defeat fascism and communism. They came home in triumph from the ferocious battlefields of World Wars I and II.

In Korea and Vietnam they fought just as bravely as any of their predecessors, but no triumphant receptions awaited them at home. They soldiered on through the twilight struggles of the cold war and showed what they were capable of in Desert Storm. The American people took them into their hearts again.

In this century hundreds of thousands of G.I.s died to bring to the beginning of the 21st century the victory of democracy as the ascendant political system on the face of the earth. The G.I.s were willing to travel far away and give their lives, if necessary, to secure the rights and freedoms of others. Only a nation such as ours, based on a firm moral foundation, could make such a request of its citizens. And the G.I.s wanted nothing more than to get the job done and then return home safely. All they asked for in repayment from those they freed was the opportunity to help them become part of the world of democracy—and just enough land to bury their fallen comrades, beneath simple white crosses and Stars of David. The volunteer G.I.s of today stand watch in Korea, the Persian Gulf, Europe and the dangerous terrain of the Balkans. We must never see them as mere hirelings, off in a corner of our society. They are our best, and we owe them our full support and our sincerest thanks.

As this century closes, we look back to identify the great leaders and personalities of the past 100 years. We do so in a world still troubled, but full of promise. That promise was gained by the young men and women of America who fought and died for freedom. Near the top of any listing of the most important people of the 20th century must stand, in singular honor, the American G.I.

General Colin Luther Powell
former Chairman of the Joint Chiefs,
now chairman of America's Promise
1937–
Army General, Desert Storm

IF WILDFLOWERS CAN SPRING
FROM VERDUN

Almost exactly four years ago, my wife and I, with our two-year-old daughter in tow, found ourselves on a terrible battleground.

The three of us were living in Germany, where I was stationed in the Army, and we had just spent Thanksgiving weekend in Paris. On the way back to our home in Germany, back to my job in a profession that must inevitably concern itself with preparations for war, my wife and I decided to make a side trip to a place whose name is forever linked to war, a name which resonates as an evocation of Europe's peculiar capacity for self-immolation: the World War I battleground of Verdun.

It is a place where the French in 1916 said of the advancing Germans, "They shall not pass." And the Germans did not, although it took something on the order of 600,000 lives to enforce that edict.

For the first time all weekend, as we drove back across the empty French countryside, the weather turned for the worse—so much so, with its rain and cold black winds, that we considered foregoing this side trip. But the chilly rain that would complicate the logistics of the visit had the additional effect of painting the area in an appropriately somber hue. So as we left the auto route and worked our way toward the battlefield my wife, Merrie, and I remarked at how "right" the day seemed—how much it cohered with the pictures our minds had always drawn of trench warfare and unfathomable carnage.

Our map led us to a corner of the battleground into which the war had concentrated particular ferocity, past hillsides carpeted with tiny crosses, to a monument which has acquired a unique status in the French psyche. It is called the Trench of Bayonets and marks the spot in the fortifications where more than 100 French infantrymen, formed up for an assault with fixed bayonets, were buried when the bunker they were massed took a direct artillery hit. Only the bayonets and the ends of the rifle muzzles were visible above the tons of muddy earth that had entombed the men.

After the battle, the French government decided that rather than exhuming the bodies, it would memorialize them where and how they had died— essentially the same way the American government, a generation later, would choose to honor the sailors of the U.S.S. *Arizona* at Pearl Harbor.

The bayonets are gone now, removed by museums and pothunters or reduced by time and the elements, but the long, low mound of dirt that filled in the trench is still spiked with the rifle muzzles, and with tiny crosses and tricolor ribbons and flowers. There is no grass. A stone memorial covers the trench, just a foot or two above the earth; its function is doubtless to protect the site from the weather, but its form works to hallow the ground. Visitors, consequently, must get down on their knees—an entirely appropriate posture—to see the trench. And this Merrie and I did, for several minutes. On this cold, wet November day, we were the only people there.

And then we both noticed, at about the same time, a faint murmuring behind us. We turned to see our daughter, Caitlin, toddling about, 20 feet or so from the memorial and utterly oblivious to its existence. She was softly singing to herself, while bending over, from time to time, to pick at the stray wildflowers—yellow and white and pale violet—which were hugging the hillside above the trench, and which were somehow responding to an impulse toward growth and procreation here on the cusp of winter, here in this place of death.

It arrested us immediately—a scene of great slaughter, a piece of ground consecrated by an accident of grim fate and by a gesture of national consciousness, a patch of earth adrift in a sea flecked with crosses—and at its epicenter, a little girl picking flowers.

Caitlin's act was certainly not part of the consecration, yet in a very real sense it validated that consecration—it further hallowed the ground. It did so precisely because this very typical little girl could just sing and pick flowers on land that had been so bitterly fought over, so bathed in blood. And because the flowers themselves, springing from an earth that has had over 50 uninterrupted years now to heal itself from the scorchings of the past, are also part of that reconsecration.

And now, four years later, even the people of the Balkans, that tortured corner of Europe where World War I ignited itself, are stumbling, ever so uncertainly and reluctantly, toward a peace of their own. Even these tentative steps would not be possible if not for the assured presence of thousands upon thousands of young American men and women. Like their fathers and grandfathers before them, who themselves ventured to Europe in 1917 and in 1944, these soldiers are not conquerors, but—and we can use this word now without a trace of cynicism or hypocrisy—peacekeepers.

The undeniable truth is that one cannot walk across Europe's battlefields without acknowledging that American soldiers—for whom conquest has never been a mission—have brought the Old World a greater measure of peace than it has ever known.

Perhaps the reach of their noble efforts can extend even so far as the genocidal Balkans. If wildflowers can spring from the slaughter-pen of Verdun, if that blood-soaked soil can see the day when it suffers no greater violence than from the pluckings of a little girl, then surely we can dare to dream of that possibility.

> Major Christopher Riley, 1997
> Originally printed in the newspaper,
> the *Iowa View*

HIS DEGREE OF ACCEPTANCE

The American soldier is a product of American society, and the Army is a microcosm of the population as a whole. Because of the nature of the Army's mission, the soldier is especially selected for physical and mental ability. He is, in this sense, an above-average citizen rather than an average one. The prestige of the soldier's job reflects this.

The American soldier is also affected by some of the differences between Army organizations and civilian life. Especially important are the system of rank and the comradeship of life among fellow soldiers. On the other hand, the Army is following the same trends in bureaucratic organizations and technological advancement as the country as a whole. The American soldier, however, differs from his national culture in his degree of acceptance of authority and patriotism.

> From the book *Taking Command*, 1967,
> by the United States Military Academy
> Office of Military Psychology and
> Leadership

AN AFFAIR OF THE HEART

Army Chief of Staff General Eric K. Shinseki
Address to the Eisenhower Luncheon
45th Annual Meeting of the Association of the United States Army
October 12, 1999, Washington D.C.
(As prepared for presentation)

[Excerpts (closing remarks)]

We are about leadership; it is our stock in trade, and it is what makes us different. We take soldiers who enter the force, and we grow them into leaders for the next generation of soldiers. Our soldiers provide back to America a corps of leaders who have a tremendous work ethic, who have a strong sense of values, who treat others with dignity and respect, who are accustomed to hard work, who are courageous, who thrive on responsibility, who know how to build and motivate teams, and who are positive role models for all around them. We provide this opportunity to American youth so that we can keep our Nation strong and competitive, and enable it to fulfill its leadership role in the community of nations. We invest today in the Nation's leadership for tomorrow.

General Shinseki

In providing this strategic edge to the Nation, we are, we have been, and we will remain a values-based institution where loyalty, duty, respect, selfless service, honor, integrity, and personal courage are the cornerstone of all that we do today and all of our future successes. Our soldiers, who exemplify these values every day, are the very best in the world; they voluntarily forego comfort and wealth, face hardship and sacrifice, confront danger and sometimes death in defense of the Nation. We owe them our unwavering support, our professional excellence, and our resolute pursuit of this vision to ensure that they remain the world's finest land force for the next crisis, the next war, and an uncertain future.

Throughout it all, soldiering will remain an affair of the heart—-it has always been that way and always will be. Soldiering will always be an affair of the heart.

THANKSGIVING IN BOSNIA, 1999

Dear Friends and Family,

Greetings from Bosnia and Happy Thanksgiving!

The soldiers here are enjoying a Thanksgiving Feast common throughout the Army on this special day. The Army tradition is to lighten the soldier's ruck sacks and duties—-and lay out a spread that surpasses any Thanksgiving meal you have ever seen. As we all take time out for this great American tradition, I thought you'd like to know how truly fortunate we are in Bosnia.

We are celebrating a feast of plenty here that our Russian allies can hardly believe—-and we see them by the dozens enjoying the day with us. This great country has much to be thankful for that the Russian soldiers can only dream about—-our wealth and bountiful food supply. To the Russian soldiers, an assignment to Multi-National Division (North) is a dream come true. Here they eat all they want, 24 hours a day, with a wide selection of drinks and menu choices. At an average meal, there are six or more main entree selections, plenty of side selections, and abundant sweets/pastries. We have a well stocked Post Exchange that tops any store in Russia. The Russians are particularly enamored with Old Spice after shave. And if the Exchange doesn't have something, just about anything can be ordered and shipped reliably and quickly. Unlike our Russian allies, we have all the latest high quality military "snivel" gear to keep us dry and warm. We have Gore-Tex coats, trousers, boots and sleeping bags. We have Kevlar helmets and protective vests. We have the best, most reliable and lethal small arms money can buy. Our HMMWV is the envy of the world—-it gets us anywhere we need to go safely and with power to spare.

We sleep in containers or small buildings with heaters and air conditioners. We have two television stations that broadcast a wide variety of sports, news and network programs. We have the Internet. We have unrestricted water and hot showers. We have fitness centers and gymnasiums with the latest workout equipment aplenty. We have a movie theater, pizza place and Burger King. We have an education center that helps soldiers get their GED and offers a variety of college courses. We have a spartan hospital that offers every required specialty and high quality medical care, along with a dental clinic that even offers cleanings. We have reliable mail service, free laundry service, and other services that make life as good as it can get.

The only thing our soldiers do not have is freedom to roam the country, drink alcohol and have the presence of our loved ones—-a small sacrifice for all the things we do have. Our soldiers are well armed and disciplined. More than any other factor, the U.S. Army has brought peace to the Balkans. We are not viewed as an "Army of Occupation," rather as guarantors of stability and peace. The savagery of war is gone, replaced with hope. The soldiers are glad to serve, and proud to be Americans.

Happy Thanksgiving and thanks to all for your continued support!

Warm Regards,
MAJ Jim Stockmoe
Eagle Base, Tuzla
Bosnia-Herzegovina, 1999

CHAPTER EIGHT

Leadership and Character

Good character provides leaders a platform from which to operate. This chapter combines the topics of leadership and character into one because of the interdependence of each on the other. This chapter also supports the notion that the principals of leadership have always been, and remain, an intensively human process, a process tied to every dimension of human emotions.

Leadership is character in action.

The Noncommissioned Officer's Guide, 1948

Leadership is intangible, and therefore no weapon ever designed can replace it.

General Omar Bradley

We must possess a set of values that instinctively guide our decisions.

General Edward C. Meyer

What lies behind us and what lies before us are small matters compared to what lies within us.

Oliver Wendell Holmes
1841–1935
American Jurist

LET THEM COME ON!

There is an interesting story about General Washington when he took command of the Continental Army at the beginning of the American Revolution. There was an immediate need for that Army. But what General Washington found at Cambridge, Massachusetts was a rather ragged body of soldiers. Some wore uniforms, others multicolored clothing from a variety of sources. Some carried guns, others sticks. Still others held farm tools. A few gripped ancient swords. In particular, there was a regiment from Connecticut that looked pretty bad. Peter Marshall, former chaplain to the United States Senate, once wrote about what General Washington saw:

The men were few ... badly armed ... and poorly dressed. They did not even stand at attention. Their ranks were ragged and they had the air of discouragement. Many of them were hungry and had gone without a decent meal for days on end.

Some were lame. They were a sorry lot. Yet when the regiment was drawn up for Washington to inspect them, the great general stood erect and, looking at them as if they were in the finest regiment in the world, he said:

"Gentleman, I have great confidence in the men of Connecticut."

Reenactment of Revolutionary War drill   Patriots then and now

One of the soldiers writing home to his family said in a letter, "When I heard Washington say that, I clasped my musket to my breast and said to myself, 'Let them come on.' "

This story illustrates a unique quality: Given the challenge, proper recognition, and sound leadership, the American soldier will have pride, endure any hardship, and undergo any sacrifice in the cause of freedom and service to country.

The worth of a state, in the long run,
is the worth of the individuals composing it.

John Stuart
1806–1873
English Philosopher and Economist

The true test of civilization is, not the census,
nor the size of cities, nor the crops—no,
but the kind of man the country turns out.

Ralph Waldo Emerson

You may be whatever you
resolve to be.

General
Stonewall Jackson

A man of character in peace is a man of courage in war. ... One does not develop character in the heat of battle or a moment of crisis. Character grows out of the steady application of moral values and ethical behavior in one's life.

General John A. Wickham, Jr.

To win, we must have leaders and commanders with fire in their bellies.

General William E. DePuy

Nations have passed away and left no traces, and history gives the naked cause to it—one single, simple reason in all cases; they fell because their people were not fit.

Rudyard Kipling
1865–1936

The heart and soul of the soldier is the key.

Ardant Du Picq

Nothing in the world can take the place of persistence. Talent will not; nothing is more common than unsuccessful men with talent. Genius will not; unrewarded genius is almost a proverb. Education will not; the world is full of educated derelicts. Persistence and determination alone are omnipotent. The slogan "press on" has solved and always will solve the problems of the human race.

Calvin Coolidge
1872–1933
30th President of the United States
(1923–1929)

General Pershing

A competent leader can get efficient service from poor troops; while, on the contrary, an incapable leader can demoralize the best of troops.

General John J. "Blackjack" Pershing
from *My Experiences in the World War*
Volume 1, 1931

Your company will be a reflection of yourself. If you have a rotten company, it's because you are a rotten captain.

Major Christian Bach

The ultimate measure of a man is not where he stands in moments of comfort and convenience, but where he stands at times of challenge and controversy.

Author Unknown

I WILL BE THERE

In the Normandy invasion, a young commander of paratroopers, Lieutenant Colonel Edward S. Krause, was given the task of capturing the main enemy communications center, the French town of Saint Mere Eglise. Three hours before the take-off he assembled his battalion, held a small American flag in front of them, and said:

This was the first flag raised over the city of Naples.
YOU PUT IT THERE.
I want it to be the first flag raised over a
liberated town in France.
The mission is that we will put it up in
Saint Mere Eglise before dawn.
YOU HAVE ONLY ONE ORDER—
TO COME AND FIGHT WITH ME
WHEREVER YOU LAND.
WHEN YOU GET TO SAINT MERE EGLISE,
I WILL BE THERE!

U.S. Army Paratroopers   World War II

CHARACTERISTICS OF LEADERSHIP

You have to lead men in war by bringing them along to endure and display qualities of fortitude that are beyond the average man's thought of what he should be expected to do. You have to inspire them when they are hungry and exhausted and desperately uncomfortable and in great danger. Only a man of positive characteristics of leadership with the physical stamina that goes with it can function under those conditions.

General George C. Marshal

The soldier is a man; he expects to be treated as an adult, not a schoolboy. He has rights; they must be made known to him and thereafter respected. He has ambition; it must be stirred. He has a belief in fair play; it must be honored. He has a need of comradeship; it must be supplied. He has imagination; it must be stimulated. He has pride; it can be satisfied and made the bedrock of character once he has been assured that he is playing a useful and respected role. To give a man this is the acme of inspired leadership. He has become loyal because loyalty has been given to him.

When all are tired, cold, and hungry at the end of the day, it is the leader who puts aside his personal discomfort to look to the needs of his soldiers.

It is not enough to fight, it is the spirit we bring to the fight that decides the issue.

General George C. Marshall

*Leadership in a democratic Army means firmness,
not harshness; understanding, not weakness; justice,
not license; humaneness, not intolerance; generosity,
not selfishness; pride, not egotism.*

General Omar Bradley

The only safe ship in a storm is leadership.

Faye Wattleton

*Commanders and their staffs should visit units two
echelons below their own. The more senior the officer
who appears with a very small unit at the front,
the better the effect on the troops. If some danger
is involved in the visit, its value is enhanced.*

General George S. Patton, Jr.

As Good As You Are

On July 7, 1944, in Normandy, France then-Colonel Robert H. York took command of the 331st Infantry Regiment of the 83rd Division. COL York was already a veteran of 11 major battle engagements and had fought in three D-Day landings at Oran, Sicily, and Omaha Beach, heading an infantry battalion of the First Division. At 32, he became one of the youngest Regimental Commanders in the Army.

Prior to his taking command, the 331st had been completely demoralized, having lost six regimental commanders in the first thirty days of combat, two killed, two relieved, and two replaced—and having suffered heavy casualties in their first engagement after landing on Omaha Beach (over 1,100 enlisted and 100 officers). Once in command COL York's leadership transformed the 331st Infantry into a hard-hitting unit that went on to fight victoriously in five major campaigns in France, Luxemburg, Belgium, and Germany to establish a bridgehead across the Elbe River, 65 miles from Berlin, two weeks before V-E (Victory in Europe) Day. The esprit de corps that prevailed in the 331st with York's leadership was unprecedented. In a matter of weeks his soldiers followed him in devoted admiration and respect.

How did he do this?

His soldiers witnessed York's genuine concern for their safety and well-being. His soldiers knew him by name; they saw him visiting each and every battalion headquarters and company; they knew he was extremely loyal to his subordinates; they knew he was brave and spent most of every day with attacking battalions and companies, generally where the action was the toughest.

One particular incident provides a good example of COL York's respect for the individual soldier. Early one morning a private, who had just returned from a patrol into enemy lines, was giving COL York a report. An officer kept butting in trying to speak to the Colonel. Colonel York kept telling the Lieutenant to wait. After getting the information from the private, Colonel York took the officer into the battalion headquarters tent and gave him a lesson in military courtesy. The radio operator on duty only heard the opening remarks—

"Who do you think you are? ... That private is as good a human being as you are! ..."

William Coffey

[Derived from oral history interviews conducted by the U.S. Army War College.]

U.S. Soldiers   World War II, Pacific Theater

U.S. Soldier
World War II,
European Theater

The Other 99

We hear about the clever man—the man who leads the line,
But seldom do we hear about—the other ninety-nine;
The men who bravely battle in—a world of enterprise,
Who form the steppingstones on which—the clever man may rise.
The wheel of life is not cast—that issues from the mould;
On each small part depends the heart—
which hath the greater hold;
The outer pinion may revolve—
and glisten in the sun,
But it's the oil-stained cogs beneath—
on which these pinions run.
Each man has got his part to play—each man can hope to shine,
But he who leads, most surely needs—the other ninety-nine.

Author Unknown

The Final Test

*The final test of a leader is that he leaves behind him
in other men the conviction and the will to carry on.*

Walter Lippmann
New York Herald Tribune,
April 14, 1945

THE MAN IN THE ARENA

It is not the critic who counts, not the man who points out how the strong man stumbled or where the doer of deeds could have done better. The credit belongs to the man who is actually in the arena; whose face is marred by dust and sweat and blood; who strives valiantly; who errs and comes short again and again ... who knows the great enthusiasms, the great devotion, and spends himself in a worthy cause; who at the least knows in the end the triumph of high achievement; and who, at the worst, if he fails, at least fails while doing greatly, so that his place shall never be with those cold and timid souls who know neither victory nor defeat.

Theodore Roosevelt
from a speech delivered at the Sorbonne, Paris
April 23, 1910

U.S. Soldier
World War II

GENERAL GEORGE PATTON—
COMBAT LEADER

In 1943, when Major General DeWitt C. Smith Jr. was a newly commissioned lieutenant, he began his World War II experience in Europe as an armored infantry rifle platoon leader and company commander in the 4th Armored Division. In campaigns extending from Normandy to Czechoslovakia, he served mainly with spearhead elements of General Patton's Third Army, including the relief of Bastogne. During the course of the war, Lieutenant Smith had several opportunities to observe General Patton, hear him speak, ponder his teachings, and receive the inspiration of his leadership. On 18 October 1979, on the occasion of a lecture at Carlisle Barracks by Mr. Martin Blumenson on the subject of General Patton's leadership, Major General Smith recorded his personal recollections of the particular traits and techniques of leadership displayed by General Patton during the Allies' historic march through the German heartland over 35 years before:

- General Patton was visible; he showed himself to his men.

- He gathered units and groups of men together whenever possible and spoke to them.

- He spent much more time praising and rewarding his soldiers than in finding fault.

- He defended his soldiers and his units to all the rest of the world.

- He decentralized soldiering in peacetime and fighting in wartime to his subordinate commanders, thus building their self-confidence, allowing them maximum freedom for initiative, and giving them the satisfaction that comes from responsibility. Along with this, he gave them the tools to do the job.

- He engaged personally in teaching and training his men.

- He turned administration over to his staff (as was always clear), saving his own time for reflecting, training, leading, and exhorting.

- He emphasized color, tradition, esprit, and unit cohesiveness.

- Through his major subordinates, he saw that the troops knew what was going on.

- He insisted on tough discipline in combat as well as training, with particular emphasis on personal cleanliness, appearance, and behavior, and maintenance of weapons and equipment.

- His combat tactics, capitalizing on speed and aggressiveness, were aimed at winning quickly, thus saving lives.

[Source: US Army War College Memorandum (Office of the Commandant), subject: Techniques of Leadership—General George Patton, dated 19 October 1979]

TAKE THAT HILL

No leader ever managed a unit up to take a hill, ... they were led there.

General Nathan Forrest
1821–1877
Confederate Army

Ability and Interest

During World War II the Army interviewed thousands of soldiers to get their ideas on leadership. The top two qualities men thought good leaders should have are ability, and interest in the welfare of the men.

*Handbook and Manual
for the Noncommissioned Officer*
1952

The Distinction

*Character is the direct result of mental attitude.
I believe that character is higher than the intellect.
I believe that leadership is in sacrifice, in self-denial,
in humility and in the perfectly disciplined will.
This is the distinction between great and little men.*

Vince Lombardi

*Even with the gifts of human understanding and of
professional competence arising from careful training,
our military leader will not be complete without the
third attribute of greatness; namely, character—
character which reflects inner strength and
justifies confidence in oneself.*

General Maxwell D. Taylor

*When supported with education,
a person's integrity can give
him something to rely on
when his perspective seems to blur,
when rules and principles
seem to waver, and when
he's faced with hard choices
of right or wrong.
It's something to keep him
on the right track,
something to keep him
afloat when he's drowning.*

Admiral James Stockdale

THOSE WHO MUST WIN YOUR BATTLES

Discussions of leadership are apt to dwell upon such
people as George Washington and Robert E. Lee
and George Patton and Admiral Nelson and
Admiral Nimitz and General Doolittle.
Not many of us need to prepare for their jobs.
The leader I prefer to consider is the sergeant who must
get his squad up a knife-edged ridge to an enemy
bunker; the commander of a small craft who must
cross a reef and touch down exactly in the right spot on
a blazing beach; the airplane pilot who must take his
plane through the middle of terrific flak straight to
the objective while paratroopers go out the door.
They are the leaders who must win your battles.

GEN W. B. Palmer
"Men Think as Their Leaders Think"
Army Information Digest, Jan 1954

The genius of a good leader is to leave behind him
a situation which common sense, without the grace
of genius, can deal with successfully.

Walter Lippman

Two Commanders

Two kinds of commander, my company needs,
One for the words, the other for deeds.
One to parade us with guidons held high,
The other to lead us when steel starts to fly.
One who will push us to get ourselves squared,
Another to pull us when we get damned scared.
One to inspect us to make us stay clean,
Another to train us and make us "real men".
A Captain who always is starched, pressed and strike,
A Captain whose boots may show wear from our hike,
A leader with ribbons displayed on his shirt,
A leader whose face with sweat streaks in the dirt.

We need a commander whose accounts are just right.
We need an old man who can teach us to fight.
Would it not fit a magnificent plan
If both our commanders could be the same man?

Private First Class David B. Farley
Company A, 1st Battalion,
30th Infantry

The wonderful thing about soldiers, is that they ...
will permit any man a fair and just time to
prove himself, provided he does his best.
After that they will take almost anything,
do almost anything, for a competent
commander who combines pride in
himself and in them with a humble
recognition of his privilege
in commanding them.

John Masters
from his book,
The Road Past Mandalay

We don't need "leaders" who stay warm on
cold days by oil barrels while their men
freeze on the grenade ranges.
If they get cold, the leader ought
to get just as cold.
And when he marches back to the
barracks with them after that
kind of day, they know
he is one of them.

Drill Sergeant Karl Baccene
in "It's Tough to Be the First Domino"
ARMY, February 1971

*T*he hardships the soldier must endure,
the leader must also endure.

What the Soldier Thinks:
A Monthly Digest of War Department Studies
on the Attitudes of American Troops, WW II
November 1944

WE WERE HERE FIRST

*S*ometime ago, a sergeant, speaking to a group of officer
candidates said: "From most of us," he said, referring to
the troops, "you can expect … courage to match your
courage, guts to match your guts— endurance to match
your endurance—motivation to match your motivation—
esprit to match your esprit—a desire for achievement to
match your desire for achievement. You can expect a love
of God, a love of country, and a love of duty to match
your love of God, your love of country, and your love
of duty. We won't mind the heat if you sweat with us.
We won't mind the cold if you shiver with us. …
Gentlemen, you don't accept us: we were here first.
We accept you, and when we do, you'll know.
We won't beat drums, wave flags, or carry you off the
drill field on our shoulders, but, maybe at a company
party we'll raise a canteen cup of beer and say,
'Lieutenant, you're o.k. …' just like that."

SGM John Stepanek
Army Digest
August 1967

*W*e must not compensate for a lack of competence
among our leaders with the bravery of our soldiers.

US Army Field Manual 100-5 Operations
(1970s version)

SOME BASICS FOR YOUNG LEADERS

There must have been millions of words written on leadership. Another thousand pages on motivation and even more on counseling. All the while behavioral scientists attempt to penetrate the human psyche to find even more ways of doing what? Getting the job done.

Modern terminology boggles the mind: directive, nondirective, electric, organizational effectiveness, synergistic communications, and so on. Add priority pressures such as what to do first, short-fuse missions, career apprehension, a family with the measles and an alcoholic squad leader—it gets to be a rather full day after day after day.

I would propose a few basics. They don't subvert the new titles nor are they a panacea for the ne'er-do-well. They're not "Brown Shoe" army either, although they have been around a long, long time. They're just statements that do not need any explanation:

- Listen to your soldiers

- Instill pride, never degrade

- Set reasonable standards

- Be hard, but be fair

- Be as good as your word

- Train hard; your life really depends on it

- Keep your soldiers informed

- Be honest in all things

- Respect all soldiers

That about covers leadership, including all the fancy words. I'm not against any method, but sometimes I (maybe you do, too) get confused with all the reinventing and new tools we have. If they do nothing else, they get us thinking about leadership and that's just great.

Command Sergeant Major Walter Krueger

WHERE ARE THE WARRIORS?

Some of the mythology that exists is that we don't have any warriors anymore in the Army, and we're more interested in managership. That's misguided logic. Whoever heard of George Patton in 1938? We've got a lot of those warriors in the ranks today. What we don't need are the headlines for them to be prominent.

If anyone asks you, "Where are the warriors in today's Army? Where are the Pattons, Bradleys, and the others?" Give them a straight answer! They are "out there," now, leading our soldiers at every level in our units! If war comes, they will emerge, just as they did in World War II.

General John A. Wickham, Jr.

An officer who will invariably assume the responsibility for failure, whether he deserves it or not, and invariably gives the credit for success to others, whether they deserve it or not, will achieve outstanding success.

General George S. Patton, Jr.

MILITARY LEADERSHIP IN A CHANGING SOCIETY

Mr. James H. Webb, Jr. (Former Secretary of the Navy)
Naval War College Conference on Ethics

November 16, 1998

My current professional endeavors offer me a great vantage point from which to observe the forces that are shaping the world. I travel a lot, and often find myself in discussions with people of widely varying backgrounds regarding the turbulence within our society, how other countries are reacting to us, and what has happened to leadership within our government. Sometimes these exchanges assist me in the conduct of my trade as a writer. At others they help me when I pursue business opportunities. And always, because of my own life's journey, they bring me to think of the United States military. Where is its place in this changing world? Where does it stand among its own people? How do those on the outside view it? Where are current defense leaders taking it? And how are its own leaders honoring their sacred duty to preserve the standards handed down through the generations?

The world has been through many changes since my time in government. Borders and regimes have fallen. Crises have come and gone. Political positions have ebbed and flowed. Weapon systems have improved and become more costly. The nature of the threat has become unduly vague. The military has shrunk and become less visible to public debate. But the basic requirements of leadership, strategy and even tactics remain constant, just as they have over the ages, in the same manner that the basic elements of human character have not altered since biblical times. And so I feel comfortable today offering you a pair of eyes that watch from the outside, whose interest in these matters is nothing more than the well-being and proper functioning of the American military, an institution into which I was born, which brought me into manhood, which tested me under fire in combat, and which, when all the rhetoric is stripped away, is the ultimate guarantor of this nation's way of life.

How does the rest of the country view you, and what you are doing? Among all the world's nations the United States is the most diverse in terms of ethnicity, longevity of citizenship, and ultimately, of viewpoint. And so it is impossible to know from aggregate numbers in polling and public opinion surveys exactly how our military is viewed, and how those views impact on an understanding of and respect for what you are doing. But I would like to address three separate components today, each of which present the military and the nation a different set of challenges. Those of the elite policy makers (including the media), the general public, and the "new Americans."

First, and most important to the formulation of military policy, are the elites. At the outset I would offer you an important touchstone. The greatest lingering effect of the Vietnam era on our society is that by default it brought about a new notion: that military service during time of war is not a prerequisite for moral authority or even respect. Indeed, every day since that era this notion has been accorded a quiet affirmation among our elites, usually whispered to one another, that some lives are worth more than others, that it is right and proper for those who are the so-called best and brightest by virtue of an elite education to be excused from the dirty work of our society. Think of the disproportionate loss to society, the logic goes, if a future Albert Einstein or Thomas Edison is killed in some fruitless foreign engagement. Or, as an old Chinese saying used to put it, one should never use good steel for nails or good men for soldiers. I myself, like the majority of this nation, subscribe to a different view—in effect the reverse of that syllogism, because when it comes to leadership as opposed to law or medicine or engineering the logic is indeed the reverse: the hotter the fire, the tougher the steel, and the more reliable the leader. And also because in a democracy it is a given that the more one has benefitted from the fruits of our nation, the greater is his obligation to serve. But it is important to recognize that our elites abandoned this position during the Vietnam War, and it has affected policy for an entire generation. As one example of this disparity, Harvard lost 691 alumni in World War Two, while in Vietnam it lost a total of 12 out of all the classes from 1962 to 1972.

This notion of special privilege has spread, not abated, over the decades following the Vietnam War. For most elites who make policy or provide commentary on it, you are little more than an intellectual issue. Just as the crisis in public education is for them a matter to be worried over in removed policy terms rather than directly experienced by their own privately schooled children, almost no one in a position to affect policy has a direct human stake in the outcome of a military engagement. It has also created a vacuum of true understanding in the highest places. Today, for the first time since the United States became a major world power, none of the principals in the national security arena—the President, the Secretary of Defense, the Secretary of State, the Director of the CIA, or the national security adviser—have served in the military. This problem might recede when the Clinton Administration leaves town, but it is unlikely to go away. Twenty years ago when I was a committee counsel in the Congress a clear majority of the Senators and Congressmen were veterans, although most of their staff were not. Similarly, a majority of the editors at the major media outlets had military service, although their reporters did not. Today, the staff members and the reporters are now the Congressmen and the editors. In the congress veterans are a distinct minority, and in the media almost no one has served.

In terms of attitude, the elites fall into three categories. Some, I should say many, do have a sympathy and respect for what you do. But with a few exceptions they lack a referent—in their own experience, among their peers, and in their families—to place what you are doing in an understandable context. A second category, despite their public rhetoric, views you to be merely firemen and policemen of a different order, hired for a job, however dangerous, and expected to do it without complaint. This notion was reinforced during the Gulf War, when the Bush Administration often pointed out with pride that the war wasn't costing the United States anything, because other countries were footing the bill. What does it make you when a national leader places your wartime service in the context of a bill for services rendered? And finally, there is a small but very powerful minority that believes you are dangerous, that you must be continually humiliated and subdued, that militarism is an American disease, that the more empowered and respected you become, the more you threaten pet political issues and even the fabric of society. Do not underestimate these people. Despite the absurdity of their views they are intelligent, well-positioned at the power centers of our culture, and intent on marginalizing your sacrifices.

This bifurcation of our society causes some otherwise well-meaning people to put modern military service into a false context. Recently William Bennett gave a lecture on ethics at the Naval Academy, in which he compared the World War Two and Vietnam generations by focusing on twin events that took place. In 1994: the 50th anniversary of the D-Day landing at Normandy, and the 25th anniversary of Woodstock. One celebration, according to Mr. Bennett, mirrored a generation that understood sacrifice and service. The other illuminated an age group consumed by drugs and self-absorption. To Mr. Bennett, who in 1969 was a student at Harvard Law School, this was probably an apt comparison. But for those who graduated from the Naval Academy during that era this speech bordered on insult.

If Mr. Bennett had wanted to reinforce the value of service and the notion of sacrifice in front of that audience, he could have compared the two elements of his own generation, and discussed what each was doing during the summer of 1969. I personally was leading a rifle platoon in the An Hoa Basin of Vietnam, and spent part of that summer in recuperation after being wounded. And I was hardly alone. Five hundred thousand other Americans— far more than turned out for the party made famous for its drugs, sex and rock and roll—were serving there with me. But who on the national scene saw this, or remembers it, even among conservative commentators? And who truly understands what it means to deploy to sea again and again in the 1990s, leaving family and friends behind for months at a time?

Next, the general public. In the aggregate they like you, they support you, and they respect you. But in reality they know less and less about what you are actually doing, and fewer and fewer among them have a human stake if what you're doing goes wrong. When we had the draft, families throughout the nation paid close attention, because nearly all of them were at risk when troops were sent into harm's way. Additionally, a constant stream of veterans was returning to communities throughout the country, and despite persistent media reports to the contrary they were bringing home a positive story about military service and the challenges of wearing the uniform. Those who are veterans are still able to communicate these messages, but with a smaller military, longer enlistments and higher retention the veteran population is dwindling. As one example, a thousand World War Two veterans are dying every day.

And what of the "new Americans?" Our country is so vastly rich and powerful, so dominant in the world's cultural centers through its impact in film, music and fashion, that it is difficult for many newcomers to understand that it was built from nothing, on the backs of individuals who carved out a wilderness, designed a unique system of government, and along the way had to be willing to take time from their lives and serve the larger good. Many recent immigrants come from cultures that do not respect their military, or from societies where the military is viewed as corrupt and authoritarian. They do not understand the deep sense of patriotism and tradition that is at the bottom of our most dedicated military people's service. Indeed, they have been given no reasons to see military service as a duty of citizenship. And a lost opportunity lurks here—the chance to embrace these new Americans as equal citizens, and to reinforce the notion that being an American brings with it a shared history, no matter at what point one's own family arrived, as well as an obligation to serve the greater good. Being an American is more than paying taxes and obeying the speed limit. The sacrifices of the past inform the greatness of the present, and the sacrifices of the present provide security for the future, and it is above all the military services which connect us all in such a way.

These are all, as we used to say in the Pentagon, disconnects. And there is a further disconnect embraced by all three of these groups, that frequently distorts or submerges the importance of national defense. It can be summarized in one word: internationalization. We live in an age of multinational corporations, heightened economic interdependence, instant global communications on the Internet. It can be argued that the ability of powerful investment engines to withhold capital or to shift its flow from one country to another is the most visible form of raw power in the world today. And people across America want a piece of the pie. They want to become well-off. They want to do business. They don't want to be told that in five or fifteen years the business they are pursuing might in some vague way hurt the country. And so in a world where the threats to our national security have become arguable and blurred, money has become amoral, refusing to recognize national borders, and investments repudiate the notion of loyalty.

Our government leaders have consciously ignored this phenomenon, hidden from it, sometimes even fed it for fear that their campaign contributions would dry up if they did otherwise. And American business has become almost a caricature of Lenin's famous taunt that the last capitalist would be hung from the rope he sold for a profit. Is it really that bad? Well, the short answer is "yes." One can see the dangers of this lack of strategic thinking in the present administration's China policy, for I cannot imagine a greater example of what can happen when conscious strategic ignorance creates a disadvantage for those who must wear the uniform. I spend a lot of time in Asia, usually with Asians rather than Americans, and it was clear that the President's announcement of a "strategic partnership" with China during his trip last summer sent chills through the region. He spent nine days in China and did not visit Japan, in my view our most important ally. His rhetoric and his actions went far beyond normal bounds to reward the policies of a repressive regime that has been a nuclear proliferator and has developed a dangerous strategic axis through the Muslim world for more than a decade. Why? Everybody knows why. Trade.

A recent *New York Times* investigation spelled out just how far this obsession with China has gone. Looser regulations regarding American export policies have enabled Chinese companies to obtain a wide range of sensitive, sophisticated technology—worth billions of dollars. The new rules allowed American companies to sell many of these products without prior government approval, and the President decided to change these rules without a rigorous review by intelligence officials or other national security experts. The new policy was anchored in the fantasy that industry executives would raise questions about their own sales, requiring them to seek a Commerce Department license only if they believed the equipment would end up in military hands. And now it's been revealed that some of the high-speed computers sold to civilian customers—ostensibly for predicting weather patterns but also capable of scrambling secret communications and even designing nuclear weapons—are being used by the Chinese Army. As my thirteen-year-old daughter would say, "like, DUH." Even those with a passing knowledge of China know that in matters of security and technology its government is a monolith, and that the Chinese military itself has operated dozens of shell corporations involved in everything from Selling AK-47s and SKS rifles on the streets of Los Angeles to obtaining just this sort of technology. And that this travesty occurred at the same time the Chinese were enabling Pakistan to develop a nuclear capability, thus setting off the dangerous exchange of nuclear explosions between Pakistan and India last summer, and were assisting Iran and North Korea with their missile programs. I can think of no greater example of calculated stupidity and unthinking betrayal over the past forty years. But who benefits from it? And who pays if these sorts of miscalculations go wrong?

A memory lurks here, of World War Two soldiers lamenting that the Japanese artillery coming their way was made from scrap metal that American businessmen had sold a few years earlier for a profit. But let us now speak of the present, and of the future. Does our nation have a strategy in the wake of the Cold War? How is the military being used, and positioned for future use? From this outside observer's studied referent, there is not a clear strategy, particularly one that is driving the makeup of our armed forces. The last clearly enunciated strategy of this sort was the Nixon Doctrine, announced in 1969, which laid down three bench marks for American defense policy: that we would provide a nuclear umbrella for our non-nuclear allies and work vigorously against nuclear proliferation, that we would honor our treaty commitments, and that we would provide assistance to other friendly nations defending themselves from external threat if such actions were in the national interest of the United States.

The American military is becoming quite sophisticated in meeting lower-end threats such as those it recently encountered in Haiti, Somalia and Bosnia, and has made impressive doctrinal strides in such areas as the potential use of force in littoral areas. But focusing on these scenarios in the absence of a clearly enunciated global strategy actually puts our overall force structure at greater risk. We can do this job well and so we fund it, but we should be careful about when we do it: the fruitless commitment to Somalia, where we have no treaties, no national interest, and initially had no forces at risk, is perhaps the classic example of how not to use the American military. On the larger scale, in the face of truly serious threats, we are the only credible guarantor of deterrence and stability in the free world. The potential for such threats is real, and their dynamics are unpredictable. Korea is as always a tinderbox. The Islamic world is galvanizing and gaining ever more sophisticated weaponry. Historical references are always flawed but Russia increasingly reminds one of Weimar Germany, and China or Japan in the 1930s.

If we cease to structure our forces in a way that can defeat these and other threats, the probability of their occurrence will increase. And to state the obvious, it is impossible to rebuild and train a larger navy in six months or a year if the world turns ugly again and requires us to sustain a large-scale military presence in a vital region. And nowhere are we so vulnerable in this new era where so few Americans understand the nature of war and military operations than in the reduced size of our navy. This is not to diminish the difficulties of the Army and the Air Force, which have seen dramatic reductions since the end of the cold war. But these changes were largely the product of our reduced presence in NATO Europe, and that presence was a historical anomaly for the United States. Never before 1949 did our country occupy large positions in foreign countries solely for the purpose of local defense. By contrast, for more than a century we have recognized that the navy connects us to the world and is essential to its day-to-day security as well as our own. Just as Russia, China and Germany are traditional continental powers, the United States is a maritime nation, by virtue of its geographical position, economic and security interests, cultural ties, and treaty obligations with other countries. The NATO reductions were actually a return to historical normality for the US military. And it should be remembered that in the decades before World War Two the navy received roughly half of the national security budget. The end of the cold war brought very few changes to the obligations faced by the navy. It must operate continuously in the present low-threat conditions, and it must be capable of doing even more at the turn of a switch. Its presence around the world on the calmest of days is a signal of global stability, a message that the United States is looking after its economic and security interests. Its ability to maneuver and respond at crisis points is the single most important measure of our day-to-day credibility.

If the threat increases, the Navy-Marine Corps doctrine of amphibious power projection in the littoral regions of the globe allows us to assert our interests without the diplomatic frustrations and operational vulnerability of ground bases. And the capability of putting a sustainable logistical train in place during major engagements, coupled with the power of the fleet, is an essential ingredient of national strategy. But what has happened to the navy in the last ten years? Our effort to build a 600 ship navy during the 1980s was in reality a rather modest comeback from a period of serious neglect. I had argued in writing—before becoming Secretary of the Navy—that we should return to historical normality by reducing our presence in NATO and increasing the size of the fleet.

The morning I resigned as Secretary rather than agreeing to a reduction in the fleet I made a half-joking comment to Larry Garrett, then my undersecretary, that I did not choose to be remembered as the father of the 350 ship navy. But never did I imagine that the Navy's leadership would allow the devastation that has now resulted in a 300 ship navy, with the numbers continuing to sink. If present construction schedules hold, we may be headed for a 200 ship navy. By FY 2001 the navy will have reduced the size of the fleet by 45 percent since my resignation—if it meets its procurement goals—and funding for procurement is lagging far behind those goals. Since 1992 alone, the size of the fleet has decreased by 31 percent while optempo has increased by 26 percent. More than half of the ships in the navy are at sea on any given day, and a majority of those are forward deployed. The aircraft mishap rate is nearly double last year's, the highest level in the last five years.

Recruitment is dramatically off, 7,000 below requirements, the worst of all the services. Enlisted retention is below requirements and all the officer warfighting communities forecast serious retention problems. Funding for ship and aircraft modernization has decreased by more than 50 percent since 1990. The people who are leaving cite more and more frequently that their greatest reason is a disappointment in the quality of leadership they are receiving from above. These are all signs of a force that is growing tired, fraying around the edges. And what is the Navy's leadership proposing in response to this dilemma? The answer on the table right now is to cut back infrastructure—that is, to size down the bases so that they meet the reductions in the fleet. In other words, rather than argue the dangerous reduction of the size of the fleet, they are accepting permanently its reduction by removing the infrastructure that supported larger numbers. Their only other substantive proposal is to bring back the 50 percent retirement package, as if 10 percent more in retirement pay alone is going to keep the overworked and underappreciated 25-year-old in the system.

Those of us who have been around for a while—including today's admirals—have seen all of this before, although not at this truly dangerous level. When I was commissioned in 1968 there were 930 combatants in the navy. We had the high optempo of Vietnam but we did not have the Indian Ocean and the Persian Gulf. In the post-Vietnam malaise the traditional strategic arguments were discredited, the careful warnings were disregarded, and by 1979 the navy had bottomed out at 479 combatants. Then the Indian Ocean commitments began after the twin crises in Iran and Afghanistan. Optempo became unbearable as it became necessary to keep carriers continually on-station. The *Independence* made a 210-day deployment with eight days ashore. The *Nimitz* made a 146-day deployment with no days ashore. Ships fell into disrepair. People voted with their feet until the navy was short 23,000 petty officers. My navy peers came up with a cynical slogan: make Commander and get your divorce.

This vision haunted me in late 1987 and early 1988 when we were faced with again reducing the size of the fleet. As we argued the issue I had my staff come up with a chart that covered several decades. On the chart I had them plot three curves: the size of the fleet, the operational commitments assigned to the navy by the national command authority, and retention. Predictably, it was shown that operational commitments did not vary with the size of the fleet. And retention went down along with the "bathtub" effect of fleet reduction. And so after three attempts to meet budget reductions without reducing the size of the fleet were rejected, I decided that I would not walk the fleet back from our goal of 600 ships, into the bathtub—where the navy now resides.

Why is this happening again? The answer is that it was allowed to happen by leaders who were unable or unwilling to make the case for a larger navy, and as a result failed to educate the congress and the public. They didn't fight at 600 ships. They didn't fight at 500. They didn't fight at 400. They're telling the world that 300 is fine and doable, while they're on the way to 200. And so I return to my initial observation. In a world where fewer and fewer policy makers have any connection to the military, and where the political process knows less and less about matters of strategy, leadership and the intricacies of force structure planning, whose duty should it be to bring forward the logic and the answers? The senior admirals should not be selling 300 ships to the navy. They should be arguing 400 ships, or more, to the nation. Those leaders who comfortably claim that the notion of civilian control precludes them from arguing their own case should study the success of the Marine Corps, for this is exactly what it did in the late 1940s when it was threatened with extinction, and in different form it is what Marine Corps leaders continue to do today. Military subservience to political control applies to existing policy, not to policy debates. The political process requires the unfettered opinions of military leaders, and military leaders who lack the courage to offer such opinions are in my view just as accountable to their people as the politicians who have secured their silence.

The silence of the admirals as the fleet shrinks and their sailors continue to do more with less has not gone unnoticed. A recent Naval Institute Proceedings article pointing out that only one in ten navy junior officers in a recent study aspires to command—and that number not even addressing the issue of quality—is an ominous warning. A lot of reasons were given, but two messages came through loud and clear. The first was that money alone won't solve the problem. Americans have never been mercenaries, and although it is the duty of their leaders to provide for their well-being, they can't simply be bought. The second was an overwhelming disenchantment with the Navy's senior leaders. I recently heard these same two messages again and again during a discussion with junior aviators in Japan. This evident breakdown in the junior officer corps is deeply troubling, for it hints of a fundamental change in the navy's culture, probably fueled in equal parts by the Goldwater-Nichols legislation and the effect of the Tailhook scandal on Navy leadership. Command is tough, risky, lonely, the most challenging job an officer can have. But it is also the very emblem of traditional military service. It is what dedicated officers have always lived for and aspired to. The greatest experience of my professional life has been the privilege of commanding marines at the platoon and company level. And what is a military service whose leaders do not aspire to command? It becomes a gutless bureaucracy, pushing papers and taking a paycheck. These young officers did not come into the navy with this attitude. The circumstances of their careers have inflicted it upon them.

When leadership fails, sometimes a fundamental shift overtakes a unit, or a military service, or a nation that is so profound that it can indeed change an entire ethos. Most often the sea of change takes place gradually, not because of decisions taken by senior leaders so much as from their inaction, an acquiescence to insistent, incremental pressures generated from the outside. Usually the leadership, reacting to and sometimes overwhelmed by these outside pressures, are the ones who comprehend the changes the least, and in some cases cannot perceive what has happened until it is too late for them to protect even their own legacy.

Let's hope that this will not be the epitaph for a United States Navy on its way to 200 ships and a third-rate future. Its history, its traditions, its special place at the center of all that is great about this country, demand that those who serve, of whatever rank and level of experience, do what they can to explain to the American people that the navy must be led from within, that what has happened over the past ten years is not right, and that what is left is not enough.

*Technology helps ... but make no mistake about it.
I don't care whether you're in a ship, a plane,
a helicopter, a tank, or running onto a beach
off a landing craft in the middle of the night,
it takes men and women of character.*

Gordon Sullivan

WHAT DOES IT TAKE TO BE SUCCESSFUL?

You've got to love being a soldier.

You've got to love being around other soldiers.

You've got to love leading, training, and caring for soldiers.

You've got to be dedicated, motivated, physically fit, mentally alert, morally straight, technically and tactically proficient.

You must believe in our nation, believe in our Army, and believe in your fellow soldier.

You've got to be all you can be; and if you're a leader, you have to want the same for all the soldiers in your charge.

Sergeant Major of the Army (SMA) Richard A. Kidd

Clutch Hitters

Any man, whatever be his rank, can command who has the courage to try and the brain to see clearly what other men miss. I am quite sure that I have known personally a greater number of emergent combat leaders than any man living. None was a genius or possessed of a better-than-average IQ. As a type, they are stolid rather than imaginative, and it is usually the lack of flair, rather than a failure to conform to what is asked of them, that denies them promotion or special recognition until their pre-eminent qualities are proved under fire. Their spirits are fanned by danger. Other men rally to them in emergency because they take positive action. There is the key word. These clutch hitters are able to fill the void caused by the failure of appointed leadership, because they do not mistake the appearance of that position for the reality.

S.L.A. Marshall

HE WHO WOULD COMMAND

Decision of character is one of the most important of human qualities, philosophically considered. Speculation, knowledge, is not the chief end of man; it is action. We may, by a fine education, learn to think most correctly, and talk most beautifully; but when it comes to action if we are weak and undecided, we are of all beings the most wretched.

*All mankind feel themselves weak, beset with
infirmities, and surrounded with dangers;
the acutest minds are the most conscious of difficulties
and dangers. They want, above all things, a leader
with that boldness, decision, and energy, which with
shame they do not find in themselves. "Give us the
man," shout the multitude, "Who will step forward
and take the responsibility." He is instantly the idol,
the lord, and the king among men. He then who
would command among his fellows, must excel them
more in energy of will than in power of intellect.*

Charles Burnap

*Common sense should be a
leadership trait.*

General Richard E. Cavazos
U.S. Army

Sincerity is the key leadership trait.

Bruce Clark

*When in war, men must die, they can't be managed
to their deaths, they must be led.*

Colonel Dandridge "Mike" Malone
U.S. Army, Infantry

You Will Have All the Credit

The battle of Gettysburg had just been fought. President Lincoln sensed an opportunity to end the war by driving hard against Lee's rear in retreat. A swift, daring attack might do it. As commander-in-chief of the army, he ordered General Meade to pursue. A friendly note in the president's handwriting accompanied the instructions:

"The order I enclose is not of record. If you succeed, you need not publish the order. If you fail, publish it. Then, if you succeed, you will have all the credit of the movement. If not, I'll take the responsibility."

You Did It

I'm just a plowhand from Arkansas, but I have learned how to hold a team together. How to lift some men up, how to calm down others, until finally they've got one heartbeat together, a team. There's just three things I'd ever say:

- If anything goes bad, I did it.
- If anything goes semi-good, then we did it.
- If anything goes real good, then you did it.

That's all it takes to get people to win football games for you.

Coach Bear Bryant

Authority is a poor substitute for leadership.

John Luther

Our militia will be heroes,
if we have heroes to lead them.

Thomas Jefferson

DON'T WAIT FOR THE PLANS

During WW II, General MacArthur called in one of his Army engineers and asked: "How long will it take to throw a bridge across the river?" "Three days," the engineer told him. "Good" snapped the general. "Have your draftsman make drawings right away." Three days later the general sent for the engineer and asked how the bridge was coming along. "It's all ready," reported the engineer. "You can send your troops across right now if you don't have to wait for the plans. They ain't done yet."

You can buy a man's time; you can buy his physical presence at a given place; you can even buy a measured number of his skilled muscular motions per hour. But you cannot buy enthusiasm ... you cannot buy loyalty ... you cannot buy the devotion of hearts, minds, or souls. You must earn these.

Clarence Francis

A Private one night saw another soldier passing and called out, "Hey, buddy, give me a light." The other soldier stopped and held out a lighted match. Raising his eyes to speak his thanks for the favor, the first soldier saw the star of brigadier general and at once apologized, "I beg your pardon, sir. I didn't mean any disrespect. I didn't notice you were a general." "That's all right," replied the general, "but you should thank God that I wasn't a second lieutenant."

Author Unknown

Morale is when your hands and feet keep on working when your head says it can't be done.

Admiral Ben Moreell

*All great leaders have
possessed the capacity of
believing in the capabilities
and talents of others.
The man who is always
disdainful of subordinates,
who constantly denigrates
their work, who always
compares their efforts
unfavorably with his own
will wind up leading no
one but himself.*

**Colonel
Theodore Roosevelt**

*Good leaders take at least a little more
than their share of blame, and a lot less
than their share of credit.*

Stephen Leacock
Economist and Humorist
1869–1944

*I want this team to win, I'm obsessed with winning,
with discipline, with achieving.
That's what this country's all about.*

George Steinbrenner
Owner of the New York Yankees

*Since the dawn of time, men have competed with
each other—with clubs, crossbows, or cannon,
dollars, ballots, and trading stamps.*

Much of mankind, of course, abhors competition,
and these remain the acted upon, not the actors.
Anyone who says there will be no competition in
the future simply does not understand the
nature of man ... men must compete.

T. R. Fehrenbach

EFFECTIVE LEADERSHIP DEMANDS A LOT OF THINGS

- Confidence—confidence in yourself, confidence in others, confidence in your cause.

- Optimism—a belief that the goal is not only good but that it will be reached.

- Knowledge—an understanding of the underlying problems, what needs to be done, and how to go about getting it done.

- Decisiveness—the ability to weigh options, make decisions, and gain the acceptance of the group.

- Openness—a respect for the opinions of all and a desire to work with people of divergent views and personalities.

- Sharing—a willingness to help with even menial tasks, to be out in front, and to support the members of the group, to plan adequately, to wait for the right time for action.

- Courage—the courage to withstand criticism, to make sacrifices, to resist pressure, and to continue in the face of adversity.

- Communication—the ability to understand what others are trying to say and to convey decisions and action plans clearly.

Leadership occasionally demands a lot of other things too. It never comes cheap.

Author Unknown

*An Army commander does what is necessary
to accomplish his mission and ...
nearly 80 percent of his mission
is to arouse morale.*

General George S. Patton, Jr.

*A leader should be doubly careful about his dress,
appearance, and deportment ...
You are always on parade.*

General George S. Patton, Jr.

*All officers ... must be vitally interested in everything
that interests the soldier. Usually you will gain a great
deal of knowledge by being interested, but, even if
you do not, the fact that you appear interested
as a very high morale influence on the soldier.*

General George S. Patton, Jr.

*Let us then rely on the
goodness of our cause,
and the aid of the Supreme Being,
in whose hands victory is to
animate and encourage us to
great and noble actions.*

**General
George Washington**

A profession is a personal thing that man acquires.
It cannot be inherited. It cannot be bequeathed.
Only he who, having made that acquisition,
puts to use that knowledge and skill with all
his ability and complete dedication of purpose
can be truly called a professional.

R. E. Onstad

He that cannot obey, cannot command.

Ben Franklin

People who try to command respect
are wasting their time.
Respect can't be commanded.
It must be earned.

Author Unknown

Take away my people but leave my factories
and soon grass will grow on the factory floors.
Take away my factories but leave my people and
soon we will have a new and better factory.

Andrew Carnegie
Owner of Carnegie Steel
1835–1919
Philanthropist

You cannot bring about prosperity by discouraging thrift.
You cannot strengthen the weak by weakening the strong.
You cannot help the wage earner by pulling down the wage
payer. You cannot help the poor by destroying the rich.

You cannot keep out of trouble by spending more than you earn. You cannot build character and courage by taking away a man's initiative and independence. You cannot help men permanently by doing for them what they could and should do for themselves.

Abraham Lincoln

A good commander is someone who can step on your boots and still leave a shine.

Author Unknown

The question: "Who ought to be boss?" is like asking "Who ought to be the tenor in the quartet?" Obviously, the man who can sing tenor.

Henry Ford

Leadership is a word and a concept that has been more argued than almost any other I know. I am not one of the desk-pounding type that likes to stick out his jaw and look like he is bossing the show. I would far rather get behind the frailties and the requirements of human nature. I would rather try to persuade a man to go along, because once I have persuaded him, he will stick. If I scare him, he will just stay as long as he is scared, and then he is gone.

Dwight D. Eisenhower

*Leadership, at its highest,
consists of getting people to work for you when
they are under no obligation to do so.*

Charles F. Kettering
1876–1958
American Electrical Engineer and Inventor

*No business can progress and grow without
leadership. In the final analysis, leadership is
the only real advantage one organization has
over another in a competitive society.*

George MacDonald
1824–1905
Scottish Novelist and Poet

*I am tired of hearing about men with "the courage
of their convictions." Nero and Caligula and Attila
and Hitler had the courage of their convictions—
but not one had the courage to examine
his convictions, or to change them,
which is the true test of character.*

Sidney Harris

*Ability may get you to the top,
but only character will keep you there.*

Author Unknown

The Seven Deadly Sins of Leadership

1. **Haughtiness**—thinking highly of oneself and poorly of others.

2. **Arrogance**—claiming much for oneself and giving little to others.

3. **Pride**—an absorbing sense of one's own greatness.

4. **Disdain**—seeing contemptuously the inferiority of others compared to oneself.

5. **Presumption**—claiming place or privilege above one's right.

6. **Assumption**—assuming superiority and privilege which others would be slow to concede.

7. **Vanity**—intensely craving admiration and applause.

Author Unknown

Formula for handling people:
1. Listen to the other person's story.
2. Listen to the other person's full story.
3. Listen to the other person's full story first.

General George C. Marshall

You do not lead by hitting people over the head.
That's assault—not leadership.

Dwight D. Eisenhower

The prime function of the leader
is to keep hope alive.

John Gardner

Ten Characteristics of a Good Leader

1. **Persistence.**　Not insistence. A strong leader hangs on a little longer, works a little harder.

2. **Imagination.**　He or she harnesses imagination to practical plans that produce results.

3. **Vision.**　The present is just the beginning. He is impressed with the possibilities of the future.

4. **Sincerity.**　He or she can be trusted.

5. **Integrity.**　He or she has principles and lives by them.

6. **Poise.**　He or she isn't overbearing, but is friendly, assured.

7. **Thoughtfulness.**　He or she is considerate, aware.

8. **Common Sense.**　Good judgement based on reason.

9. **Altruism.**　He or she lives by the Golden Rule.

10. **Initiative.**　He or she gets things started–now!

Author Unknown

*Two qualities make the difference between
leaders and men of average performance.
They are curiosity and discontent.
I have never known an outstanding
man who lacked either.
And I have never known a man of small
achievement who had both.*

Charlie Brower

*Leadership is the art of changing a group from
what it is into what it ought to be.*

George Herbert

Rudeness is a little person's imitation of power.

Henry Ford
1863–1947
Industrialist, Automobile Manufacturer

We flatter ourselves by claiming to be rational and intellectual beings, but it would be a great mistake to suppose that men are always guided by reason. We are strange, inconsistent creatures, and act quite as often, perhaps oftener, from prejudice or passion. The result is that you are more likely to carry men with you by enlisting their feelings, than by convincing their reason.

John Lubbock

Character is much easier kept than recovered.

Thomas Paine
1737–1809
Political Philosopher, Author

The badge of rank which an officer wears on his coat is really a symbol of servitude—servitude to his men.

General Maxwell D. Taylor
Army Information Digest
June 1953

*V*alues are at the core of everything our
Army is and does. Your commitment to living
and teaching the Army's core values is critical
to our success today and tomorrow.

General Dennis J. Reimer

*S*oldiers ask only a few things of us.
They ask for responsible and inspired leadership
with a vision for what is right.

General John A. Wickham, Jr.

*H*istory does not long entrust the care of
Freedom to the weak or the timid.

Dwight D. Eisenhower

CHAPTER NINE

Freedom and Liberty

This chapter provides speeches, quotes, and stories about the origins of American liberty, the price already paid for our freedoms, and America's heartfelt embrace for the freedoms we all enjoy.

Remember, officers and soldiers, that you are fighting for the blessings of liberty.

**General
George Washington**

General George Washington
Continental Army
1732–1799
1st President of the United States
(1789–1799)

GIVE ME LIBERTY

Excerpts, from Patrick Henry's speech before the Virginia Convention, March 1775

Patrick Henry
1736–1799
Statesman and Orator

If we wish to be free—if we mean to preserve inviolate those inestimable privileges for which we have been so long contending—if we mean not basely to abandon the noble struggle in which we have been so long engaged, and which we have pledged ourselves never to abandon until the glorious object of our contest shall be obtained—we must fight! I repeat it, sir, we must fight! An appeal to arms and to the God of hosts is all that is left us! They tell us, sir, that we are weak; unable to cope with so formidable an adversary. But when shall we be stronger? Will it be the next week, or the next year? Will it be when we are totally disarmed, and when a British guard shall be stationed in every house? Shall we gather strength by irresolution and inaction?

Shall we acquire the means of effectual resistance by lying supinely on our backs and hugging the delusive phantom of hope, until our enemies shall have bound us hand and foot? Sir, we are not weak if we make a proper use of those means which the God of nature hath placed in our power. The millions of people, armed in the holy cause of liberty, and in such a country as that which we possess, are invincible by any force which our enemy can send against us. Besides, sir, we shall not fight our battles alone. There is a just God who presides over the destinies of nations, and who will raise up friends to fight our battles for us. The battle, sir, is not to the strong alone; it is to the vigilant, the active, the brave.

Besides, sir, we have no election. If we were base enough to desire it, it is now too late to retire from the contest. There is no retreat but in submission and slavery! Our chains are forged! Their clanking may be heard on the plains of Boston!

The war is inevitable—and let it come! I repeat it, sir, let it come.

It is in vain, sir, to extenuate the matter. Gentlemen may cry, Peace, Peace—but there is no peace. The war is actually begun! The next gale that sweeps from the north will bring to our ears the clash of resounding arms! Our brethren are already in the field! Why stand we here idle? What is it that gentlemen wish? What would they have? Is life so dear, or peace so sweet, as to be purchased at the price of chains and slavery? Forbid it, Almighty God!

I know not what course others may take but as for me; give me liberty or give me death.

Thomas Jefferson
1743–1826
Author of the Declaration of Independence
3rd President of the United States
(1801–1809)

*Eternal vigilance is the
price of liberty. ...
If a nation expects to be
ignorant and free,
in a state of civilization,
it expects what never was
and never will be.*

Thomas Jefferson
letter to Colonel Charles Yancey
January 6, 1816

*In order for the tree of
liberty to survive
it must be watered by
the blood of its patriots
of each generation.*

Thomas Jefferson
in a letter to James Madison
1778

*Liberty, when it begins to take root,
is a plant of rapid growth.*

George Washington

The Cause of All Mankind

It is a common observation here (Paris) that our cause is the cause of all mankind, and that we are fighting for their liberty in defending our own.

Benjamin Franklin
in a letter to Samuel Cooper
1777

Benjamin Franklin
1706–1790
*American Statesman,
Inventor, and Writer*

FROM THE BEGINNING ...

Preamble to the Declaration of Independence
1776

When, in the course of human events, it becomes necessary for one people to dissolve the political bands which have connected them with another, and to assume among the powers of the earth the separate and equal station to which the laws of nature and of nature's God entitle them, a decent respect to the opinions of mankind requires that they should declare the causes which impel them to the separation. We hold these truths to be self-evident: that all men are created equal, that they are endowed by their Creator with certain inalienable rights, that among these are life, liberty, and the pursuit of happiness, that to secure these rights governments are instituted among men.

We ... solemnly publish and declare, that these colonies are and of aright ought to be free and independent states ... And for the support of this declaration, with a firm reliance on the protection of divine providence, we mutually pledge our lives, our fortunes, and our sacred honour.

From the Declaration of Independence, 1776

Independence Hall, Philadelphia

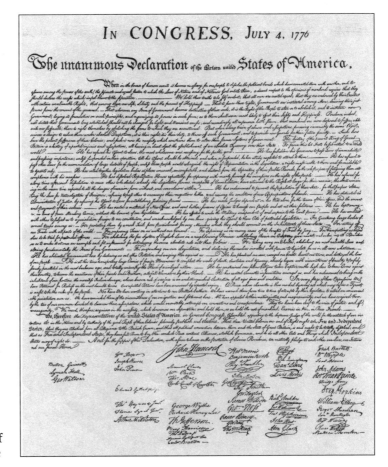

Declaration of Independence

We the People of the United States, in Order to form a more perfect Union, establish Justice, insure domestic Tranquility, provide for the common defense, promote the general Welfare, and secure the Blessings of Liberty to ourselves and our Posterity, do ordain and establish this Constitution for the United States of America.

Opening statement from the
Constitution of the United States of America,
1787

THE PRICE THEY PAID FOR FREEDOM

The Declaration of Independence marked the birth of America, but it was a painful and costly birth. The fifty-six courageous men who signed the declaration paid the price for being freedom fighters through hardship, sacrifice, and death. What kind of men were they? Who were those founding fathers of this nation who met in Philadelphia during the summer of 1776? More than half were lawyers or judges. More than a dozen were merchants, none were farmers or large plantation owners. Among the others were doctors, politicians, a minister, and a poet-musician-philosopher. Benjamin Franklin, at 70, was the oldest; nineteen were under 40; three were in their 20s. All but two had wives. They were men of means, respected in their communities, who enjoyed much ease and luxury in their personal lives. Almost all were men of learning and accomplishment, not wild-eyed rabble-rousers.

The signers of the Declaration of Independence had security, but they valued liberty more. John Adams said to his wife Abigail,

> I am well aware of the toil, and blood, and treasure, that it will cost to maintain this declaration, and support and defend these states; yet, through all the gloom I can see the rays of light and glory. I can see that the end is worth more than all the means.

The men understood well the struggle facing them when they took up arms to win freedom from an oppressive government. The penalty for treason was death by hanging. Even before the declaration was published with their names signed below it, the British tracked every member of Congress suspected of having put his name to treason. John Hancock already had a price of 500 pounds on his head. Every signer became a wanted man. While declaring their independence from England, the founders of America also declared their dependence upon God as the author of their being and the source of such wisdom and moral leadership as would be needed to create and sustain a new nation. The Declaration of Independence has four clear references to a deity. They concluded their statement with these words:

> For the support of this declaration, with a firm reliance on the protection of the Divine Providence, we mutually pledge to each other our lives, our fortunes and our sacred honor.

Of the fifty-six, few would survive for long and one-fourth of them would lose their lives as a direct consequence of the War for Independence. Five were captured by the British and tortured before they were executed as traitors. Nine were killed in battle or died from wounds or from battle's hardships. Twelve had their homes, from Rhode Island to Charleston, sacked, looted, and occupied or burned by the enemy. Two lost their sons in the Continental Army. One had two sons captured. Carter Braxton of Virginia, a wealthy planter and trader, saw his ships swept from the seas by the British navy. He sold his home and properties to pay his debts, and died in rags.

Thomas McKean was so hounded by the British that he was forced to move his family almost constantly. He served in Congress without pay and his family was kept in hiding. His possessions were taken from him and poverty was his reward. Vandals or soldiers or both looted the properties of Ellery, Clymer, Hall, Walton, Gwinett, Heward, Ruttledge and Middleton. At the Battle of Yorktown, Thomas Nelson, Jr. noted that British General Cornwallis had taken over the Nelson home for his headquarters. The owner quietly urged General George Washington to open fire, which was done. The home was destroyed and Nelson died impoverished seven years later.

Francis Lewis had his home plundered and his properties destroyed. The enemy stole everything they could and burned the rest to the ground. His wife was held prisoner in a filthy, unheated room, without even a bed. After several months of captivity, she was exchanged for two British prisoners, but died from her abuse.

John Hart was driven from his wife's bedside as she was dying. Their 13 children fled for their lives. His fields and his grist mill were laid waste. For more than a year, he lived in forests and caves. When he returned home after the war, he found that his wife was dead, his children vanished, and his farm destroyed. A few weeks later he died from exhaustion and a broken heart. Norrish and Livingston suffered similar fates. Thomas Lynch, Jr., had his health broken from privation and exposure while serving as a company commander in the military.

Someone once said,

> To be born free is a great privilege; to die free is a great responsibility.

When the British tried to seize American arms and munitions in Lexington, Massachusetts and in Williamsburg, Virginia because tyrants fear an armed populace a conflict began which "fired the shot heard round the world." Our benefactors in that struggle are not only those who took up arms against tyranny in defense of freedom and individual rights, but also those who took up the pen to give voice to the idea of liberty. To those who sacrificed to create our country and preserve it for posterity, the end was worth the painful means. Their bold, new vision of freedom gave us a nation which shines for the rest of the world like the beacon held by the Statue of Liberty. Where would we citizens of these United States of America be today if there had not been those who counted the cost of freedom and willingly paid that great price? Can we preserve their legacy?

Freedom is not free.

Author Unknown

The Blessings of Liberty

General George Washington
1732–1799
Continental Army

Never has New York seen a more brilliant military pageant than assembled off Gravesend during July and August, 1776, when British General Howe and his forces arrived from Halifax and was joined by his brother, Lord Howe, admiral of the British fleet, with between three and four hundred ships, with the Germans hired to aid the British in subduing the colonists. Sir Henry Clinton also arrived with troops from the south, and fully 30,000 veteran soldiers stood ready to annihilate the American Army, which never attained greater numbers than 18,000 men. The English planned to seize New York and then the rest of the country, quickly subdue the Colonials, and bring the war to a speedy end. As they landed and established themselves in and around New York, General Washington kept close watch upon their movements. He had 9,000 men in a fortified camp at Brooklyn, and on August 22, when he learned that the enemy had landed 10,000 men and 40 cannon at the lower end of Long Island, he (General Washington) endeavored to encourage his men in the following brief address:

*T*he enemy have now landed on Long Island
and the hour is fast approaching on which
the honor and success of this army and
the safety of our bleeding country depend.
Remember, officers and soldiers, that you are
freemen fighting for the blessings of liberty—
that slavery will be your portion and that
of your posterity if you do not acquit
yourselves like men.

General George Washington

True Liberty

True liberty is the being governed by laws of our own making. But as it would be impossible to collect together all the individuals of a whole State in order to frame laws for the benefit of the whole, the only remedy [is] for the inhabitants of every County to choose persons from amongst themselves, in whom they can confide; which persons so elected, shall make laws to bind the whole. And if, on trial, it appears that the wisdom or integrity of those elected few, or any of them, does not answer your expectations, you have an opportunity at the next annual election to turn them out, and put others in their room and more to your liking. This is true constitutional liberty, and this is the liberty for which you are now contending; and I tell you, my lads, when once you part with the foundation stone of happiness, you become slaves immediately, and all the effects of your industry and labour will be to aggrandize court officers and not for the advancement of yourselves or families. Learned men might tell you a great deal more on this subject, and give you more enlarged account of constitutional liberty; but be assured, so long as you have a sufficient check on your lawmakers, or rather, so long as you have the making of your own laws as a people, so long you are perfectly safe, and no longer. Now the King of England has sent over fleets and armies to compel us to give up this invaluable privilege into his hands; but with the blessing of God, we will maintain it against him and all the world so long as we have a man left to fire a musket. You must know, that if once they can establish the right to make laws for us, without our consent, from that moment our lives, our property, all that is worth possessing in the world, will be entirely at their mercy. This country, thus attacked, determined to defend itself against the invader. Thirteen States united themselves for this purpose, each State delegated its powers to certain Gentlemen, who were to represent the whole Country, and conduct this grand struggle for liberty, just as your Assembly represents the several

Counties of this State. Thus is the Continental Congress formed; and tho' the King in his speech, and the writers he employs, perpetually tell us that we are under a tyrannic government, that our leaders are arbitrary and will conduct us to ruin; yet, when we know that these Gentlemen are of our own appointment, and that we can remove them whenever we please, we are sure there is no danger; we have the staff in our hands, and have nothing to fear. ... You are now on your way to the Camp [Valley Forge], when you arrive there you will see your countrymen, like the armies of Israel, covering the mountains; they have built themselves a city on the banks of the Schuylkill, and endure all the hardships of their homely situation with cheerful patience; and what is it you think that blunts the keen edge of the northern winds, and makes content to smile on those frozen hills? I tell you it is the love of that liberty I have set before you, it is the consciousness of the justice of our cause. Men induced by such principles, laugh at danger, and surmount every difficulty.

From a Continental Army Sergeant
about the Ordeal at Valley Forge
1778

*Don't interfere with anything in the Constitution.
That must be maintained, for it is
the only safeguard of our liberties.*

Abraham Lincoln

*God grants liberty only to those who love it
and are always ready to guard and defend it.*

Daniel Webster
June 3, 1834

*All our freedoms are a single bundle,
all must be secure if any is to be preserved.*

Dwight David Eisenhower
General of the Army

*T*he only sure bulwark of continuing liberty is a
government strong enough to protect the interests
of the people, and a people strong enough and
well enough informed to maintain its
sovereign control over the government.

Franklin Delano Roosevelt

Live Forever or Die by Suicide

*A*ll the armies of Europe, Asia,
and Africa combined, with all the
treasure of the earth (our own
excepted) in their military chests;
with a Buonaparte for a commander,
could not by force, take a drink
from the Ohio River or make a
track on the Blue Ridge
in the trial of a thousand years.

*A*t what point then is the approach of
danger to be expected? I answer, if it ever
reach us, it must spring up amongst us.
It cannot come from abroad.
If destruction is to be our lot, we must
ourselves be its author and finisher.
As a nation of freemen, we must live
through all time, or die by suicide.

Abraham Lincoln
January 27, 1838

The spark of liberty in the mind and spirit of man cannot be long extinguished, it will break into flames that will destroy every coercion which seems to limit it.

President Herbert Clark Hoover
1874–1964
31st President of the United States
(1929–1933)

We must be the great arsenal of democracy.

Franklin Delano Roosevelt

General Douglas MacArthur

A man who will not protect this freedom does not deserve to be free.

General Douglas MacArthur
1880–1964
American Five-Star General
Army Chief of Staff
(1930–1935)

FIGHTING ETERNALLY

*There are those in this country today who ask me
and other veterans of World War Number One,
"What did it get you?"... The thing they forget is
that liberty and freedom and democracy are so
very precious that you do not fight to win them
once and stop. ... Liberty and freedom and
democracy are prizes awarded only to those
peoples who fight to win them and then
keep fighting eternally to hold them!*

Alvin York, 1941
from the book
Sergeant York: An American Hero

Sergeant Alvin York
World War I

MAN'S ETERNAL DESIRE

Mr. President, the most powerful single force in the world today is neither communism nor capitalism, neither the H-bomb nor the guided missile—it is man's eternal desire to be free and independent. The great enemy of that tremendous force of freedom is called, for want of a more precise term, imperialism—and today that means Soviet imperialism and, whether we like it or not, and though they are not to be equated, Western imperialism. Thus the single most important test of American foreign policy today is how we meet the challenge of imperialism, what we do to further man's desire to be free. On this test more than any other, this nation shall be critically judged by the uncommitted millions in Asia and Africa, and anxiously watched by the still-hopeful lovers of freedom behind the Iron Curtain. If we fail to meet the challenge of either Soviet or Western imperialism, then no amount of foreign aid, no aggrandizement of armaments, no new pacts or doctrines or high-level conferences can prevent further setbacks of our course and to our security.

Senator John Fitzgerald Kennedy
United States Senate
Washington D.C.
July 2, 1957

We in this country, in this generation, are—by destiny rather than choice—the watchman on the walls of world freedom. We ask, therefore, that we may be worthy of our power and responsibility, that we may exercise our strength with wisdom and restraint, and that we may achieve in our time and for all time the ancient vision of peace on earth and goodwill toward men.

Prepared by President John F. Kennedy for delivery at the
Dallas Trade Mart luncheon November 22, 1963
(the day he was assassinated)—undelivered

LET THE WORD GO FORTH

John Fitzgerald Kennedy
1917–1963
35th President of the United States
(1961–1963)

[Engraving on the granite near President John F. Kennedy's gravesite, chosen by Mrs. Kennedy from his inaugural address.]

Let the word go forth from this time and place to friend and foe alike, that the torch has been passed to a new generation of Americans.

Let every nation know whether it wishes us well or ill that we shall pay any price, bear any burden, meet any hardship, support any friend, oppose any foe to assure the survival and success of liberty.

Now the trumpet summons us again not as a call to bear arms, though arms we need, not as a call to battle, though embattled we are, but as a call to bear the burden of a long twilight struggle, a struggle against the common enemies of man, tyranny, poverty, disease and war itself.

*In the long history of the world only a few generations
have been granted the roll of defending freedom in its
hour of maximum danger. I do not shrink from
this responsibility, I welcome it.*

*The energy, the faith, the devotion which we bring
to this endeavor will light our country and
all who serve it, and the glow from that
fire can truly light the world.*

*And so my fellow Americans, ask not what your country
can do for you, ask what you can do for your country.
My fellow citizens of the world, ask not what America
can do for you, but what together we can do
for the freedom of man.*

*With good conscience our only sure reward, with
history the final judge of our deeds, let us go forth
to lead the land we love, asking His blessing and
His help but knowing that here on earth
God's work must truly be our own.*

———————— ★ ————————

COMBAT GRAFFITI

*For those who fight for it,
freedom has a flavor the
protected will never know.*

Written on a C-ration box found
after the siege of Khe Sahn,
Vietnam, 1968

**North Vietnamese artillery shells explode on the beleaguered
Marine base at Khe Sanh on February 21, 1968.**   Khe Sanh was
considered to be strategically important and had to be held at any cost.

SYMBOL OF FREEDOM

To oppressed peoples all over the world, our soldiers are a symbol of freedom. ... After a long and empty night of uncertainty and fear, the East Germans on one refugee train to the west finally crossed the border at the town of Hof. Someone on the train asked doubtfully, "Are we really in the west?" Just then, in the early light of dawn, they looked out to see soldiers of the 2nd Armored Cavalry Regiment patrolling the border. At that instant, a cry of joy went up, "There are the Americans. We are free."

General Carl E. Vuono

In this critical time in the affairs of the world, it is vital that the democratic nations show their concern for the well-being of men everywhere and their desire for a better life for mankind.

**President
Harry S. Truman**

Harry S. Truman
1884–1972
33rd President of the United States
(1945–1952)

If liberty is to be saved, it will not be by doubters,
men of science, or the materialists: it will be by
religious convictions; by the faith of the individuals
who believe that God wills men to be free.

Henri Frederick Amiel

The years ahead will be great ones for our country,
for the cause of freedom and the spread of civilization.
The West will not contain Communism, it will
transcend Communism. We will not bother
to denounce it, we'll dismiss it as a sad,
bizarre chapter in human history whose
last pages are even now being written.

President Ronald Reagan
Notre Dame University
May 17, 1981

It is the Soviet Union that runs against the tide of
history. ... [It is] the march of freedom and democracy
which will leave Marxism-Leninism on the ash heap
of history as it has left other tyrannies which stifle the
freedom and muzzle the self-expression of the people.

President Ronald Reagan
Speech to Britain's Parliament
1982

SOME LIGHTS SEEM ETERNAL

The poet called Miss Liberty's torch, "the lamp beside the golden door." Well, that was the entrance to America, and it still is. And now you really know why we're here tonight.

The glistening hope of that lamp is still ours. Every promise, every opportunity is still golden in this land. And through that golden door our children

can walk into tomorrow with the knowledge that no one can be denied the promise that is America.

Her heart is full; her torch is still golden, her future bright. She has arms big enough to comfort and strong enough to support, for the strength in her arms is the strength of her people. She will carry on in the eighties unafraid, unashamed, and unsurpassed.

In this springtime of hope, some lights seem eternal; America's is.

President Ronald Reagan
Republican National Convention
speech, August 23, 1984

History tells us liberty is never free and every generation must make a down payment of service and perhaps sacrifice for its sake. If we enjoy peace today, it is because of our military strength and because of those who served before us. If we want peace for our children and our children's children, we as a people must remain very vigilant, militarily and economically strong, and led in every walk of life by people of character.

General John A. Wickham, Jr.

Freedom can be lost in a single generation. ... All any nation can give to each succeeding generation is the possibility of freedom. ... It is my prayer that our people will always remember: freedom is never free.

General John A. Wickham, Jr.

*I*t is almost uncanny how the three underlying principles
of our founding fathers have remained unchanged over the
years—our commitment to be independent, our will to win,
and our determination to fight to retain our inalienable
rights. ... We all need to understand our heritage as
soldiers in order that we may be better protectors of our
nation's sacred trust. ... We owe our nation, our children,
and grandchildren the debt of ensuring that each of
our soldiers knows what it is they are protecting and
guarding and why. ... Our children and grandchildren
will flourish and remain as strong, dedicated,
and morally sound as we are today, providing
the will is never lost for the cause of freedom.

SMA Glen E. Morrell
"What Soldiering Is All About"
ARMY, Oct. 1986

*W*e like living right, and being free.

Merle Haggard
from the lyrics "Okie from Muskogee"

*T*he triumph of the United States and our allies is the
triumph of a simple set of concepts—liberty, rule of law,
respect for the individual—treating all our people—all
races, all genders—with dignity and respect. We won—
and are winning—because the ideas—the foundations—
of our way of life are better than anything else devised
by man. The thing that motivates us to persevere and
patiently confront aggressive designs at every turn is an
abiding faith in our ideas of liberty and democracy.

Gordon Sullivan

This country gave me my freedom,
it doesn't owe me anything else.

Author Unknown

LIBERTY, NOT ENSLAVEMENT

Two weeks after Pearl Harbor in a speech broadcast from York Institute in Jamestown, Sergeant York said,

Our hands are on the plow and we dare not,
cannot turn back from our determination
to rid the world of the Hitler menace.
Life, not death; liberty, not enslavement;
the pursuit of happiness, not the pursuit
of sorrow and misery, will keep democracy
fighting until victory is assured.

This War Is Everybody's War

Wars are not won by men alone. Men must have materials with which to fight, and materials cost money. Sergeant York worked hard to sell Americans on the importance of buying war bonds during WW II. In a radio program sponsored by the War Bond Office of the Eighth Corps area, he said,

This war is everybody's war. The sooner everybody is wholeheartedly behind it, the sooner it will be over. It will never be finished quick as long as we put more store by our private, personal, and selfish wants than our national liberty and democracy. And the way I see it, liberty and democracy are prizes that come only to people who fight to win them and then keep on fighting eternally to hold them. Though all of us may not be front line fighters, all of us can still help with the fight. We can buy war bonds to the limit just as those American fighting men keep fighting to the limit. Men couldn't win with their bare hands in 1918. Men can't win with their bare hands today.

Sergeant Alvin York

*A*merica has proved that it is practicable to elevate the
mass of mankind—the laboring or lower class—to raise
them to self-respect, to make them competent to
act a part in the great right and the great duty of
self-government; and she has proved that this may be
done by education and the diffusion of knowledge.
She holds out an example a thousand times more
encouraging than ever was presented before to those
nine-tenths of the human race who are born
without hereditary fortune or hereditary rank.

Daniel Webster

*I*nterwoven is the love of liberty with every
ligament of the heart.

George Washington

*I*f the true spark of religious and civil liberty be kindled,
it will burn. Human agency cannot extinguish it.
Like the earth's central fire, it may be smothered for a time;
the ocean may overwhelm it; mountains may press it down;
but its inherent and unconquerable force will heave both
the ocean and the land, and at some time or another,
in some place or another, the volcano will break
out and flame to heaven.

Daniel Webster

The Dream of Freedom

History is a ribbon, always unfurling; history is a journey. And as we continue our journey, we think of those who traveled before us. We stand together again at the steps of this symbol of our democracy. Now we hear again the echoes of our past: a general falls to his knees in the hard snow of Valley Forge; a lonely President paces the darkened halls, and ponders his struggle to preserve the Union; the men of the Alamo call out encouragement to each other; a settler pushes west and sings a song, and the song echoes out forever and fills the unknowing air. It is the American sound. It is hopeful, big-hearted, idealistic, daring, decent, and fair. That's our heritage; that is our song. We sing it still. For all our problems, our differences, we are together as of old, as we raise our voices to the God who is the Author of this most tender music. And may He continue to hold us close as we fill the world with our sound—sound in unity, affection, and love—one people under God, dedicated to the dream of freedom that He has placed in the human heart, called upon now to pass that dream on to a waiting and hopeful world. God bless you and may God bless America.

President Ronald Reagan
closing remarks from his
Second Inaugural Address
January 21, 1986

A Concert of Free Peoples

It is a fearful thing to lead this great peaceful people into war, into the most terrible and disastrous of all wars, civilization itself seeming to be in the balance. But the right is more precious than peace, and we shall fight for the things which we have always carried nearest our hearts—for democracy, for the right of those who submit to authority to have a voice in their own governments, for the rights and liberties of small nations, for a universal dominion of right by such a concert of free peoples as shall bring peace and safety to all nations and make the world itself at last free.

Woodrow Wilson

President Woodrow Wilson
1856–1924
28th President of the United States
(1913–1921)

Liberty has constraints, but no frontiers.

David Lloyd George
1863–1945
British Statesman

OPPORTUNITY UNDER LIBERTY

In a clearing of the forests of Kentucky stands a crude log cabin. It is bare within and forbidding without. It speaks of the deepest poverty. Stretched upon the bare earth floor in the cabin lies a ragged untaught boy, poring, by the flickering light of the fireplace, over a borrowed book. He lifts his eyes to gaze upon the burdened form of his pioneer mother, and I hear him say:

> Life is hard. The future seems hopeless. My fathers fought in the American Revolution. They helped adopt the Constitution of America. They gave allegiance to a government, not by men but by laws which should be of equal application to all. Clad in the skins of animals, they penetrated the wilderness. With rifle nearby, they hewed logs for their cabins, cleared lands for their fields, and built homes for their children. Their eyes held a constant vision in which all men should be free to work out their own destiny, to plan their own lives in their own way, to possess the fruits of their own toil, and to stand or fall by their own efforts. Poor and humble though I am, I have a chance. In my country no doors are barred to me because I am poor. I can work. Be the reward much or little, it will be mine. I can learn; the knowledge will give me power. Thank God, I have a chance.

And the ragged boy rose to become the rail-splitter, the country store-keeper, the small town lawyer, the advocate of a great cause, the exemplar of individual liberty under the law, the great American President, the emancipator of a race, the defender and preserver of the American Union. This is the triumph, in the life of one man, of a human soul given equal opportunity under liberty.

by Arthur M. Hyde
former Governor of Missouri and
Secretary of Agriculture under
President Hoover

[From the book, *The Public Speaker's Treasure Chest,* by Herbert V. Prochnow, Harper & Brothers Publishers, New York, © 1942]

*Yesterday the greatest question was decided which
ever was debated in America; and a greater perhaps
never was, nor will be, decided among men.
A resolution was passed without one dissenting colony,
that these United Colonies are, and of right
ought to be, free and independent states.*

John Adams
Letter to Abigail Adams, July 3, 1776
1735–1826
2nd President of the United States
(1797–1801)

*I have but one lamp by which my feet are guided,
and that is the lamp of experience.
I know no way of judging of the future
but by the past.*

Patrick Henry
Speech at the Virginia Convention
St. John's Episcopal Church, Richmond, Virginia
March 23, 1775

A PLACE WE CANNOT HELP BUT LOVE

*We know what works: Freedom works. We know
what's right: Freedom is right. We know how to secure
a more just and prosperous life for man on Earth:
through free markets, free speech, free elections, and
the exercise of free will unhampered by the state.
For the first time in this century, for the first time in
perhaps all history, man does not have to invent a
system by which to live. We don't have to talk late into
the night about which form of government is better.
We don't have to wrest justice from the kings.
We only have to summon it from within ourselves.*

*We must act on what we know. I take as my guide the
hope of a saint: In crucial things, unity; in important
things, diversity; in all things, generosity.
America today is a proud, free nation, decent and civil,
a place we cannot help but love. We know in our
hearts, not loudly and proudly, but as a simple fact,
that this country has meaning beyond what we see,
and that our strength is a force for good.*

President George Herbert Bush
from his Inaugural Address, January 20, 1989
1924–
41st President of the United States
(1989–1993)

CHAPTER TEN

Patriotism

An American patriot is one who loves, supports, and defends our nation. Patriotism is the process of loving, supporting and defending the same. This chapter provides stories, lyrics, poems and commentaries on the uniqueness and special qualities of American patriotism. From civilian to soldier, from children to elders, from sea to shining sea, this chapter echoes those heartfelt feelings that show the love we all have for our country.

A citizen's proudest privilege is to bear arms under his country's flag.

General George S. Patton, Jr.
1885–1945
Commander of the Third Army, WW II

**Soldiers of the Army's 82nd Airborne Division
proudly display their colors.**

PRESERVING THE REPUBLIC

Liberty Bell   Hung in Independence hall in 1753, the bell was rung in July 1776 to proclaim the Declaration of Independence.

You must have ambition, but it must be fired by patriotism.

General Creighton Abrams

It is the manners and spirit of a people which preserve a republic in vigor.

Thomas Jefferson

Our Constitution is an actual operation; everything appears to promise that it will last; but nothing in this world is certain but death and taxes.

Benjamin Franklin
in a letter to M. Leroy, 1789

AN AMERICAN WITHOUT RESERVE

I was born an American; I live an American; I shall die an American; and I intend to perform the duties incumbent upon me in that character to the end of my career. I mean to do this with absolute disregard of personal consequences.

What are the personal consequences? What is the individual man, with all the good or evil that may betide him, in comparison with the good or evil which may befall a great country, and in the midst of great transactions which concern that country's fate?

Let the consequences be what they will, I am careless. No man can suffer too much, and no man can fall too soon, if he suffer, or if he fall, in the defense of the liberties and constitution of his country.

Daniel Webster
1782–1852
Secretary of State
(1841–1843 and 1850–1852)

MEMORIAL DAY

Memorial Day, originally called Decoration Day, is a day set aside for remembrance of those who have died in our nation's service. Memorial Day was first proclaimed on 5 May 1868 by General John Logan, in his General Order Number 11, and was first observed on 30 May 1868; when flowers were placed on the graves of Union and Confederate soldiers. The South, at first, refused to acknowledge, Memorial Day, honoring their dead on separate days until after WW I. It is now observed in almost every state of the union on the last Monday of every May. Since the Civil War more than 1.1 million veterans, both women and men, have lost their lives in service to America. Indeed the Civil War alone accounted for more than 600,000 dead.

The following is the verbatim order establishing Decoration Day, as written in 1868:

General Order
No. 11
Headquarters, Grand Army of the Republic
Washington, D.C., May 5, 1868

I. The 30th day of May, 1868, is designated for the purpose of strewing with flowers or otherwise decorating the graves of comrades who died in defense of their country during the late rebellion, and whose bodies now lie in almost every city, village, and hamlet churchyard in the land. In this observance no form or ceremony is prescribed, but posts and comrades will in their own way arrange such fitting services and testimonials of respect as circumstances may permit.

We are organized, comrades, as our regulations tell us, for the purpose, among other things, "of preserving and strengthening those kind and fraternal feelings which have bound together the soldiers, sailors, and marines who united to suppress the late rebellion." What can aid more to assure this result than by cherishing tenderly the memory of our heroic dead, who made their breasts a barricade between our country and its foe? Their soldier lives were the reveille of freedom to a race in chains, and their death a tattoo of rebellious tyranny in arms. We should guard their graves with sacred vigilance. All that the consecrated wealth and taste of the Nation can add to their adornment and security is but a fitting tribute to the memory of her slain defenders. Let no wanton foot tread rudely on such hallowed grounds. Let pleasant paths invite the coming and going of reverent visitors and fond mourners. Let no vandalism or avarice or neglect, no ravages of time, testify to the present or to the coming generations that we have forgotten, as a people, the cost of free and undivided republic.

If other eyes grow dull and other hands slack, and other hearts cold in the solemn trust, ours shall keep it well as long as the light and warmth of life remain in us.

Let us, then, at the time appointed, gather around their sacred remains and garland the passionless mounds above them with choicest flowers of springtime; let us raise above them the dear old flag they saved from dishonor; let us in this solemn presence renew our pledges to aid and assist those whom they have left among us as sacred charges upon the Nation's gratitude—the soldier's and sailor's widow and orphan.

II. It is the purpose of the Commander-in-Chief to inaugurate this observance with the hope it will be kept up from year to year, while a survivor of the war remains to honor the memory of his departed comrades. He earnestly desires the public press to call attention to this Order, and lend its friendly aid in bringing it to the notice of comrades in all parts of the country in time for simultaneous compliance therewith.

III. Department commanders will use every effort to make this order effective.

> By command of:
> John A. Logan, Commander-in-Chief
>
> N. P. Chipman, Adjutant-General

*P*atriotism is easy to understand in America;
*it means looking out for yourself by
looking out for your country.*

President Calvin Coolidge
1872–1933
30th President of the United States
(1923–1929)

THE AMERICAN'S CREED

I believe in the United States of America as a government of the people, by the people, for the people; whose just powers are derived from the consent of the governed, a democracy in a republic, a sovereign Nation of many sovereign States; a perfect union, one and inseparable; established upon those principles of freedom, equality, justice, and humanity for which American patriots sacrificed their lives and fortunes.

I therefore believe it is my duty to my country to love it, to support its Constitution, to obey its laws, to respect its flag, and to defend it against all enemies.

William Tyler Page
Written in 1917
Accepted by the United States
House of Representatives on April 3, 1918

[Historical Notes: The American's Creed was a result of a nationwide contest for writing a National Creed, which would be a brief summary of the American political faith founded upon things fundamental in American history and tradition. The contest was the idea of Henry Sterling Chapin, Commissioner of Education of New York State. Over three thousand entries were received, and William Tyler Page was declared to be the winner. James H. Preston, the mayor of Baltimore, presented an award to Page in the House of Representatives Office Building on April 3, 1918. The Speaker of the House of Representatives and the commissioner of education of the state of New York accepted the Creed for the United States, and the proceedings relating to the award were printed in the Congressional Record of April 13, 1918. It was a time when patriotic sentiments were very much in vogue. The United States had been a participant in World War I only a little over a year at the time the Creed was adopted.

The author of the American's Creed, William Tyler Page, was a descendant of John Page, who had come to America in 1650 and had settled in Williamsburg, Virginia. Another ancestor, Carter Braxton, had signed the Declaration of Independence. Still another ancestor, John Tyler, was the tenth president of the United States. William Tyler Page had come to Washington at the age of thirteen to serve as a Capitol Page. Later he became an employee of the Capitol building and served in that capacity for almost sixty-one years. In 1919 he was elected clerk of the House. Thirteen years later, when the Democrats again became a majority party, they created for Page the office of minority clerk of the House of Representatives. He held this position for the remainder of his life.

Referring to the Creed, Page said: "It is the summary of the fundamental principles of the American political faith as set forth in its greatest documents, its worthiest traditions, and its greatest leaders." His wording of the Creed used passages and phrases from the Declaration of Independence, the Preamble to the Constitution, Lincoln's Gettysburg Address, and Daniel Webster's reply to Robert Y. Hayne in the Senate in 1830.]

*Our graduates seldom amass great wealth,
but just as seldom do they display weakness or
indifference to their duties as citizens.
They are trained to be soldiers, if there be need for
soldiers, but what is far more important,
they are trained to be good citizens, strong and
of the type so urgently needed to promote
the welfare of this country of ours
in its democratic progress.*

General George C. Marshall
Speaking to a national radio audience from
the Virginia Military Institute
November 11, 1940

Talk About Heaven

The following is a veteran's reply to Dear Abby, about a letter complaining that America is going to hell, April 1982

DEAR ABBY: I am retired, have a good income and am in good health. I play golf every day, have a roof over my head and have a supermarket to shop for food without having to farm and raise it myself.

I have an electric stove to cook my food, and a washer and dryer to do my laundry instead of a washboard and tub. I have nice clothes and shoes on my feet and don't have to go barefoot as I did when I was a child.

I have a nice bathroom and don't have to go outside in the cold as I did when I was a child. I bathe in a bathtub with plenty of hot water whenever I feel like it instead of in a washtub behind a pot-bellied stove on Saturday night as I did when I was a child.

I am not locked up in a prison or a mental hospital as some people are. I am free to go where I want. I have a television set and stereo that kings could not enjoy years ago.

I have a car for transportation instead of a horse and buggy. I was married for 22 years to a woman who was as beautiful as a movie star. I went through World War II without a scratch. Talk about Heaven. America is Heaven!

THINKING OUT LOUD

*All must admit that the reception of the teachings
of Christ results in the purest patriotism,
in the most scrupulous fidelity to public trust,
and in the best type of citizenship.*

President Grover Cleveland
1837–1908
22nd and 24th President of the United States
(1885–1889 and 1893–1897)

*Not until I went into the churches of America and
heard her pulpits flame with righteousness did
I understand the secret of her genius and power.
America is great because America is good,
and if America ever ceases to be good,
America will cease to be great.*

Alexis deTocqueville
1805–1859
French Author
Wrote extensively about the American People
and their political institutions

The Things That Make A Soldier Great

The things that make a soldier great and send him out to die,
To face the flaming cannon's mouth, nor ever question why,
Are lilacs by a little porch, the row of tulips red,
The peonies and pansies, too, the old petunia bed,
The grass plot where his children play, the roses on the wall:
Tis these that make a soldier great. He's fighting for them all.

Tis not the pomp and pride of kings that make a soldier brave;
Tis not allegiance to the flag that over him may wave;
For soldiers never fight so well on land or on the foam
As when behind the cause they see the little place called home.
Endanger but that humble street whereon his children run—
You make a soldier of the man who never bore a gun.
What is it through the battle smoke the valiant soldier sees?
The little garden far away, the budding apple trees.
The little patch of ground back there, the children at the play,
Perhaps a tiny mound behind the simple church of gray.
The golden thread of courage isn't linked to castle dome
But to the spot, where'er it be—the humble spot called home.
And now the lilacs bud again and all is lovely there,
And homesick soldiers far away know spring is in the air;
The tulips come to bloom again, the grass once more is green,
And every man can see the spot where all his joys have been.
He sees his children smile at him, he hears the bugle call,
And only death can stop him now—he's fighting for them all.

Edgar A. Guest
from the book, *Poems of Patriotism*

VETERANS DAY

In 1921, an unknown World War I American soldier was buried in Arlington National Cemetery. This site, on a hillside overlooking the Potomac River and the city of Washington, became the focal point of reverence for America's veterans.

Similar ceremonies occurred earlier in England and France, where an unknown soldier was buried in each nation's highest place of honor (in England, Westminster Abbey; in France, the Arc de Triomphe). These memorial gestures all took place on November 11, giving universal recognition to the celebrated ending of World War I fighting at 11 A.M., November 11, 1918 (the 11th hour of the 11th day of the 11th month). The day became known as "Armistice Day."

Armistice Day officially received its name in America in 1926 through a Congressional resolution. It became a national holiday 12 years later by similar Congressional action. If the idealistic hope had been realized that World War I was "the War to end all Wars," November 11 might still be called Armistice Day. But only a few years after the holiday was proclaimed, war broke out in Europe. Sixteen and one-half million Americans took part. Four hundred seven thousand of them died in service, more than 292,000 in battle.

Realizing that peace was equally preserved by veterans of WW II and Korea, Congress was requested to make this day an occasion to honor those who have served America in all wars. In 1954 President Eisenhower signed a bill proclaiming November 11 be changed from Armistice Day to Veterans Day.

On Memorial Day 1958, two more unidentified American war dead were brought from overseas and interred in the plaza beside the unknown soldier of

World War I. One was killed in World War II, the other in the Korean War. In 1973, a law passed providing interment of an unknown American from the Vietnam War, but none was found for several years. In 1984, an unknown serviceman from that conflict was placed alongside the others. To honor these men, symbolic of all Americans who gave their lives in all wars, an Army honor guard, the 3d U.S. Infantry (The Old Guard), keeps day and night vigil.

A law passed in 1968 changed the national commemoration of Veterans Day to the fourth Monday in October. It soon became apparent, however, that November 11 was a date of historic significance to many Americans. Therefore, in 1978 Congress returned the observance to its traditional date.

Author Unknown

War Is an Ugly Thing

War is an ugly thing but not the ugliest of things; the decayed and degraded state of moral and patriotic feelings which thinks that nothing is worth war is much worse.

U.S. soldier standing over a dead Japanese soldier   South Pacific, World War II

*A man who has nothing for which he is willing
to fight, nothing which is more important than
his own personal safety, is a miserable creature
and has no chance of being free unless
made and kept so by the exertions of
better men than himself.*

John Stuart Mill

GOD BLESS AMERICA

*God bless America,
Land that I love,
Stand beside her and guide her
Thru the night with a light from above.*

*From the mountains to the prairies,
To the oceans white with foam,
God bless America,
My home, sweet home.*

America, the Beautiful

O beautiful for spacious skies,
For amber waves of grain,
For purple mountain majesties
Above the fruited plain.
America! America! God shed His grace on thee,
And crown thy good with brotherhood
From sea to shining sea.

Pikes Peak seen through "Gateway Rock"   Garden of
the Gods, Colorado Springs, Colorado

O beautiful for pilgrim feet,
Whose stern impassion'd stress
A thoroughfare for freedom beat
Across the wilderness.
America! America! God mend thine ev'ry flaw,
Confirm thy soul in self-control,
Thy liberty in law.

[These words were penned, originally as a poem, by Katharine Lee Bates
following her visit to the summit of Pikes Peak on July 22, 1893.]

God Bless the U.S.A.

If tomorrow all the things were gone
I'd worked for all my life,
And I had to start again
with just my children and my wife,
I'd thank my lucky stars
to be living here today,
'Cause the flag still stands for freedom
and they can't take that away.

I'm proud to be an American
where at least I know I'm free,

And I won't forget the men who died
who gave that right to me,
And I gladly stand up next to you
and defend her still today,
'Cause there ain't no doubt I love this land
God Bless the U.S.A.

From the lakes of Minnesota
to the hills of Tennessee,
Across the plains of Texas
from sea to shining sea.
From Detroit down to Houston
and New York to L.A.,
There's pride in every American heart
and it's time we stand and say:

I'm proud to be an American
where at least I know I'm free,
And I won't forget the men who died
who gave that right to me,
And I gladly stand up next to you
and defend her still today,
'Cause there ain't no doubt I love this land
God Bless the U.S.A.

Lee Greenwood

The American Eagle

When God made the clam
He guaranteed him absolute economical and social security.
He built the clam a house, a shell, to protect him from his enemies.
When hungry, the clam simply opens his shell and food rushes in for him.
He has no worries.
He doesn't fight anybody.
He's not going anywhere.
But, when God made the eagle,
He gave him the sky as a domain.
The eagle then nested on the highest crag,
Where the storms threaten every day.
For food he flies through miles of rain, snow, sleet and wind.

He screams his defiance at the elements,
and goes about his own business,
building his own life.
When aroused, he's a vicious foe for his enemies.
The eagle, not the clam, is the emblem of America!

Author Unknown

You're the Finest

In just 200 years, your country,
through freedom and hard work,
has changed the world.
In agriculture, industry, education, medicine, law,
transportation, and on and on.
No country can match America's record in religious freedom,
civil freedom, human rights, the importance
and dignity of the individual.
We do have our differences.
But when we join together in times of crisis,
our strength is awesome.
Among all the world's nations,
America still stands out front.
You're an American.
You're the finest ever—
and don't you ever, ever forget it.

Reprinted with permission from Harry J. Gray
Former Chairman of United Technologies Corporation.
This message was published in the *Wall Street Journal,* 1980

Pledge of Allegiance

I pledge allegiance to the flag
Of the United States of America
And to the republic for which it stands,
one Nation under God, indivisible,
with liberty and justice for all.

[The "Pledge of Allegiance" was first published in a magazine called "The Youth's Companion." In 1892 Authorship was claimed for both James B. Upham and Francis Bellamy. In 1939 the United States Flag Association ruled that Bellamy was the author of the original pledge. The words, "under God" were added on June 14, 1954.]

*A person gets from a symbol
the meaning he puts into it.*

The United States Supreme Court

COMMENTARY ON THE
PLEDGE OF ALLEGIANCE

As a schoolboy in Vincennes, Indiana, one of Red Skelton's teachers explained the words and meaning of the Pledge of Allegiance to his class. The teacher felt his pupils were bored reciting the pledge every morning, so he decided to explain to his students what the lines they were mumbling meant. Skelton later wrote down, and eventually recorded, his recollection of this lecture. During the presentation of his CBS television show on the night of January 14, 1969, Mr. Skelton read his version of the "Pledge of Allegiance" to the flag. He immediately received 200,000 requests for it; he recorded it and the record was widely played throughout the country. Mr. Skelton's meaning follows.

I   Me; an individual; a committee of one.

Pledge   Dedicate all of my worldly goods to give without self-pity.

Allegiance   My love and my devotion.

To the Flag   Our standard; Old Glory; a symbol of Freedom; wherever she waves there is respect, because your loyalty has given her a dignity that shouts, "Freedom is everybody's job."

United   That means that we have all come together.

States   Individual communities that have united into forty-eight great states. Forty-eight individual communities with pride and dignity and purpose. All divided with imaginary boundaries, yet united to a common purpose, and that is love for country.

And to the Republic   Republic—a state in which sovereign power is invested in representatives chosen by the people to govern. And government is the people; and it's from the people to the leaders, not from the leaders to the people.

For which it stands

One Nation   One Nation—meaning, so blessed by God.

Indivisible   Incapable of being divided.

With Liberty   Which is Freedom; the right of power to live one's own life, without threats, fear, or some sort of retaliation.

And Justice   The principle, or qualities, of dealing fairly with others.

For All   For All—which means, boys and girls, it's as much your country as it is mine.

And now, boys and girls, let me hear you recite the Pledge of Allegiance:

I pledge allegiance to the Flag of the United States of America, and to the Republic, for which it stands; one nation, indivisible, with liberty and justice for all.

Since I was a small boy, two states have been added to our country, and two words have been added to the Pledge of Allegiance: "Under God." Wouldn't it be a pity if someone said that is a prayer, and that would be eliminated from schools, too?

Red Skelton

———————— ★ ————————

Thank God! I—I also—am an American!
Daniel Webster

———————— ★ ————————

One country, one constitution, one destiny.
Daniel Webster
from a speech on March 15, 1837

———————— ★ ————————

CHAPTER ELEVEN
Caring and Compassion

This chapter provides stories, quotes, and articles about the caring and compassion displayed by Americans in both peace and war. It is a chapter that talks about those soldiers who really give a damn about their fellow man and soldier. This chapter describes a very unique and important quality that every good leader needs to practice, namely, the ability and willingness to take care of the troops.

President Abraham Lincoln
1809–1865
16th President of the United States
(1861–1865)

With Malice toward none;
With charity for all;
With firmness in the right, as
God gives us to see the right,
Let us strive on to finish
the work we are in;
To bind up the nation's wounds;
To care for him who shall
have borne the battle,
And for his widow,
And his orphan—
To do all which may achieve
and cherish a just and lasting
peace among ourselves,
And with all nations.

From President Lincoln's
Second Inaugural Address
March 4, 1865

LETTER FROM PRESIDENT LINCOLN

Abraham Lincoln
1809–1865

To Mrs. Lydia Bixby

Executive Mansion,
Washington, November 21, 1864

Dear Madam,

I have been shown in the files of the War Department a statement of the Adjutant General of Massachusetts, that you are the mother of five sons who have died gloriously on the field of battle.

I feel how weak and fruitless must be any words of mine which should attempt to beguile you from the grief of a loss so overwhelming. But I cannot refrain from tendering to you the consolation that may be found in the thanks of the Republic they died to save.

I pray that our Heavenly Father may assuage the anguish of your bereavement, and leave you only the cherished memory of the loved and lost, and the solemn pride that must be yours, to have laid so costly a sacrifice upon the altar of freedom.

Yours, very sincerely and respectfully,
Abraham Lincoln

[In reality, only two of Mrs. Bixby's sons had died in action, but Lincoln was unaware of this when he wrote the letter.]

When the Army of Northern Virginia surrendered,
large numbers of the rebel soldiers came over to us.
We were glad to see them. They had fought bravely,
and were as glad as we that the war was over. ...
We received them kindly, and exchanged pocket knives
and sundry trinkets, that each could have something
to carry home as a reminiscence of the great event.

Theodore Gerrish
20th Maine Volunteers, Civil War, from the book Rank and File

*T*he *American people desire and are determined to work,*
for a world in which all nations and all peoples
are free to govern themselves as they see fit,
and to achieve a decent and satisfying life.
Above all else, our people desire and are determined to
work for peace on earth, a just and lasting peace.

President Harry S. Truman

A SOLDIER'S STORY, WW I

Actual Combat Photo   World War I

It was a few weeks before Christmas 1917. The beautiful snowy landscapes of Europe were blackened by war. The trenches on one side held the Germans and on the other side the trenches were filled with Americans. It was World War I. The exchange of gunshots was intense. Separating them was a very narrow strip of no-man's-land. A young German soldier attempting to cross that no-man's-land had been shot and had become entangled in the barbed wire. He cried out in anguish, then in pain he continued to whimper. Between the shells all the Americans in that sector could hear him scream. When one American soldier could stand it no longer, he crawled out of the American trenches and on his stomach crawled to that German soldier.

When the Americans realized what he was doing they stopped firing, but the Germans continued. Then a German officer realized what the young American was doing, and he ordered his men to cease firing.

Now there was a weird silence across the no-man's-land. On his stomach, the American made his way to that German soldier and disentangled him. He stood up with the German in his arms, walked straight to the German trenches and placed him the waiting arms of his comrades. Having done so, he turned and started back to the American trenches.

Suddenly there was a hand on his shoulder that spun him around. There stood a German officer who had won the Iron Cross, the highest German honor for bravery. He jerked it from his own uniform and placed it on the American, who walked back to the American trenches. When he was safely in the trenches, they resumed the insanity of war.

[This story appeared in "Moments of Christmas," by Robert Strand, New Leaf Press, 1993. Reprinted with permission.]

*F*ar *from being a handicap to command,*
compassion is the measure of it.
For unless one values the lives
of his soldiers and is
tormented by their ordeals,
he is unfit to command.

General Omar N. Bradley
1893–1981
Led U.S. First Army invasion of Normandy,
1944

General Omar Bradley

Tie My Boot

When General Matthew B. Ridgway took command of a demoralized U.S. 8th Army during the Korean War, he immediately went to the front and visited with his soldiers. Once, on a wet, dark morning, he stood beside a road as a group of tired Marines moved by, carrying heavy loads. One young Marine, too laden to bend down, was tripping over the laces of his boot which had become untied. In the semidarkness, he called to the stationary group, "Hey, would one of you sons-a-bitches tie my boot?" The commander of the Eighth Army knelt in the mud and tied the Marine's boot.

General Matthew Ridgway
Korean War

General Ridgway did it not for show, nor because he was a general. He tied that Marine's boot because he was a soldier first, a member of a team, a soldier who had the impulse to help a fighting man, a man in trouble.

CARING AND THE ART OF COMMAND

Excerpts from a speech by General Melvin Zais
U.S. Army (Retired), March 1977

... obviously I could go on in the same vein but I will stop providing you with pearls of wisdom and I will elaborate at some length on the one piece of advice which I believe will contribute more to making you a better leader and commander—will provide you greater happiness and self-esteem and at the same time advance your career more than any other advice which I can provide you. And it doesn't call for a special personality, and it doesn't call for any certain chemistry. Any one of you can do it and that advice is—**You must care**. The Chief of Staff of the Army in a recent speech said it another way—"You must give a damn."

Let's talk a little more about caring. You'll find that at this school and any other service school that you might attend, beginning at your basic course and winding up at war college level that you spend about 80% of your time on tactics, strategy, weapons, planning, writing. I'm being very generous here.

And you spend about 20% of your time on people matters. And I note that here at the Armed Forces Staff College with this Delos C. Emmons Lecture Series, that the worm is turning a little bit from when I made this first observation after many years in the service school system. It's an interesting phenomena and a paradox that we go to school after school after school and spend about 80% of our time on tactics, weapons, logistics and planning and about 20% on people matters and then we go to our units and what do we do? We spend about 80% of our time on people matters and about 20% of our time on tactics, weapons, logistics, etc. Just think about it. You're young officers mostly here, majors and lieutenant colonels but you have all commanded companies; some hope to command battalions; many have been S-3s and execs; some have commanded smaller ships; some have commanded air squadrons. Where does your time go? Just reflect on it. You're dealing with grievances; you're inspecting barracks; you're inspecting latrines; you're checking mess halls, supply rooms, day rooms. You're worrying about laundry; you're worrying about pay; you're greeting new officers and new non-commissioned officers and new soldiers; you're saying goodbye to officers and non-commissioned officers. You're officiating at the promotions of your officers and your non-commissioned officers; you're officiating at the demotions of certain non-commissioned officers; you're dealing with the pass policy and complaints; you're dealing with awards; you're engaging in a great deal of correspondence; you're visiting the guard house; you're going to chapel on Sunday. Even if you're not religious, you're going there because you think you should as a good leader because you should do it as an example to your men. Those are the things that you're dealing with in command and you must care about your soldiers and your sailors and your airmen. Now think to yourself, all of you are saying to yourself right now, "Well, I care. What's this guy talking about?" Well, there are degrees of caring. There are degrees of personal sacrifice to reflect the amount of caring that you do. And there's an attitude that you have to develop in yourself. How do you know if you care? You're sitting out there wondering "Do I care. Do I *really* care?" How do you know if you care?

Well, for one thing, if you care, you listen to your junior officers and soldiers. When I say listen, I don't mean that stilted baloney that so may officers engage in and stand up to an enlisted man and say "How old are you son? Where are you from? How long have you been here? Thank you very much. Next man." That's baloney. That's form. That's posed. I can remember when I asked my son when he was a cadet at West Point how he liked his regimental Commander and he paused a while and, with that clean-cut incisiveness with which most midshipmen and cadets evaluate people, he said to me "he plays the role." Wow, that was damning! "He plays the role." I noticed this officer in later life and he postured a great deal and he always stood with his knees bent back and he always turned one toe out and he always wore special little things around his collar and he always turned sideways. I knew what he [my son] meant when he said "He plays the role."

Well, I'm not talking about that kind of stuff. I'm talking about listening. Because a young soldier won't come out and tell you that everything is all wrong. He'll be a little hesitant. If you ask him if he is getting along all right, if he just shrugs, he's getting along lousy. If he's not enthusiastic in his response, there's something wrong and you better dig a little deeper. You care if you listen to him. Really listen, you care if you really wonder what he's doing on his off duty activities. When you're about to tee off on Saturday afternoon, when you're at the club at happy hour, when you're going or coming home from church on Sunday, if you're wondering, if there is a little creeping nagging in the back of your head about, "I wonder, I wonder what the soldiers are doing. I wonder." Do you do that? What are your airmen doing? What are your sailors doing? Where do they go? You care if you go in the mess hall and I don't mean go in with white gloves and rub dishes and pots and pans and find dust. You care if you go into the mess hall and you noticed that the scrambled eggs are in a big puddle of water and that 20 pounds of toast have been done in advance and it has been laying there hard and cold. And the bacon is laying there dripping in the grease and the cooks have all their work done way ahead of time. The cold pots of coffee are sitting on the tables getting even colder. If that really bothers you, if it really gripes you, if you want to tear up those cooks, you care. It's little things.

When I was in Vietnam a Quartermaster Captain was bragging to me about the ice cream that they made at Camp Evans and were taking out to the soldiers on the fire bases. I said, "That's great." He said "Sir, would you like to see what we're making?" I said, "I'd like to see very much." And I went there and they had these machines and they were pouring ice cream into these gallon containers. He was very proud. He says, "We get it out there everyday." I said, "That's great. What do you carry it out there in?" He said "Oh these containers." I said, "Yeah, but how do the soldiers eat it? You know, they're all in little dugouts. They're not all lined up in a mess hall. They don't have mess kits out there and things like that." He said, "I know, Sir." I said, "I know how they eat it. They pass that thing around and they stick their fingers in it and each one grabs some." I said, "Get some Dixie cups and send them." He said "Dixie cups?" I said, "Yeah, Dixie cups."

I use these little elementary things because I'm trying to illustrate a point. When you're getting ready for the annual IG inspection and you know these guys are "GI-ing" the barracks and you know they're working like hell and it's Sunday night, If you'll get out of your warm house and go down to the barracks, and wander in to see them work. And just sit on the foot locker. You don't have to tell them they're doing a great job. Just sit on the foot locker and talk to one or two soldiers and leave. They'll know that you know that they're working like hell to make you look good. If, as I mentioned earlier, on Sunday and holidays you're concerned. If you take your kids and wife and you go to the mess hall. If even before that, you wander around and see if they're making that place look decent, you care. If you have a fine, uncommonly good looking non-commissioned officer with muscles rippling down his

cheeks and a strong neck and clean as a whistle, trim as can be, shoulders back, the look of tigers in his eyes and he says to you "Captain, don't worry about it. I guarantee I'm going to take care of it." If you don't check to see whether he is making these guys do pushups until they're dizzy and sweating and about to pass out, if you don't wonder—is this guy getting sadistic pleasure from pushing these guys around, if you don't make it your business to make it known throughout your outfit that you won't put up with that crap, then you don't care. But if that worries you when you wonder, then you go and check and you ask questions and you make sure. You care.

If you look out your window before a parade and you see that the troops are lined up there, 15, 20, or 30 minutes before, windy, rainy, hot, whatever it may be, if it doesn't really boil you to see that, you don't care. But if it does, you care because the only reason, the only reason the soldiers stand around and wait is because some dumb jerk officer didn't plan it right or he planned it such a way that the troops have to pay for him not missing a deadline. You care if just before a jump or just before assault on a hot landing or just before takeoff from an aircraft carrier or just before a close support raid, you care if you wander down to where these guys are and you notice that their Adam's apples are bobbing a little, you notice that they are a little pale, and you notice that they are yawning a lot. People yawn when they are scared. And it really helps scared soldiers and scared Lieutenants and scared Captains and Majors and Commanders and Lieutenant Commanders and it helps anybody when you're scared and getting ready to do something more difficult for somebody to come around who is senior to you, whom you respect and admire to let you know that he knows, that he cares. You have got to seek out these situations wherever it is tough for your men. Be there and understand and be sympathetic and give a pat and it has got to bother you in your belly when you walk down the line and you see all these lads waiting, they're sitting under the wing of the plane or they're sitting near a chopper and they're loaded and the sweat is coming down their faces and they're really scared and you can smell it in their breath. I can tell you, you can smell fear in a man's breath but you'll never know it unless you get close enough to them to smell it. And if it bothers you and if you try to help him that way, you care. I can't make you do this. But you really, you really need to like soldiers. You need to be amused at their humor, you need to be tolerant of their bawdiness, you have to understand that they're as lousy as you let them be and as good as you make them be. You just have to really like them and feel good about being with them.

When I was commanding the 101st Airborne Division, I used to write a column every week. It was in a paper called *The Screaming Eagle.* The name of the column was called "Lucky Eagle Says." I tried to get some message to my soldiers. I tried to get some direct communication to them. My code name was "Lucky Eagle." The code name for the fellow before me was "Bold Eagle." I figured if I was bold, my soldiers would know it. I didn't have to put it in my code name so I named myself Lucky Eagle on account of soldiers are superstitious and soldiers are always scared about something and if they wanted to be associated with anything, they like to be associated with luck. This is what I wrote in this column and I saved it. I said:

> You cannot expect a soldier to be a proud soldier if you humiliate him. You cannot expect him to be brave if you abuse and cower him. You cannot expect him to be strong if you break him. You cannot ask for respect and obedience and willingness to assault hot landing zones, hump back-breaking ridges, destroy dug-in emplacements if your soldier has not been treated with the respect and dignity which fosters unit esprit and personal pride. The line between firmness and harshness—between strong leadership and bullying, between discipline and chicken, is a fine line. It is difficult to define but those of us who are professionals and who have also accepted a career as leaders of men must find that line. It is because judgment and concern for people and human relations are involved in leadership that only men can lead men and not computers.
>
> I enjoin you to be ever alert to the pitfalls of too much authority. Beware that you do not fall in the category of the little man with a little job with a big head. In essence, be considerate, treat your subordinates right and they will literally die for you.

I wanted all my officers and non-commissioned officers to know I felt that way.

Now I want to close by stating that if you care, I guarantee you a successful career. I won't guarantee that you will be a general or admiral but I guarantee that you will improve your chances ten fold. So it is in your self-interest. Even if you do not become a flag officer you will still be happy in the devotion, love and affection of your men and you will like yourself better.

I sincerely believe that to be a successful leader in the idealistic sense—you must care.

Those who care about people deeply, in peace time and war time, are those who are going to capitalize on that unit and are going to be very successful.

Looking back over 35 years as an officer, as leader and led, I have oftentimes "taken pulse" on how I thought I was doing. There were times when I didn't quite measure up to the high standard of personal and professional excellence that I had set for myself, times when I knew I had to work harder to improve myself. You know how I could tell? I could see it in the eyes of those around me. ... You can fool bosses, and at times even peers, but you can't fool your subordinates. Look into their eyes— you'll really learn something.

General John A. Wickham, Jr.

You must ... love being a soldier; love being around other soldiers; love leading, training, and caring for soldiers and their families; be technically and tactically proficient; be dedicated, motivated, physically fit, mentally alert, and morally straight; believe in your fellow soldier, in your Army, and in your nation; strive to be all you can be. And, if you're a leader, want the same for those in your charge.

SMA Richard A. Kidd
"Being a Soldier," *Soldiers Magazine*
May 1994

Seniors, not superiors.

We and us, not I or me.

Do the best you can and look after your soldiers.

General Richard E. Cavazos
USA, Retired

One of the enduring memories of this war will be the images of America's soldiers moving into battle with an iron determination to crush the enemy and, only hours later, treating defeated Iraqi prisoners with dignity and respect.... We equally honor the unsung heroes of Desert Storm—the soldiers who manned the ramparts of freedom in other regions of the world, the soldiers who provided invaluable support for our forces in the desert, and the soldiers who maintained undiminished readiness for contingencies worldwide.

General Carl E. Vuono

When soldiers of the 4-32 Armor, 3rd Armored Division began to take prisoners, the Iraqi soldiers started yelling and screaming at my soldiers, "Don't shoot us, don't shoot us," and one of my soldiers said, "Hey, we're from America, we don't shoot our prisoners." That sort of stuck with me.

1SG Dennis L. DeMasters
in TRADOC Pamphlet 525-100-4
Leadership and Command on the Battlefield:
Noncommissioned Officer Corps, 1994

THERE IS ALWAYS SOMEONE WHO WILL HELP

In the mid '80s a young soldier wrote a letter to General John A. Wickham, Jr., then-Chief of Staff of the Army. It was a letter about the two-way commitment between the Army, its soldiers, and their families. This soldier had recently suffered a serious brain injury during a parachute jump and medical experts were doubtful about his survival. But he did live, and he wrote the following letter:

Life's difficulties are always cropping up, but in the Army people make up for the things that go wrong. There is always someone who will help in the Army. When the doctors thought I would never make it, my unit never gave up.

They were with me and supported me. They stayed behind me and my family the whole way. Words cannot express my thanks and the thanks of my wife for the care that my company commander, my first sergeant, and my buddies showed during the most difficult time in our lives.

That's what the Army is all about, taking care of each other. I appreciate what the Army is doing for families. And, you know what? I'm proud to be a soldier.

PROUD TO BE AN AMERICAN: WITNESS TO KOSOVAR'S ARRIVAL

by First Lt. Mike Nachshen, USAF, Special to the American Forces Press Service, McGuire Air Force Base, N.J.

I was on the flight line helping escort about 325 reporters when Tower Air 747, call sign Kosovo One, touched down May 5 (1999) at 4:18 P.M.

As the wide-bodied plane descended with a manifest of more than 400 Kosovar refugees, a hush fell over the assembled reporters. The only sound was that of the aircraft's wheels making contact with the tarmac.

What struck me was that I was watching history in the making, and that I was playing a small (extremely small) part in this momentous event. A few moments later, the first refugees began departing the plane and boarding buses that would take them to their temporary home at nearby Fort Dix.

I was less than 100 feet from the refugees, and was able to see their faces as they stepped off the plane. The first person I saw walk down the stairs was a little boy, probably 7 or 8 years old. His face and clothes were dirty, he clutched a ragged teddy bear in his right hand and a small blue plastic bag in his right—at that moment in time, that was everything he owned.

He squinted into the bright light at the hundreds of reporters, VIPs and uniformed people there and made his way toward the bus. Then a woman, holding the hands of her two small children, walked off the plane, followed by a man bent with old age who wore a traditional skullcap on his head.

As the refugees continued to disembark, I tried to put myself in their shoes. I tried to imagine what it must have been like to be chased out of their homeland at gunpoint, to see loved ones murdered and raped and homes burnt to the ground, to walk hundreds of miles to a squalid refugee camp, then board a plane and, finally, arrive in a country where there would be enough to eat, a bed to sleep in, and a military that protects, not persecutes, its citizens.

I think I must have got a speck of dust in my eyes, because they started to water and wouldn't stop. About an hour later, I was in a gym in the Fort Dix Kosovar compound, informally dubbed "The Village."

As various officials briefed the new arrivals, I found myself looking at our Kosovar guests. I think they were bewildered, overwhelmed—and touched— by all the attention they were receiving.

I watched small children play. They ran around, wrestled with each other, played tag, and did everything they could do to drive their mothers nuts. What really struck me was that these kids, despite what they'd been through, played the same way American kids do.

Then, the floor of the gym was swarming with large men wearing black suits and sunglasses, speaking into hand-held microphones and looking everywhere for bad guys.

Moments later, First Lady Hillary Clinton took the mike. She talked for about 10 minutes—I don't remember everything she said, because what stands out in my mind happened after she started to leave. As she headed toward the door, the refugees stood up, and started chanting "U-S-A, U-S-A."

Everyone was on their feet, from little old ladies in babushka scarves to teenagers wearing blue jeans and Miami Dolphin jackets. The gym was shaking from their enthusiastic clapping and foot-stomping.

I can't tell you how proud I felt at that moment. Even now, days after the event, I can still hear them chanting and can still see them on their feet, cheering with everything they had. Words, and the television footage that has dominated the evening news, cannot capture the outpouring of emotion in that room.

I'm sure they felt relief and gratitude because they were no longer in harm's way, but I also think they felt something more. I think these people were genuinely ecstatic about being in America, a country that espouses the values of liberty, equality and justice, a country with laws that protect people against the kind of hatred the Kosovars escaped.

And a country willing to take a stand, and lead our NATO allies against a brutal dictator who uses thug-like tactics to accomplish his goals. It's probably safe to say that every other airman and soldier in the gym was caught up in the pep-rally feel of the moment. Several GIs were shouting and clapping along with the refugees.

I also think there must have been a lot of dust in the room, because the three soldiers standing next to me were rubbing their eyes. As I listened to these people who had been chased out of their homeland fill the gym with their voices, I realized that this was why I had joined the Air Force—to serve my country and make the world a better, safer place.

I have never felt more proud to wear my uniform, and I have never felt so proud to be a citizen of America—the greatest country in the world.

[First Lt. Mike Nachshen is deputy chief of public affairs at McGuire Air Force Base, N.J.]

A CALL FOR HELP

by Theresa Morel Hudler, Waldorf, Maryland
©1995, GUIDEPOSTS, New York, NY

A rainstorm had just ended that late January 1968 morning when the UH-1 "Huey" helicopter settled into the mud by the 12th evacuation hospital at Cu Chi ("KooChee"). The chopper was a troop carrier, a "slick," not the medevac type we were used to. It was full of wounded men who only minutes before had been in battle. Their comrades had hastily loaded and flown them to us. Most would remain with us, but the urgent cases would be flown to another unit not far from Cu Chi.

Nurses and medics ran under the rush of blades to lift the wounded through the open sides of the helicopter. Triage was begun. There was the sickly smell of blood and mud, the shouts of medics, the moan of men in pain, the down-winding whine of the chopper's engine.

I had just finished my 12-hour shift and should have been headed back for the nurses' barracks, but someone called to me.

"Lt. Morel, come here, please! Tell us what to do with this one!" I slopped through the mud to a medic standing beside a low stretcher.

Crouching beside the soldier on the stretcher, I observed a massive head wound. He would die if we did not get him to a head-trauma unit. I motioned for the IV equipment and leaned toward the soldier's ear.

"Don't worry, sweetheart; we'll get you out of here. We'll get you someplace safe. Just hang on."

Glancing up through the confusion, I saw crew members heading back to their "slick."

"Wait!" I yelled. "Wait! We have to take this man on and take him up north!"

I jumped to my feet and ran toward the chopper, waving. The pilot glanced at his crew; flying wounded was not their usual duty. He looked back at me and nodded.

Soon hands lifted the litter and slid it into the open chopper, loading it against a projecting bulkhead near the rear. It took up all but a few inches of the width of the chopper's floor. The door gunners, heads bulky in huge protective helmets, climbed up onto narrow benches behind the litter, facing outward, sliding in behind mounted M-60 machine guns.

It was not common for nurses to fly evacuation runs, and I had never been in a helicopter before, but there was no one else free to go. I scrambled up onto the metal floor behind the pilot and co-pilot's seats. Someone tossed me a flak jacket and a standard steel-pot helmet. I noticed the gunners and pilots hooking their helmet headsets into connectors. The crew would now be able to communicate with each other. I had no headset, no ear protectors. My helmet flopped back and forth as I struggled to snap the drab flak jacket over my fatigues and then checked that the patient's IV was securely attached to a hook overhead.

The co-pilot told me to bang on his seat if I needed something once we were airborne. He would then swing his helmet mike out so I could speak into it.

I sat down flat on the vibrating metal floor, my back to the pilots' seats. The doors had been left open; it was as if the chopper had no sides. Sweat trickled down my face and under my uniform. I watched my patient closely as the engine wound up to full pitch. The helicopter lifted up slowly just above the trees, the nose dropping a bit. It moved forward. We were flying.

The engine and rotors throbbed through the metal roof and the wind rushed past the open doors. The sounds were deafening. The roar increased as we began to move a hundred miles an hour following the contours of the terrain, up and over the jungle trees, down over rice patties and fields.

Suddenly the pilots shouted something about enemy troops below. Simultaneously the gunners opened up with their machine guns. The pilots began to fly evasive maneuvers—banking the chopper steeply first to one side and then the other. The staccato pounding of gunfire, the roar of the wind and the whine of the engine made an earsplitting clash.

I forced myself to concentrate on my patient. Hours earlier, I had begun my shift with my daily visit to the chapel area. Now I was praying again, crying out silently: *Oh dear God! Don't let him die here in all this! Let us get him to a safe place!*

Suddenly I noticed that the IV had come loose from his arm. He would die! I banged on the pilot's seat to get him to level off, but he could not hear me.

I clawed across the pitching deck to the litter. As I leaned over to reach for the IV needle, my helmet slipped forward. It would come off and hit the wounded man! I pulled it off with one hand and flung it behind me.

Now I was bent over, helmetless, tearing tape with my teeth and the one hand, trying to hold the IV in with the other, screaming silently over and over, *Oh dear God, don't let him die here! Don't let him die here!*

Suddenly the gunner on my left stopped firing. He pivoted sharply 90 degrees and bent over until his head covered mine and his mouth was within an inch of my ear. *Why is he here? Does he want to speak to me?* I wondered in the split second he was poised there. Then there was a Ping and a Pang. A bullet headed for my left temple ricocheted off his helmet with enough force to knock him out. The gunner slumped unconscious over me and my patient.

His weight was suffocating us. I shoved his body to the left and he rolled onto the litter handles, inches from the open door. I didn't know if he was tethered or secured in some way or not, so I grabbed him with my left hand, still holding the IV needle with my right. I was crying.

Oh dear God, he'll fall out! Don't let him fall out! Help us dear God! The prayer screamed through my heart.

It was a little while—a minute? an hour?—before the other gunner realized what had happened. He spoke to the pilots on his mike and they broke off the fight and flew straight to the field hospital. We landed. I unclenched my cramped fingers from the gunner's fatigues and the patient's IV.

Medics pulled the gunner down and placed him on a stretcher, then slid the patient's litter to the ground. I headed first to my patient. The IV was still attached and he was stable, still alive. Before I turned away I touched his arm. "Peace," I whispered.

He was rushed off. I never learned if he survived.

I ran to the other litter and bent over the gunner, grabbing his wrist, feeling for a pulse.

With his helmet off, there was no sign of a wound. In fact, he was only dazed.

His eyes opened and focused on me as I bent over him.

"What is it?" he asked. "What do you want?" This was the soldier whose helmeted head covered my bare one in a single bullet-splintered second. I just looked at him; what did he mean?

He spoke again, struggling to rise up on his elbow: "You called me!"

A few days later the gunner and I met to talk over what had happened. The Tet offensive was now fully under way. He offered me the bullet-scarred helmet as a souvenir, but I insisted that he keep it. I do not remember his name. But over the years, even as I repressed most of my Vietnam memories, I always remembered that when I needed protection, a gunner heard a call for help so loudly and clearly over the cacophony of noises in the helicopter, that he stopped firing, turned, and bent down to see what I wanted. Yet, tearing tape with my teeth I had not spoken a word. I had only prayed in silence to a God who had heard and answered me.

Editor's Postscript:

For many years following her months in Vietnam, Theresa Hudler repressed her war memories. Then in the 1990s she found a deeper faith in God and, through prayer, was able to face and leave the pain of them behind. As this book is being published, she is in training to become a permanent medical missionary to Vietnamese refugees living just over the border in Cambodia, not more than 20 miles from Cu Chi.

And They Have Names

By people, I do not mean "personnel." I do not mean
"end strength." I do not mean "percent of fill"
or any of those other labels which refer to people
as a commodity. I mean living, breathing,
serving human beings. They have needs and
interests and desires. They have spirit,
and will, and strengths, and abilities.
They have weaknesses and faults.
And they have names.

General Creighton Abrams

A Soldier's Scraps

It would take a pretty tough guy not to feel his heart go out to the shivering, little six-year-old squeaker who stands barefoot in the mud, holding a bit tin bucket so the dogface can empty his mess kit into it. Many soldiers, veterans of the Italy campaign and thousands of similar buckets, still go back and sweat out the mess line for an extra chop and hunk of bread for those little kids.

But there is a big difference between the ragged, miserable infantryman who waits with his mess kit, and the ragged, miserable civilian who waits with his bucket. The doggie knows where his next meal is coming from. That makes him a very rich man in this land where hunger is so fierce it makes animals out of respectable old ladies who should be wearing cameos and having tea parties instead of fighting one another savagely for a soldier's scraps.

Sergeant Bill Mauldin
from his book *Up Front,* 1945

*A man who is good enough to shed his blood
for his country is good enough to be given
a square deal afterwards.*

Theodore Roosevelt, 1903
1858–1919
26th President of the United States
(1901–1909)

With this statement, the Pilgrims of Plymouth Colony enacted into law the first veteran's benefit recorded in America. The year was 1636, and the Colony was engaged in a conflict with the Pequot Indians. History shows that since that first simple declaration of concern, the American people have continued and strengthened their efforts to compensate for the losses and to minimize the disadvantages suffered by those who have responded to the nation's call to serve.

*If any man shalbee set forth as a souldier
and shall be returned maimed,
he shalbee maintained competently
by the Collonie during his life.*

CHAPTER TWELVE

Training

Live to train, train to fight, fight to win is the focus of this chapter. Training is the one indispensable element of combat readiness, and training for combat readiness remains this country's best guarantee for a credible military deterrence and combat victory in the event of war.

American soldiers prepare to cover the body of a fallen comrade. Another pays his last respects. Vietnam War

A dead soldier who has given his life because of failure of his leader is a dreadful sight before God. Like all soldiers, he was tired before he died, and undoubtedly dirty, and possibly frightened to his soul and there he is on top of all that ... never again to see his homeland. Don't be the leader who failed to instruct him properly, who failed to lead him well. Burn the midnight oil, that you may not in later years look at your hands and find his blood still red upon them.

James Warner Bellah

IF WE ARE PREPARED ...

*To be prepared for war is one of the most
effectual ways of preserving peace.*

George Washington

*Our object ought to be to have a good army
rather than a large one.*

George Washington
15 September 1770

Elihu Root
*American Statesman
and Diplomat*

*The peace, prosperity and honor
of our country will one day
lie in your hands. ...
Before you leave the Army,
according to all precedents
in history, you will be
engaged in another war.
It is bound to come
and will come.
Prepare your country
for that war.*

Elihu Root 1903
1845–1937
*Secretary of War (1905–1909)
Senator (1909–1915)*

*We don't want any more wars, but a man is
a damn fool to think there won't be any more of them.
I am a peace-loving Quaker, but when war breaks
out every damn man in my family goes.
If we're ready, nobody will tackle us.*

MG Smedley Butler
October 1931

*We have had the
lesson before us over
and over again—
nations that were not
ready and were unable
to get ready found
themselves overrun
by the enemy.*

Franklin D. Roosevelt
1882–1945
*32nd President of
the United States
(1933–1945)*

President Franklin Delano Roosevelt
1940

*The instruments of battle are valuable only
if one knows how to use them.*

Ardant Du Picq

John Wayne
"The Duke"
1906–1979

*War is tough …
it's tougher
if you're stupid.*

John Wayne
in the movie
Sands of Iwo Jima
1949

Units fight well because of pride and training.

T. R. Fehrenbach
from his book
This Kind of War

WOULD THE LIEUTENANT LIKE TO LEARN …

When I was a new second lieutenant, I was assigned to the weapons platoon, 57 millimeter recoilless rifle and 60 millimeter mortars. I didn't know much about these weapons. I knew a mortar from a recoilless rifle, but that was it. However, I had a Sergeant Putnam—Sergeant First Class Putnam. … Putnam realized how "green" I was. He did a couple of things for me that symbolize how NCOs can teach and how officers can learn.

He realized that "how I was received" by the platoon was going to be crucial. So—before I even met the platoon—he came to me that first night and said, "It would be useful for the lieutenant to know the roster of men, and here it is. Tomorrow, when I introduce the platoon to the lieutenant, it would be useful if the lieutenant knew the names." So I picked up the roster and I memorized the names. The next day, when he introduced me to the platoon, I called the names off by memory. The soldiers stood up so I could associate the names and faces, and they were impressed that I had made the effort to know them. They thought I knew enough to care, but in fact, Sergeant Putnam was teaching me to care.

The second thing Putnam realized was that I didn't know "my elbow from my ear" about the weapons. He said, "Would the lieutenant like to learn about the weapons in the platoon?" "Yes, I would." So he picked a place in the field—and why he picked that place, I didn't understand at first—he selected a muddy field that was right behind the latrine. ... Why did he pick that place? Because after supper everybody in the company, including soldiers in the platoon, went into that latrine. There, looking out over the screens, they saw me in the mud taking instruction from the experienced platoon sergeant, learning their weapons as well as they knew them.

Clever, Putnam—he was teaching, and fortunately, I was listening and learning. Sharing with your fellow soldiers your knowledge, experience, and standards of excellence is the greatest legacy you can leave with them. The same is true with the officers you teach. And we never get too old to learn a little more.

> **General John A. Wickham, Jr.**
> *Chief of Staff, U.S. Army*

*Y*ou can tell the difference when a brigade
or battalion commander comes in ...
with a long-term approach rather than
to try to run 100 miles an hour.
It puts him in a teaching mode opposed
to in a directive mode.
I believe that's very critical ...
because you have to develop subordinates ...
that is our principal responsibility.

General Richard E.Cavazos
USA, Retired

*L*ife on the battlefield is short for the unprepared. ...
He who prepares only for a short war
is likely to get one.

General Edward C. Meyer

THE WARRIOR ETHIC

**Tanker of the 1st Cavalry Division prepares for combat
during Operation Desert Shield**

*Training is not done in a sterile environment
of cold calculating management.
Training has to be rooted in deep ideals
and beliefs—something worth dying for.
The warmth of service to those beliefs—
love of country, pride and belief in each other—
yes, duty, honor, country—
that's the warrior ethic.*

**General
Richard E. Cavazos**
USA, Retired

*W*hen fear kicks in,
training takes over.

[from a young sergeant,
wounded during Desert Storm]

1SG Dennis L. DeMasters
in TRADOC Pamphlet 525-100-4
Leadership and Command on the Battlefield:
Noncommissioned Officer Corps, 1994

*S*trong leadership that develops
*effective teams is the key
to success in battle.*

FM 22-102
Soldier Team Development

*M*ost of the things that are really
worth knowing cannot be taught.

Albert Einstein
1879–1955
American Physicist

*I*n no other profession are the penalties for
*employing untrained personnel so appalling
and so irrevocable as in the military.*

Douglas MacArthur
1933

**Unit patch, 82nd
Airborne Division**
18th Airborne Corps,
US Army

*The 82nd had been one of the great fighting divisions of
World War I. ... It was a proud division, but it was a
name, a legend, a memory only in February of 1942. ...
To both General [Omar] Bradley and me it seemed vitally
important to ... plant in each man's mind the idea
that valor endured from generation to generation. ...
One of the first things we did, therefore, was to invite the
grand old soldier [Alvin] York down from his home in
Tennessee to tell the massed division about that great fight.
... Sergeant York's visit had a great deal to do with
the early inculcation of that supreme confidence,
that magnificent esprit, which later was to be the
hallmark of the airborne. He created in the minds
of youngsters of every station and class, the conviction
that an aggressive soldier, well trained and well
armed, can fight his way out of any situation.*

General Matthew B. Ridgway
from *Soldier: The Memoirs of Matthew B. Ridgway,*
1956
Commander 82nd Airborne Division, WW II
Commander 8th US Army, Korean War
Supreme Commander of NATO forces in Europe
(1951–1953)
Army Chief of Staff
(1953–1955)

CHAPTER THIRTEEN
Honor and Honoring

This chapter discusses and describes those values and characteristics which we hold in our hearts as the most vitally important elements of our individual character (honor). It also provides discussion on those same elements of character that we value about other people (honoring). Also included in this chapter are items on remembering, pride, and values.

A soldier is many things to many people: someone's son or daughter, a husband or wife, a father or mother, a friend, an acquaintance. A soldier is a citizen among other citizens, and a servant. It is in the role of servant that the soldier observes a fundamental difference: their fellow citizens have entrusted them with the power to protect "their lives ... their fortunes ... and their sacred honor.

General John A. Wickham, Jr.
Army Chief of Staff, (1983–1987)

**Soldiers of the U.S. Army's Old Guard
prepare for ceremonies**

ABOVE ALL OTHER CONSIDERATIONS

Honor cannot be defined satisfactorily
because it is a belief that is intangible;
one that exists in the minds of men.
An honorable man must be one who believes
in strict conformity to that which is right;
one who shrinks from any thought of acting
other than in a straightforward manner in which
no attempt is made or intended to deceive;
and one who will uphold his convictions
above all other considerations.

Bugle Notes, 1954

War must be carried on systematically,
and to do it you must have men of character
activated by principles of honor.

When men are employed and have the incitements of
military honor to engage their ambition and pride, they
will cheerfully submit to inconveniences, which in a
state of tranquility would appear insupportable.

George Washington

Taps

Day is Done
Gone the Sun
From the Lake
From the Hill
From the Sky
Rest in Peace
Soldier Brave
God is Nigh.

Fading Light
Dims the Sight,
And a Star
Gems the Sky,
Gleaming Bright,
From Afar,
Drawing Nigh,
Falls the Night.

Thanks and Praise,
For our Days,
Neath the Sun,
Neath the Stars,
Neath the Sky,
As we Go,
This we Know,
God is Nigh.

Author Unknown

MG Butterfield, 1863
Composer of "Taps"

STAND FAST TO THE UNION

President Lincoln,
Speech to the 148th Ohio Regiment
Washington DC, August 31, 1864

Soldiers of the 148th Ohio: I am most happy to meet you on this occasion. I understand that it has been your honorable privilege to stand, for a brief period, in the defense of your country, and that now you are on your way to your homes. I congratulate you, and those who are waiting to bid you welcome home from the war; and permit me, in the name of the people, to thank you for the part you have taken in this struggle for the life of the nation. You are soldiers of the Republic, everywhere honored and respected. Whenever I appear before a body of soldiers, I feel tempted to talk to them of the nature of the struggle in which we are engaged. I look upon it as an attempt on the one hand to overwhelm and destroy the national existence, while, on our part, we are striving to maintain the government and institutions of our fathers, to enjoy them ourselves, and transmit them to our children and our children's children forever.

To do this the constitutional administration of our government must be sustained, and I beg of you not to allow your minds or your hearts to be diverted from the support of all necessary measures for that purpose, by any miserable picayune arguments addressed to your pockets, or inflammatory appeals made to your passions or your prejudices.

It is vain and foolish to arraign this man or that for the part he has taken, or, has not taken, and to hold the government responsible for his acts. In no administration can there be perfect equality of action and uniform satisfaction rendered by all. But this government must be preserved in spite of the acts of any man or set of men. It is worthy [of] your every effort. Nowhere in the world is presented a government of so much liberty and equality. To the humblest and poorest amongst us are held out the highest privileges and positions. The present moment finds me at the White House, yet there is as good a chance for your children as there was for my father's.

Again I admonish you not to be turned from your stern purpose of defending your beloved country and its free institutions by any arguments urged by ambitious and designing men, but stand fast to the Union and the old flag. Soldiers, I bid you Godspeed to your homes.

THE GETTYSBURG ADDRESS

Address delivered by President Abraham Lincoln at the dedication of the cemetery at Gettysburg:

Four score and seven years ago, our fathers brought forth upon this continent a new Nation, conceived in Liberty, and dedicated to the proposition that all men are created equal. Now, we are engaged in a great Civil War, testing whether that Nation, or any nation so conceived and so dedicated, can long endure. We are met on a great battlefield of that war. We have come to dedicate a portion of that field as a final resting place for those who gave their lives that that Nation might live. It is altogether fitting and proper that we should do this.

But, in a larger sense, we cannot dedicate, we cannot consecrate, we cannot hallow this ground. The brave men, living and dead, who struggled here, have consecrated it far above our power to add or detract. The world will little note nor long remember what we say here, but it can never forget what they did here. It is for us, the living, rather to be dedicated to the great task remaining before us; that from these honored dead, we take increased devotion to that cause for which they gave the last full measure of devotion; that this Nation, under God, shall have a new birth of freedom; and that government of the people by the people and for the people shall not perish from the earth.

President Abraham Lincoln
1809–1865
16th President of the United States
(1861–1865)

Abraham Lincoln
November 19th 1863
Gettysburg, Pennsylvania

DEDICATION CEREMONY SPEECH

General Douglas MacArthur Corridor at West Point

Mr. Secretary, Mrs. MacArthur, guests here on the platform, and you ladies and gentlemen, and you of the Armed Forces. We honor today the memory of Douglas MacArthur and the legend that was his life. It was a legend that began on cavalry outposts in the Old West, where the son of a Civil War hero and Medal of Honor winner first heard the sounds of drums and shouted cadence. He would hear those sounds again when he was graduated from West Point with one of the highest academic averages in history and with the academy's greatest honor—First Captain of the Corps, Douglas MacArthur.

As a young officer on a secret and highly dangerous intelligence mission in Mexico, he would win his first recommendation for the Medal of Honor. Wounded twice in France during World War I, he would be decorated repeatedly for his gallantry under fire and become one of the youngest and most popular generals in American history.

As a superintendent of the Military Academy, he would bring much needed reform to the West Point curriculum, up-grading scholastic standards

General Douglas MacArthur
Korean War, 1950

while emphasizing the importance of sports. Words he spoke then are even now inscribed at West Point in stone: "Upon the fields of friendly strife are the seeds that upon other fields, on other days, will bear the fruits of victory."

In the early thirties, as the youngest Army Chief of Staff in history, he warned the Congress of the need for military readiness and a modern Army featuring strong armored and air forces. While bearing the brunt of a Japanese attack in 1942, he would win the Medal of Honor for his heroic defense of the Philippines. When ordered by President Roosevelt to leave the islands, he would thrill the free world with his defiant pledge, "I shall return."

During his brilliant military campaigns of the South Pacific, his island-hopping, hit-them-where-they-ain't strategy, won quick victories with limited resources—victories that saved thousands of American lives, electrified his countrymen and confounded the enemy.

As a postwar ruler of Japan, he showed himself a wise and compassionate statesman who won forever the affection of the Japanese people even as he brought about one of the most remarkable achievements in the history of self-government.

Then, in Korea, in the face of brutal aggression, he accomplished one of the most brilliant maneuvers in military history—the Inchon landing. In 1951, before a joint session of Congress, he would give one of the most memorable speeches in American history, a speech in which he warned, and we must always remember, "In war indeed there can be no substitute for victory."

It is true this brilliant career sometimes aroused envy in lesser men, but the general sought to leave intrigue to headquarters staff and politicians. He was always a front-line general, a leader of fighting men. Once, at a remote airfield in New Guinea, an officer spotted him near the front lines and rushed up to him. In a worried voice he pointed to a spot of jungle 50 yards away and said, "Excuse me, sir, but we killed a sniper in there only a few minutes ago." The general answered, "Fine, son, that's the best thing to do with them."

Even at the age of 82 he was giving the same inspiring example to young soldiers. The Class of 1962 at West Point will never forget the words they heard from him one May afternoon, words that he began with a bit of humor. He said, "As I was leaving the hotel this morning, a doorman asked me, 'Where are you headed for, General,' and I replied 'West Point'. He remarked, 'Beautiful place. You ever been there before?' " But then came that unforgettable speech, a speech in which he reminded those young soldiers that "duty, honor, country" were three hallowed words that reverently dictate what you ought to be, what you can be, and what you will be. They are your rallying points, he said, "to build courage when courage seems to fail; to regain faith when there seems to be so little cause for faith; to create hope when hope becomes forlorn." He spoke of his pride in the Long Gray Line that has never failed us. He told the cadets that his last waking thought would be of the corps and the corps and the corps.

He was extraordinarily proud of his country's uniform. He said of it once, "I suppose in a way this has become a part of my soul. It is a symbol of my life. Whatever I've done that really matters, I've done wearing it. When the time comes it will be in these that I journey forth. What greater honor could come to an American and a soldier."

Well, today a new generation of young officers are asked to defend our nation just as a new generation of young Americans to whom World War II, Korea and even Vietnam are not even within memory, seek to define their own ideals and search for their own answers to ageless questions. Surely as the tide of time recedes from his era, this new generation will see in Douglas MacArthur an unflinching idealist, an eloquent warrior, a visionary soldier, a gentle conqueror, an authentic American hero.

And the general had some words for you young men. He said once that being young meant a temperamental predominance of courage over timidity and an appetite for adventure over love of ease. He added that nobody grows old by merely living a number of years; people grow old by deserting their ideals.

As long as America affords her brave a place of honor; as long as we as a people seek to keep alive the ideals of selflessness and freedom; as long as we look to the wise and the just for inspiration, our thoughts will turn to the General and the General and the General.

Thank You.

Remarks by President Ronald Reagan
The Pentagon,
September 10, 1981

AT A BASE OVERSEAS

For Our Soldiers

'Twas the night before Christmas at the base over seas, And the sentry was lonely in snow to his knees.

The plane over Greenland just circling around, The sweep of the radar not making a sound. The cook's in Alaska, the baker's in Guam, preparing Christmas dinner for those far from home. All over the world, airmen, soldiers, and sailors en masse, protecting our future, our present, our past.

Some sit in a movie they've seen twice before, Thinking of loved ones and Christmas—and more. Because of these women, and men far from home, our Christmas is peaceful with no combat zones. At dinner this Christmas, remember in prayer.

Author Unknown

I CAME TO SEE MY SON'S NAME

[This article was provided courtesy of the Virtual Wall, Vietnam Veterans Memorial, which can be found at <www.VirtualWall.org>.]

by Jim Schueckler

My job as a volunteer "visitor guide" was to help people find names on the "Moving Wall," a replica of the Vietnam Veterans Memorial in Washington, DC. More importantly, I gave visitors a chance to talk. While searching the directory or leading a visitor to the name they sought, I would quietly ask, "Was he a friend or a relative?" Over the six days, I began conversations that way with several hundred people. Only a handful gave me a short answer; almost everyone wanted to talk. Each had their own story to tell. For some, the words poured out as if the floodgates of a dam, that had been closed for thirty years, had just burst open. For others, the words came out slowly and deliberately between long pauses. Sometimes, they choked on the words, and they cried. I also cried as I listened, asked more questions, and silently prayed that my words would help to heal, not to hurt. "I came to see my son's name." I heard those and similar words from several parents who came to the Moving Wall. Their son had died in a war that divided our country like no other event since the Civil War. He died in a war that some Americans had blamed on the soldiers, who were called to fight it. Some young men had no choice; they were called by the draft. Others, including some 30,000 women, were called differently, by a sense of duty to their family and nation. Our culture mourns and respects our dead; but in the shadow of that bitter war, the sacrifices, of those who died and of their families, were not given dignity. Mothers and fathers came to see that their sons had not been forgotten, that their names were remembered on that Wall, that someone else cares.

A frail and elderly mother came to the Moving Wall in a wheelchair. As we looked for her son's name, she described his interests during high school and then the agonizing days when she was first told that her son was injured, then missing, then classified as "lost at sea." She asked me to thank all the other people who helped bring the Moving Wall to Batavia.

" 'Til death do us part" came abruptly to thousands of marriages because of that war. I met two widows of men whose names are on the Wall. One woman showed me a picture of her husband and a separate picture of their daughter ... a daughter that her husband never met ... a girl who grew up without a father. I was painfully aware that, had some Viet Cong soldiers been slightly better marksmen, my wife and son might have come to the Wall to see my name.

Sisters and brothers came to see a name. One brother so close in age that "People were always calling us by the other's name, and we both hated it." A sister said, "I was so much younger than him, I didn't realize why my Mom was crying when we said goodbye to him at the airport."

One brother confided that, although he had not been a war protester, his feelings and his first confrontation with the Wall in Washington were almost identical to those of the brother in the play "The Wall, a Pilgrimage." He said, "It was as if the actor had reached into my soul and exposed every one of my feelings about my brother and the war."

A group of four people stood near one panel. I offered to make a rubbing of a name. The man pointed to the name Paul D. Urquhart.

I asked, "Is that Captain Paul Urquhart, the helicopter pilot?" The man nodded and said, "He's my brother." I explained that I flew with Paul on his first tour in Vietnam and read that he had been shot down during his second tour. Paul's brother said that he and his family came from Pennsylvania on the anniversary date of Paul's becoming Missing In Action. I made a rubbing of Paul's name and added a rubbing of the Army Aviator wings from my hat, a symbol we had both worn so proudly so long ago.

Aunts and uncles also came to see a special name on the Wall. One aunt said, "He stayed overnight at our house so much that one neighbor thought he was our son." An uncle lamented, "I took him hunting. I was the one who taught him to like guns."

Cousins came to the Wall; and many said, "He was like a brother."

One man asked me to look up the name Douglas Smith.

I asked back, "Do you mean Doug Smith, a Marine, from North Tonawanda High School?"

The man introduced me to his wife, Doug's cousin. She was pleased to be able to talk about Doug with a classmate who remembered him. I showed her Doug's name on my own personal list.

Veterans came to see the names of their buddies. Most of them were eager to tell me about their friend or how he died. Many remembered the day in great detail and spoke of what's called "survivor's guilt …".

"He went out on patrol in my place that day" or "If I hadn't been away on R & R (rest and recuperation), he wouldn't be dead."

Others were bothered that they couldn't remember much about their friend because they had tried to "block it out" for so many years. Another man said, "I lost a few good friends while I was there (Vietnam), but I don't want to find just their names because I feel the same about all 58,000 of these names."

"Tree-line vets" are men or women who have finally been able to go to a Moving Wall location but are terrified of coming close enough to actually see some names that have been haunting them so many years. One such veteran stood for a long time some fifty feet from the Wall. My brothers, Vic and Chris, talked with him. After awhile, he and Vic were able to laugh about some of their common Marine Corps experiences; and then they were finally able to approach, see, and touch, those names together.

Many people came to the Wall in the privacy or serenity of darkness. Our security men reported that there were only a few minutes each night that the Wall had no callers at all. One visitor spent several hours in the middle of the night standing in front of a certain panel. Whenever anyone came close, he would move away. When alone again, he would move back to that panel to continue his silent vigil. Still others came in the darkness before dawn to watch the break of a new day over the Wall.

One vet came in a wheelchair. He could not talk or walk; but, with great effort, Peter's shaking hand could scrawl messages on a pad. The nurse who pushed his wheelchair said that Peter had been excited about the Moving Wall visit since he first read about it in the *Daily News*.

Peter came to see the name of his friend that he thought had died in 1975, but he could not remember the man's name. They had been high school buddies and joined the Army together. They went to boot camp and Vietnam together. Peter saw his friend die.

At the bottom of Panel 1 West, I squatted down and read off the names of the small number of men and one American woman who died in Vietnam in 1975. Peter did not recognize any of the names.

The EDS computer operators ran a search but found no Vietnam casualties from Peter's small home town. We asked if his friend might have come from another town, and Peter wrote "Wales?". The computer search gave one name, but he was killed in 1968. I went back to Peter and asked, "Was his name Eric Jednat."

The shock on Peter's face, and then his tears, told us that we had found the right name. We moved to Panel 53 West, where we turned the wheelchair so Peter could touch his friend's name.

Many people came who were not related to, but knew one or more of the men named on the Wall. A high school teacher told me, "I taught four of these boys."

Others said,

"He was the little boy who lived across the street."

"We were going steady in high school."

"He delivered my newspapers."

"I was his Boy Scout leader."

"He went to our church."

"I worked with his mother at the time he was killed."

"My son played football with him."

"We were classmates for twelve years."

There were hundreds of similar, personal connections between the visitor and one or more names on the Wall.

To other visitors, the names were not as personal but still were significant ...

"I didn't know him, but I remember how it shocked
the town when he died."

"I just wanted to pay my respects."

"I didn't know any of them, thank God."

"I came to show support for the vets who came back."

"My son went to Vietnam, but he came back OK."

Others expressed amazement ...

"I wanted to see the names of the seven young men from Holley.
I can't believe our little village lost so many boys."

"I had no idea so many lost their lives."

"Such a waste. Such a terrible, terrible waste."

"I hope and pray we never go through that kind of war again."

"Is this the price of peace?"

Some visitors asked rhetorically,

"Will mankind ever learn?"

Two weeks after the visit of the Moving Wall to Batavia, a friend told my wife, "I don't understand all the concern about the Moving Wall; why don't people just forget about that dirty war?"

For many, the Moving Wall does not need to be explained. Those who do not understand are, perhaps, more fortunate than those who do.

AMERICA'S BATTLE

The speech below was presented at the 55th Anniversary of World War II at the Marine Corps Memorial, Arlington, VA February 20, 2000. The introduction was made by Iwo Jima veteran Major General Fred Haynes, U.S. Marine Corps (Retired).

General Haynes: *"John Bradley is the second man from the right, the Pharmacist Mate, the only Navy man in this magnificent statue which represents everything that all of us here, our children, our grandchildren stand for. We have with us today his fourth child, third son, James Bradley, who will talk to us a little about what this represents. I present James Bradley."* (See pages 78 and 79, Chapter 2, for photos of the flagraising.)

(Bradley rises from his seat and strides across the wet grass to the podium. Silently he turns away to gaze at his father's enormous bronze likeness. He turns back to the audience and begins.)

So there's my dad in the tallest bronze monument in the world, but that's about all we knew growing up. He wouldn't talk about Iwo Jima; he would always change the subject. After he died, I phoned my mother and asked her to tell me everything that dad ever told her about Iwo Jima. She said, 'That won't take long, because he only talked about it once—on our first date. For seven or eight disinterested minutes and then never again in a 47-year marriage did he say the words, Iwo Jima.'

After his funeral, we were in for some surprises. My brothers and my mother were searching for his will in his office. They opened a closet door. In that closet were two large brown boxes. We were surprised that in those boxes he had secretly saved memories of 50 years of being a flagraiser. Then the next day we were in for another surprise. My father's Captain on Iwo Jima phoned my mother and asked her if she knew that my father had been awarded the Navy Cross for valor two days before the flag raising. She said no. My father had kept his heroism a secret from his wife, from his family, and his community for half a century.

I burned with curiosity and went on a quest. I phoned mayor's offices and sheriff's departments all across the country, looking for the relatives of these six guys. I interviewed hundreds of you Iwo Jima veterans and I learned a lot.

I learned how young you were. My dad is not the guy putting the pole in the ground; he's the next guy up. But behind him, obscured by him, on the other side, is Rene Gagnon.

Rene Gagnon, at that moment, had a photo of his girlfriend in his helmet. He needed the protection because he was scared. He was 17 years old.

Ira Hayes, the last man on the statue whose hands cannot reach the pole. Proud of being with you Marines, he wrote home from the boat taking him to

Iwo Jima: 'These boys I'm with are all good men. I would not take 1000 dollars to be separated from them.'

I learned how eager you boys were to serve. Harlon Block, at the base of that pole, enlisted in the United States Marine Corps with all of the senior members of his high school football team.

I learned how determined you were on Iwo Jima. My dad wrote a letter home three days after the flag raising. He wrote, "I didn't know I could go without food, without water, or sleep for three days, but now I know it can be done."

I learned about leaders. Ira Hayes is the last guy up there. The next guy you're looking at is Franklin Sousley. Behind Franklin, obscured by Franklin, is my hero—Mike Strank. Where is Mike's right hand? Mike's right hand is not on the pole. Mike is behind his boys. He's the Sergeant. He's the Marine leader and his right hand is gripping the right arm of Franklin Sousley, a young boy. Mike is helping Franklin lift a heavy pole; a Marine leader caring for his boys. Three weeks before Iwo Jima, his Captain said that he wanted to promote Mike Strank. Mike turned it down on the spot saying, "I promised my boys I'd be there with them."

And I learned about the heartbreak that you went through. Franklin Sousley, the second figure in. Franklin was fatherless at the age of nine. He was dead on Iwo Jima at the age of nineteen. His aunt told me that when the telegram arrived at the General Store in Hilltop, Kentucky a young, barefoot boy ran that telegram up to his mother's farm. The story is that the neighbors could hear his mother scream all night and into the morning. The neighbors lived a quarter of a mile away.

I learned about the challenges that you faced. You did the impossible. You fought an underground, unseen enemy. I learned that the Air Force bombed Iwo Jima more than any spot in the Pacific and only rearranged the sand. I learned that the Navy lobbed shells the size of Volkswagens—with the power to re-sculpture Mount Suribachi—and didn't kill anybody.

It took you guys to win a battle that historians describe as "American flesh against Japanese concrete."

I have been to Iwo Jima. It's five miles long. If you're in a car going 60 miles an hour, it takes you 5 minutes to conquer it. It took you—slogging, fighting, dying—36 days.

I learned that my father's company, named "Easy" Company, had 84 percent casualties. Sixteen percent of my dad's buddies made it off unharmed.

Bob Schmidt told me that when they buried the dead on Saipan, they buried by individual grave. When they buried on Iwo Jima they buried by row—rows of a hundred boys. He told me that they needed surveyors to mark the lines.

Corpsman Hoopes instructed me, "You tell your readers that my uniform was caked with blood and it cracked. And it was not my blood."

I learned about the buddyhood and bravery that won the battle of Iwo Jima. Jack Lucas, here in the front row, jumped on the beach without a rifle.

And the reason he didn't have a rifle is because he wasn't supposed to be there. He stowed away to go fight the battle of Iwo Jima. And a couple days later jumped on two grenades to save his buddies.

Nurse Norma Crotty is in the audience and I interviewed her. She was an "Angel in the Air," flying down to evacuate the grievously wounded. She evacuated Navy personnel, Army personnel—all over the Pacific. She was a nurse for 50 years caring for civilians and military.

I asked, "Nurse Norma, was there anything different about those Iwo Jima Marines?" And she said, "Yes, I'll never forget them. It was their spirit. I evacuated boys from other battles that were beaten, but those Marines had Esprit de Corps. Those boys were burned. They were bruised. But I never saw a Marine who was beaten."

I think it's time we Americans put this battle into perspective. This is not just a big battle of the Pacific, or an important battle of World War II. This is unique. This is above and beyond. This is "America's Battle."

America's Battle, what else can you call a battle that in one day had more casualties than two and a half months at Guadalcanal? Normandy was terrible, but at the end of one day, at the end of 24 hours, you and I could have had a tea party on the beaches of Normandy. It was completely safe. Boys died on the beaches of Iwo Jima—on the beaches—for two weeks.

America's Battle. What else can you call the only battle that when Franklin Delano Roosevelt saw the casualties he gasped, and he cried?

TIME Magazine, March 5th, 1945, wrote, "no battle of World War II—not even Normandy—was watched with as much interest as the battle of Iwo Jima."

America's Battle ...

(Bradley gazes at the Iwo Jima veterans in the audience and beckons to them.)

Hey guys listen up! George Washington. Thomas Edison. Hank Aaron. You Marines and Corpsmen who won America's Battle.

I would like to salute you guys, but I know how difficult that is because you are as humble as you are brave. Jessie Boatright said to me, "You know Bradley, you think we did something special out there in the Pacific, but we were just ordinary guys. Ordinary guys just doing our duty."

Yes, well, I'm more in synch with the words of Tex Stanton. I often call Tex Stanton when I need advice with my writing. And he always picks up on the first ring. He doesn't leave his chair very often. Because Mr. Stanton has no legs. He left those on Iwo Jima 55 years ago.

Mr. Stanton said to me, "You know Bradley, heroism on that island was a funny thing. You had to be observed, and you had to be written up, and if you got a medal your citation said that you did something above and beyond. Well Bradley," he said, "I saw a lot of heroes on Iwo Jima and the way I figure it, if you got through one day on that island you were doing something above and beyond just to survive."

I would like to salute you guys. You guys who won America's Battle. You ordinary guys. You heroes of Iwo Jima.

After a silent pause Bradley turns to gaze at the six bronze figures for a moment and then walks across the wet grass to his seat.

WHAT IS A VETERAN?

Some veterans bear visible signs of their service: a missing limb, a jagged scar, a certain look in the eye. Others may carry the evidence inside them: a pin holding a bone together, a piece of shrapnel in the leg—or perhaps another sort of inner steel: the soul's ally forged in the refinery of adversity. Except in parades, however, the men and women who have kept America safe wear no badge or emblem. You can't tell a vet just by looking. What is a vet?

He is the cop on the beat who spent six months in Saudi Arabia sweating two gallons a day making sure the armored personnel carriers didn't run out of fuel.

He is the barroom loudmouth, dumber than five wooden planks, whose overgrown frat-boy behavior is outweighed a hundred times in the cosmic scales by four hours of exquisite bravery near the 38th parallel.

She—or he—is the nurse who fought against futility and went to sleep sobbing every night for two solid years in DaNang.

He is the POW who went away one person and came back another—or didn't come back *at all.*

He is the Quantico drill instructor that has never seen combat—but has saved countless lives by turning slouchy, no-account rednecks and gang members into Marines, and teaching them to watch each other's backs.

He is the parade-riding Legionnaire who pins on his ribbons and medals with a prosthetic hand.

He is the career quartermaster who watches the ribbons and medals pass him by.

He is the three anonymous heroes in The Tomb Of The Unknowns, whose presence at the Arlington National Cemetery must forever preserve the memory of all the anonymous heroes whose valor dies unrecognized with them on the battlefield or in the ocean's sunless deep.

He is the old guy bagging groceries at the supermarket—palsied now and aggravatingly slow—who helped liberate a Nazi death camp and who wishes all day long that his wife were still alive to hold him when the nightmares come.

He is an ordinary and yet an extraordinary human being, a person who offered some of his life's most vital years in the service of his country, and who sacrificed his ambitions so others would not have to sacrifice theirs. He is a soldier and a savior and a sword against the darkness, and he is nothing more than the finest, greatest testimony on behalf of the finest, greatest nation ever known. So remember, each time you see someone who has served our country, just lean over and say Thank You. That's all most people need, and in most cases it will mean more than any medals they could have been awarded or were awarded.

Author Unknown

A MESSAGE FROM A CITIZEN: "THANKS"

I was too tired to hit the commissary after work, so I stopped off at the grocery store to do a little shopping, hoping their crowd would be smaller. Much to my dismay it was packed. As I walked around with the basket with the funky wheel, I couldn't help but notice the looks I drew. I thought it might be the basket or maybe because I was in uniform. Whatever the case, the looks became stares, and I became increasingly uncomfortable. I muddled through the express lane; the cashier never even shared a word with me; and I couldn't help but notice the rolling eyes and shake of the head as I nervously fumbled for my debit card. I was really feeling outside of my element navigating through the sea of civilians without another blue suit in sight. I just wanted to get out of there or, at least, out of uniform. As I dodged cars toward my parking space, I heard a voice from a distance call out, "Sir! Oh, sir!" I saw a young woman and her daughter bravely cross lanes of traffic to get to me, and for a split second I thought they had mistaken me for the police (or a bus driver). But then what she said to me hasn't left me and probably never will. "I just wanted to thank you for all that you sacrifice in order to serve our country," she said. "We just wanted to tell you we appreciate you." Then her 3-year-old said, "Thanks for keeping us safe." I was speechless. In two seconds my 15 years of service flashed before my eyes. I've endured places with no hot water, no heat in the winter nor coolness from the beating sun in the summer. I've shoveled snow, packed sandbags and loaded pallets in searing heat for operations Desert Shield and Desert Storm. I've been face down in the dirt more often than I care to remember and have been pushed to my physical limit often. As a recruiter in my hometown I've had kids throw things at me, steal from me and mock me. Many counselors have disdained me, and parents cursed me. But never, never ever had anyone come up to say "Thank you" until that night outside the store. I'm certain that lady would want me to pass on her message. We've all been through a lot—civilian and military alike.

At times we feel misunderstood, at times even shunned and persecuted by the very same society we protect. But there are many out there who certainly appreciate our service.

> Senior Master Sgt. Carl Cooper
> Air Education and Training
> Command

[Sergeant Cooper's commentary originally appeared in the April 16, 1999 "Wingspread" newspaper, Randolph Air Force Base, Texas.]

The Deep-Seated Pride

Whether in war or peace, soldiers who have passed through the ranks of the United States Army in service to their country look back on that experience with a high sense of pride. ... Veterans ... never seem to lose the deep-seated pride that comes from serving one's country.

General John A. Wickham, Jr.

In honor of all women who served in the Armed Forces to preseve America's Freedom   Courtesy of VFW Post 4051, Colorado Springs, Colorado. Commander Duane Knutson

A Thank You to a Vietnam
Medal of Honor Recipient

On behalf of all Americans, and especially on behalf of your platoon members who are here today, I thank you for what you mean to our country. Thank you for what you gave that day and what you have given every day since. Thank you for reminding us that being American has nothing to do with the place of your birth, the color of your skin, the language of your parents or the way you worship God. Thank you for living the enduring American values every day. Thank you for doing something that was hard, because no one else was there to do it. Thank you for looking out for people when no one else could be there for them. You have taught us once again that being American has nothing to do with place of birth, race or ethnic origin, or religious faith. It comes straight from the heart. And your heart, sir, is an extraordinary gift to your country.

President William Clinton

[February 8, 2000 remarks by President Clinton in presentation of the Medal of Honor to Alfred Rascon for extraordinary heroism in Vietnam, March 16, 1966.]

LONG MAY IT WAVE ...

A foreign diplomat who often criticized American policy once observed a United States Marine perform the evening colors ceremony. The diplomat wrote about this simple but solemn ceremony in a letter to his country:

During one of the past few days, I had occasion to visit the U.S. Embassy in our capital after official working hours. I arrived at a quarter to six and was met by the Marine on guard at the entrance of the Chancery. He asked if I would mind waiting while he lowered the two American flags at the Embassy. What I witnessed over the next 10 minutes so impressed me that I am now led to make this occurrence a part of my ongoing record of this distressing era.

The Marine was dressed in a uniform which was spotless and neat; he walked with a measured tread from the entrance of the Chancery to the stainless steel flagpole before the Embassy and, almost reverently, lowered the flag to the level of his reach where he began to fold it in military fashion.

MY BROTHER FOR ETERNITY

[Poem, recited at the dedication of the
USS *Arizona* memorial in 1962.]

*Shall ne'er go by,
from this day to the ending of the world,
but we in it shall be remembered.
We few, we happy few, we band of brothers;
for he that today sheds his blood for me,
shall be my brother for eternity.*

USS *Arizona*, **burning and slipping into the sea**
Morning of December 7, 1941

He then released the flag from the clasps attaching it to the rope, stepped back from the pole, made an about face, and carried the flag between his hands—one above, one below—and placed it securely on a stand before the Chancery. He then marched over to the second flagpole and repeated the same lonesome ceremony. On the way between poles, he mentioned to me very briefly that he would soon be finished.

After completing his task, he apologized for the delay—out of pure courtesy, as nothing less than incapacity would have prevented him from fulfilling his goal—and said to me, "Thank you for waiting, Sir. I had to pay honor to my country."

I have had to tell this story because there was something impressive about a lone Marine carrying out a ceremonial task which obviously meant very much to him and which, in its simplicity, made the might, the power and the glory of the United States of America stand forth in a way that a mighty wave of military aircraft, or the passage of a super-carrier, or a parade of 10,000 men could never have made manifest.

In spite of all the many things that I can say negatively about the United States, I do not think there is a soldier, yea, even a private citizen, who could feel as proud about our country today as that Marine does for his country.

One day it is my hope to visit one of our embassies in a far-away place and to see a soldier fold our flag and turn to a stranger and say, "I am sorry for the delay, Sir. I had to honor my country."

Author Unknown

YOUNG AMERICAN PATRIOTS

The following letters are from American youth to soldiers, sailors, airmen and marines, and are evidence that the profession of arms is still held in high regard. (Their last names and hometowns have been removed to protect the children.)

3/31/99
Name: Andrea
Age: 16

Your Letter to the Soldiers:

Dear Soldiers:

Hi! My name is Andrea,
I'm a 16 year old Sophomore from Indiana. I want to thank you for your willingness to serve our Country. I admire you all for everything you do. I

have always had a love for the Armed Forces, only because of what it stands for, freedom. Stay proud! God Bless.

Andrea
Lt. U.S. Civil Air Patrol

03/28/99
Name: Justin
Age: 5

Your Letter to the Soldiers:

I like how you fight. Be careful. I want to be a soldier. What do you do. Thank you for fighting, Justin

03/26/99
Name: Coleman
Age: 4

Your Letter to the Soldiers:

Hello, My name is Coleman and I live in Washington. My daddy was in the Navy before I was born. I think it's really neat that you are in the military. I pray for you to all be safe at night. God Loves you and so do I. Thank you.

03/26/99
Name: Craig
Age: 14

Your Letter to the Soldiers:

Hey I just want to thank you for putting your life on the line everyday to protect those who can't fight for themselves. I know it must be hard being away from your family so I hope this ends soon. good luck Godspeed and GOOD HUNTING!!!

03/25/99
Name: Amber
Age: 11

Your Letter to the Soldiers:

Thank you for protecting our country. Good luck on your missions. We always need you there to watch over our country and are thankful you are there for us. I have 4 brothers, and 2 sisters and I am glad that you are protecting them too. My wish is for everyone to one day get along, so we don't have to have war. And the world will last for our kids and their kids. Thank you!

Amber,
Ohio

03/15/99
Name: Jennifer
Age: 15

Your Letter to the Soldiers:

I hope all of you are safe and when you guys come home you aren't missing anything. Just be careful and watch what you do. I have faith in you guys in taking care of each other and yourself.

02/10/99
Name: Zachary
Age: 13

Your Letter to the Soldiers:

Dear Soldier,
I would like to thank you for going over seas to defend democracy. When I grow up I want to be a Marine or be in the Army. I hope you have a short time over there and will return to our country. If the person reading is a marine; Semper Fi!

01/02/99
Name: Leigh Ann
Age: 11

Your Letter to the Soldiers:

Dear Soldier or Sailor,

I think you have a great job. I know you do good work protecting our country. I hope you had a good Christmas. I am sorry if you did not get to spend it with your family. I hope you will get to come home soon, wherever you live. Is it dangerous where you are? Do you see many children there? I hope you keep safe and keep them safe. If you can, let me know.

12/21/98
Name: John
Age: 13

Your Letter to the Soldiers:

My name is John. Thank you for making so many sacrifices including giving up your holidays with your families to keep the world peaceful and to protect our country. I appreciate everything you are doing for us. I hope that you will be able to come home soon to your families.
God Bless you.

12/20/98
Name: Kelsey
Age: 4

Your Letter to the Soldiers:

I want yous to be safe and I love yous, thank yous all you do.

12/20/98
Name: Tyler
Age: 9

Your Letter to the Soldiers:

I'm sorry you can't be with your families on the holidays, but thank you for fighting to make the world a safer place for me and my sister to live in.

12/19/98
Name: Gretchen
Age: 9

Your Letter to the Soldiers:

I don't know exactly what you are doing but we all thank you for helping the world be safe. If you have any kids I will pray for them. We hope that you won't be there long!!!!!! I will pray for you.

LOVE,
Gretchen

12/19/98
Name: Chris
Age: 12

Your Letter to the Soldiers:

Good luck in your battles and remember if you die you are still American heroes and you will always be a hero. Goodbye and good luck and merry Christmas.

[These letters were provided courtesy of Support Our Soldiers (SOS). SOS is a website dedicated to our service members; their web address is <sos@opsos.org>.]

EARN THIS

As you know, I am a doctor specializing in Emergency Medicine in the Emergency Departments of the only two military Level One trauma centers. They are both in San Antonio, TX and they care for civilian emergencies as well as military personnel. San Antonio has the largest military retiree population in the world living here because of the location of these two large military medical centers. As a military doctor in training for my specialty I work long hours and the pay is less than glamorous. One tends to become jaded by the long hours, lack of sleep, food, family contact and the endless parade of human suffering passing before you. The arrival of another ambulance does not mean more pay, only more work. Most often it is a victim from a motor vehicle crash. Often it is a person of dubious character who has been shot or stabbed. With our large military retiree population it is often a nursing home patient.

Even with my enlisted service and minimal combat experience in Panama prior to medical school, I have caught myself groaning when the ambulance brought in yet another sick, elderly person from one of the local retirement centers that cater to military retirees. I had not stopped to think of what citizens of this age group represented.

I saw *Saving Private Ryan*. I was touched deeply. Not so much by the carnage in the first 30 minutes but by the sacrifices of so many. I was touched most by the scene of the elderly survivor at the graveside asking his wife if he'd been a good man. I realized that I had seen these same men and women coming through my Emergency Department and had not realized what magnificent sacrifices they had made. The things they did for me and everyone else that has lived on this planet since the end of that conflict are priceless.

Situation permitting I now try to ask my patients about their experiences. They would never bring up the subject without the inquiry. I have been privileged to an amazing array of experiences recounted in the brief minutes allowed in an Emergency Department encounter. These experiences have revealed the incredible individuals I have had the honor of serving in a medical capacity, many on their last admission to the hospital.

There was a frail, elderly woman who reassured my young enlisted medic trying to start an IV line in her arm. She remained calm and poised despite her illness and the multiple needle-sticks into her fragile veins. She was what we call a "hard stick." As the medic made another attempt I noticed a number tattooed across her forearm. I touched it with one finger and looked into her eyes. She simply said "Auschwitz." Many of later generations would have loudly and openly berated the young medic in his many attempts. How different was the response from this person who'd seen unspeakable suffering.

A long-retired Colonel who as a young USN officer had parachuted from his burning plane over a pacific island held by the Japanese. Now an octogenarian, his head cut in a fall at home where he lived alone. His CT scan and suturing had been delayed until after midnight by the usual parade of high priority ambulance patients. Still spry for his age, he asked to use the phone to call a taxi to take him home then realized his ambulance had brought him without his wallet. He asked if he could use the phone to make a long distance call to his daughter who lived 70 miles away. With great pride we told him that he could not as he'd done enough for his country and the least we could do was get him a taxi home, even if we had to pay for it ourselves. My only regret was that my shift wouldn't end for several hours and I couldn't drive him myself.

I was there the night MSG Roy Benavidez came through the Emergency Department for the last time. He was very sick. I was not the doctor taking care of him but I walked to his bedside and took his hand. I said nothing. He was so sick he didn't know I was there. I'd read his Congressional Medal of Honor citation and wanted to shake his hand. He died a few days later.

The gentleman who served with Merrill's Marauders, the survivor of the Baatan Death March, the survivor of Omaha Beach, the 101 year old World War I veteran, the former POW held in frozen North Korea, the former Special Forces medic now with non-operable liver cancer, the former Viet Nam Corps Commander.

I remember these citizens. I may still groan when yet another ambulance comes in but now I am much more aware of what an honor it is to serve these particular men and women. I am angered at the cut backs, implemented and proposed, that will continue to decay their meager retirement benefits.

I see the President and Congress who would turn their back on these individuals who've sacrificed so much to protect our liberty. I see later generations that seems to be totally engrossed in abusing these same liberties won with such sacrifice. It has become my personal endeavor to make the nurses and young enlisted medics aware of these amazing individuals when I encounter them in our Emergency Department. Their response to these particular citizens has made me think that perhaps all is not lost in the next generation.

My experiences have solidified my belief that we are losing an incredible generation and this nation knows not what it is losing. Our uncaring government and ungrateful civilian populace should all take note. We should all remember that we must "Earn this."

Rangers Lead the Way!

CPT Stephen R. Ellison, M.D.

Just A Simple Soldier

He was getting old and paunchy and his hair was falling fast
And he sat around the Legion telling stories of the past,
Of a war that he had fought in and the deeds that he had done
In his exploits with his buddies; they were heroes, everyone.

And 'tho sometimes to his neighbors, his tales became a joke,
All his buddies listened, for they knew whereof he spoke.
But we'll hear his tales no longer, for old Bob has passed away
And the world's a little poorer, for a soldier died today.

No he won't be mourned by many, just his children and his wife,
For he lived an ordinary very quiet sort of life,
He held a job and raised a family, quietly going on his way;
And the world won't note his passing; 'tho a soldier died today.

When politicians leave this earth, their bodies lie in state,
While thousands note their passing and proclaim that they were great,
Papers tell of their life stories from the time that they were young,
But the passing of a soldier goes unnoticed, and unsung.

Is the greatest contribution to the welfare of our land
Some jerk who breaks his promise and cons his fellow man?
Or the ordinary fellow who in times of war and strife
Goes off to serve his Country and offers up his life?

The politician's stipend and the style in which he lives
Are sometimes disproportionate to the services he gives,
While the ordinary soldier, who offered up his all,
Is paid off with a medal, and perhaps a pension small.

It's so easy to forget them, for it was so long ago
That our Bob's and Jim's and Johnny's went to battle, but we know
It was not the politicians, with their compromise and ploys,
Who won for us the freedom that our country now enjoys.

Should you find yourself in danger with your enemies at hand,
Would you really want some cop-out with his ever waffling stand?
Or would you want a soldier who has sworn to defend
His home, his kin, and country, and would fight until the end?

He was just a common soldier and his ranks are growing thin
But his presence should remind us, we may need his like again.
For when countries are in conflict, then we find the soldier's part
Is to clean up all the troubles that the politicians start.

If we cannot do him honor while he's here to hear the praise,
Then at least let's give him homage at the ending of his days.
Perhaps just a simple headline in the paper that might say:

OUR COUNTRY IS IN MOURNING, FOR A SOLDIER DIED TODAY.

Author Unknown

SGT(P) DONALD WAYNE SLOVER

Subject: Letter about SGT Slover

Dear America:

    I am writing this letter to extend thanks to all the American people who still, despite the recent headlines undermining the ethics and morality of the military, understand that our jobs and way of life are necessary to preserve the "American" way of life. I once thought that "America" viewed us as most media portrays us; immoral, unethical, and uncivilized. My recent travels led me to conclude that the opposite is true. You, the American people, that honor and respect what we do, deserve a public "thank you." Just a few weeks ago, a tragedy embedded itself in the tall evergreen forests at the Joint Readiness Training Center in Fort Polk, LA. As a tank slowly slalomed through the trees after sunset on January 14, 1998, the tank commander fell victim to the inherent danger of the military. SGT(P) Donald Wayne Slover passed away that night as he was guiding his tank through the thickest of trees, fog, and rain. The tank's edge clipped and uprooted a tree, which sent it crashing to the ground. The medics, arriving on site only minutes later, felt SGT(P) Slover's last pulse. As one of two military escorts, I was required to accompany the remains from the training area to the burial site, ensuring the proper and unimpaired delivery to the next of kin. The obligation required a two day journey from Fort Hood, TX, to Williamsburg, KY, via Fort Polk, LA. Loading, unloading, and transportation of the remains required our physical presence. This particular trip entailed a three hour van ride, a connecting flight in Atlanta in route to Knoxville, and a one hour drive to Williamsburg, KY. Upon boarding our initial flight out of Houston we informed the flight attendant of our duties. After explaining that it was necessary for us to depart the plane first upon landing (so as not to delay the cargo personnel unloading the casket), two gentlemen offered their seats in the first row of the plane for our last row seats. This gesture left me speechless. I'm not so sure they even knew our purpose for having to be first off the plane, but with no questions immediately sacrificed their front row seats. After arriving in Atlanta, we were escorted by airport personnel off the plane and down to the tarmac. Standing in our dress green uniforms, we watched as the airline employees carefully unloaded the casket onto the cargo truck. The truck drove off to the departing gate and we made our way back inside the terminal. We met the cargo truck at the departure gate and again were escorted down to the tarmac to supervise the loading of our final flight. Following the loading, we turned and headed back to the terminal. As we made that walk, I noticed that we were being watched by the crowd awaiting the outbound flight. Not thinking much about it at the time, I scurried out of the cold and awaited the boarding call. We boarded the plane and again informed the flight attendant of our duties and departure requirements. The flight was booked, every seat filled, and she told us that she would make an announcement upon landing that we were to exit the plane first. Having been on full flights before, I was for certain that this announcement would be ignored. Passengers are normally elbow deep in the overhead compartments as soon as the wheels touch the ground. I was 100% positive I would be the last person off that flight. But I took my seat in the back of the plane, my partner 10 rows in front, and with all of my military skills tried to devise a plan that could project me to the front of that plane upon landing. I concluded that even generals would have a rough time planning such an operation. As the plane touched down in Knoxville, the flight attendant gave the standard "keep your seat-belts fastened until the captain turns off the seat-belt sign" announcement. She then led into the fact that two military escorts were on-board and that everyone must remain in their seats until we departed the plane. The plane parked and to my astonishment, not a soul moved. I'd never witnessed such absolute silence in my life. Many of the passengers turned their heads to the rear of the plane but not a sound was made as myself and the other escort donned our jackets, grabbed our bags, and headed down the aisle. I realized then that all eyes were on us. As we neared the exit an older gentleman leaned toward us and broke the silence with something I will never forget, "God bless you both," he said. I am, sir, most truly blessed. I have been afforded the opportunity to work alongside some of the greatest sons and daughters of our nation. We know and understand that each day presents the possibility of injury and/or death and we take all precautions to prevent them. But we sacrifice that possibility because you depend on us. We train through the roughest of conditions, with minimum sleep and limited resources, anywhere at anytime, to ensure we are always ready. We, sir, are most honored that you entrust us to defend your country. So I'm writing this letter to say thanks. Thank you Delta Airlines, thank you gentlemen for your seats, thank you sir for your blessings, and thank you America for your support. You see ... we as soldiers don't expect you to understand the ways in which we live, train, and fight; we just ask for a thank you from time to time. A little appreciation from the people we're defending weighs more than a chestful of awards and medals. SGT(P) Donald Wayne Slover gave his life training to defend the very code of morality and ethics he exemplified and believed in. SGT(P) Slover believed in the Army and his country. I worked alongside SGT(P) Slover for over a year. He was good at his job and he loved it. He never complained and always did what was asked of him. SGT(P) Slover always maintained the courage of his convictions. I hope he lied [sic] to rest knowing he was appreciated. If not, we failed as a nation and we owe it to him. SGT(P) Slover ... thank you! You will be missed!

Daniel Ashley
1-10 Cavalry, 4th Infantry Division
READY AND FORWARD

'Twas the Night Before Christmas

T'was the night before Christmas, he lived all alone,
In a one bedroom house made of plaster and stone.

I had come down the chimney with presents to give,
And to see just who in this home did live.

I looked all about, a strange sight I did see,
No tinsel, no presents, not even a tree.

No stocking by mantle, just boots filled with sand.
On the wall hung pictures of far distant lands.

With medals and badges, awards of all kinds,
A sober thought came through my mind.

For this house was different, it was dark and dreary.
I found the home of a soldier, once I could see clearly.

The soldier lay sleeping, silent, alone.
Curled up on the floor in this one-bedroom home.

The face was so gentle, the room in such disorder,
Not how I pictured a United States soldier.

Was this the hero of whom I'd just read?
Curled up on a poncho, the floor for a bed?

I realized the families that I saw this night,
Owed their lives to these soldiers who were willing to fight.

Soon, 'round the world the children would play,
And grown-ups would celebrate a bright Christmas day.

They all enjoyed freedom each month of the year,
Because of the soldiers, like the one lying here.

I couldn't help wonder how many lay alone,
On a cold Christmas Eve, in a land far from home.

The very thought brought a tear to my eye,
I dropped to my knees and started to cry.

The soldier awakened and I heard a rough voice,
"Santa don't cry, this life is my choice.

I fight for freedom, I don't ask for more,
My life is my God, my Country, my Corps."

The Soldier rolled over and drifted to sleep,
I couldn't control it, I continued to weep.

I kept watch for hours, so silent and still,
As we both shivered from the cold night's chill.

I didn't want to leave on that cold, dark night,
This Guardian of honor so willing to fight.

Then the soldier rolled over, with a voice soft and pure,
Whispered, "Carry on Santa, it's Christmas Day, all is secure."

One look at my watch, and I knew he was right,
Merry Christmas my friend, and to all a good night.

Author unknown

The Eagle

He clasps the crag with crooked hands;
Close to the sun in lonely lands,
Ringed with the azure world he stands.

The wrinkled sea beneath him crawls;
He watches from his mountain walls,
And like a thunderbolt he falls.

Alfred (Lord) Tennyson

*It is, in a way, an odd thing to honor those who
died in defense of our country, in defense of us,
in wars far away. The imagination plays a trick.
We see these soldiers in our mind as old and wise.*

Memorial Day, May 29, 2000   Courtesy of VFW Post 4051, Colorado Springs,
Colorado. Commander Duane Knutson

We see them as something like the
Founding Fathers, grave and gray haired.
But most of them were boys when they died,
and they gave up two lives—the one they were
living and the one they would have lived.
When they died, they gave up their chance to be
husbands and fathers and grandfathers.
They gave up their chance to everything
for our county, for us.
And all we can do is remember.

President Ronald Reagan
from the book
The Wisdom and Humor of
the Great Communicator

[Commenting on his return to Little Round Top, Gettysburg, Pennsylvania, in 1913. Chamberlain was awarded the Medal of Honor for his service there.]

Mortal After All

I went—it was not long ago—
to stand again upon that crest
whose one day's crown of fire has passed
into the blazoned
coronet of fame.

I sat there alone on the storied crest,
till the sun went down
as it did before over the misty hills,
and the darkness crept up the slopes,
till from all earthly sight I was
buried as with those before.

But oh, what radiant companionship
rose around,
what steadfast ranks of power,
what bearing of heroic souls.
Oh, the glory that beamed
through those nights and days.

Joshua Lawrence
Chamberlain

Nobody will ever know it here!
I am sorry most of all for that.
The proud young valor that
rose above the mortal,
and then at last was mortal after all.

Joshua Lawrence Chamberlain

THANK YOU FOR LISTENING

I like to go to the library at lunchtime sometimes, and today was one of those times. While walking amongst the books, I saw a small bent-over old man, hobbling along with a cane, ear piece, and assorted other body append-ages visible beneath his shirt. He had on a "World War II Veteran" baseball cap, so I asked him which branch he was in. "Army Air Force," was the reply. "Were you ever in the service?" he asked. "Yes, I was a helicopter pilot in Viet-nam," I replied. "Where were you stationed?" I asked. "Europe." "What did you do?" He points to the tie-tac he was wearing, "Recognize this?" It was a B-24 Liberator. "Sure, my Dad was in the Pacific. Who were with you with?" He pulls a business card out of his decrepit old wallet. It says: John F. Barnacle, 450th "COTTONTAILS" Bomb Group, 15th A.F. Air Forces Escape and Eva-sion Society, Air Forces Gunners Association, D.A.V.–AM. LEG.–V.F.W., Huntsville, AL 35810. I asked John, "So, what did you do?"

He replied, "Ball Turret Gunner. I don't want to bore you, but, would you like to hear my story?" "I sure would." He then regaled me with his story, of how he enlisted in the Guard in '38, and got called to active duty in October '40. He started out in B-25s as a waste gunner. He was still in the States, out drinking with a bunch of guys one night, and one of them got drunk and told him about this special unit that Col. Jimmy Doolittle was forming up down at Eglin. John bummed a flight down to Eglin. He reported to the operations Ma-jor, and told him wanted to volunteer for the special unit he heard about. The Major told him he had to wait for the Col. to come back. Later that afternoon Doolittle landed, in his own personal P-40 that he flew. John reported to Doolittle and told him that he wanted to join his outfit. Doolittle told him to get the hell out his office. He already had more guys wanting to commit sui-cide than he needed. That's how John missed the Tokyo raid. So, John re-turned back to his base, only to get disciplined with 120 days of KP and guard duty for running off to Jimmy. He then volunteered to train as part of the first two Heavy Bomber crews for the 450th. He was the small guy, so he got the ball turret. John then told me; of the day—one of many days—in which he personally shot down 5 German fighters, a mixture of ME-109s and FW-190s;

of how he was wounded three times; of the day his B-24 got shot down over Yugoslavia, and he spent 30 days in E&E with Tito's partisans before he was repatriated to the Allies; of how they refused to let him return to combat because of the rule that shot down and returned airman might reveal info about the resistance; of about how he went back to the States, and trained new crewmen for the B-29; and how they refused to let him volunteer to be B-29 crewman in the Pacific—they said he had had too much already. He then showed me his beat-up old "Caterpillar Club" card, that he received for having his life saved by a parachute in March 1944. He had a gleam in his eyes, and that faraway look that warriors get when remembering. I know the look. I was silent, a little dumbstruck. He then hooked his cane on his arm, and took my hand in both of his. He started shaking my hand vigorously, and with tears in his eyes said, "Thank you for listening to my story." I was getting a little misty eyed too. I thanked him profusely for sharing it. This just happened within the past hour. I wrote this as a memorial to this great, and aged warrior. They are dying off fast. I also wrote it because I saw myself—all of us—a few years down the road, as old men, (I mean really old men) forgotten by everybody. I hope somebody wants to hear my story someday. I hope somebody will stop and care. I am a little misty eyed again.

> Robert Glasier, Maddog 19
> Greyhound 19, 240th Attack
> Helicopter Company
> (AHC), Republic of Vietnam (RVN)

U.S. Marines Vietnam War

The Six O'Clock News

For us it was the six o'clock news.
For them it was reality.

We called for pizza.
They called for medics.

We watched children play.
They watched children die.

We learned of life.
They learned of death.

We served dinner.
They served their country.

Our passion was success.
Theirs was survival.

We forgot.
They can't.

Author Unknown

THEY LOVED GOD, COUNTRY, AND OUR NAVY

Admirals: FYI, a very noteworthy and moving piece follows. As many of you know, JFK is operating in the Gulf and lost an S-3 along with the pilot and NFO several days ago (the rear two stations were unoccupied). The pilot's father is RADM Pat Moneymaker, USN (Ret), former Blue Angel Commanding Officer (CO), Commander of the Air Group (CAG), and Commander Naval Space Command, and a man who touched many in the Navy during his career with his energy and enthusiasm. Below are the comments and eulogy by JFK CO and CAG ... well worth the read and will perhaps cause you, as they did for me, to stop for a second and think about this busy world and all that we do and stand for. We're truly blessed to have such fine leadership and dedication in our Navy. This scenario has played out many times on many ships, but thru the wonders of modern at sea email connectivity, we can almost be there too.

FYI, "Carlos" is RADM Johnson,

V/R, Deputy

Sent: Wednesday, November 17, 1999

Subject: Eulogy

    Dear Phil: thank you all so much for your expressions of condolences and support. You have no idea how much they mean to me and the team out here in the North Arabian Gulf. We had a very nice memorial service for Mat Moneymaker and Mike Meschke on the flight deck late this afternoon. As if even the Arabian Gulf understood, we saw rain showers throughout the morning ... truly fit my mood ... but we steered a southerly course to avoid the rain by the time of the ceremony. We were all in our Blues; the overcast skies muted the strength of the sun and made for a balmy, subdued sunset. I shut down the radars and the bridge navigated us such that the wind dropped to zero, so the setting was peaceful and calm.

    Carlos gave a very moving speech, which he finished by reading the poem "Freedom isn't free." His wisdom and fatherly counsel reassured those in attendance that we can—and must—press on from this tragic event. CAG Pat Walsh then got up, and delivered what I think is one of the finest eulogies I have ever heard ... I have copied it and attached it at the bottom of this email. If words can adequately express the vision and ideals that have lasting meaning in life, then surely the words below must be the of the highest order.

    Billy Valentine said the sad farewells from the squadron, and then had 3 of his officers who knew Mat and Mike the best get up and tell a few stories about their lost friends. They were sad, sweet, compassionate stories from men who in the last 48 hours have come to recognize their own mortality ... and the importance of their extremely rare skills. I was moved by the depth of their passion, and their commitment to carrying on where their fallen comrades had left off. Finer men cannot be found, I believe. With all of our ego, false bravado, and human frailties, Naval Aviation remains a profession of the highest calling ... and of those, only a very few will ever share the sheer joy and simultaneous terror of tactical jet aviation. It is the best of times, and sometimes the worst of times ... and it is the exhilaration of life at the farthest edge. For this, and a million other reasons, we are resolved to pick ourselves up and press on.

CAG Walsh's Comments:

    It is an honor to speak to you on behalf of our fallen comrades. Today we celebrate their life and legacy, their commitment and dedication to principles that you and I hold dear, and many, many wonderful memories. As I think of Mat and Mike in the spirited and compressed lives that we lead at sea, I am reminded of the words of Lord Byron when he wrote that the "days of our youth were the days of our glory." These were gentlemen of impeccable character,

**Sailor paying tribute
to a fallen comrade**

honor, and youthful vitality; both were noble officers of courage and outstanding repute. They loved God, country, and our Navy, and I had the pleasure of their company. The privilege that I have had, and now the burden that I carry, has been the charge to guide them, lead them, and return them home to their loved ones. I have asked for the opportunity to speak to you this evening not only to give this testimonial on behalf of my colleagues, but also to offer my profound admiration and gratitude to the families who shared their sons, their husband, and their fiancé, with us.

Today is especially difficult for me, because Mat's father taught, led, and shepherded my peers and friends. Today, I am reminded of all that his father had done for me with his example, dedication, and selfless service to this family that you and I belong [to] and hold dear. Whether you realize it, sense it, or understand it completely, you are part of a great circle of community, history, and tradition, where one generation cares for and nurtures the next. Mat's father had done that for me, and I am charged to do that for you.

Mat had a passion for life and he eagerly anticipated each new challenge. He was a scuba diver, rock climber, world-class collegiate swimmer, triathlete, and seaplane pilot. Shawn Inman, "Catbox", told me that it was an inspiration and honor to serve with Mat. He always had time to look after Sailors and made every effort to keep them challenged and headed in the right direction. The air wing respected Mat for his qualities as a naval officer, his skills as a pilot, and capabilities as an LSO.

The Mauler ready room, in typical good humor, noted that Mat never wore a watch, always had his alarm clock set on the wrong time, but somehow managed to get where he needed to go. They noted that his clock ticked with the sounds of the ship, the noise of the catapults calling him to the platform, and the excitement of going flying. I agree with them that most of us will simply remember Mathew as the nicest guy we will ever meet. We know that he will continue to watch over us, just as he did from the platform on many a dark, stormy night, keep us safe and bring us home.

Mike jump-started his naval career with ten years aboard fast attack and boomer submarines before he joined the ranks of aviators, and then hunted the very submarines he served aboard. Mike was an avid scuba diver and outdoorsman. He was practical and technical in his approach to aviation, and was tops in his class. The Maulers tell me that behind his gentle shyness and quiet demeanor was a "Clydesdale," a nickname that he earned a long time ago because his hard-charging work ethic and steadfast reliability was rock-steady, like that of the famous family of horses. The airwing respected Michael because he dedicated himself to others, and was a relentless problem-solver who always tried to make life better for everyone.

I will think of them both often in the days to come. I will think of their professionalism as I prepare for tomorrow's combat operations and how they would want me to focus on the important national commitment that you and I must face. We will remember their gifts of innocence and laughter as the Thanksgiving and Christmas holiday season approaches. And, you and I will remind each other of how much better our lives were for having them both here.

There is another reason why I will always remember these men and all that they have stood for and represent. In three short weeks, I will have a son. My wife, Andy, and six-year old daughter, Jennifer, anxiously await his arrival next month. I am already proud of the little man who will carry on my family name and legacy; and, I already have great expectations for him. I want him to have a passion for life to enjoy it to its fullest whether that means surfing clouds or surfing the sea. At the same time, I want and hope that he will think in terms larger than himself and that he surrounds himself with people in a community that have a sense of history, of obligation to each other, and a soul. I don't care whether he wears a watch or if he has an alarm clock, but I hope people admire and respect him for his skills, competence, capabilities, and personal code of ethics. I hope that they will think of him as a "Clydesdale" who always tries to make life better for everyone. I do not know if you realize it or not, but he already has a head start. You see, my wife and I decided last Spring on the name of our son who will be born in a few short days. We wanted a name, steeped in biblical tradition that would serve as a reminder to us each time we called him that this person was a wonderful gift from God. The reason why I will remember this day, this moment, and these gentlemen for the rest of my life is because soon, I will have a son named Matthew Michael.

With the good Lord's help, my son will have a happy and full life. I can think of no greater act than for him to someday wear our country's uniform.

I use the announcement of his birth as an opportunity to turn to you today, and remind you that you will teach, guide, and shepherd our children through adversity and difficult days such as today. Tell them what you learned today, that a soldier becomes a warrior when he has experienced both the triumph of life and victory, but also the stinging, searing finality of death itself. Then, when a soldier is emotionally tattered, physically drawn, mentally fatigued, and he wants to withdraw to the deep, dark corners of solitude and despair, he realizes he must summon up the strength within himself; his ship and shipmates depend on him. It is only when he has experienced both the triumph of life and tragedy of death that he is a true warrior.

Sunday, many of us became older, wiser, and aware of our own mortality; we became warriors. I can tell you that when the time comes for my son to leave home, I pray that there will be shipmates ... someone just like Mat and Mike ... who will help him to pursue his dreams, guide him as he faces his own adversities, and shepherd him into manhood.

Now I ask that you set aside your doubts and fears, your trepidation and anxieties, and that you look inside yourself and summon up the courage of the long blue line, and join me on our combat mission over the beach tomorrow.

[end of eulogy]

A Guy Who Wanted To Live

When you lose a friend you have an overpowering desire to go back home and yell in everybody's ear, "This guy was killed fighting for you. Don't forget him—ever. Keep him in your mind when you wake up in the morning and when you go to bed at night. Don't think of him as the statistic which changes 38,788 casualties to 38,789. Think of him as a guy who wanted to live every bit as much as you do. Don't let him be just one of 'Our Brave Boys' from the old home town, to whom a marble monument is erected in the city park, and a civic-minded lady calls the newspaper ten years later and wants to know why that 'unsightly stone' isn't removed."

Sergeant Bill Mauldin
from his book *Up Front*
1945

No person was ever honored for what he received. Honor has been the reward for what he gave.

Calvin Coolidge

Surely every post ought to be deemed honorable in which a man can serve his country.

George Washington

Honor is the quality of personal integrity ... It is won slowly by a lifetime of small decisions where one puts the virtues of compassion and justice ahead of his own advancement.

Commonweal

Honor lies in honest toil

Grover Cleveland

One of the greatest sources of energy is pride in what you are doing.

Ben Franklin

National honor is national property of the highest value.

James Monroe
First Inaugural Address, March 4, 1817
1758–1830
5th President of the United States
(1817–1825)

He was a foe without hate, a friend without treachery,
a soldier without cruelty, and a victim without
murmuring. He was a public officer without vices,
a private citizen without wrong, a neighbor without
reproach, a Christian without hypocrisy, and a man
without guilt. He was a Caesar without his ambition,
Frederick without his tyranny, Napoleon without his
selfishness, and Washington without his reward.

Benjamin H. Hill
in his tribute to Robert E. Lee

Remember, remember always that all of us,
and you and I especially, are descended from
immigrants and revolutionists.

Franklin Delano Roosevelt
Address to Daughters of the American Revolution
April 21, 1938

Humility must always be the portion of any man
who receives acclaim earned in the blood of his
followers and the sacrifices of his friends.

Dwight D. Eisenhower
Address at Guildhall on receiving the
Freedom of the City of London award
July 12, 1945

ONE GROUP OF MEN

*If you ever think the world is a rotten place,
go to the cemetery overlooking the
beach at Normandy (Omaha Beach)
and see what one group of men
did for another.*

Andy Rooney
about D-Day

The American Cemetery in Colleville-sur-Mer, Normandy, France
contains the graves of 9,386 American GIs.

*Responsible citizenship in a free
country means what it says.
It means conducting one's self responsibly,
in the interest of others as well as self.*

Dwight D. Eisenhower

ON WHOSE SHOULDERS WE STAND

This is the first time in history that this ceremony has been held, as you have been told, on this West Front of the Capitol. Standing here, one faces a magnificent vista, opening up on this city's special beauty and history. At the end of this open mall are those shrines to the giants on whose shoulders we stand. Directly in front of me, the monument to a monumental man: George Washington, Father of our country. A man of humility who came to greatness reluctantly. He led America out of revolutionary victory into infant nationhood. Off to one side, the stately memorial to Thomas Jefferson. The Declaration of Independence flames with his eloquence. And then beyond the Reflecting Pool the dignified columns of the Lincoln Memorial. Whoever would understand in his heart the meaning of America will find it in the life of Abraham Lincoln. Beyond those monuments to heroism is the Potomac River, and on the far shore the sloping hills of Arlington National Cemetery with its row on row of simple white markers bearing crosses or Stars of David. They add up to only a tiny fraction of the price that has been paid for our freedom. Each one of those markers is a monument to the kinds of hero I spoke of earlier. Their lives ended in places called Belleau Wood, The Argonne, Omaha Beach, Salerno and halfway around the world on Guadalcanal, Tarawa, Pork Chop Hill, the Chosin Reservoir, and in a hundred rice paddies and jungles of a place called Vietnam. Under one such marker lies a young man—Martin Treptow—who left his job in a small town barber shop in 1917 to go to France with the famed Rainbow Division. There, on the western front, he was killed trying to carry a message between battalions under heavy artillery fire. We are told that on his body was found a diary. On the flyleaf under the heading, "My Pledge," he had written these words:

> America must win this war. Therefore, I will work, I will save, I will sacrifice, I will endure, I will fight cheerfully and do my utmost, as if the issue of the whole struggle depended on me alone.

The crisis we are facing today does not require of us the kind of sacrifice that Martin Treptow and so many thousands of others were called upon to make. It does require, however, our best effort, and our willingness to believe in ourselves and to believe in our capacity to perform great deeds; to believe that together, with God's help, we can and will resolve the problems which now confront us.

And, after all, why shouldn't we believe that? We are Americans. God bless you, and thank you.

> President Ronald Reagan
> Closing remarks from his
> First Inaugural address
> January 20, 1981

CHAPTER FOURTEEN

Old Glory, Allegiance, and Citizenship

The American flag, and all that it represents, is the focus of this chapter. The allegiance displayed by Americans throughout our history has been the result of pride, love of country, and a sense of one's citizenship.

The Star Spangled Banner

Oh, Say, can you see, by the dawn's early light
What so proudly we hailed at the twilight's last gleaming?
Whose broad stripes and bright stars, through the perilous fight,
O'er the ramparts we watched were so gallantly streaming!
And the rocket's red glare, the bombs bursting in air,
Gave proof through the night that our flag was still there;
Oh, say, does that star-spangled banner yet wave
O'er the land of the free, and the home of the brave?

On that shore dimly seen through the mists of the deep,
Where the foe's haughty host in dread silence reposes,
What is that which the breeze, o'er the towering steep,
As it fitfully blows, now conceals, now discloses?
Now it catches the gleam of the morning's first beam,
In full glory reflected now shines on the stream;
Tis the star-spangled banner; oh, long may it wave
O'er the land of the free, and the home of the brave!

And where is that band who so vauntingly swore
That the havoc of war and the battle's confusion
A home and a country should leave us not more?
Their blood has washed out their foul footstep's pollution.
No refuge could save the hireling and slave
From the terror of flight, or the gloom of the grave;
And the star-spangled banner in triumph doth wave
O'er the land of the free, and the home of the brave.

Francis Scott Key

["Then, in that hour of deliverance, my heart spoke" wrote Francis Scott Key, of the British attack in September 1814. "Does not such a country, and such defenders of their country, deserve a song?"]

Francis Scott Key had a friend, a physician in the rural Baltimore area, named Dr. William Beanes. Legend has it that the little known Dr. Beanes managed to get himself captured and imprisoned by the British on one of their frigates that was engaged in a siege of Fort McHenry.

As was the custom, Key went to the officer of the ship and proceeded to bargain for the freedom of his friend. He managed to persuade the British to let him go, but only after the current battle was over. He was, therefore, on the deck of the ship while it was firing at the American-held Fort McHenry, in the Baltimore Harbor. The firing ended during the night. He waited and watched, with the ultimate dawn bringing the revelation that the flag was still flying. This sight inspired the song that became our National Anthem.

THERE IS BUT ONE FLAG

*A flag is the emblem of sovereignty—a symbol and
guarantee of protection. Every nation and people
are proud of the flag of their country.
England, for a thousand years boasts her Red flag
and Cross of St.George; France glories in her Tri-color
and Imperial Eagle; ours the "Star-spangled Banner,"
far more beautiful than they—this dear old flag!—
the sun in heaven never looked down on so proud a
banner of beauty and glory. Men of the Black Brigade,
rally around it! Assert your manhood, be loyal to duty,
be obedient, hopeful, patient. Slavery will soon die;
the slaveholders' rebellion, accursed of God
and man, will shortly and miserably perish.
There will then be through all the coming ages,
in very truth, a land of the free—one country, one flag,
one destiny. I charge you, Men of the Black Brigade
of Cincinnati, remember that for you, and for me,
and for your children, and your children's children,
there is but one Flag, as there is but one Bible,
and one God, the Father of us all.*

James Lupton
Acting Camp Commandant
presenting the National flag to The Cincinnati Black Brigade
September 4, 1862

MIKE CHRISTIAN'S FLAG

[From a speech made by CAPT John S. McCain, USN, (Ret.) and current Senator from Arizona.]

As you may know, I spent five and one half years as a prisoner of war during the Vietnam War. In the early years of our imprisonment, the NVA kept us in solitary confinement or two or three to a cell. In 1971 the NVA moved us from these conditions of isolation into large rooms with as many as 30 or 40 men to a room. This was, as you can imagine, a wonderful change and was a direct result of the efforts of millions of Americans on behalf of a few hundred POWs 10,000 miles from home. One of the men that moved into my room was a young man named Mike Christian. Mike came from a small town near Selma, Alabama. He didn't wear a pair of shoes 'til he was 13 years old. At 17, he enlisted in the US Navy. He later earned a commission by going to Officer Training School. Then he became a Naval Flight Officer and was shot down and captured in 1967.

Mike had a keen and deep appreciation of the opportunities this country—and our military—who provide for people who want to work and want to succeed. As part of the change in treatment, the Vietnamese allowed some prisoners to receive packages from home. In some of these packages were handkerchiefs, scarves and other items of clothing. Mike got himself a bamboo needle. Over a period of a couple of months, he sewed the American flag on the inside of his shirt. Every afternoon, before we had a bowl of soup, we would hang Mike's shirt on the wall of the cell and say the Pledge of Allegiance. I know the Pledge of Allegiance may not seem the most important part of our day now. But I can assure you that in that stark cell it was, indeed, the most important and meaningful event.

One day the Vietnamese searched our cell, as they did periodically, and discovered Mike's shirt with the flag sewn inside and removed it. That evening they returned, opened the door of the cell, and for the benefit of all of us, dragged Mike Christian outside and beat him severely for the next couple of hours. Then they opened the door of the cell and threw him in; we cleaned him up as well as we could. The cell in which we lived had a concrete slab in the middle on which we slept as well as we could. Four naked light bulbs hung in each corner of the room. As I said, we tried to clean up Mike as well as we could. After the excitement died down, I looked in the corner of the room and, sitting there beneath that dim light bulb with a piece of red cloth, another shirt, and his bamboo needle, was my friend, Mike Christian. He was sitting there with his eyes swollen almost shut from the beating he had received, making another American flag.

He was not making the flag because it made Mike Christian feel better. He was making that flag because he knew how important it was to us to be able to pledge our allegiance to our flag and country.

So the next time you say the Pledge of Allegiance, you must never forget the sacrifice and courage that thousands of Americans have made to build our nation and promote freedom around the world.

You must remember our duty, our honor, and our country.

I pledge allegiance to the flag of the United States of America and to the republic for which it stands, one nation, under God, indivisible, with liberty and justice for all.

JUST ASK PERMISSION

To those who want to burn the flag, just ask permission.

Does the first Amendment gives us the right to desecrate the American flag? Or is the flag a sacred symbol of our nation, deserving protection by law? Tough call? "The Solution" For those who want to light Old Glory on fire, stomp all over it, or spit on it to make some sort of "statement," I say let them do it. But under one condition: they MUST get permission from three sponsors.

First, you need permission of a war veteran. Perhaps a Marine who fought at Iwo Jima? The American flag was raised over Mount Surabachi upon the bodies of thousands of dead buddies. Each night spent on Iwo meant half of everyone you knew would be dead tomorrow, a coin flip away from a bloody end upon a patch of sand your mother couldn't find on a map. Or maybe ask a Vietnam vet who spent years tortured in a small, filthy cell unfit for a dog. Or a Korean War soldier who helped rescue half a nation from Communism, or a Desert Storm veteran who repulsed a bloody dictator from raping and pillaging an innocent country. That flag represented your mother and father, your sister and brother, your friends, neighbors, and everyone at home. I wonder what they would say if someone asked them permission to burn the American flag?

Next, you need a signature from an immigrant. Their brothers and sisters may still languish in their native land, often under tyranny, poverty and misery. Or maybe they died on the way here, never to touch our shores. Some have seen friends and family get tortured and murdered by their own government for daring to do things we take for granted every day. For those who risked everything simply for the chance to become an American ... what kind of feelings do they have for the flag when they Pledge Allegiance the first time? Go to a naturalization ceremony and see for yourself, the tears of pride, the thanks, the love and respect of this nation, as they finally embrace the American flag as their own. Ask one of them if it would be OK to tear up the flag.

Last, you should get the signature of a mother. Not just any mother. You need a mother of someone who gave their life for America. It doesn't even have to be from a war. It could be a cop. Or a fireman. Maybe a Secret Service or NSA agent. Then again, it could be a common foot soldier as well. When that son or daughter is laid to rest, their family is given one gift by the American people; an American flag. Go on. I dare you. Ask that mother to spit on her flag.

I wonder what the founding fathers thought of the American flag as they drafted the Declaration of Independence? They knew this act would drag young America into war with England, the greatest power on earth. They also knew failure meant more than just a disappointment. It meant a noose snugly stretched around their necks. But they needed a symbol, something to inspire the new nation. Something to represent the seriousness, the purpose and conviction that we held our new idea of individual freedom. Something worth living for. Something worth dying for. I wonder how they'd feel if someone asked them permission to toss their flag in a mud puddle?

Away from family, away from the precious shores of home, in the face of overwhelming odds and often in the face of death, the American flag inspires those who believe in the American dream, the American promise, the American vision ... Americans who don't appreciate the flag don't appreciate this nation. And those who appreciate this nation appreciate the American flag. Those who fought, fought for that flag. Those who died, died for that flag. And those who love America, love that flag—and defend it.

So if you want to desecrate the American flag, before you spit on it or before you burn it ... I have a simple request. Just ask permission. Not from the Constitution. Not from some obscure law. Not from the politicians or the pundits. Instead, ask those who defended our nation so that we may be free today. Ask those who struggled to reach our shores so that they may join us in the American dream. And ask those who clutch a flag in place of their sacrificed sons and daughters, given to this nation so that others may be free. For we cannot ask permission from those who died wishing they could, just once ... or once again, see, touch or kiss the flag that stands for our nation, the United States of America.

by Mr. Tom Atkins

[Mr. Atkins is the Editor of the Common Conservative, which can be located at <commonconservative.com>.]

OH, SAY CAN YOU SEE

It is half time of the Super Bowl [January 2000] and I just received a call from an old friend … a retired first sergeant who had to call and let me know what he saw at one of your local bars this evening. It seems this bar was having a dart tournament prior to the game and had quite a crowd of folks including some Fort Eustis soldiers in civilian clothes. Well the tournament was pretty much over as the game was getting ready to start and the TVs were all turned to the game when Faith Hill began to sing the National Anthem. My retired friend was deep in a conversation with someone at the bar when his wife said "Look over there." On the other side of the bar were all the soldiers standing at attention as Faith Hill sang the National Anthem. The conversation ended as everyone stood. When Ms. Hill finished the bar patrons did not applaud but the conversation turned to how the Army was doing a good job of raising great Americans who understood what it meant to be a soldier and what it meant to be an American. Steve, the game was great but it sure won't top that story. My friend thinks the soldiers were from BNCOC [Basic Non-Commissioned Officers Course], but he is not sure.

Author Unknown

*The things that the flag stands for were created
by the experiences of a great people.
Everything that it stands for was written by their lives.
The flag is the embodiment, not of sentiment,
but of history. It represents the experiences made
by men and women, the experiences of those
who died and lived under that flag.*

Woodrow Wilson
June 14, 1915

CHAPTER FIFTEEN
Setting the Example

F ollow Me and Do as I do are the focus of this short and final chapter. Those who
have set the example for others to follow are the leaders who have always made
the difference between success or failure and between victory or defeat.

*To share a common lot,
and participate in the inconveniences
which the Army are obliged to
undergo has been with me
a fundamental principle.*

General George Washington
Continental Army

TAKING CARE OF HIS MEN

Throughout his tenure as Commander-in-Chief of the Continental Army, General Washington's loyalty to his soldiers never wavered. Time and again, General Washington was the last to leave the field of battle or last to cross a river in retreat always ensuring that the men in his command were taken care of first.

One of the most notable instances of General Washington's leadership and loyalty was at Valley Forge during the winter of 1777–1778. Supplies and shelter were almost non-existent and the winter was very bitter. General Washington had his men fell trees and build cabins for shelter. Until then, the soldiers had been sleeping in little more than tattered tents.

Only after his men had built their log cabins did General Washington occupy the building designated for his headquarters.

We want a clean Camp, clean clothes, well-dressed victuals. However deeply involved in rags our Army may be we still can do our best to appear decently attentive to our behavior in these regards. ... Sergeants and Corporals are to set example for the men.

**General
George Washington**
1778,
Ordeal at Valley Forge

Example is the best general order.
General George Crook, 1970

ONLY THE ROCKS LIVE FOREVER

This is a personal perspective on ideals for leaders in terms of values and attitudes. My hope is that these thoughts will be remembered and will be of some future use as a simple guide and framework of life.

Lame Beaver, an Indian warrior, said, "Only the rocks live forever." Clausewitz stated that the leader must stand like a rock on which the waves break in vain. George Patton said that a military officer or noncommissioned officer must be a rock to withstand the storms and tests of time.

I have selected three rocks to serve as a beacon for the leader. Rocks to provide strength and be a bulwark against the temptations and ordeals of life.

The first rock comes from the study of military history. Most historians differ on the great leaders of the past. My selections on the basis of leadership are: Hannibal of Carthage, George Washington, Napoleon Bonaparte, Robert E. Lee, and George Patton. In attempting to find a common thread from comprehensive study of these five, I have selected an excerpt from Freeman's last volume on Lee.

> And if one, only one, of all myriad incidents of his stirring life had to be selected to typify his message, as a man, to the young Americans who stood in hushed awe that rainy October morning as their parents wept at the passing of the Southern Arthur, who would hesitate in selecting that incident? It occurred in Northern Virginia on his last visit there. A young mother brought her baby to him to be blessed. He took the infant in his arms and looked long at it and then at her and slowly said, "Teach him he must deny himself." That is all. There is no mystery in the coffin at Lexington there in front of the windows that look to the sunrise.

The second rock is—Be a Sam Damon. Of course many have never read "Once an Eagle" by Anton Myrer. His book is an historic novel about two professional soldiers, Courtney Massengale and Sam Damon. The former is a careerist, ticket-puncher, self-seeker, and a political officer. The latter is a real soldier of great integrity, loyalty, courage, dedication, knowledge, and selflessness. It is a simple comparison of extremes. Sam Damon is the ideal. Among his traits, selflessness is key and foremost. Emulate his qualities and true leadership.

Football and coaching is the source of the third rock. It comes from the late great Paul "Bear" Bryant and his guiding principle for his player on the field and for life. Ask any former Alabama, Texas A&M, Kentucky, or Maryland athlete who played under this magnificent leader from Moro Bottom, Arkansas and they all relate the same message, "Always show your class." There is also no secret under the hickory tree in Birmingham.

There they are. Deny yourself. Be a Sam Damon. Always show your class.

These three rocks have a great utility and value for all walks of life, far beyond my ability to relate them. I hope that they will serve you forever. God bless you.

Robert Lee Powell
Colonel, Infantry

A BUNCH OF UNITED STATES MARINES

Chaplain's Thought

Last Thursday morning I was one of more than 300 runners in the National Security Agency (NSA) Armed Forces Week 5K run (Ft. Meade, MD). It was pretty crowded at the start, but things thinned out after about five minutes or so, and I took my bearings. Perhaps 200 yards ahead of me was a group of maybe 8 Marines or so who were obviously running together. I decided that a good goal would be to beat them, which seemed reasonable as I am a macho Air Force Chaplain and they were only a bunch of United States Marines. I kept them in sight for the next couple of miles, but the longer the race went on, the younger those guys got. It became apparent to me in the last half mile that I was not going to catch them, and I resigned myself to finishing well behind them. Then I noticed that one of their teammates was struggling and was gradually dropping off the pace. I panted out a word of encouragement as I caught him and realized that he was not about to give up. Within 100 yards of the finish line I saw a strange sight. The entire group of Marines made a U-turn in the road and were running back towards me. As they ran past me I noted their well-chiseled muscles and the determined set of their jaws. I glanced over my shoulder in time to see them rally around their buddy to provide the emotional support of the team so that they could all finish together. I was impressed. No way would they leave a struggling comrade behind. As I entered the finishing chute I murmured a prayer, "God, I'm glad those guys are on our side." And so it was that I learned a theological truth from the U.S. Marines that is as vivid as any my seminary professors ever taught,

> If anyone sees his brother in need but has no pity on him, how can the love of God be in him? Let us not love with words or tongue but with actions and in truth.

John 3:17,18

Last Thursday I witnessed "a few good men" in action. They reminded me of the strength of being a team, and that words without actions are pretty much useless.

Thanks Marines.

A message from Chaplain Johnson
LtCol, USAF

As I grow older I pay less attention to what men say.
I just watch what they do.

Andrew Carnegie

CLOSING THOUGHTS

*The willingness with which our young
people are likely to serve in any war,
no matter how justified,
shall be directly proportional as
to how they perceive the veterans
of earlier wars were treated and
appreciated by their nation.*

President

George Washington

*We will always remember.
We will always be proud.
We will always be prepared,
so we may always be free.*

**President
Ronald Reagan**

BIBLIOGRAPHY

A Doughboy with the Fighting Sixty-ninth: A Remembrance of World War I. Albert M. Ettinger and A. Churchill Ettinger. Shippensburg, PA: White Mane, 1992.

America Goes to War. Bruce Canton. 1958.

Army Digest. August 1967, pp. 5–6, quote from SGM John Stepanek.

Being a Soldier, Soldiers Magazine. SMA Richard A. Kidd. May 1994.

Bradley. 1951.

Brave Men. Ernie Pyle. NY: William Sloane, 1947.

Combat Force Journal. February, 1954.

Commander's Call, Nov–Dec 1980, DA PAM 360-857, Part I. Developed by Military Review, July 1980.

Front and Center. COL Daniel T. Chapman. Article entitled "Last Night's Artillery Battle." 1991.

Gordon R. Sullivan: The Collected Works 1991–1995.

Guideposts for a Proud and Ready Army, dated 01 March 1985. Developed by John A. Wickham Jr., General, United States Army Chief of Staff.

Hope is Not a Method: What Business Leaders Can Learn from America's Army. Gordon R. Sullivan and Michael V. Harper. NY: Random House, 1996.

It's Tough to Be the First Domino. LTC Tom Hamrick. ARMY (Feb 1971): 39–41.

Leadership and Command on the Battlefield: Noncommissioned Officer Corps. TRADOC Pamphlet 525-100-4. 1994.

Men Against Fire: The Problem of Battle Command in Future War. Col S.L.A. Marshall. The Infantry Journal and William Morrow & Co., NY. 1947.

Men Think as Their Leaders Think. General W. B. Palmer. Army Information Digest, January 1954.

Meyer, General Edward C., United States Army Chief of Staff, June 1979– June 1983.

New York Herald Tribune. Walter Lippmann. Article entitled *"The Final Test."* April 14, 1945.

Once An Eagle. Anton Myrer.

Poems of Patriotism. Edgar A. Guest.

Rank and File: The Common Solider at Peace and War 1642–1914. Compiled by T. H. McGuffie. London: Hutchinson, 1964.

Sergeants on Training. SGT Michael Davis, in Sergeants' Business, Jul–Aug 1988.

Sergeant York: An American Hero. David D. Lee. Lexington, KY: University Press of Kentucky, 1985.

Soldier: The Memoirs of Matthew B. Ridgway. General Matthew B. Ridgway. 1956.

SMA Kidd Defines Roles, Sentinel magazine, March 12, 1993, by SMA Richard A. Kidd.

Strand, Robert. *"A Soldier's Story, WW I."* New Leaf Press.

Taking Command, the Art and Science of Military Leadership. Developed by the Armed Forces leader by Office of Military Psychology and Leadership, United States Military Academy. Stackpole Books, © 1967 by Stackpole Company.

Techniques of Leadership—General George Patton. The US Army War College Memorandum (Office of the Commandant). October 19, 1979.

The G.I. Journal of Sergeant Giles. Compiled and edited by Janice Holt Giles. Boston: Houghton Mifflin, 1965.

The Public Speaker's Treasure Chest. Herbert V. Harper & Brothers Publishers. New York & London, © 1942.

The Road Past Mandalay. John Masters.

The Wisdom and Humor of the Great Communicator. President Ronald Reagan.

This Kind of War. T. R. Fehrenbach.

Thunderbolt: General Creighton Abrams and the Army of His Times. Lewis Sorley.

Today's Youth Share Desire For Stricter Rules. General Charles Krulak. As printed in the *Richmond Times-Dispatch,* June 20, 1999.

To Hell and Back. Audie Murphy. Blue Ridge Summit, PA: Tab Books. 1988 (reprinted from 1949).

Up Front. Bill Mauldin. NY: World. 1945.

Vouno, General Carl E., *Collected Works of the Thirty-first Chief of Staff,* General, United States Army. 1991.

What Soldiering Is All About. SMA Glen E. Morrell. ARMY (Oct 1986): 39–42.

What the Soldier Thinks: A Monthly Digest of War Department Studies on the Attitudes of American Troops. Chief of Staff, General G. C. Marshall.

Wickham, General John A., Jr. *Collected Works of the Thirtieth Chief of Staff.* United States Army. 1987.

PERMISSIONS ACKNOWLEDGMENTS

Every effort has been made to ensure that required permissions for all material were obtained. The editor and Graphics West, Inc., cannot take responsibility for any errors or omissions. Please contact Purple Mountain Publishing concerning any errors or omissions. Those sources not formally acknowledged here will be included in future printings of this book.

Grateful acknowledgment is made to the following to reprint previously published and unpublished material:

Adkins, Tom. For the article entitled "Burn That Flag." Reprinted with permission from Mr. Adkins in a letter dated May 30, 2000.

Baker, Vernon. For speech entitled "I Will Fight For You," as published in The Retired Officers Association's (TROA) magazine, *The Retired Officer Magazine*. Reprinted with permission by Ms. Heather Lyons, Managing Editor to *The Retired Officer Magazine*, on behalf of Mr. Baker, in a letter dated July 11, 2000.

Bradley, James. For the speech entitled "America's Battle." Reprinted with permission from Mr. Bradley. Verbal permission was provided to William Coffey Sr. by Mr. Bradley on May 30, 2000 in Newton, Connecticut.

Clough, Jonathan, Major, USAF. For the letter to Professor Van Wormer responding to an editorial in the US News and World Report. Reprinted with permission by Major Clough in a letter dated June 2, 2000.

Ellison, Stephen, Captain, MD, USA. For use of the letter entitled "Earn This." Reprinted with permission of CPT Stephen Ellison, in a letter dated August 4, 2000.

Glasier, Robert. For the article entitled "Thank You For Listening." Reprinted with permission from Mr. Glasier in a letter dated October 5, 2000.

Gray, Harry J. For use of the poem "You're the Finest." Reprinted with permission of Ms. Sandy Sweeney, Assistant to Harry J. Gray, on his behalf, in a letter dated July 25, 2000.

Guideposts Book & Inspirational Media. Article entitled "A Call for Help." Reprinted with permission from *Guideposts* magazine. Copyright 1995 by Guideposts, Carmel, New York, 10512. Permission letter dated July 21, 2000.

Krulak, Charles, General (USMC). For article and all speeches by GEN Krulak. Reprinted with permission by Ms. Mary Glackin and Ms. Kimberly Schleifer, on behalf of General Krulak, in a letter dated July 15, 2000.

Kushner, Hal, M.D. For use of his speech entitled "Dr. Hal Kushner, POW." Reprinted with permission of Dr. Kushner in a letter dated July 12, 2000.

Moros, Melyssa. For use of letters entitled "Young American Patriots," from the Support Our Soldiers (SOS) website. Reprinted with permission of Ms. Melyssa Moros in a letter dated May 28, 2000.

Mouer, Dan. For use of the article "What is a Vietnam Veteran." Reprinted with permission from Mr. Dan Mouer, in a letter dated July 11, 2000.

New Leaf Press, Mr. Jim Fletcher, Editor of New Leaf Press, for use of the article from Robert Strand's article "A Soldier's Story, WW I," from his book, *Moments of Christmas,* in a letter dated August 6, 2000.

Perot, Ross. Foreword of this book. Reprinted with permission of Mr. H. R. Perot, in a letter by Mr. Perot dated July 10, 2000.

Plumb, Charles. For use of story entitled "Who Packs Your Parachute," Reprinted with permission by Mr. Plumb in a letter dated July 27, 2000.

Powell, Colin L., General, USA (Ret.). For letter written by GEN Powell and entitled "GI." Reprinted with permission of F. William Smullen, Chief of Staff to GEN Powell, on his behalf, in a letter dated July 13, 2000.

Reader's Digest. The Reader's Digest Association, Inc. For article by Mr. B. T. Collins entitled "The Courage of Sam Bird," reprinted with permission by Ms. Sandra M. Hill, Director, Magazine Rights, on behalf of *Reader's Digest.*

Riley, Christopher, MAJ, USA (Ret.). Article entitled "If Wildflowers Can Spring From Verdun" is reprinted with MAJ Riley's permission in a letter dated July 14, 2000.

Rogers, Bernard W., General, USA (Ret.). All quotes and speech "A Contribution to Every Citizen." Reprinted with permission of General Bernard W. Rogers, in a letter dated July 19, 2000.

Schueckler, Jim. For the article entitled "I Came To See My Son's Name." Reprinted with permission of Mr. Schueckler in a letter dated June 4, 2000.

Shinseki, Eric, General, USA. Speech entitled "An Affair of the Heart." Reprinted with acknowledgment, as public domain information, from LTC Lewis M. Boone, Special Assistant to the Chief of Staff, Army, in a letter dated June 23, 2000.

Stockdale, James B., Vice Admiral, USN (Ret.). For his quote, reprinted with permission of VADM Stockdale in a letter dated June 17, 2000.

Sullivan, Gordon R., General, USA (Ret.). All quotes. Reprinted with permission of General Gordon R. Sullivan, in a letter dated August 3, 2000.

Schwarzkopf, H. Norman, General, USA, (Ret.). All quotes and letters reprinted with permission of Lynn Williams, Chief of Staff to GEN Schwarzkopf, on his behalf, in a letter dated July 26, 2000.

Tanney, Tom. For use of letter entitled "Fighting For My Flag." Reprinted with permission of Mr. Tanney in a letter dated June 14, 2000.

Univeral Music Publishing Group, © Copyright 1984. Songs of Univeral, Inc. a division of Univeral Studios, Inc. (BMI) International Copyright Secured. All Rights Reserved. For use of words by Lee Greenwood, "God Bless the USA." Reprinted with permission in a letter dated August 30, 2000, by Mr. Paul E. Brooks, Coordinator, Motion Picture & Television Music.

Universal Press Syndicate. For article entitled "Talk About Heaven," a Dear Abby article. Reprinted with permission of Ms. Raegan Marshall, Permissions Coordinator for Universal Press Syndicate, in a letter dated August 21, 2000.

Van Wormer, Katherin. Letter to *US News and World Report*. Reprinted with permission from Professor Van Wormer, in a letter dated October 13, 1999.

Wall Street Journal, The, Dow Jones & Company, Inc. for use of the article entitled "Still the Noblest Calling" by J. D. Wetterling. Reprinted with permission by Ms. Lisa Rossi, Reprint Permissions Coordinator, Editorial Page, on behalf of *The Wall Street Journal*, in a letter dated July 6, 2000. Permission was also received by Mr. J. D. Wetterling.

Walsh, Pat, Captain, USN. For the eulogy entitled "They Loved God, Country, and Our Navy." Reprinted with permission by Captain Walsh, in a letter dated June 6, 2000.

Welsh III, Mark A., Brigadier General, USAF. Speech entitled, "Just People, and Feelings, and Sounds," reprinted with permission from BG Welsh, in a letter dated July 5, 2000.

INDEX BY AUTHORS AND TITLES

PATRIOT
HEARTS

To order copies of *Patriot Hearts* using a check or money order, write to:

Purple Mountain Publishing
P.O. Box 77019
Colorado Springs, CO 80970-7019

Price for softcover book is $16.95 and for hardcover is $23.95. Please add $2.95 per book for shipping and handling. This S/H cost applies to U.S. addresses, including APO/FPO, Puerto Rico, Guam, American Samoa, and other U.S. Protectorates. Shipping and handling for international addresses is $7.00 per book. Please make checks or money orders payable to "Purple Mountain Publishing".

For additional information on where to order *Patriot Hearts* (i.e., book stores, additional web sites) please refer to Purple Mountain Publishing's web site at <http//hometown.aol.com/patriothearts> for the most updated information on telephone numbers and web sites to order from.

Purple Mountain Publishing is currently soliciting letters, speeches, stories, quotes, poems, etc., similar to those found in this book, for the sequel, *More ... Patriot Hearts*. Payment may be made for submissions on a case by case basis, especially for original, unpublished works with copyright release permission. If you wish to submit a photograph with your material, a copyright release will be required for publication. Items can be sent to:

Purple Mountain Publishing
P.O. Box 77019
Colorado Springs, CO 80970-7019
or
e-mailed to PurpleMTPub@aol.com.

If you wish to have any photograph returned, please provide a return address and a request for its return.

**Purple Mountain
Publishing**